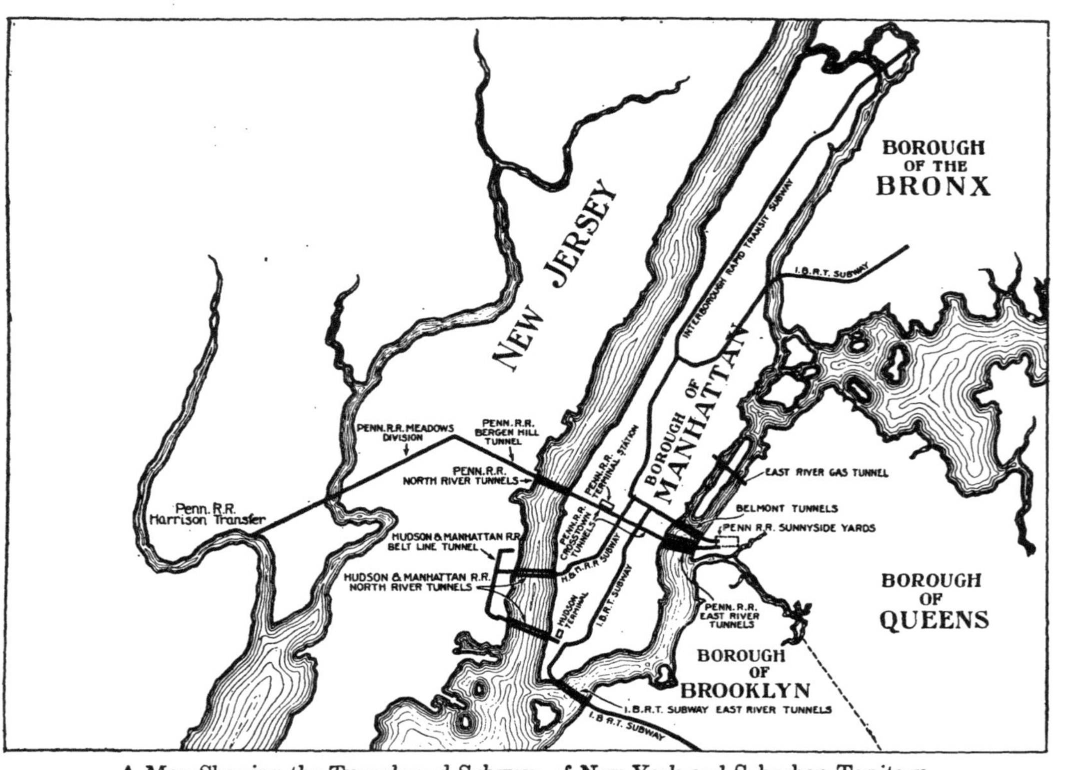

A Map Showing the Tunnels and Subways of New York and Suburban Territory.

Frontispiece.

THE SUBWAYS AND TUNNELS OF NEW YORK

METHODS AND COSTS

WITH AN APPENDIX ON TUNNELING MACHINERY AND METHODS AND TABLES OF ENGINEERING DATA

BY

GILBERT H. GILBERT, LUCIUS I. WIGHTMAN

AND

W. L. SAUNDERS

FIRST EDITION

FIRST THOUSAND

NEW YORK

JOHN WILEY & SONS

LONDON: CHAPMAN & HALL, LIMITED

1912

THE SCIENTIFIC PRESS
ROBERT DRUMMOND AND COMPANY
BROOKLYN, N. Y.

TRIBUTE

No record of tunneling under the rivers surrounding New York is complete without a tribute of admiration and respect to the genius and ability shown by the men who were the architects and builders. It has for a long time been an easy matter to tunnel through rock. The power drill simply added to the efficiency of rock tunneling and in doing this it was made possible to build great tunnels for railways, aqueducts, etc., within a reasonable time and at reasonable expense.

To build and maintain tunnels through silt or other alluvial material, especially tunnels of large diameter, was a problem which had not been solved by engineers as late as 1874. At that time Mr. Delos E. Haskin came to New York from San Francisco, where he had made a fortune, every dollar of which he lost in an effort to prove the practicability of tunneling under the Hudson River and through the silt by means of compressed air. Though Haskin did not live to enjoy the fruits of his work, he proved the practicability of his scheme in a general way and to him belongs the credit as the genius who pushed the idea to the front.

Next came Mr. Charles M. Jacobs, who combined the genius and enthusiasm of Haskin with the ability of the engineer. Mr. Jacobs built the first tunnel under the rivers about New York, namely, the East River Gas Tunnel from New York to Brooklyn. After this he took up with enthusiasm the completion of the old Haskin tunnels, maintaining with earnest zeal the practicability of the scheme, modified on lines of his own experience, until he succeeded in completing these and the Pennsylvania tunnels, which are described in this volume. In the darkest days of tunneling under these rivers Mr. Jacobs never lost courage. When the work began he was on the job at all times, and his genius and engineering capacity are shown throughout this great work. He has now returned to his home in England, and well does he deserve the reputation and wealth which he has achieved.

Mr. William G. McAdoo, with great foresight and ability, planned and executed that gateway to New York, through tunnels under the Hudson, which is called the McAdoo System. Of these three men Haskin was the enthusiast, Jacobs the engineer and McAdoo the business man.

W. L. SAUNDERS.

PREFACE

THE system of subways and tunnels in and about New York City is the result of traffic conditions which are entirely without parallel in any other city of the world. The island of Manhattan, comprising the Borou h of Manhattan of the City of New York, is a little less than twelve miles in length and, at the widest point, a trifle over two miles in width; yet it is the business center of a population aggregating probably close to six millions. The census of 1910 credits New York City with a population of something over four millions. But when to this figure are added the inhabitants of the adjacent cities in New Jersey, New York and Connecticut which are within commuting distance, six millions is probably a fair estimate of the population, the business pivot of which is found in the island of Manhattan. The actual business center for this vast number may be further restricted to a section south of 42d Street, the upper part of the island being principally residential in character.

A consideration of these figures will reveal the magnitude and complexity of the traffic problem in New York City. The East River intervenes between Manhattan and the Boroughs of Brooklyn and Queens, and the suburban towns of Long Island, New York Bay separates the Borough of Richmond (Staten Island). The Hudson River divides the industrial and suburban territories of New Jersey from New York. On the north, the Harlem River divides the Borough of the Bronx, and the towns of New York State and Connecticut, from their business center.

Every business day in the year a vast tide of humanity converges on the business center of New York City. Throughout the business day a large percentage of these business men and women, and shoppers, must be furnished quick and safe transportation within the limits of the island. Every evening this tide diverges to its homes. This morning and evening migration must all be accomplished within the space of an hour or so. The magnitude of the transportation problem here presented has called for the greatest engineering genius and almost unlimited capital; and its solution—by no means complete as yet—finds its beginning in the transit system of which the New York subway, and the North and East River tunnels with their connections, are a part.

The ferry systems from New Jersey, Long Island and Staten Island have reached the limit of their capacity. The East River bridges furnish relief to the situation, but are by no means sufficient. The elevated and surface car systems of New York and Brooklyn have been extended to their practical limit. With surface, above-surface, and over-water means of transit incapable of further expansion, the only alternative was to make use of the subterranean and subaqueous territory underlying and adjacent to the greater city. The subways, and subaqueous and land tunnels, in and about New York City may be considered as simply a beginning of a vast system of sub-surface transportation which must develop with the growth of population.

The present Interboro Rapid Transit Subway consists of a trunk line starting in Brooklyn, passing under the East River, entering Manhattan at the Battery, and following the backbone of the island to its northern extremity, with a branch to the Bronx passing under the Harlem River.

The Pennsylvania Railroad and Long Island Railroad system comprises a series of surface, subaqueous and subterranean lines starting at Harrison, N. J., crossing the meadows on the surface, penetrating Bergen Hill by tunnel, plunging beneath the Hudson, or North River, through two subaqueous tunnels, traversing Manhattan through the crosstown tunnels, passing beneath the East River through four subaqueous tunnels, and emerging on the surface at Long Island City. This system may be said to properly include the great Pennsylvania Passenger Terminal in New York City, with its sub-surface yards. Its object is not only to give quick access to the heart of Manhattan for the commuting service of Long Island and portions of New Jersey, but to provide also a city terminal for the Pennsylvania through traffic from the West.

The so-called McAdoo System is for suburban service entirely. It includes: A sub-surface belt line, or tunnel, along the Jersey shore connecting three railroad terminals; four subaqueous tunnels under the Hudson; and a line of subway from the terminus of two of its Hudson River tunnels northward under Manhattan Island.

Under the East River are the Belmont tunnels, completed but not yet in operation, from Long Island to Manhattan. They will, probably, later be made a part of the great traffic arteries of New York.

The tunnel and subway system serving the population centering in New York thus includes: One complete subway system connecting three boroughs; eight subaqueous tunnels under the East River; six subaqueous tunnels under the Hudson River to the mainland; two subaqueous tunnels under the Harlem River to the Bronx; the belt-line tunnels and the New York subway of the McAdoo System; and the Bergen Hill and crosstown tunnels of the Pennsylvania Railroad.

In the aggregate these enterprises probably involve as much capital as the building of the Panama Canal—and possibly even more. They have encountered at every stage obstacles stupendous in magnitude and difficulty, and calling for engineering methods beyond all precedent. They represent engineering and contract achievement of such vast importance that they mark a new era in construction work.

The authors here acknowledge their indebtedness to the many engineers and contractors whose records and papers have furnished so much of the information in these pages. Individual credit has been given in many places throughout the book. But in many cases the authority is not stated, simply because the data given is a compilation from a number of sources. Acknowledgment is also made to the Ingersoll-Rand Company and to the Cameron Steam Pump Works for photographs and tables of engineering information; to the American Society of Civil Engineers for the use of many valuable plates and illustrations; and to *Compressed Air Magazine*, from which several important papers, with their illustrations, have been taken.

THE AUTHORS.

CONTENTS

CHAPTER XIX

CHAPTER XX

CHAPTER XXI

APPENDICES

APPENDIX A

APPENDIX B

APPENDIX C

APPENDIX D

APPENDIX E

APPENDIX F

APPENDIX G

APPENDIX H

APPENDIX I

APPENDIX J

APPENDIX K

APPENDIX L

APPENDIX M

APPENDIX N

SUBWAYS AND TUNNELS OF NEW YORK

CHAPTER I

TOPOGRAPHY, GEOLOGICAL FORMATION AND HISTORICAL DATA

The island of Manhattan is a rocky ridge lying north and south and having an area of approximately 14,000 acres or 22 square miles. It is in the upper end of New York Bay, between the Hudson River on the west and the East River on the east, with the Harlem River and Spuyten Duyvil Creek, small connecting tideways, separating it from the mainland on the north and northeast.

Manhattan Island, as well as the adjacent country to the north and east, is principally a formation of rock composed chiefly of gneiss and mica schist, with heavy seams of coarse-grained dolomitic marble and thinner layers of serpentine running through it. These rocks are supposed to be Lower Silurian in character. Rocks of the Lower Silurian era are mainly sandstone, shales, conglomerates and limestones; but Professor Newberry holds that they have so great a similarity to some portions of the Laurentian Range in Canada, that it is difficult to evade the conviction that they are of the same period.

The deep troughs, through which the Hudson and East Rivers find their way through New York harbor to the ocean, are supposed by the same authority to have been excavated during the late Tertiary period when Manhattan Island and the other islands in New York Bay stood much higher than they do now, when Long Island did not exist, and when a great sand plain extended beyond the Jersey coast some eighty miles seaward.

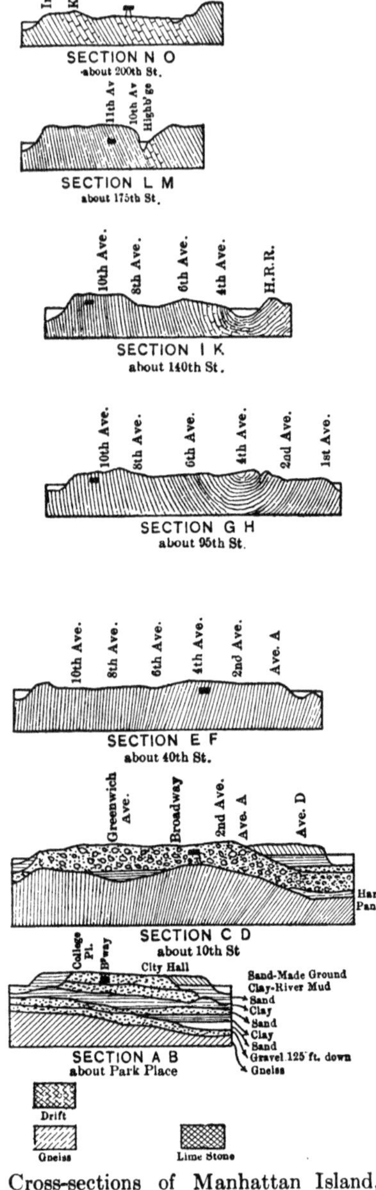

Cross-sections of Manhattan Island, showing Geological Formations.

For half its length northward from its lower point, Manhattan Island slopes on either side from a central ridge. On the upper half of the island the ground rises precipitously from the Hudson River in a narrow line of hill which on the eastern side sinks rapidly to a plain known as the Harlem Flats, bordering on the Harlem and East Rivers. The surface throughout the island is rocky, with the exception of this plain.

The district beyond the Harlem River, as far north as Yonkers, is traversed by lines of rocky hills trending north and south. Some idea of the varied outline which was once characteristic of the whole island can be gathered from the present surface formation of Central Park. The bed of the Hudson River is a deposit resulting from the washing away of the rocks of the upper river in the form of silt, shale, sandstone or other sedimentary or metamorphic rock, and a trap rock of the Palisades formation.

NOTE. From Dana's Geology; Newberry's Geological History of New York Island; Edwin L. Godkin, Encyclopedia Britannica; Report of the Chamber of Commerce of the State of New York, 1905.

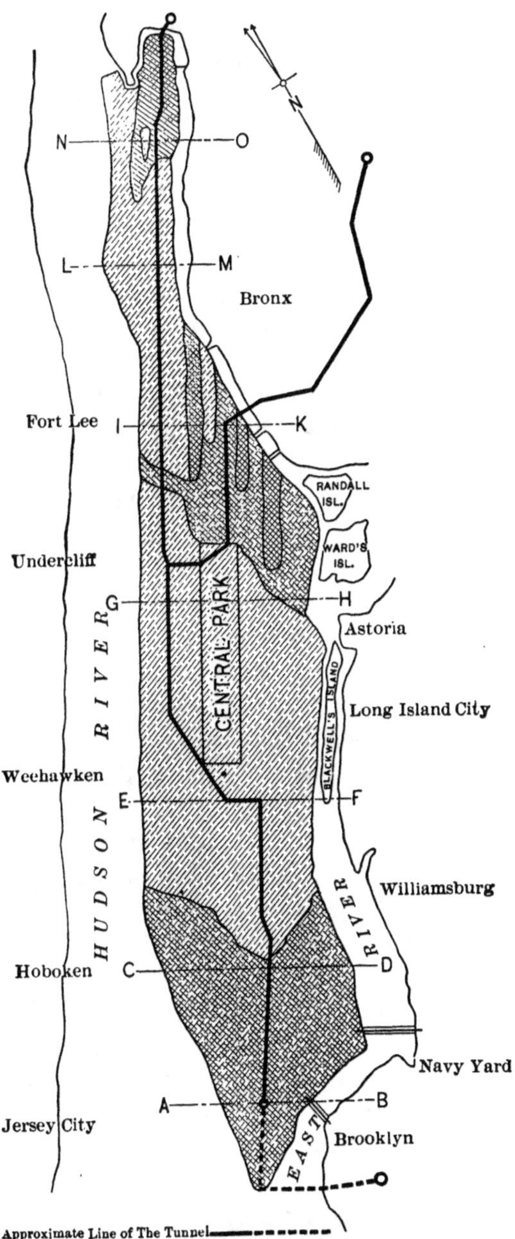

Geological Map of Manhattan Island, with Route of the Original Rapid Transit Subway.

From the first settlement of Manhattan Island by the Dutch, two or three years after Hudson's visit in 1609, until 1700, the population had become about 21,700 In 1800 this had grown to 60,500; in 1820 to 124,000. From that time the population has increased until it has successively covered the district south of Wall Street, south of Canal Street, south of 23d Street, south of 42d Street, south of the Harlem River; and it now extends north of the Harlem along the Hudson River well toward Yonkers, and on the east toward Long Island Sound.

The population of the municipality is, as already stated, approximately four millions.

The first settlement was at the extreme southern end of the island The commerce of that day was gathered at this point, and this section remains to-day the great center of finance, trade and commerce. The metropolitan center, including the nearby cities of New Jersey, New York and Connecticut, embraces a total population of probably six millions and is, with the exception of London, the largest center of population in the world. The growth from south to north, covering an extent of more than ten miles, has been restricted on the eastern and western sides by the East and Hudson Rivers. The conditions of growth and population have demanded rapid and certain means of travel between the different sections and the general center.

At the beginning of the last century small stages met all transit requirements. With the advent of steam ferries, about 1820, transportation across the rivers was facilitated. In 1850 stage and omnibus lines served the population and were a little later superseded by tram cars.

Rapid transit in a sense somewhat approaching the present understanding of the term was introduced in 1875, when trains were brought into the Grand Central Station at 42d Street over a four-track system. A short section of elevated railroad had been erected in Greenwich Street in 1870. Ten years later elevated railway structures had been completed to the Harlem River. The opening of the Brooklyn Bridge in 1883, and the further extension of the system of elevated roads, brought the outlying districts within reasonable traveling time of New York City. In 1884 the cable system of propelling street cars was introduced, to be later displaced by electric railway systems.

From 1868 to 1900 many projects and schemes were put forth to improve transit facilities Among the first was the Beach Pneumatic, incorporated in 1868, and known as the Broadway Underground Railway. It was the only one upon which constructive work was actually done. The charter of this company provided that, to demonstrate the practicability of its plans "to transmit letters, packages and merchandise, etc., it must first lay down and construct one line of said pneumatic tubes, etc." A full-sized section of the tunnel was built on the lines adopted and is to-day in good condition. In 1873 this company's charter was amended to permit it to construct, maintain and operate an underground railway for the transportation of passengers and property. It was proposed to operate the tunnel by means of compressed air, a car circular in cross-section being used, approximately fitting the interior of the tube. It was pointed out that by this means the obnoxious gases from the combustion of coal in locomotives would be done away with.

Work was begun on the tunnel at the corner of Broadway and Warren Street, and a section was built under Broadway to the southern side of Murray Street. The straight portions of the tunnel were lined with brick to a diameter of eight feet in the clear; the curved portions were of cast iron. The tunnel was built by means of a shield, which was forced forward two feet at a time by hydraulic jacks.

Early in 1870 the tunnel was open for inspection. A car was run from one end to the other with the object of demonstrating the safety and practicability of the plan. The work done failed of successful issue. Engineers were divided in opinion as to the possibility of building an underground tunnel under narrow streets in front of such massive structures as the Astor House. Owing to this difference of opinion on the part of the experts financial support could not be obtained and the project was dropped.

In 1871 the Gilbert Elevated Railroad was chartered for the purpose of constructing a pneumatic tube railway. It was proposed to erect a pneumatic tube, supported from arches above the street. It was claimed that the road would be noiseless and the train out of sight. This plan was found impracticable and too expensive, and it was decided to build the tube without a top, and to operate a steam road in the trough thus formed. Finally the trough also was abandoned and the plan resolved itself into a simple elevated railroad, the outgrowth of which are the present elevated railway systems of the city.

CHAPTER II

THE ORIGINAL HUDSON TUNNEL

In 1871 D. C. Haskins conceived the idea of building a tunnel under the Hudson River. In making a trip from the Pacific Coast via Omaha he had been struck with the system of building piers for a railway bridge over the Missouri River. This system was the forming of caissons made up of a number of iron rings bolted together and constituting a cylinder which could be lengthened by the addition of rings as the caisson descended. Air locks and compressed air were used, the material within the caisson being excavated by hand till a bed rock foundation was reached.

From a study of this work Mr. Haskins conceived the idea that iron cylinders fitted with air locks could be placed horizontally, and tubular tunnels under the Hudson River could be started from the bottom of a shaft by using compressed air to prevent the inflow of earth and water. As the material was excavated in front of the tunnel the latter was to be advanced by the addition of rings of the diameter of the finished tube. Work on such a tunnel under the Hudson River to connect New Jersey and New York was commenced on the New Jersey side in November, 1874. The bed of the Hudson is a silt deposit, which when dry is an impalpable powder, but when saturated with water is as fluid as quicksand. When a certain degree of moisture is carried by this material it has a consistency approximating that of clay. This latter characteristic was taken advantage of by maintaining an air pressure in the heading equal to the hydrostatic head outside, when the material to be excavated formed a barrier against the entrance of water, thus permitting the heading to be advanced. The work began with sinking a shaft 38 feet in outside diameter, lined with 4 feet of brick work to a depth of 54 feet below mean high water. On opposite sides of the shaft, in the direction of the length of the tunnel, false pieces of elliptical form, 26 feet high and 24 feet wide, were built. These were to be removed to permit the passage of the tunnel. An air lock, 6 feet in diameter by 15 feet long, was attached to the shaft cylinder above the false piece on the east side. A temporary working entrance to the tunnel was formed of eleven rings, each 2 feet wide, but of different diameters. The tops of these rings were in the same horizontal line, forming a cone-shaped chamber with steps of 18 inches leading to the air-lock.

From the base of this cone, which was 20 feet in diameter, two parallel single track tunnels were started. As the largest ring was not large enough to take in both tunnels, a ring of a diameter equal to the exterior of the north tunnel was built and lined with 2 feet of brick work. Regular tunnel work was then commenced. Silt was excavated till the top center plate of a new ring could be placed and bolted to the one behind; then plates were bolted to either side of this top plate until the ring was completed. When four rings of plate, equal to 10 feet of section, had been placed, and the heading cleared out, the masonry was laid. The plates were of quarter-inch iron, 2½ feet in width by 3½ feet in length, flanged on all four sides with angle iron. The tunnels were 18 feet high by 16 feet wide, inside dimensions.

The air pressure was kept about equal to the hydrostatic head, amounting to 18 pounds at the shaft and increasing to 36 pounds at a distance of 1600 feet. No fixed rule could be given to govern the air pressure, but it was found generally that a little less than the hydrostatic pressure at the axis of the tunnel gave the best results under ordinary conditions. The excavated chamber was 23 feet in diameter, so that the difference of water pressure between the top and bottom of the chamber was about 11 pounds per square inch. Under these conditions some air escaped through the roof and some water entered through the bottom. Excessive pressure resulted in an increased discharge of air through the roof, causing the silt to dry out and drop into the tunnel. If this mass was sufficient a blow-out and consequent flooding resulted.

When the north tunnel had been advanced over a quarter of a mile the south tunnel was started, and when this had been carried forward some distance both tunnels were bulkheaded; and work on the removal of the temporary entrance was commenced.

A serious blowout occurred in July, 1880. The doors of the airlocks had become wedged by falling earth and plates, cutting off the escape of the men, twenty of whom were drowned. This accident had an unfavorable effect upon the financial aspect of the undertaking.

The New York end was started by sinking a timber caisson 48 by 29½ feet to a depth of 56 feet below high water, where it was fully imbedded in sand. Through the west side of this caisson, on the line of the tunnel, an opening was cut and roof plates of the tunnel put in and braced. Plates were added till a section 12 feet long had been built, when an iron bulkhead was constructed. In building additional sections the same system was adopted. As each section of the iron tube was completed it was cleaned out and the brick lining laid. This was the first and only instance of building a subaqueous tunnel in sand without the aid of a shield.

S. Pearson & Son of England assumed the contract in 1888, Sir John Fowler and Sir Benjamin Baker acting as consulting engineers. The shield method of driving was adopted and heavy iron plates were substituted for masonry. The light boiler plate lining was no longer required. The work was stopped through lack of capital and unsuccessful attempts were made at various times to resume the operations until the early part of 1902. In that year the franchise and property of the tunnel company were acquired by the New York and New Jersey Railroad Company, and operations were again started. In 1905 the New York and New Jersey Railroad Company disposed of their interests to the Hudson Company, who have since completed the tunnels. The completion of this work, which is now known as the McAdoo System, is described in another chapter.

CHAPTER III

THE EAST RIVER GAS TUNNEL

THE first completed tunnel under the East River, that of the East River Gas Company, for the transmission of illuminating gas from the gas works on Long Island for distribution throughout Manhattan, was of unusual interest and importance in that its successful completion demonstrated the entire possibility of constructing similar tunnels under the same waterway wherever they may be required; and also in that the progress of the work revealed the peculiar conditions and the special difficulties which might be expected to be encountered in similar undertakings in the same neighborhood.

This tunnel was not as large in section as would be required for a standard railroad, or even for trolley cars and general traffic, but it was still large enough to reveal all the difficulties which a larger construction would have involved. The rock section was required to be 8½ feet high and 10 feet wide, and the heading was driven the full width. The location of the tunnel is from Webster Avenue, Ravenswood, Long Island, under both channels of the East River, with Blackwell's Island between them, to Seventy-second Street, Manhattan. The roof grade of the tunnel was 40 feet below the lowest point in the bed of the river, which was in the west channel and 111 feet below mean high water mark. The water in the east channel was not more than half as deep as that in the west channel so that the depth of ground over the tunnel was there much greater.

Preliminary investigation revealed bed rock on both sides of the river only a few feet below the surface and also on the island; and drill soundings made with difficulty in both channels seemed to show from two to five feet of sand and gravel at the bottom and then solid rock, so that the driving of the tunnel was expected to be a clean and uninterrupted job straight through and the contract for the job was placed on that basis.

Work was begun by the contractors, McLaughlin, Reilly & Co., at the Long Island end June 28, 1892. Bed rock was found 9½ feet below the surface, being a compact gneiss almost approaching granite. Work commenced on the New York end July 10. The rock here was the regular micaceous gneiss known as " New York rock." The rock in the New York shaft was straight grained with a dip of about 10 degrees from the vertical, striking nearly north and south and becoming harder as the depth increased. No water or any abnormal difficulties were encountered and the bottom of the shaft was reached at the end of October, 139½ feet below the surface. At the Long Island shaft the progress was not so rapid. The rock was seamy and much water was encountered. There was no reliable water supply for the boilers and the water obtainable, although not salt, was entirely unfit for use and there were numerous stoppages during the entire continuance of the work on account of the water supply.

The care and precision with which the line was laid are indicated by the fact that when the headings met, 1678 feet from the New York shore, the lines were within ½ inch of each other laterally and 1¼ vertically.

Two Ingersoll-Sergeant compressors were installed at each end of the tunnel, and drills of the same company were employed throughout the work. On the New York end the driving of the heading proceeded to a distance of 348 feet, when a seam of decomposed rock was struck, a straight face across the heading. After advancing into this 9 feet it was found unsafe to proceed, the ground finally having reached " about the consistency of soup." A steel air lock 6 feet in diameter and 10 feet long, was made and fastened solidly in the rock. Working under air pressure was commenced, the initial pressure being 35 pounds; electric lighting was installed.

The heading was enlarged and changed to a circle 12 feet in diameter. The tunnel in this part was lined as it advanced with light plates of wrought iron connected with angle irons, and 12 inches of brick work was laid inside the plates. One-half of the thickness of the brick was subsequently removed and a lining consisting of cast iron segments bolted together finished the job.

The working air pressure was ultimately raised to 48 pounds, which was higher than men had ever worked in before, and they began to experience serious difficulty in continuing the work. Four deaths in all resulted from the air pressure, and there were no other deaths or accidents in the entire progress of the work. The first man to die was a foreman. The second man had been long out of employment and was in very low condition. He died in the air lock after his first shift of two hours. The third man became paralyzed from his shoulders down and died soon after. The fourth man died nearly a year after the others.

In connection with this feature of the work the following rules for men working in compressed air were formulated by Dr. Andrew H. Smith of the Presbyterian Hospital:

1. Never enter the air lock with an empty stomach.

2. Use as far as possible a meat diet, and take warm coffee freely.

3. Always put on extra clothing when coming out, and avoid exposure to cold.

4. Exercise as little as possible during the first hour after coming out, and lie down if possible.

5. Use intoxicating liquors sparingly. Better not at all.

6. Take at least eight hours sleep every night.

7. See that the bowels are evacuated every day.

8. Never enter the lock if at all sick.

9. In exit from the air lock, the time occupied should be five minutes for each atmosphere above the normal.

The earliest injurious effect experienced is an itching caused by air globules in the capillaries, which may be quickly cured by inducing profuse perspiration.

The "bends," a more serious trouble, is an intense rheumatic pain in the joints caused by air globules in the sockets.

Paralysis leaves lasting injury and is usually the cause of death when it occurs.

A highly steam heated dressing room was found beneficial, with copious supplies of hot, strong coffee.

For pressures up to 30 pounds the men worked two shifts of four hours each, with one hour of rest between. For the highest pressure the men worked only 1½ hours at a time, and 4½ hours for the entire day.

The information herein contained is mostly abstracted from the report of the chief engineer, Mr. Charles M. Jacobs, Mem. Inst. C.E., Mem. Inst. M.E. The following narration of a bit of experience of Sunday, March 26, 1893, is quoted from the report.

"In order to keep an exact record of the air pressure I had fitted up an Edison automatic recording pressure gage with high and low pressure alarm bells attached. The foreman of the contractors with the engineer had broken the lock and removed the pencil. The fires were nearly out and the compressors were stopping, the pressure having fallen 11 pounds. A large quantity of soft ground had worked into the heading, entailing more exercise of ingenuity and determination to get things going right again. A great cavity had washed in and the water was bringing it down continuously."

In the progress of the work serious troubles occurred with the contractors, who finally abandoned the entire contract. At one point they had to be restrained by injunction from removing their compressors at a critical time. The air pressure would not have been maintained and a general collapse might have resulted. The matter became a subject of litigation.

At the Long Island end of the work the troubles had their own individuality. Bad and insufficient water for the boilers caused frequent stoppages, while it was essential to keep the pumps active to prevent drowning out. The first soft ground was met 253 feet from the shaft, and at 285 feet a green, slimy, and almost liquid material began oozing out, which so embarrassed the contractors that they then abandoned the work, allowing the heading to fill with water.

The stringency of the money market in 1893 was another incident which caused a cessation of all operations for a couple of months.

A neighboring picnic place, "Jones's Woods," took fire and with it was destroyed the entire plant at the New York end, and before pumps and compressors could be installed the heading was drowned out again.

The time of greatest anxiety, difficulty and risk was when, in advancing the shield at the New York end, a shelving bank of rock was found in front of the bottom of the shield, while at the top was the softest black mud. It was necessary to blast out this rock in the floor in advance of the shield and to get through the bulkhead which had been put in when the work had been abandoned. Direct communication was opened with the river, so that refuse and even live crabs came into the tunnels. The leakage of air was so great that both compressors at the limit of their speed had difficulty in maintaining the pressure of 48 pounds. The difficulties continued until the shield was entirely entered into the black mud, when the pressure was reduced and the shield was advanced at the rate of 6 feet per day. The shield was pushed forward by twelve hydraulic jacks with a combined thrust of 600 tons. The second soft place extended 98 feet. The rock ahead was badly seamed, but finally became solid again and then in two weeks 101 feet and 94.6 feet advance respectively was made, which rate had never been surpassed in that class of rock.

The headings met July 11, 1894, 1676 feet from the New York shaft. The total distance from shaft to shaft was 2550 feet, so that two-thirds of the length was driven from the New York end. When working in solid rock the average progress was 69 feet per week. Bonuses were given to foremen and to some of the gang leaders.

Considering the unexpected difficulties encountered and the delays from so many different causes, the total time from the beginning to the completion of the tunnel, a few days over two years, must be considered remarkable, and could only have been possible with constant resourcefulness and untiring push. After the ends met there was little more to be done and in a very short time a 36-inch gas main was laid with an uninterrupted motor car track at the side of it.—From *Compressed Air Magazine*.

CHAPTER IV

MANHATTAN-BRONX DIVISION OF THE NEW YORK SUBWAY

In January, 1890, the contract for the Manhattan-Bronx division of the New York subway was awarded and the work of construction was undertaken by the Rapid Transit Subway Construction Company. The work was to be done in four sections, as follows:

Section 1 extended from the southern terminus at City Hall to and including the station at 59th Street and Broadway; it comprised five miles of four-track subway.

Section 2 included all railroad from the north end of the 59th Street station to and including the station at 137th Street and Broadway; and on the east side from the junction of 103d Street and Broadway to and including the station at 135th Street and Lenox Avenue. This section comprised 3.43 miles of two-track subway and 0.51 mile of three-track viaduct.

Section 3 included all railroad on the west side, northward from the station at 137th Street and Broadway, to and including the station at Fort George; and on the east side from the station at 135th Street and Lenox Avenue, to and including the station at Melrose Avenue. This comprised 4.32 miles of two-track subway.

Section 4 comprised the remainder of the road, from Fort George to Kingsbridge on the west side and from Melrose Avenue on the east side, including 5.29 miles of two-track viaduct.

The prices to be paid were as follows:

Section 1	$15,000,000
Sections 1 and 2	26,000,000
Sections 1, 2 and 3	32,000,000
Sections 1, 2, 3 and 4	35,000,000

The cost of equipment was estimated at $6,000,000.

Note. From Report of the Chamber of Commerce of New York State, 1905; The New York Subway, issued by the Interborough Rapid Transit Company.

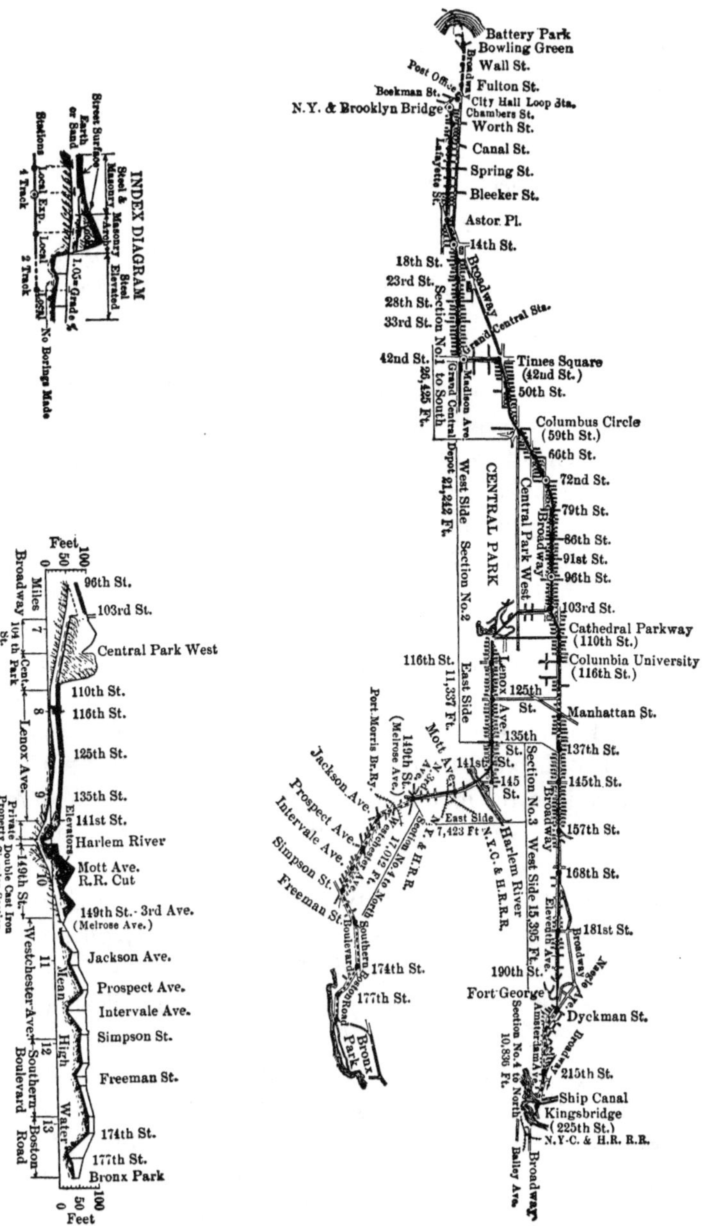

Map of the New York Rapid Transit Subway in Manhattan and The Bronx, with Contour of the Lenox Avenue Branch.

Five designs were adopted in the construction of the Manhattan-Bronx Division of the subway, as follows:

For a length of 10.6 miles or 52.2 per cent of the total length of the road, the typical section has a flat roof near the surface with I-beams connected by concrete arches forming the roof and sides, supported by bulb angle columns between the tracks.

In the Battery Park loop, for a short distance on Lenox Avenue and in the Brooklyn portion of the Brooklyn extension (later discussed), a flat roof of reinforced concrete is supported by bulb angle columns between the tracks.

For a distance of 4.6 miles or 23 per cent of the total length, concrete-lined tunnel was used, of which 4.2 per cent was concrete-lined open cut work and the remainder rock tunnel.

An elevated road on a steel viaduct was used for about five miles or 24.6 per cent of the total length.

Under the Harlem River, and under the East River for the Brooklyn extension, cast iron tubes were used. The construction of the typical subway has been carried out by a variety of methods adapted to the different situations in accordance with the views of the sub-contractors doing the work. The work was done in open excavation by the "cut and cover" system. The distance from the street level to the rock surface below determined the manner of excavating trenches. In some places the rock came to the surface; in other places the subway was entirely in water-bearing loam or sand. The natural difficulties of construction were increased by the network of sewers, water and gas mains, steam pipes, pneumatic tubes, electric conduits, etc., which filled the streets. The surface roads and their conduits still further complicated the problem.

In some places the columns of the elevated roads had to be shored temporarily. Where the subway passed close to the foundations of high buildings the shoring and other precautionary measures to insure safety were both intricate and costly; and a large proportion of the route was close to the surface, which entailed the removal and reconstruction in many places of the underground mains and ducts and of the projecting

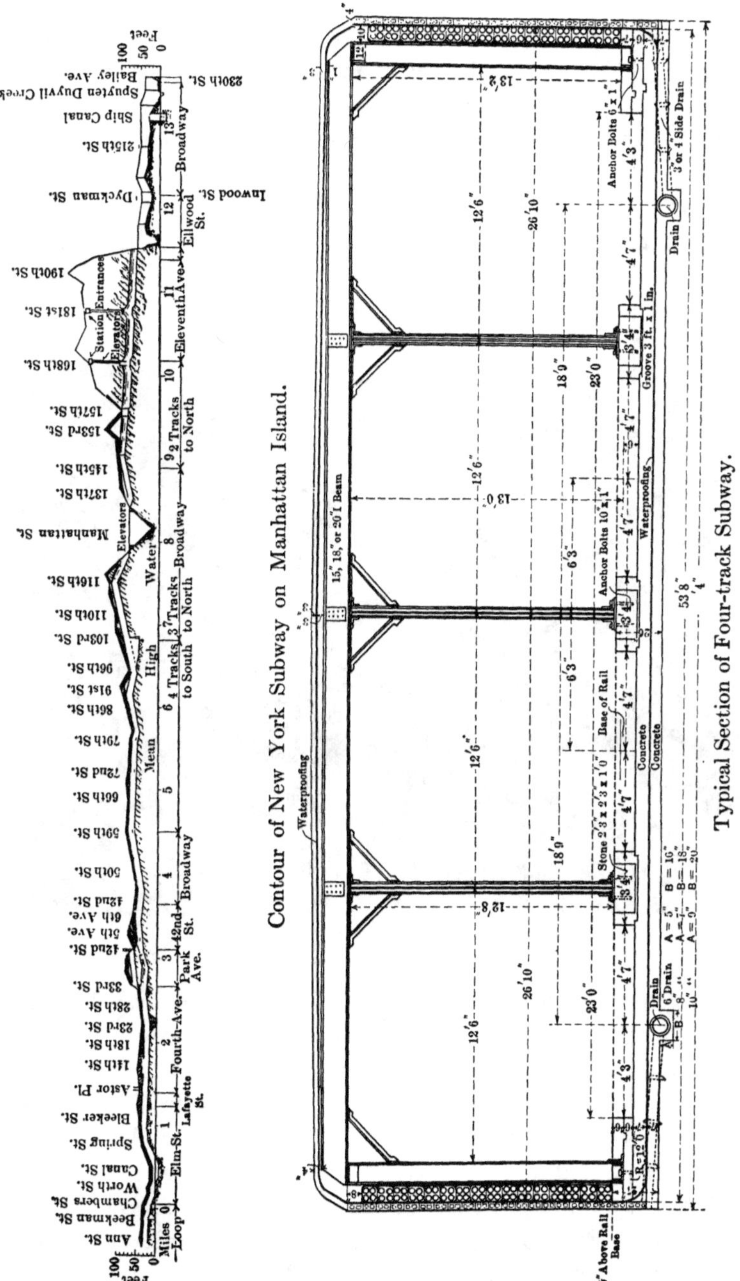

Contour of New York Subway on Manhattan Island.

Typical Section of Four-track Subway.

vaults and buildings, and required the underpinning of walls. Provision also had to be made for the maintenance of traffic upon the streets under which the subway was being built. Small sections or areas of these streets were floored or bridged to form a roadway for traffic while excavation was going on beneath. Where the rock came to the surface it was necessary to divert the electric surface roads to the side of the street; for attempts to remove the rock from beneath the tracks

Subway Construction at Union Square and Fourth Avenue.

destroyed the yokes of the surface road. Open trench work was adopted where the roadway was sufficiently wide to permit traffic at the sides. In the case of surface tracks overlying the area to be excavated the tracks were hung from the lower chords of trusses supported at their ends on crib work.

Between 33d and 42d Streets under Park Avenue, between 116th and 120th Streets under Broadway, between 157th Street and Fort George under Broadway and Eleventh Avenue, and between 104th Street and Broadway under Central

Park and Lenox Avenue, the road is in a rock tunnel lined with concrete. The section on the west side between 157th Street and Fort George constitutes the second longest double-track rock tunnel in the United States, the Hoosac Tunnel only exceeding it in length.

From 116th Street to 120th Street on Broadway the tunnel is 37½ feet in width—one of the widest concrete arches in the world. On the Lenox Avenue section from Broadway and 103d

Subway Tunnel Heading at 116th Street and Broadway: Timbering in Soft Ground Over Rock.

Street to Lenox Avenue and 110th Street under Central Park, a two-track tunnel was driven through micaceous rock by taking out top headings and two full-width benches, the work being done from two shafts and one portal. All drilling for the headings was done by an eight-hour night shift, using percussion drills. The blasting was done early in the morning and the day gang removed the spoil, which was hauled to the shafts and the portal in cars drawn by mules. A large part of this rock was crushed for concrete. The concrete floor was the first part of the lining to be put in place. Rails were laid on it for a traveler having molds attached to its sides, against which the walls were built. A similar traveler followed with the centering for the arch roof, a length of about fifty feet being completed at each operation.

On the Park Avenue section from 34th Street to 41st Street two separate double-track tunnels were driven below, and one on either side of, a double-track electric railway tunnel.

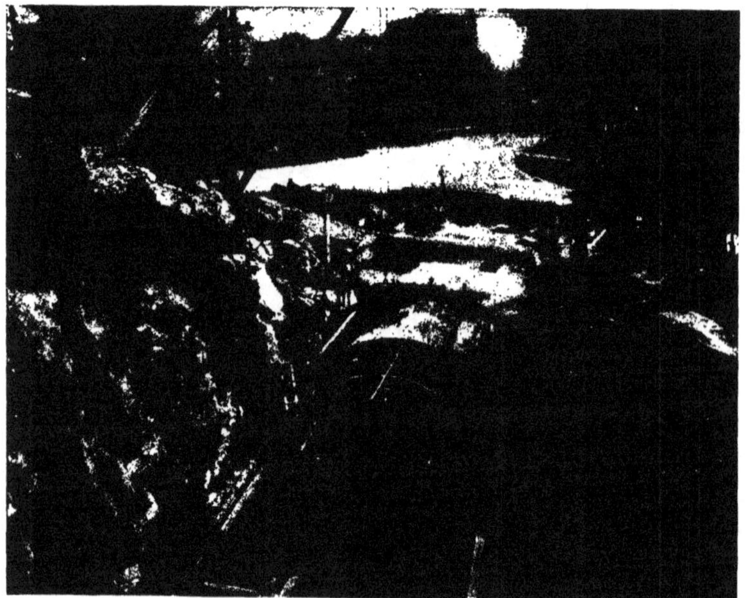

Open Cut Subway Construction in Central Park, Lenox Avenue Branch.

This work was done from four shafts, one at each end of each tunnel. At first top headings were driven at the north end of both tunnels and at the south end of the west tunnel; at the south end of the east tunnel a bottom heading was driven. The system of driving at the south end of the west tunnel was later changed from a top to a bottom heading. The rock in this section was irregular and the inclination of the strata gave rise to serious danger from slips.

The headings of the west tunnel met in February and those of the east tunnel in March, 1902. The enlargement of the tunnels to the full section was then commenced. A disturbance above the surface of the east tunnel resulted in damage to several house fronts. The portion of tunnel affected was bulkheaded at each end, packed with rubble and grouted with Portland cement mortar injected under pressure through pipes sunk from the street surface. When the interior was firm the tunnel was re-driven, using much the same methods employed in earth tunnels where the arch lining is built before the central cone has been removed. To avoid further settlement of the earth the work was done slowly. When the lining had been completed Portland cement grout was again injected under pressure through holes left in the roof until further movement of the fill above was prevented.

The tunnel between 157th Street and Fort George, already referred to as the second longest two-track tunnel in the United States, was put through in a short time and without any special difficulty. The tunnel was driven from two portals and two shafts, the latter at 168th and 181st Streets. The heading was carried north and south from each shaft.

The Harlem River is crossed by a tunnel of twin single-track cast-iron cylinders 16 feet in diameter. The approaches on both sides are double-tracked concrete arch structures. The total length of the section is 1500 feet, of which 641 feet are of the cast-iron cylinder construction. Instead of employing the usual methods by the use of shields and compressed air, these subaqueous tunnels were formed by dredging a trench in the bed of the river, in which a caisson was built, within which the excavation was made. The bed of the Harlem River at this point is of mud, silt and sand, much of which was so nearly fluid that it was removed by a jet process. The maximum depth of excavation was about fifty feet. The trench was 50 feet wide and carried to a grade of 39 feet below low water, this grade being about 10 feet above the subgrade of the tunnel. The War Department required that there be a depth of 20 feet over the tunnel at low water and that during construction half of the width of the river should be left free for navigation.

To support a working platform three rows of piles were driven on each side of the trench from the west bank to the middle of the river, there being 38 feet in the clear between the platforms. A pile foundation was then made over the area to be covered by the subway. The piles were driven with 6 feet 4 inches transversely and 8 feet longitudinally between centers. They were then cut off 11 feet above the center line of each tube and capped with 12-inch square timbers. A caisson in which

Concrete Arch Subway Construction in Open Cut.

to excavate the remaining material and place the iron and concrete was formed of 12-inch sheet piles for the sides and a heavy timber roof. As a guide and steadiment for the sheet piling which formed the sides of the caisson, a frame-work was built and sunk over the pile foundations. Transverse trusses were connected longitudinally at their outer ends by eight timbers 12 inches square, so arranged that two timber stringers, separated to permit the passage of and to form a guide for the sheet piles, were bolted to the upper and lower chords at each end. The sheathing was driven to a depth of 10 to 15 feet below the bottom of the finished tunnel. The roof, formed of three courses of 12-inch square timbers, separated by a 2-inch plank and thoroughly caulked, was then floated into position over the piles, loaded with earth and sunk. Three timber shafts, 7×17 feet in plan, passed through this roof. Work in this caisson was carried on under air pressure, part of the spoil being blown out by water jets and the remainder removed through the air-locks in the shafts. When the excavation had been completed the piles were braced, the concrete and cast-iron lining put in place, and the piles cut off as the concrete bed was laid up to them.

The eastern half of this tunnel was a modification of the plan just described. The side walls of the caisson were formed of sheet piling, but for a roof the permanent upper half of the tunnel of iron and concrete was used. The trench was dredged nearly to subgrade. Steel pilot piles with water jets were driven in advance of the wooden sheet piles. If boulders were encountered they were drilled and blasted. The steel piles were pulled by a hoisting engine and the wooden piles driven in their place. When the piling was finished a pontoon 35 feet by 106 feet and 12 feet deep was built between the working platforms. Upon a false deck or floor the upper half of the cast-iron shells was assembled, their ends closed by steel diaphragms, and the whole covered with concrete. The pontoon was then submerged several feet, parted at the center and each half drawn endwise from beneath the floating top of the tunnel. The latter was then loaded and carefully sunk in place, the connection with the shore section being made by a diver and access through the roof being provided by a special opening. When in place men entered through the shore section, cut away the floor or wooden bottom and completed the caisson so that work could proceed. Three of these caissons were required to complete the east end of the crossing.

The construction of the approaches to the sub-river tunnel was carried out between heavy sheet piling. The excavation was very wet and in places over 40 feet in depth.

The following data cover the essential features involved

in the building of the Manhattan-Bronx section of the subway, the approximate quantities of excavation and materials being from the chief engineer's report:

The total length of this section of the subway is 109,570 feet.

The total amount of excavation was 2,990,016 cubic yards of which 1,700,228 cubic yards were earth, 921,182 cubic yards were open cut rock work, and 368,606 cubic yards were rock tunnel.

Cameron Pump for Drainage in Harlem River Tunnel, New York Subway.

The cost of excavating was about one-third of the total amount of the contract. The time required for excavating was two-thirds of the time allotted for the completion of the job.

The quantities of the principal materials used in construction were approximately as follows: steel, 65,000 tons; cast iron, 8,000 tons; concrete, 489,122 cubic yards; brick, 18,519 cubic yards; water-proofing materials, 775,795 square yards.

The total length of track is 305,000 feet, of which 245,000 feet are underground and 60,000 feet above ground. The contract time was four and one-half years.

CHAPTER V

BROOKLYN-MANHATTAN DIVISION OF THE NEW YORK SUBWAY

In September, 1902, the contract for the Brooklyn-Manhattan branch of the subway was awarded to the Rapid Transit Subway Construction Company for $3,000,000. The route to be followed was to be from the junction of Park Row under Broadway, Bowling Green, Battery Place, State Street and Battery Park, with a loop under Battery Park and Whitehall Street. From there it was to pass under the East River to Furman Street, Brooklyn, and thence under Joralemon and Fulton Streets and Flatbush Avenue to the junction of Flatbush and Atlantic Avenues. The entire line is underground. At the Battery the Brooklyn line passes under the Manhattan line to avoid a grade crossing. The estimated cost of road and equipment was from $8,000,000 to $10,000,000.

Three types of construction were used in the Manhattan-Brooklyn Division, as follows:

Typical flat-roof steel beam subway from the Post Office to Bowling Green.

Typical reinforced concrete subway in Battery Park, Manhattan, and from Clinton Street to the terminus in Brooklyn.

Two single-track cast-iron lined tubular tunnels from Battery Park under the East River and under Joralemon Street to Clinton Street, Brooklyn.

Under Broadway, Manhattan, the work was through sand. The congested surface traffic, the net-work of sub-surface structures, and the high buildings adjacent, made this one of the most difficult portions of the road to build. Because of the heavy surface traffic it was required that during construction the street should be maintained in a condition which would not impede this traffic during the day time. This was provided for by making openings in the sidewalks near the curb at two points and erecting temporary working platforms over the street, 16 feet from the surface.

Excavation was done by the ordinary drift and tunnel method. The excavated material was hoisted from the openings to the platforms and discharged into wagons. On the street surface, over and in advance of the excavation, temporary plank

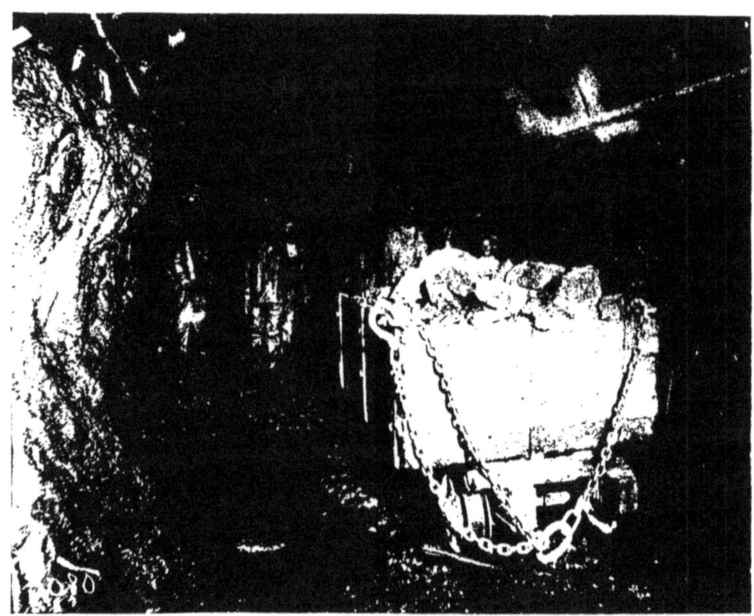

Drilling and Mucking in East River Subway Tunnel.

decks were placed and maintained during the drifting and tunneling operations, and after the permanent subway structure had been erected up to the time when the street surface was permanently restored. As the roof of the subway was only five feet from the street surface, gas and water mains and conduits had to be arranged for. These were carried temporarily on a trestle work over the sidewalks and when the subway structure was completed they were restored to their former position.

From Bowling Green, south along Broadway and State Street and in Battery Park, where the subway was in reinforced concrete, the "cut and cover" method was employed, the

Driving Sheet Piling with an Ingersoll-Rand Sheet Pile Driver on Subway Construction in Brooklyn.

elevated and surface railway structures being temporarily supported by wooden and steel trusses and permanently supported by foundations resting on the subway roof. From Battery

Place, south along the loop, the greater portion of the excavation was below mean high-water level, and necessitated the use of heavy tongue-and-groove sheathing and the continuous operation of two centrifugal pumps to keep the work dry.

The tubes or tunnels under the East River, including the approaches, were each 6544 feet in length. They were formed of cast-iron sections bolted together and had an inside diameter

Ingersoll-Rand Rock Drills in Heading of One of the East River Subway Tunnels.

of 15½ feet. They were reinforced by grouting outside of the plates and lined inside with beton to the depth of the flanges.

From the Manhattan side to the middle of the East River the tunnels were in rock and the ordinary rock tunnel drift method was employed, the work being carried on under air pressure. On the Brooklyn side beneath the river the formation was sand and silt. Four shields weighing 51 tons each were used and a hydraulic pressure of about 2000 tons provided to force them forward; two shields, working from Garden Place toward the center of the river, were operated under air pressure in water-bearing sand. The river tubes have a 3.1 per cent grade, and at the deepest point in the middle of the river the depth is about 94 feet below mean high water.

The typical subway of reinforced concrete from Clinton Street to the terminus at Flatbush Avenue was constructed by the method already described in connection with the Manhattan-Bronx Division. From Borough Hall to the terminus the route of the subway is directly below an elevated structure, which was temporarily supported by timber bracing having its bearing on the street surface and upon the tunnel timbers. Permanent support was provided by means of masonry piers built upon the roof of the subway structure.

Along this portion of the route are surface electric roads operated by an overhead trolley on tracks of the ordinary tie construction. Little difficulty was experienced in taking care of these during the construction of the subway. Work was carried on day and night, the excavation being expedited by using flat cars on the surface trolley roads for removing the spoil. Spur tracks were built for this purpose and most of this removal was done at night.

CHAPTER VI

COMPRESSED AIR IN THE SUBWAY CONSTRUCTION: COST OF EXCAVATION IN THE NEW YORK SUBWAY

THE original plan of the general contractor on the New York subway work, Mr. John B. McDonald, was to install air com-

Ingersoll-Rand Corliss Compressor Used in Subway Construction at the Battery Park Plant. This Compressor was one of those used in building the Jerome Park Reservoir.

pressing plants at convenient points along the line of construction and to dispose of the air power to the sub-contractors. This project, however, was not carried out. The sub-contractors installed their own compressor plants, either as individuals or by a number of them uniting to build a plant for their own use. The installation and use of central air compressing plants to provide power for the work may be accepted as the factor that made possible the building of the subway within the specified limits of time and cost. It is to be regretted that no record was kept of the actual cost of operation of these plants. Nor were there any steam plants working under similar conditions with which comparison could be made. There can be no doubt, however, that the advantages of compressed air were a controlling influence in hastening this important work. To illustrate the advantages of a central air compressing plant over the use of scattered, direct steam driven machines, the following comparison is given showing the decrease in operating costs secured by converting the steam plants of the Gray Canon Quarries near Cleveland, O., to a centralized compressed air plant. The table given below is a comparison of average daily fuel and labor charges against the power system during the month of April, 1903, when operating by steam and during the corresponding month of 1904, when operating by compressed air.

	1903		1904	
Coal consumption	50 tons run-of-mine at $2	$100.00	15½ tons slack at $1.60	$ 24.80
Labor and attendance, channelers	16 machines at $10	160.00	12 machines at $10	120.00
Labor and attendance, drills	15 machines at $3	45.00	9 machines at $3	27.00
Firemen at hoists	9 men at $1.25	11.25		
Firemen at pumps and drill boilers	2 men at $2	4.00		
Firemen at mill, 12-hour shift	2 men at $1.25	2.50		
Boiler repair gang		5.00		
Locomotive repair and rental		10.00		
Coke for reheaters		....		1.00
Total charge, labor and fuel		$337.75		$172.80

The total daily saving in labor and fuel by means of compressed air was $164.95, corresponding to a total saving in a year of 300 days of $49,485.00.

The reduction in the number of machines operated in 1904 is due to the fact that a high and constant air pressure was always available and enabled the lesser number of machines to do more work than was performed by the greater number in 1903, when operating under the lower and fluctuating steam pressure. It is assumed in the table that the minor charges for lubrication and waste are the same.

The coal consumption was a matter of absolute record. In 1903, run-of-mine coal was used, delivered to 31 boilers, and broken, scattered and wasted in cartage. In 1904 slack coal was handled, at minimum cost.

Another fact worthy of note is that the steam plants replaced by the new air system were, in most cases, operating under conditions of average fuel and steam economy. The boilers at the hoists were of good tubular type, in standard brick settings and well housed. The channelers carried their own boilers of standard locomotive type. Yet even with these favorable conditions for fuel economy the saving in coal consumption has been as indicated in the table above. The tabulated comparison is a statement of fact, but it fails to bring out two points of vital importance, viz., the output of rock, when using air, was greater than when using steam; and this increased output was secured with a force reduced by 75 men. Figuring these men at the average daily wage paid, the daily saving already shown is brought up to $275.00.

The result is due to the fact that a full working day of ten hours is secured. When the throttles are opened a full working pressure is available and maintained throughout the working day. There is no delay in starting due to fluctuating boiler pressure. There is no labor employed in wheeling coal, in moving water barrels and pipe to keep pace with machines. There is no steam or smoke settling in the work and interfering with the hoisting. There is no water to be blown out or draining gangs to look after the pipes to avoid freezing. The working conditions are in every way improved.

Cost of Rock Excavation in Open Cut: New York Subway. The results here given were secured under fair average conditions, using air driven rock drills, loading the spoil into self-dumping buckets carried by cableways, and dumping into wagons.

The cost of drilling, blasting and disposing of the spoil was, in mica schist, from $2.25 to $2.40 per cubic yard, varying with the length of haul and the depth of cut. This high cost per cubic yard was due to inefficient labor, to the restriction of city ordinances limiting the amount of explosive used at a blast, and to the great amount of trimming and sledging of rock.

The average scale of wages was, for an 8-hour shift, as follows:

Foremen	$3.50 to $4.00
Laborers	1.50
Teams and drivers	4.50
Drillers	2.75
Drillers' helpers	1.50
Hoist runners	3.00
Compressor engineers	4.00
Firemen	2.00
Carpenters	3.50
Timber handlers	2.00
Smiths	2.75
Smiths' helpers	1.50
Water boys	.75

In the cost per cubic yard as here given allowance has been made for all charges, including interest and depreciation.

The depth of excavation was from twenty-five to forty feet and the average width about forty feet. Laborers handled and loaded something less than two cubic yards per shift; this small performance to be accounted for by the sledging and plug-and-feather work required after blasting, to make the rock of a size that could be loaded into the buckets by hand. The cost of hauling about one mile was from 55 to 65 cents per cubic yard. The average weight of 40 per cent dynamite used per cubic yard was three-fifths of a pound, dynamite costing 12½ cents per pound.

Cost of Earth Work: New York Subway. The earth excavation in the lower part of the city was usually performed under the most difficult conditions. It was required that the street traffic should not be interfered with during the day time; that surface car tracks should be diverted or supported; and that the net-work of mains, conduits and sewers should be kept operating during construction.

The cost of earth excavation under these conditions was from $3.50 to $3.70 per cubic yard. In places where the work was in sand, the cost of shoring and supporting the mains, pipes and conduits was 50 cents per cubic yard. In the sections in the upper part of the town where the traffic was less and the conditions more favorable, the cost varied between 75 and 95 cents per cubic yard. This was in earth, ploughed and shoveled into wagons, the wagons being pulled out of the cut by power or snatch teams.

Under conditions where the surface tracks required more support, where the mains and conduits were more numerous, and where the spoil was dumped at sea, the cost increased to $1.25 to $1.60 per cubic yard. The charge for hauling to sea by barge was 60 cents per wagon load, equivalent to about 30 cents per cubic yard. The contractors were paid from $2.00 to $2.50 per cubic yard according to the difficulties of excavation.

Cost of Concrete: New York Subway.

In foundations .... $4.50 to $4.75 per cubic yard
Roof and side arches............. 7.50 to 8.00 per cubic yard
Average cost per cubic yard in
arches, foundations and covering 6.00

Cost of Brick Work: New York Subway.

In backing .... $10.50 to $11.00 per cubic yard

CHAPTER VII

THE PENNSYLVANIA RAILROAD DEVELOPMENTS IN AND NEAR NEW YORK CITY

The North River Bridge Company projected the building of a great suspension bridge across the North or Hudson River to enable all of the railroads terminating on the west shore of the river to enter New York City at the foot of West Twenty-third Street. The Pennsylvania Railroad Company gave this project its support by agreeing to pay its pro rata share for the use of the bridge, but the other railroads declined to participate and the plan was abandoned.

The Pennsylvania Railroad having acquired control of the Long Island Railroad, and having decided to establish terminal facilities in New York City proper, undertook the project of connecting New Jersey, Manhattan Island and Long Island by a system of tunnels. New operating conditions, resulting from the application of electric traction to the movement of heavy railroad trains, which were initiated in tunnel operation by the Baltimore & Ohio Railroad and subsequently studied and adopted by railroads in Europe, had eliminated the difficulties of ventilation connected with steam traction through tunnels and also made possible the use of grades which had been practically prohibitive with the steam locomotive.

Under the new plan the main line of the Pennsylvania Railroad connects with the tunnel system by a surface line beginning near Newark, N. J., which crosses the Hackensack Meadows, passes through Bergen Hill and under the North River, Manhattan Island, and East River in tunnels, to a large terminal yard known as Sunnyside Yard in Long Island City

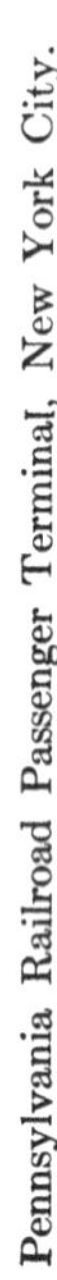

Pennsylvania Railroad Passenger Terminal, New York City.

The estimated cost of the New York tunnel extension and station, including the interchange yards at Harrison, N. J., and Sunnyside, L. I., was $100,000,000.

This system is essentially one for handling passenger traffic, but the Pennsylvania Railroad has not only the legal power but also the facilities for making it a through route for freight if desired. The requirements include handling the heaviest through express trains as well as the more frequent and lighter trains for local service. The following summary of the various divisions of the line will give a comprehensive idea of the general features of the project.

The Meadows division includes the interchange yard at Harrison, near Newark, N. J., adjoining the tracks of the present New York division of the Pennsylvania Railroad. It also includes a double-track railroad across the Hackensack meadows to the west side of Bergen Hill, a total distance of 6.04 miles. The construction throughout this division is embankment and bridge work.

The North River division commences at the west side of Bergen Hill and passes through the hill in two single-track rock tunnels to a large permanent shaft at Weehawken, near the west shore of the North River; and thence eastward a distance of 224 feet to the Weehawken shield chamber. It then passes under the North River through two cast iron, concrete-lined, single-track tunnels having an outside diameter of 23 feet, to a point under Thirty-second Street near Eleventh Avenue, in New York City. It continues thence through two single track tunnels of varying cross-section, partly constructed by the cut-and-cover method, to the east side of Tenth Avenue. Here it enters the station yard and terminates at the east building line of Ninth Avenue. The work in this division includes the station yard excavation and walls from Tenth Avenue to Ninth Avenue, and the retaining walls and temporary underpinning of Ninth Avenue. The aggregate length of line in this division is 2.76 miles.

The New York Terminal Station and its approaches extend from the east line of Tenth Avenue eastward to a point in Thirty-second and Thirty-third streets, distant respectively 292 feet and 502 feet eastward from the west line of Seventh Avenue. This division includes also the construction of subways and bridges for the support of Thirty-first and Thirty-third streets and Seventh, Eighth and Ninth avenues. Work classified under this division comprises also the Terminal Building between Seventh and Eighth avenues; the foundations for the Post Office to be erected west of Eighth Avenue; the service power house in Thirty-first Street between Seventh and Eighth avenues; the power house in Long Island City; and the traction system, tracks, signals and miscellaneous facilities required in the physical construction of the entire terminal railroad ready for operation.

The terminal station is of steel skeleton construction with masonry curtain walls, all supported by a system of columns reaching to rock foundation. The building covers two city blocks and one intersecting street and has an area of about eight acres. It is 774 feet long, 433 feet wide, with an average height above the street of 69 feet and a maximum of 153 feet. The main waiting room is 277 by 103 feet and 150 feet high. The concourse is 340 feet by 210 feet in size.

The level of the track system below the street surface varies from 39 to 58 feet, and is from 7 to 10 feet below mean high water in the harbor. This necessitated the establishing of an elaborate system of drainage over the entire station yard area.

To accelerate the loading and unloading of trains, high platforms are constructed in the station on a level with the floors of the cars in order to avoid the use of car steps and to increase the traffic capacity of the station. Access to the street is gained by elevators and stairways. There are twenty-one standing tracks at the station and eleven passenger platforms providing 21,500 feet of platform adjacent to passenger trains. Within the station area, which from Tenth Avenue to the normal tunnel sections east of Seventh Avenue comprises 28 acres, there is a total of about sixteen miles of track.

The service plant for the accommodation of machinery for lighting, heating and ventilating the station, and for operating the interlocking switch and signal system, is located in an independent building south of the station.

The power house to supply the electrical energy for the operation of the tunnel lines and the Long Island Railroad is located in Queens Borough on property adjoining the present Long Island station, near the East River. As at present designed the dimensions of the structure are 200 by 262 feet outside. It accommodates six generating units of 5500 k.w. (the standard capacity adopted for traction work) and two units of 2500 k.w. for lighting. The ultimate capacity of this station when fully extended will be about 105,000 k.w.

The East River division begins at the eastern limits of the New York station in Thirty-second and Thirty-third streets, including also the excavation work and retaining walls for the station site and yard to the track level westward to Ninth Avenue. It extends eastward from the station through tunnels, partly three-track and partly so-called twin tunnels to Second Avenue. Thence the line curves to the left under private property to the permanent shafts a short distance east of First Avenue. From this point four single-track, cast iron, concrete-lined tunnels 23 feet in outside diameter cross under the East River, and after passing through permanent shafts near the bulkhead line reach the surface in Long Island City from 3000 to 4200 feet east of the East River. The eastern portals of these tunnels are in the Sunnyside yard. The total length of this division is 4.48 miles.

The total length of the entire line included in the Pennsylvania extensions into New York City is 13.66 miles. There are 6.78 miles of single-track tube tunnels and the average length of the tunnels between portals is 5.56 miles.

In all parts of the work problems were encountered requiring for their solution large expenditures and much engineering skill; but many of the difficulties had been frequently met in previous engineering experience and the methods of overcoming them were well understood. Thus in the Meadows division a long and heavy embankment (part of which was on submerged meadow land) and many bridge foundations had to be constructed. In the Bergen Hill tunnels a very tough trap rock was encountered. In the tunnels under New York City the work was much complicated and its cost greatly increased by the necessity of caring for sewers, water and gas pipes, and foundations of adjacent buildings. Many troublesome problems were also met in the construction of the tunnels connecting the East River with the Sunnyside yard. The novel features of the project, however, were the great tunnels carrying the line under the North and East rivers.

The maximum grade west of the terminal station occurs on the New York side of the North River. It is 2 per cent in the west-bound and 1.93 per cent in the east-bound tunnels. The ruling grades for the ascending traffic are 1.32 per cent in the west-bound and 1.93 per cent in the east-bound tunnels. In the tunnels east of the terminal station the ruling grade is 1.5 per cent for both east-bound and west-bound traffic. These grades would be objectionable, if not prohibitive, with steam locomotives under heavy traffic, but the development of the electric locomotive has rendered operation over these grades entirely practicable.

From the junction with the Pennsylvania Railroad, near Harrison, N. J., to Woodside, L. I., a distance of 13.66 miles, there is an average of 1.5 curves per mile. The line has a total curvature of 230 degrees and the maximum curvature is 2 degrees.

The character of the material through which the subaqueous tunnels were constructed differed greatly in the two rivers. The bed of the North River at the level of the tunnels consists of silt, composed principally of clay, sand and water. The bed of the East River at the working point is made up of a great variety of materials, including quicksand, sand, boulders, gravel, clay and bed-rock. When the method of construction had to be decided upon for these divisions of the work there were no thoroughly satisfactory precedents to follow in either case. The gas tunnel under the East River, the partly constructed Hudson tunnels under the North River, the St. Clair tunnel under the St. Clair River, the Blackwell and several other tunnels under the Thames River in London, supplied much useful information.

Most of the methods proposed involved temporary structures or the use of a floating plant in the navigable channels of the river. After full consideration of the subject, however, it was decided to adopt the shield method with compressed air for the construction of the sub-river tunnels. This was the only method recommended by the chief engineers and had the great advantage of conducting all operations below the bottom of the river, thus avoiding any obstruction of the channels.

Experience has shown that it is much more difficult to construct tunnels in such materials as were encountered in the East River and on the New Jersey side of the North River than in the more homogeneous material which was found in the greater part of the North River work. During the progress of construction under the East River there were frequent blowouts through fissures opened in the river bed; and the bottom of the river over the tunnel had to be blanketed continually with clay to check the flow of the escaping air from the shield.

In view of the serious difficulties which is was thought might be encountered in the application of the shield method to the East River work, several other methods for the execution of this division received special consideration. One of these was the freezing process, and an extended experiment was made to prove its possibilities. A pilot tunnel 7½ feet in diameter was driven into the bed of the East River for a distance of 160 feet. Circulating pipes were established in it and brine, at a very low temperature, was passed through them until the ground was frozen for a distance of about 15 feet around the tunnel. Observations were carefully made to determine the rate of cooling and other important points connected with the process. It was found, however, that the construction of the tunnels was progressing satisfactorily by the shield method; and as so much time was required to freeze the material as to make the freezing process of no advantage in this particular case, the experiment was discontinued.

The sub-river tunnels consisted of a cast iron shell of segmental bolted type with an outside diameter of 23 feet and lined with concrete having a normal thickness of 2 feet from the outside of the shell. Through each plate of the shell there is a small hole, closed with a screw plug, through which grout may be forced into the surrounding material. Each tunnel contains a single track.

A concrete bench, the upper surface of which is 1 foot below the axis of the tunnel, is built on each side of the track, the distance between the bench faces being 11 feet 8 inches. Within these benches are ducts carrying the electric cables. The principal object in adopting single-track tunnels instead of a larger two-track section was to avoid the danger of accidents due to the obstruction of both tracks by derailment or otherwise.

The tunnels are just large enough to allow the passage of the train with perfect safety, for it was believed that with such an arrangement the motion of the trains would secure a thorough ventilation. Experience seems to justify this assumption; but in order to insure thorough ventilation under unusual conditions, such as the stoppage of trains in the tunnels, a complete ventilation plant is provided for each tube. Furthermore the rapidity and safety of construction were increased by making the tunnels as small as possible; since one of the difficulties in the shield method of tunnel driving is the difference in hydrostatic pressure between the top and bottom of the shield, which increases with the diameter of the tunnel.

The concrete lining was introduced to insure the permanency of the structure, to strengthen it from outward pressure and to guard it against injury from accidents which might occur in the tunnel. At points where unusual stresses were anticipated, as where the tubes pass from rock into soft ground, the shell is composed of steel instead of cast iron plates. One of the most important questions connected with the design of these tunnels was their probable stability under long, continued action of heavy and rapid railroad traffic. The tunnels are lighter than the materials which they displace when the weight of the heavy, live load is included.

Some idea of the increase in passenger traffic resulting from the establishment of the tunnel line may be obtained by comparing the proposed daily train movement from the new terminal station with the train movement at other important railroad stations as given below.

	Total trains in and out for 24 hours.	Movement at maximum hour.
Jersey City	281	29
Broad Street, Philadelphia	538	48
Union Station, St. Louis	462	89
South Terminal Station, Boston	861	87
Grand Central, New York	357	44
Pennsylvania Station, New York	500	50

From Proceedings Am. Soc. C.E., Sept., 1909. "The New York Tunnel Extension of the Penn. R. R.," by Chas. W. Raymond, M. Am. Soc. C. E.

CHAPTER VIII

BERGEN HILL TUNNELS OF THE PENNSYLVANIA RAILROAD

THESE two single-track, parallel tunnels, each 5920 feet in length, are on the west shore of the Hudson River, and penetrate Bergen Hill, which is a dyke of trap rock forming a southern extension of the Hudson River Palisades. The contractors on this work were the John Shields Construction Company and William Bradley. The work was contracted for January 20, 1906, and was completed December 31, 1908.

Starting west from the Weehawken shaft the tunnels passed through a fault for a distance of 400 feet. The broken ground in this fault consists of decomposed, sandstone, shale, feldspar, calcite, etc., interspersed with masses of harder sandstone and baked shale, gradually merging into a compact granular sandstone. The trap rock is encountered about 940 feet from the shaft. The full face of the tunnel is in trap rock at about 1000 feet from the shaft and continues in this formation to the western portal. Sandstone and trap rock are of the Triassic period, the latter being classified as diabase. The character of the trap rock varied. In places a very hard, fine-grained trap, almost black, was found, having a specific gravity of 2.98 and weighing 186 pounds per cubic foot. In this rock the average time required to drill a 10-foot hole with a No. 34 " Slugger " drill under 90 pounds pressure was 10 hours. The remainder of the trap varied from this extremely hard quality, due to different amounts of quartz and feldspar, down to a coarse-grained rock resembling a light colored granite and quite hard.

The speed of drilling the normal trap in the heading was approximately 20 to 25 minutes per foot as compared to 60 minutes per foot as noted above in the harder rock. The larger amounts of feldspar and quartz gave a greater brittle-

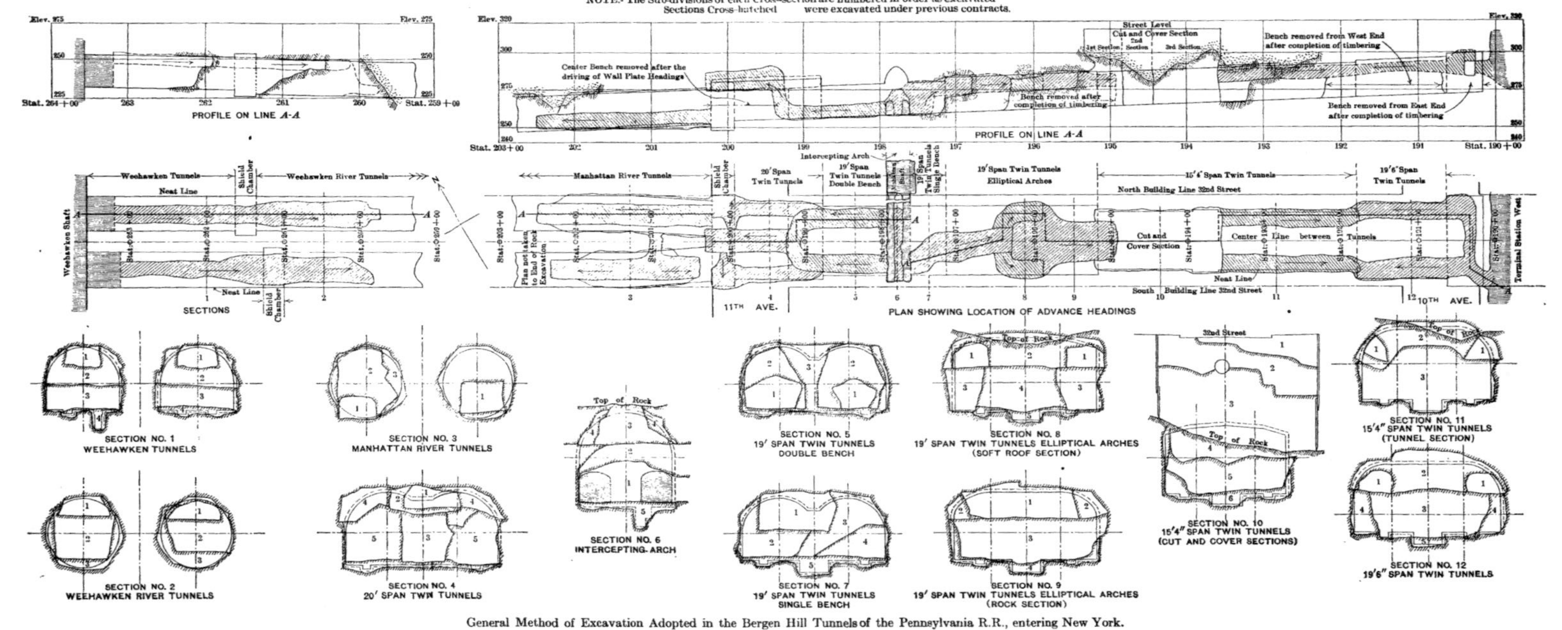

General Method of Excavation Adopted in the Bergen Hill Tunnels of the Pennsylvania R.R., entering New York.

ness in the latter case, and made easier drilling. The normal trap has a specific gravity of from 2.85 to 3.04 and weighs from 179 to 190 pounds per cubic foot.

These tunnels were excavated entirely by the center top heading method, which has found almost universal application in the United States. The drills used throughout the work

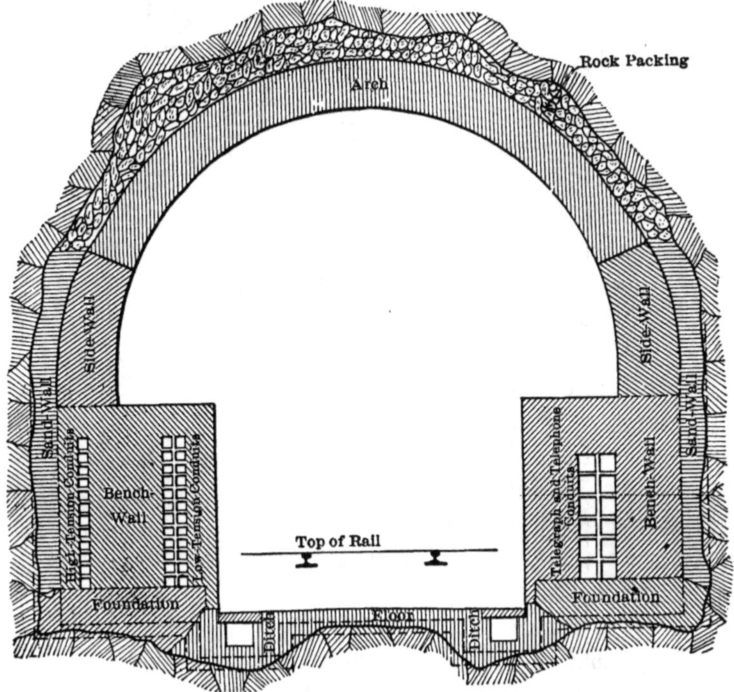

SKETCH SHOWING DIVISION OF LINING, FOR PURPOSES OF CONSTRUCTION, AND NAMES OF SECTIONS

Typical Cross-section of P.R.R. Bergen Hill Tunnels

were No. 34 Rand " Sluggers " with a $3\frac{5}{8}$-inch cylinder diameter. The steel used was " Black Diamond," $1\frac{3}{8}$-inch octagon section. These were from 2 to 12 feet in length. The bits started with a diameter of $2\frac{3}{4}$ to 3 inches, which was held to a depth of about 6 feet, when it was gradually decreased to from $1\frac{3}{4}$ to $2\frac{1}{4}$ inches at the bottom of a 12-foot hole. There was an average of one sharpening for each foot drilled and about one-quarter of an inch of steel was used for each sharpening. The quantity of steel used, lost or scrapped, was one foot for every 10 cubic yards of rock excavated, equivalent to 1.2 inches per cubic yard. An " Ajax " drill sharpener was used and proved very satisfactory.

On the bench rubber and cotton hose covered with woven marline, 3 inches in inside diameter, was used in 50-foot lengths. For the drills the same style of hose was used, one inch in diameter and in 25-foot lengths; and for the steam shovels 2½-inch hose was used in 50-foot lengths. Hose coverings of wound marline and of woven marline with spiral steel wire covering were tried. But they were not satisfactory owing to the unwinding of the marline and to the bending of the steel covering.

The average quantity of powder used was 2.9 pounds per cubic yard. Both 40 and 60 per cent dynamite were used, the latter being exclusively employed in the latter part of the work. The rock broke well. In sandstone the weight of powder used per cubic yard was much greater than in trap.

In drilling the central shaft a 6-hole cut was made on the center line, later enlarged by making 18 holes to a depth of 6 feet. In a 24-hour day the average advance was 4 feet. In the shaft the drills were run by steam until a depth of 150 feet had been reached, when compressed air became available. Four drills were used until compressed air was adopted, after which six were operated.

The drills were at work 5.2 hours per 8-hour shift. They were actually " hitting the rock " 2.5 hours per shift. The average depth drilled per hour during the time of 5.2 hours was 2.66 feet. The average footage drilled per hour, all delays included, was 1.64 feet. The following figures give the estimated cost per drill per day:

Drill runner, 1 at $3.50 per day	$3.50
Helper, 1 at $2.00 per day	2.00
Nipper, 1/5 at $1.75 per day	0.35
Heading foreman, 1/12 at $5.00	0.42
Walking boss, 1/50 at $7.50 per day	0.15
Blacksmith, 1/12 at $4.00 per day	0.34

Blacksmith's helper, 1/12 at $2.00 per day	0.16
Machinist, 1/12 at $3.00 per day	0.25
Machinist's helper, 1/24 at $1.75 per day	0.07
Pipe fitter and helper, 1/50 at $5.00 per day	0.10
Oil, waste, smith coal, etc	0.24
Drill steel, 6 inches per shift	0.24
Cost per shift	$7.78

The average footage drilled per cubic yard was 5 feet; the number of feet drilled per drill per shift was 10.5 to 12; the number of yards excavated per drill per shift was 3.5; the cost of drilling per yard was $2.22. In the foregoing the quantities paid for have been the basis of estimate; the quantities taken out were 10 per cent more than paid for.

The following table gives a comparative record of the Bergen Hill tunnels and the Simplon tunnel. The formation in the Italian end of the Simplon was an antigoric gneiss, a very hard rock.

	Bergen Hill	Simplon
Drill set up in heading, percentage total elapsed time	50%	60%
Actually drilling the rock, percentage of total elapsed time	50%	50%
Average advance per round (attack)	8.5 ft.	3.8 ft.
Average time for each attack	36 hrs.	5 hrs.
Average advance per day of 24 hours	5 ft.	18 ft.
Depth of holes	10 ft.	4.6 ft.
Diameter of holes	2¾ ins.	2¾ ins.
Lineal feet drilled per hour, per drill	2.7	7
Lineal feet drilled per cubic yard	5	6
Pounds of dynamite per cubic yard	3.4 to 5.7	8½
Average depth drilled with one sharpening	12 ins.	6½ ins.

Note. From paper by W. F. Lavis, before the American Society of Civil Engineers, April 6, 1910.

The conditions affecting the disposal of the muck after blasting were not the same at the two ends of the Bergen Hill tunnels. On the eastern end the grade descended toward Weehawken, and at the western end there was an ascending grade. At Weehawken the mouth of the tunnels was at the bottom of a shaft 80 feet deep. The muck in the tunnel cars was hoisted by elevators to a platform at the top, from which it was dumped into standard gage cars and later hauled to the crusher or storage pile, some 500 feet distant. At the western end the cars were hauled directly to the surface through the approach cut; and the material, except that which was required for concrete and rock packing, was hauled from 1000 to 3000 feet across the Hackensack Meadows. The disposal tracks were of 36-inch gage and were generally laid with 60-pound rails.

Except for about 1000 feet in each tunnel at the Weehawken end, where the muck was loaded by hand, four steam shovels operated by compressed air were used, one in each working face. Three 30-ton "Vulcan" and one 38-ton "Marion" shovels were used. These were on a standard gage track, and during blasting operations were moved 300 to 500 feet back from the face. At Weehawken empty cars of an average load capacity of one cubic yard were pushed to the shovels by hand from the storage tracks. When loaded they were started down grade by the bucket and coasted to the storage track near the shaft. The unloaded cars were hauled back to the storage track by mules, one mule handling two cars. When the tunnels were in full working order sixty muck cars were in use, about evenly divided between the two tunnels.

When mucking by hand the mucking gangs consisted of from 15 to 20 men. The maximum output per shift was 50 cubic yards and the average 35 cubic yards. The maximum output of any of the shovels was 159 cubic yards per shift and the best average in any one month was 60 cubic yards per shift. As the shovels were generally idle for one shift out of three, the quantity actually handled averaged 90 cubic yards per shift during the shifts that the shovels were at work. These quantities are "place measurement" and equal to about twice "car measurement." The shovels at both ends were usually worked

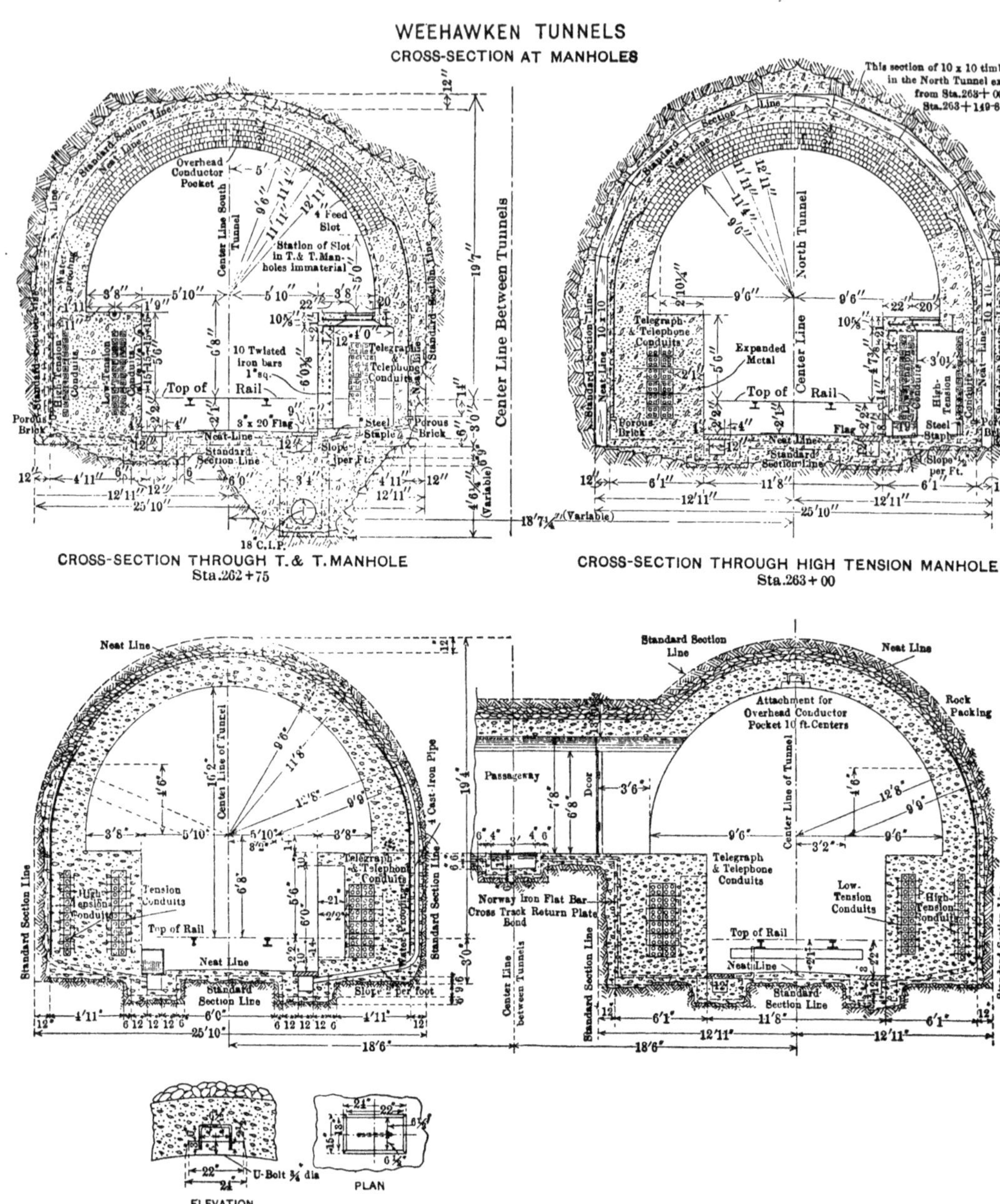

U-BOLT ATTACHMENT FOR OVERHEAD CONDUCTOR POCKET

Typical Dimensioned Cross-Sections, Bergen Hill Tunnels of the Pennsylvania R.R.

with day crews—one night crew worked the shovels in either tunnel as occasion required.

At the Hackensack or western end one-way dump cars were used having a capacity of four cubic yards. These were hauled by dinky locomotives, of which there were three, and later four, in use. To haul the cars outside to the dumps and crusher one 15-ton, 10 by 16-inch, Porter locomotive was used. In the tunnels three 12-ton, 9 by 14-inch, Vulcan locomotives were used. About thirty Allison dump cars were on the job, of which there were generally three to six undergoing repairs. The work was usually arranged so that the heavy mucking shifts alternated in the two tunnels. Two engines were then worked in the one tunnel and a single engine in the other tunnel. Generally four cars were hauled out together.

The muck from the central shaft headings was loaded by hand into cars, which were then taken to a platform 20 feet above the surface by a double elevator and dumped into storage bins or wagons.

The method by which the best results were obtained was as follows: A full round was blasted every thirty-six hours, securing an advance of 9 feet of full tunnel section. During the first shift of three, when the blasting had been completed and the lights strung, the shovel moved forward, cleaning the floor to the main pile of muck. The material from the blast was scattered from 150 to 300 feet back from the face. During this shift also the drillers mucked the heading and set up the drills, the muckers helping to carry the drills and their columns. During the second shift the main pile of muck was disposed of, leaving not more than two or three hours' work for the shovel on the third shift. This left nearly the whole of the third shift for drilling the lift holes.

At Weehawken difficulty was encountered from the fog and smoke in the tunnels after blasting. This was aggravated on days when the barometric pressure outside was low. A 6-foot fan, driven by an electric motor, was installed in the cross-passage 900 feet from the shaft (the heading being at that time about 300 feet in advance of this point) to force the air from the south into the north tunnel, drawing it in at the mouth of the south tunnel and discharging it at the mouth of the north tunnel, thus insuring a circulation in both tunnels. The fan was moved ahead to the next cross-passage when the work had progressed far enough. The compressed air discharged from the drills kept the headings, as well as that part of the tunnel between the headings and the fan, fairly clear.

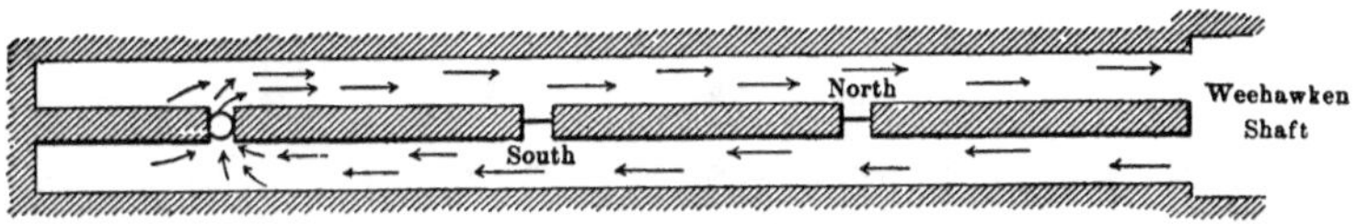

Method of Ventilation, Bergen Hill Tunnels.

The total elapsed time from starting at the Weehawken end to the completion of the excavation was almost exactly three years. The total number of days actually worked was 940, giving an average progress of 6.26 feet per working day at each of the two tunnels. Omitting the central shaft headings this gives an average rate of progress for each working face of 3.13 feet per day. At the Weehawken end the total number of days worked was 763, divided as follows: In timbered section, 186 days and about 426 feet, giving an average rate of 2.3 feet per day in each tunnel; in hard sandstone, 176 days and about 563 feet, at an average rate of 3.2 feet per day in each tunnel; in hard trap rock, 112 days and about 267 feet, giving an average rate of 2.4 feet per day in each tunnel; in ordinary trap rock, 289 days and about 1316 feet, the average rate being 4.55 feet per day in each tunnel.

The best month's work was in the Hackensack end, in trap rock, and was as follows: May, 1907, working in the south tunnel from the portal to the central shaft headings, 139 lineal feet, equivalent to about 5 feet of heading per day; November, 1907, enlargement of headings, 176 lineal feet, equivalent to 6 feet per day; April, 1908, working from the central shaft headings to the Weehawken headings in the north tunnel, 145 lineal feet or 5.2 feet per day.

In the central shaft headings during April, 1907, 122 feet of lineal heading, averaging 3.8 cubic yards per lineal foot, were taken out in the south tunnel. This is equal to 5 feet per day for the 24 days worked.

The best week's work at either of the main working faces, when the full section was being excavated in trap rock, was 803 cubic yards, equal to 41.8 lineal feet of full section tunnel, or an average of 6 lineal feet of full section per day.

The largest number of cubic yards taken out in any one week from one working face was 1087, equal to about 56.6 lineal feet of full section or an average of 8.1 lineal feet of full section per day.

The largest yardage for the whole work in any one week was 3238 cubic yards from four working faces—two faces at the Weehawken end in full section and two faces at the Hackensack bench and enlargement. This was equivalent to 168.4 lineal feet of full section tunnel or an average of 6 lineal feet per day from each working face.

The plant first installed at Weehawken and taken over by the contractor who finished the work was composed very largely of second-hand material. Eventually most of it had to be replaced. Insufficient and inefficient plant, and delay in installation, were largely responsible for the small progress made at the beginning of the work. An endeavor to continue the use of this plant not only caused added delay, but also involved a large expense. The plant installed by the original contractor proved inadequate to supply the air for the shovels and drills. The latter equipment consisted of two shovels requiring 1100 cubic feet per minute and 20 Rand "Slugger" drills using 2088 cubic feet of free air per minute. An arrangement was made with the O'Rourke Construction Company, then at work on the sub-river tunnels, to provide 4000 cubic feet of free air per minute at 100 pounds; and the old plant was shut down. The air compressing plant which finally supplied the air for the Bergen Hill tunnels was built by the Ingersoll-

Rand Company. The air was compressed to 40 pounds by low pressure machines, one being used all the time and two when necessary. These compressors were of the Corliss steam driven duplex type, with cross-compound steam cylinders and simple duplex air cylinders. Each unit had a capacity of nearly 4000 cubic feet of free air per minute. This air at 40 pounds was delivered to an Ingersoll-Rand high pressure machine of the same general type, having cross-compound Corliss steam cylinders 14 and 26 by 36 inches, with piston inlet air cylinders 13¼ inches in diameter. This machine compressed to 100 pounds. The capacity of this high pressure machine taking air at atmospheric pressure was 920 cubic feet per minute at 85 r.p.m. Taking air at 40 pounds from the low pressure machines, and working at a somewhat higher speed, this compressor alone supplied all the air used at the Weehawken end (approximately 4000 cubic feet per minute) from December, 1906, to November, 1907. With very few exceptions the pressure was steadily maintained at from 90 to 100 pounds and there was no breakdown of any kind.

At the Hackensack end the old plant was also found inadequate and a new installation was made in another situation, as it was found that the old site in the meadows was on soft ground and the vibration of passing trains caused the settling of foundations and the breaking of steam pipes. The new plant included two pairs of Stirling boilers with a total capacity of 2000 h.p. Eight compressors were installed, all of the Ingersoll-Rand straight-line steam driven type, 24 and 24 by 30 inches, each with a rated capacity of 1250 cubic feet of free air per minute. Seven of these were generally worked to the limit of their capacity to supply the necessary air.

The maximum requirements of air at the Hackensack or western end were originally estimated as follows:

Central shaft, four headings..........	24 drills
Hackensack end, two working faces.....	20 drills
	44 drills

	Cu. Ft. Free Air per Min.
44 Slugger drills	4,350
2 steam shovels	1,600
Pumps and machine shops (estimated)	1,000
4 hoisting engines, placing concrete	2,000
4 derricks	2,000
Total	10,950

The rated total capacity of the eight compressors was 10,000 cubic feet of free air per minute. It was considered that not more than two-thirds of the machine equipment would be working at the same time. The actual air requirement, therefore, was estimated to be about 8000 cubic feet of free air per minute, leaving a margin of one spare compressor for emergencies. The heaviest actual requirement, therefore, was approximately as follows:

	Cu. Ft. Free Air per Min.
40 drills	3828
2 shovels	1600
Pumps and machine shop (estimated)	1000
2 derricks	1000
Total	7428

After November, 1907, when the enlargement of the central shaft heading had been completed, the air requirements fell off to the following figures:

	Cu. Ft. Free Air per Min.
32 drills	2958
2 shovels	1600
Pumps, etc.	1000
3 hoisting engines on concrete, each working one-third time	500
2 derricks	1000
Total	7058

The average number of drills per shift was about 25 at the two working faces. There were also 5 to 10 drills used for trimming and cleaning up for concrete, with say an average of 7. This made a total of 32 drills in operation.

In lining and otherwise completing the interior of the tunnels the following quantities of the various materials were used, the figures being given per lineal foot of completed tunnel:

Concrete	7.64 cu.yd.
Rock packing	3.22 cu.yd.
Paid for	1.48 cu.yd.
Outside standard section	1.74 cu.yd.
Iron and steel	44.2 lbs.
Vitrified conduits	84.0 duct ft.
Water proofing	13.0 sq.ft.
Flags	3.3 sq.ft.

The quantities of some of the main items of materials in the Bergen Hill tunnels are as follows:

Excavation	263,000 cu.yd.
Cement used (concrete and grout)	95,000 bbls.
Concrete	95,000 cu.yd.
Dynamite for blasting	600,000 lbs.
Structural steel	50,000 lbs.

The foregoing figures are taken from a paper by Mr. W. F. Lavis, M. Am. Soc. C.E., on the New York Tunnel Extension of the Pennsylvania Railroad Bergen Hill Tunnels in the Proceedings of the American Society of Civil Engineers for February, 1910.

CHAPTER IX

NORTH RIVER TUNNELS OF THE PENNSYLVANIA RAILROAD

THE section described in this chapter is that lying between Tenth Avenue, New York, and the large shaft built by the Pennsylvania Railroad Company at Weehawken, N. J. It thus comprises the tunnels passing under the North or Hudson Rivers. The O'Rourke Engineering and Construction Company were the contractors. The subject will be treated in the following order, viz., shafts, plant and river tunnels.

Two shafts were provided, one on the New York side and one on the New Jersey side. They were placed as near as possible to the point at which the disappearance of the rock from the tunnels made it necessary to start the portion of the work which must be driven by shields.

The Manhattan shaft was located about 100 feet north of the tunnel center and there is nothing out of the ordinary about its construction. It was 55 feet deep, with a cross-section of 32 by 22 feet. The amount of excavation involved, including drifts, was 2010 cubic yards. The shaft was lined with concrete reinforced with steel beams down to solid rock, the amount of concrete used being 209 cubic yards. The cost of the shaft was 33½ cents per cubic foot. The first 13 feet of depth was in filled, or made, ground, and below that the materials encountered were red mica schist and granite. The total cost to the company was $12,943.

The Weehawken shaft was a comparatively large piece of work. Its depth was 76 feet and its dimensions at the top were 100 by 154 feet, reducing to 56 by 116 feet at the bottom. The total amount of excavation was 55,315 cubic yards, composed of sand and decomposed trap and sand rock. The cost of excavation per cubic foot was 33.7 cents. The shaft was lined with 9810 cubic yards of concrete with steel tie-rods in the rock. This shaft was started June 11, 1903, and completed September 1, 1904, at a total cost to the railroad of $166,163. It was located over the tunnels and included both of them. All work was carried on from these two shafts.

The installation of the power plant on the Manhattan side occupied the time from May, 1904, to April, 1905. Air pressure was on the tunnels on the New York side on June 25, 1005, and on the Weehawken side on the 29th of the same month. While the plants in both cases were almost identical local conditions necessitated some changes in arrangement.

The main items and the cost of the separate items in one power house are as follows:

3 500 h.p. Stirling water tube boilers........	$15,186
2 Blake feed pumps......................	740
1 Worthington surface condenser...........	6,539
2 General Electric circulating pumps, electric.	5,961
3 low pressure compressors, Ingersoll-Rand...	33,780
1 high pressure compressor, Ingersoll-Rand...	6,665
3 Blake hydraulic power pumps.............	3,075
2 General Electric electric generators and engines	7,626
Total	$79,572

The following gives a summary of the total cost of one plant:

Total cost of main items of plant..........	$ 79,572
Cost of four shields, appurtenances and demolition (including repairs)................	105,560
Cost of piping to drills, derricks and miscellaneous plant.........................	101,818
Cost of installation, including preparation of site	39,534
Total prime cost of one power house plant..	$324,484

At each shaft there were three Class "F" Stirling boilers rated at 500 h.p. Each boiler had 5000 square feet of heating surface and 116 square feet of grate area, with independent smoke stacks, 54 inches in diameter and 100 feet in height above grate level. Shaking grates were used and firing was done by hand. There were four doors to each furnace. An average of 20 tons of buckwheat coal was used in 24 hours, at each plant. The average steam pressure carried was 135 pounds.

There were two feed pumps at each plant having a free discharge capacity of 700 cubic feet per minute, the size being 10 and 6 by 10 inches.

At each plant there were three Ingersoll-Rand low pressure compressors used to supply air to the working chambers of the subaqueous shield-driven tunnels. They were also used on occasion to supply air to the high pressure compressors when the latter were hard pressed by an unusual demand for increased high pressure air. These machines were of a new design, of duplex Corliss type with cross-compound steam cylinders, designed to work condensing but capable of operating non-condensing. The air cylinders were single stage duplex. Steam cylinders were 14 and 30 inches in diameter by 36 inches stroke. Air cylinders were 23½ inches in diameter and had a combined capacity of 35.1 cubic feet of free air per revolution. While the machines were capable of running at 135 r.p.m., their normal speed was about 125 r.p.m., at which the free air capacity was 4389 cubic feet per minute or 263,340 cubic feet per hour. The steam pressure was 135 pounds and an air pressure of 50 pounds could be obtained from each compressor.

One high pressure Ingersoll-Rand compressor of cross-compound Corliss steam driven type was located in each of the plants. The capacity was about 1100 cubic feet of free air per minute when running at 85 revolutions and using atmopsheric air for the intake. When taking air at 30 pounds from the low pressure compressors the capacity was 3305 cubic feet per minute per machine. With a low pressure compressor running at 125 r.p.m. it furnished enough air at 30 pounds to supply the high pressure compressor running at 85 r.p.m. With a high pressure machine delivering at 150 pounds the combined capacity of this arrangement was 4389 cubic feet of free air per minute.

The air was delivered into a receiver 4 feet 6 inches in diameter by 12 feet high.

There were two Worthington surface condensers at each plant, each with cooling surface sufficient to condense 22,500 pounds of steam per hour, with water at 30 degrees Fahrenheit, maintaining a vacuum of 26 inches with the barometer at 30 inches. Each condenser was fitted with a horizontal direct

Interior of Weehawken Air Compressor Plant for P.R.R. North River Tunnels.

acting vacuum pump. Two 8-inch centrifugal circulating pumps driven by 36 h.p. direct current motors, running at 220 volts and 610 r.p.m., were placed on a nearby wharf and supplied salt water for the condensers directly from the Hudson River.

To operate the tunneling shields three hydraulic power pumps with 15-inch duplex cylinders and water rams $2\frac{1}{8}$ by 10 inches were installed at each power house, capable of giving a pressure of 6000 pounds per square inch. One pump was used for each tunnel and the third was held in reserve. The usual working pressure carried was 4500 pounds.

Electric light and power were supplied by two direct current generators, delivering at 240 volts through a two-wire system. These units were driven direct by a vertical tandem compound engine 10 and 20 by 14 inches, giving 150 h.p. at 250 r.p.m.

The following is the cost of operating one power house plant during the period of driving the shields, excavating and metal lining, in a 24-hour day:

No.	Labor	Rate per day	Amount
6	Engineers	$3.00	$18.00
6	Firemen	2.50	15.00
2	Oilers	2.00	4 00
2	Laborers	2.00	4.00
4	Pumpmen	2.75	11.00
2	Electricians	3.50	7.00
1	Helper	3.00	3.00
	Total per day		$62.00
	Total per 30 days		$1860.00

Supplies

Coal, 14 tons per day	$3.25	$45.50
Water	7.00	7.00
Oil, 4 gals. per day	.50	2.00
Waste, 4 lbs. per day	.07	.28
Other supplies	....	1.00
Total per day		$55.78
Total per 30 days		$1673.00
Cost of labor and supplies for one day		117.78
Cost of labor and supplies for 30 days		3533.00

The cost of operating the power plant for 24 hours during the period of concrete lining was $28.00 for labor, and $61.00 for supplies. The decrease in labor cost is due to a reduction in working force as but two engineers, two firemen, two pumpmen, one foreman electrician, one electrician and one laborer were required. The increase in cost of supplies is due to an increased water consumption.

Crushed rock for concrete was made from the trap rock excavated from the Bergen Hill tunnel. The crushing plant consisted of one No. 6 and one No. 8 Austin crusher, driven by a single cylinder, horizontal steam engine of 120 h.p. The plant was capable of crushing 225 cubic yards of stone in 10

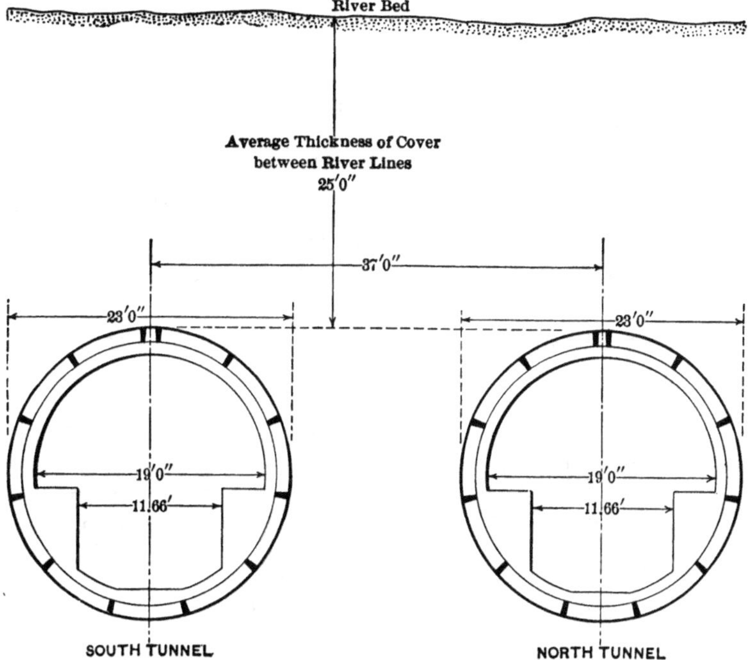

Typical Cross-section of North River Tunnels Showing Relative Positions.

hours. Stone from the pile was loaded by hand into scale boxes, which were lifted by two power operated derricks into a chute above the No. 6 crusher. From this crusher the stone was hoisted 60 feet by a bucket conveyor to a screen above the stone bin. This screen was in the form of a chute placed at 45 degrees and perforated with 2½-inch round holes. As the material passed over this chute the smaller stone dropped into the bin and the larger stone passed over into the No. 8 crusher, from which it was carried by a second conveyor to the bin. The stone was loaded into dump cars of 3 cubic yards' capacity through a sliding door in the bottom of the stone bin, and was hauled by a steam dinky engine either direct to the Weehawken shaft or to scows for transportation to New York.

The average force employed at the rock crushing plant was as follows:

1 foreman at	$3.00	
24 laborers at	1.75	Loading scale boxes for derricks.
2 laborers at	1.75	Feeding crushers.
4 laborers at	1.75	To keep screens clear.
1 engineer at	4.00	
2 engineers at	3.50	On derricks.

Owing to the constant breakdown of machinery, chutes, etc., which is inseparable from stone crushing work, a repair gang was always at work, consisting of either three carpenters or three machinists.

The approximate cost of the crushing plant was as follows:

Machinery	$5,850
Lumber	3,305
Labor for erecting	3,999
Total	$13,154

The cost of the crushed stone at Weehawken was about 91 cents per cubic yard, made up as follows:

Cost of stone	22 cents
Labor in operation of plant	31 "
Plant supplies	11 "
Plant depreciation	27 "
Total	91 cents

The crushed stone of the Manhattan shaft cost about $1.04 per cubic yard, the difference of 13 cents as compared with the Weehawken cost being made up by the cost of transfer across the river, amounting to 8 cents, and cost of transfer from the dock to the shaft, amounting to 5 cents. The stone for crushing was purchased from the contractor on the Bergen Hill tunnels.

In the design of the tunneling shields for driving the tunnels under the river the chief points to be kept in mind were ample strength, easy access to the working face combined with ease and quickness of closing the diaphragm, and general simplicity. Four of these shields were used, one at each end of each of the tunnels.

They were 15 feet 11$\frac{7}{16}$ inches long, exclusive of the hood, and 23 feet 6$\frac{1}{4}$ inches in external diameter. The outer skin or shell was 2$\frac{1}{8}$ inches thick, made up of two $\frac{3}{4}$-inch plates with a $\frac{5}{8}$-inch plate between, butt-jointed and flush-rivetted inside and out. The interior framing consisted of two floors and three vertical partitions, forming nine compartments giving access to the face. They were provided with pivoted segmental doors. Forward of the back end of the jacks the shield was stiffened by an annular girder surrounding the skin, and in the space between the stiffeners were set 24 hydraulic rams, used to force the shield ahead by pressure exerted against the last erected ring of the metal lining.

A cast steel segmental cutting edge was attached to the periphery of the forward end of the shield. The maximum and minimum overlap of the shield over the metal lining of the tunnel was 6 feet 4$\frac{1}{4}$ inches and 2 feet, respectively. To pass through the varying ground before entering the true sub-river silt, a detachable hood in nine sections was extended 2 feet 1 inch beyond the cutting edge and from the top down to the level of the upper platform.

The weight of the structural portion of each shield was 135 tons; of the hydraulic rams and erectors 58 tons; and of the complete shield 193 tons. The hydraulic apparatus was designed for a maximum pressure of 5000 pounds per square inch and a test pressure of 6000 pounds. Each of the 24 rams was 8$\frac{1}{2}$ inches in diameter by 38 inches stroke. The average pressure used upon them was 3500 pounds per square inch. With

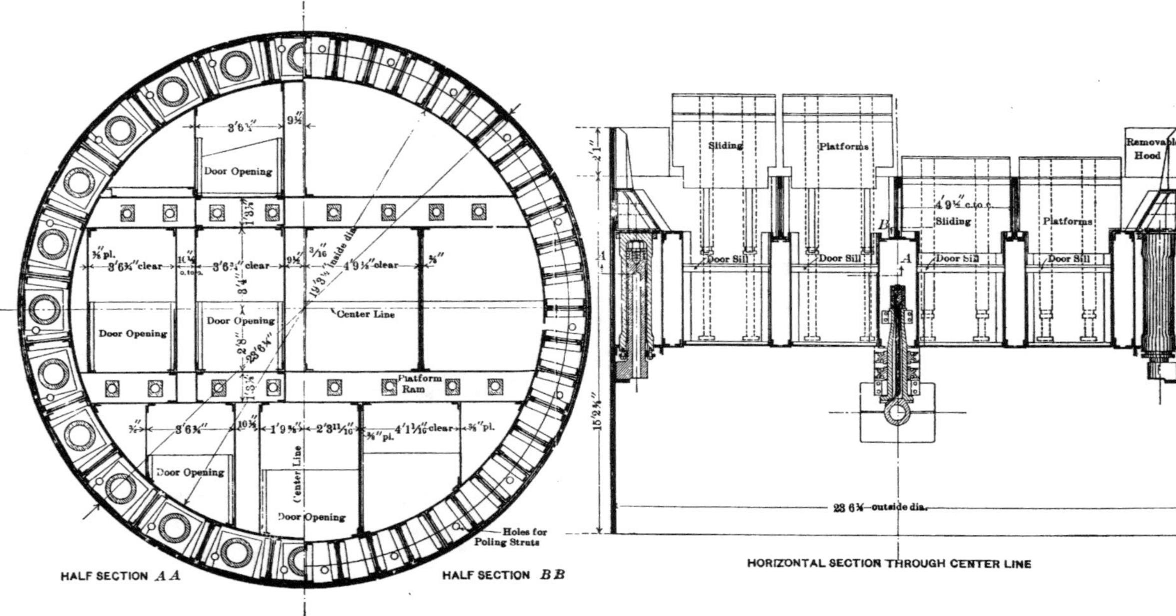

Shield Used in Driving the North River Tunnels of the Pennsylvania R.R.

a water pressure of 5000 pounds per square inch the force of one ram was 275,000 pounds and of the total number of 24 rams 6,600,000 pounds or 3300 tons, giving an equivalent pressure of 15,200 pounds per square foot of face, or 105 pounds per square inch. The rams developed a tendency to bend under

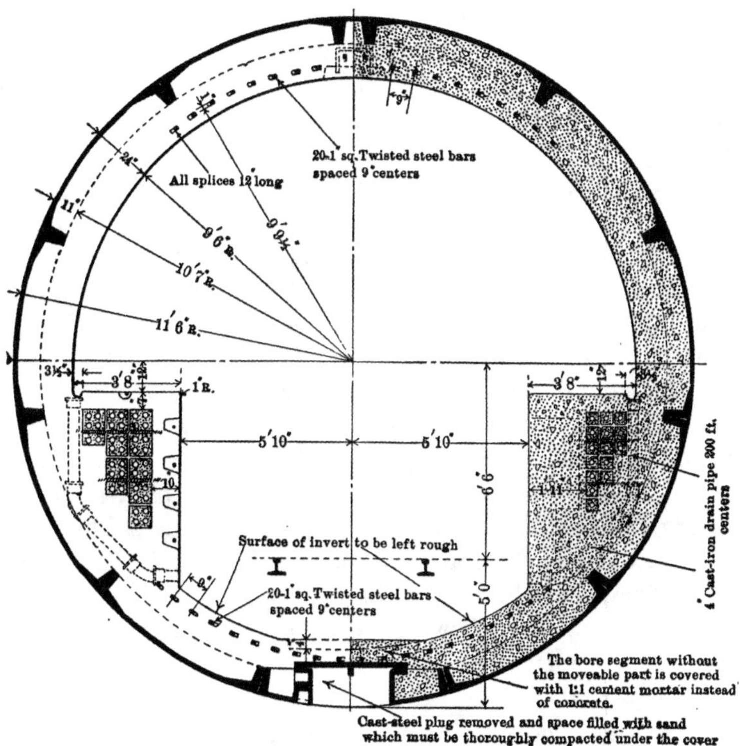

Cross-section of P.R.R. North River Tunnel, Showing Construction and Dimensions.

the severe test of moving the shield, all closed, through the river silt. It is probable that a piston 10 inches in diameter would have been better adapted for this work than those of 8½ inches used.

The floors of the two platforms, of which there were eight,

formed by the divisions of the platforms by the upright framing, could be extended forward 2 feet 9 inches in front of the cutting edge or 8 inches in front of the hood. This forward movement was produced by hydraulic jacks. The sliding platform could sustain a load of 7900 pounds per square foot, which equalled the maximum head of ground and water combined. Each sliding platform was actuated by two single-acting rams, 3½ inches by 2 feet 9 inches. With a hydraulic pressure of 5000 pounds the forward force of each pair of rams on each platform was 96,000 pounds. As the area of the nose of the platform was 1060 square inches the reaction was 90 pounds per square inch or 13,040 pounds per square foot.

Each shield was fitted with a single erector mounted on the rear of the diaphragm. This consisted of a box-shaped frame mounted on a central shaft revolving on bearings attached to the shield. Inside of this frame was a differential hydraulic plunger, 4 inches and 3 inches by 48 inches stroke. To the plunger head were attached two channels sliding inside the box frame, and to the projecting end of these the grips were attached. The opposite end of the box frame carried a counterweight which balanced about 700 pounds of the tunnel segment at a radius of 11 feet. The erector was revolved by two single-acting rams fixed horizontally to the back of the shield above the erector pivot, operating through double chains and chain wheels keyed to the erector shaft. With a hydraulic pressure of 5000 pounds the following are some of the figures connected with the erector:

Weight of heaviest tunnel segment.......	2,584 lbs.
Weight of erector plunger and grip......	616 "
Total weight to be handled by the erector ram..........................	3,200 "
Total force in erector ram moving from center of shield......................	35,000 "
Total force in erector ram moving toward center of shield.....................	27,500 "

Maximum net weight at 11 ft. radius to be handled by turning rams............	1,884 lbs.
Total force of each rotating ram at 5000 lbs per square inch....................	80,000 "
Load at 11 ft. radius equivalent to above..	3,780 "

CHAPTER X

NORTH RIVER TUNNELS OF THE PENNSYLVANIA RAILROAD
(*Continued.*)

ON the New York side the shields were built inside the iron lining of the shield chambers, and no false work was required as the necessary tackle was simply slung from the iron lining. On the Weehawken end erecting was done in the bare rock excavation and false work was required. To assemble and rivet each shield took about two weeks, the riveting being done with pneumatic tools using compressed air from the tunnel supply. When the structural steel work was completed the shields, weighing 113 tons each, were jacked to grade level. While the hydraulic fittings were being put in, the shields were moved forward on a cradle built of concrete with imbedded steel rails, upon which the shield was driven for the distance in which the tunnel was in solid rock. The installation of the hydraulic fittings took from four to six weeks per shield and brought the finished weight up to 193 tons.

When the shield was finished and in position the first two rings of the segmental tunnel lining were erected in the tail of the shield. These were firmly braced to the rock and chamber lining. The shield was then shoved ahead by its own jacks and another ring erected, and this process was continued indefinitely. In the description of the methods of work in the shield-driven tunnel which follows, the subject will be discussed in different sections determined by the different conditions met at the working face.

In working in a full rock face, excavation so far as possible was done before the shields were installed. On the New York side about 146 feet of tunnel was completely excavated, with 71 feet of bottom heading beyond that. At the Weehawken end 58 feet of tunnel and 40 feet of heading were driven. This was done to avoid handling the rock through the narrow shield doors. Test holes were driven ahead to determine the depth of rock cover. At Weehawken on February 14, 1905, a blast broke through the rock and the mud flowed in, filling the tunnel for half its height for a distance of 300 feet back from the face.

Through rock section the shield was moved upon either two or three rails imbedded in concrete. Where the full tunnel section had been excavated it was only necessary to trim off the small projections of rock. In the portions where a bottom heading only had been driven, excavation was completed just in front of the shield, the drilling below axis level being done in the heading and above that from the front sliding platforms. Shallow holes were drilled and spaced closely; light charges of powder only being used to lessen the chance of damage to the shield. In this work the small shield doors hampered operations and larger bottom openings, which would permit of subdivisions or of being partly closed in soft ground, would have been an advantage. But owing to the greater part of the rock having been excavated before the shields were installed the quantity thus handled was small. The space outside the lining was grouted with a one-and-one mixture of Portland cement and sand. Large voids were hand packed with stone before grouting.

A typical working gang is given herewith. Two gangs were worked in each shield in 24 hours in 10-hour shifts. This portion of the work was done under normal air pressure.

General

Tunnel superintendent, ½ time....	$200.00	per month
Assistant superintendent..........	5.00	per day
General foreman................	5.00	"
Electrician, ½ time..............	3.50	"
Electrician's helper, ½ time.......	3.00	"
Pipe fitter, ½ time...............	3.00	"
Pipe fitter's helper, ½ time.......	2.75	"

Total.........................About $20 per shift.

Drilling

Foreman	$5.00	$ 5.00
3 drillers	4.00	12.00
3 drillers' helpers	3.00	9.00
1 nipper	2.50	2.50
1 water boy, ½ time	2.50	1.25
1 powder boy, ½ time	2.75	1.38
Cost per shift		$31.13

Mucking

Foreman	$3.50	$3.50
8 muckers	2.75	22.00
Cost per shift		$25.50

Erecting Iron and Driving Shields

1 erector runner	$4.00	$4.00
3 iron workers	3.00	9.00
Cost per shift		$13.00
Cost of shield gangs per shift		$89.63

The rate of progress obtained was 4.2 feet per day per shield where most of the excavation had been done beforehand and 2.1 feet per day per shield where no advance excavation had been done.

When the shields had gotten far enough away from the shield chambers, and before rock cover was lost, the first air-lock bulkhead walls were put in. These walls and their fittings were designed to withstand an air pressure of 50 pounds per square inch. They were all of concrete 10 feet thick with the exception of the first two, which were only 8 feet thick. Each had three locks capable of holding men. In addition, pipes were built in to give access to the cables and to pass pipes, rails, etc., in and out. When each tunnel had been advanced about 1200 feet from the first wall a second wall like the first was built. Thus there were two of these bulkhead walls at each end of each tunnel, making 8 in all. The second bulkhead was simply an added safeguard to the tunnel and permitted the air pressure at the face to be reduced between the walls, thus lowering the pressure in stages. The exercise in walking between the bulkheads in the lower pressure was found to be beneficial to the health of those working in the compressed air.

When rock cover became dangerously thin air pressures of from 12 to 18 pounds were used, this being found sufficient to stop the water coming from the gravel on top of the rock. When the surface of the rock was first penetrated the soft face was held by horizontal boards braced from the shield until the latter could be advanced. These braces were then taken out and replaced by others. As the amount of soft ground in the face increased the system of timbering was gradually changed to one using 2-inch poling boards resting on top of the shield and supported at the face by vertical breast boards, which, in turn, were held by walings 6 by 6 inches braced through the upper doors to the iron lining and from the sliding platforms to the shield. In driving through this mixed ground, involving rock and mud, a typical working gang was as follows. In this part of the work three shifts of 8 hours each were employed.

GENERAL

⅓ tunnel supt..........	$300 per month	$4.00 day
Asst. supt............................		5.00 "
General foreman........................		5.00 "
½ electrician...........	$3.50 "	1.75 "
½ electrician's helper....	3.00 "	1.50 "
½ pipe fitter	3.25 "	1.63 "
½ pipe fitter's helper....	3.00 "	1.50 "
Cost per 8-hour shift...		$20.38

DRILLING

Foreman............................		$5.00 day
2 drillers..............	$3.25 per day	6.50 "
2 drillers' helpers......	3.00 "	6.00 "
Cost per 8-hour shift...		$17.50

TIMBERING

2 timbermen..........	$2.50 per day	$5.00 day
2 timbermen's helpers..	2.00 "	4.00 "
Cost per 8-hour shift...		$9.00

MUCKING

Foreman...............................		$ 3.50 day
6 muckers.............	$2.75 per day	16.50 "
Cost per 8-hour shift...		$20.00

ERECTING IRON AND DRIVING SHIELD

Erector runner......................		$3.50 per day
3 iron workers.........	$3.00	9.00 "
Cost per 8-hour shift...		$12.50
Total cost of labor per 8-hour shift..		79.38

The average rate of progress was 2.6 ft. per day.

Tunneling in a full face of sand and gravel was encountered only at Weehawken, and two systems of timbering were used. In the first the ground was excavated 2½ feet ahead of the cutting edge, the roof being held by longitudinal poling boards resting on the outside of the shield skin at their back ends, and on vertical breast boards at the forward ends. When the upper part of the face was dry it was held by vertical breast boards from the sliding platforms and through the shield doors to cross timbers in the tunnel. The lower part, which was always wet, was held by horizontal breast boards braced through the lower shield pockets to cross timbers in the tunnel.

As soon as the rock surface was penetrated, and the sand and gravel encountered, the escape of air was enormously increased. It was found impossible to maintain the required pressure even with the three compressors working to the limit of their capacity, each compressing 4400 cubic feet of free air per minute or 13,200 cubic feet in all.

To decrease this leakage of air a large quantity of straw and clay was used in front of the breasting. This diminished the loss of air, but a large quantity still escaped through the joints of the iron lining, so that these had to be plastered with Portland cement. Even then the loss was too great and it was necessary to shut down one tunnel and deliver all the air to the other. This allowed a pressure of 10 pounds to be maintained which, though less than the hydraulic head, was sufficient to permit progress to be made. The timbered face

Interior of Shield in P.R.R. North River Tunnel, Showing Silt Entering Through One Open Door.

was never grouted, for though this would have reduced the loss of air, it would have cut down the rate of progress very much.

The abnormally increased demand upon the air compressors to supply the necessary air to maintain the pressure in the tunnel subjected the machines to a most severe and extended test of reliability under conditions involving extreme speed and greatly augmented load. A breakdown would have meant the loss of the working face. This extreme condition was maintained until the silt, which lay above the sand and gravel, showed in the roof, when the escape of air was immediately reduced, and it became possible to work the two faces simultaneously.

In driving these faces a typical gang for an 8-hour shift was as follows:

GENERAL

⅓ General supt.	$300.00 per month	$4.00	per day
Assistant supt.		5.00	"
General foreman		5.00	"
½ electrician and helper	$3.50 and $3.00	3.25	"
½ pipe fitter and helper	3.25 and 3.00	3.13	"
Cost per 8-hour shift		$20.38	"

TIMBERING

3 timbermen	$2.50	$7.50	per day
3 timbermen's helpers	2.00	6.00	"
Cost per 8-hour shift		$13.50	"

MUCKING

Foreman		$3.50
6 muckers	$2.75	16.50
Cost per 8-hour shift		$20.00

ERECTING IRON AND DRIVING SHIELD

Erector runner		$3.25
Foreman		4.00
4 ironworkers	$3.00	12.00
Cost per 8-hour shift		$19.25
Total cost of labor 8-hour shift		$73.13

The average rate of advance in sand and gravel was 5.1 feet per day for each shield. As soon as the silt was encountered in the upper part of the face the speed increased to 7 feet per day per shield.

In passing under the river wall at Weehawken, where the bulkhead consisted only of a crib-work supported on piles, the latter obstructed the advance of the shield but were easily cut out. On the New York side the conditions were not so favorable. Here the heavy masonry bulkhead was supported on piles and rip-rap. The top of the shield came about 6 feet above the bottom of the rip-rap and the open spaces between the stones allowed a free flow of water directly from the river. As soon as the cutting edge entered the rip-rap there was a blowout, the air escaping freely to the ground surface behind the bulkhead and to the river in front of it. Clay puddle or mud, made from the excavated silt, was used in large quantities to fill the voids between the stones in the working face. The excavation of this rip-rap was carried on by the removal of one stone at a time, the spaces between the newly exposed stone being immediately plugged with mud. When the shield had advanced its own length in the rip-rap another place for the escape of air was exposed at its rear end. This leakage was stopped with mud and cement sacks at the forward end of the last ring of the tunnel.

As long as the shield was stationary it was possible, by using these methods and by exercising care, to prevent the excessive loss of air, but while the shield was being shoved ahead the difficulties were much increased, as the movement of the shield displaced the bags and mud as fast as they were placed. It was only by shoving slowly and having a large number of men looking out for leaks and stopping them that excessive air loss could be avoided.

In erecting the iron lining, as a segment was placed in position it was necessary to clean off the forward surface of the previous ring and the adjacent portion of the tail of the shield. This was always accompanied by a slight blow and for some time the air pressure in the tunnel dropped from 25 to 20 pounds. In other words, every time a segment was placed the air pressure dropped from greater than the balancing pressure to less; and on two occasions the blow became so great, and the tunnel pressure was so much reduced, that the water from the river rushed in and was not stopped until it had risen about 4 feet in the tunnel invert. On such occasions the surface of the river was greatly disturbed, often rising more than 20 feet in the air in the form of a geyser. A large quantity of grout (about 2500 barrels of cement and a similar amount of sand in the north tunnel, and 1000 barrels in the south tunnel) was used at this point. It was forced through the tunnel lining immediately behind the shield, greatly reducing the loss of air and binding the rip-rap together.

When the shield had traveled 25 feet through the rip-rap the piles supporting the bulkhead were met. One hundred of these, spaced on three-foot centers, were cut out of the path of the shield in a distance of 35 feet. In passing through the piling no timbering was done and the piles supported the face effectively.

When the river line had been passed the blow still continued, and as there was no heavy ground above the tunnel the light silt was carried away into the water by the escaping air. At one time the cover over the crown of the tunnel was reduced to such an extent that for a distance of 30 feet there was less than 10 feet of very soft silt overlying and in some places none at all. The shield was stopped and the air pressure reduced to less than the balancing pressure. The blow then stopped and about 28,000 cement bags filled with mud were dumped into the hole. They were then weighted down with rip-rap. This sealed the blowout and the work was continued without further disturbance from this source. The working force employed here was similar to that employed in the sand and gravel sections.

CHAPTER XI

NORTH RIVER TUNNELS OF THE PENNSYLVANIA RAILROAD
(*Continued.*)

In the North River tunnels, between Tenth Avenue and the large shaft at Weehawken, N. J., Ingersoll-Rand drills, sizes A-86, C-24, E-24 and F-24, were used. While the air pressure at the power house was 100 pounds, the effective pressure at the drills was only 80 pounds. The drill steel used was 1⅛ to 1⅜-inches, octagon. The holes were started with a 3¼-inch diameter and bottomed at 2⅝-inch diameter at a depth of 10 feet. The powder used on the New York side, because of the proximity of buildings and lack of heavy rock cover, was 40 per cent forcite. The holes were closely spaced and light charges of explosive used.

The amount of excavation done was 11 per cent greater than that paid for. For a period covering five months and 12,900 cubic yards of excavation the record of drilling, and amount of powder used per cubic yard of excavation, were as follows:

Portion of excavation.	Feet of hole drilled per cu. yd. of excavation.			Pounds of powder used per cu. yd. of excavation.		
	15′ 14″ Span Twin T.	19′ 6″ Span Twin T.	24′ 6″ Span Twin T.	15′ 4″	19′ 6″	24′ 6″
Wall plate heading (1)...	13.00	10.97	10.97	3.77	2.85	2.85
Total heading..........	7.87	8.17	7.81	2.31	2.02	1.78
Bench and raker bench (1)	5.97	6.15	7.56	0.94	0.93	1.13
Trench (1)............	9.82	15.96	18.10	1.84	2.49	2.73
Average for section (1)...	6.69	7.43	8.95	1.28	1.30	1.45
Actual amount (2)......	.82	7.27	8.95	1.22	1.24	1.27

In the foregoing table the items marked (1) give the figures from a typical cross-section; the item marked (2) gives the actual amount of drilling done and powder used per cubic yard for the whole period of five months. But as this included 280 feet of heading and only 220 feet of bench, the average figures (especially for explosives) are too low.

The following figures cover the cost of drilling and blasting in the rock tunnel excavation under Thirty-second Street, east of the cut-and-cover section. They cover five months of time and 11,649 cubic yards of material paid for. The total amount of drilling done was 86,749 feet in 3206 drill shifts of 10 hours each. The average footage of hole per man per hour was 3.02 in the heading and 2.71 on the bench. The cost of labor only for drilling and sharpening steels was $25.283, equivalent to 29 cents per lineal foot or $2.17 per cubic yard paid for. The total amount of powder used was 14,444 pounds, representing a cost of 14 cents per cubic yard, with dynamite at 11 cents per pound. The table below gives an analysis of the drilling operations:

	One heading.		Bench.		Center trench.	
					Mica schist.	
	Quartz.	Hard mica schist.	Quartz.	Mica schist medium.	Soft.	Medium.
	Hrs. M.	Hrs. M.	Hrs. M.	Hrs. M.	Hrs. M.	Hrs. M.
Setting up	0.38	0.15	1.23	1.10	1.58	1.10
Drilling	4.52	8.0	5.57	6.08	5.53	6.40
Necessary delay	1.40	1.45	2.23	1.50	1.33	1.17
Unnecessary delay	......	......	0.15	0.12	0.06	0.10
Taking down machine	0.05	......	0.5	0.07	0.12	0.20
Loading and firing	0.04	......	0.07	0.07	0.30	0.23
Total drilling	7.19	1.00	10.0	9.34	9.12	10.00
Mucking	2.41	......	......	0.26	0.48	......
Total	10.00	10.00	10.00	10.00	10.00	10.00
Feet drilled per shift	22.00	42.00	25.9	22.22	22.00	26.44
Feet drilled per working hour	2.86	4.20	2.59	2.32	2.39	2.64

The foregoing figures are the result of 67 observations. It was found that the average time and percentage per 10-hour shift for each operation were as follows:

Setting up	1 hr.	8 min.	or	11.3%
Drilling	5 "	58	"	59.7
Necessary delay	1 "	53	"	19.9
Unnecessary delay	0 "	07	"	1.1
Taking down machine	0 "	09	"	1.5
Loading and firing	0 "	12	"	2
Total drilling	9 "	27	"	94.5
Mucking	0 "	33	"	5.5

While the shield chambers were being excavated bottom headings were run along the lines of the river tunnels, and continued until the lack of rock cover prevented their being driven further. The typical working force in the shield chambers was as follows:

Drilling and Blasting—Ten-hour Shifts

1 foreman	at $3.50	$3.50
6 drillers	" 3.00	18.00
6 drillers' helpers	" 2.00	12.00
1 blacksmith	" 3.50	3.50
1 smith's helper	" 2.25	2.25
1 powder man	" 2.00	2.00
1 water boy	" 2.00	2.00
1 nipper	" 2.00	2.00
1 machinist	" 3.00	3.00
1 machinist's helper	" 1.80	1.80
		$50.05

Mucking

1 foreman	at $3.00	$3.00
16 muckers	" 2.00	32.00
		$35.00

ANALYSIS OF COST OF DRILLING

Item of cost.	Cost per foot of hole drilled.				Cost per drill shift.			
	15′4″	19′6″	24′6″	Average.	15′4″	19′6″	24′6″	Average.
Drilling labor	$0.25	$0.28	$0.31	$0.28	$6.95	$ 7.75	$ 7.60	$7.45
Sharpening	0.02	0.02	0.01	0.016	0.53	0.42	0.34	0.43
Drill steel (5″ per drill shift)	0.007	0.007	0.006	0.007	0.19	0.20	0.15	0.19
Drill repairs	0.002	0.02	0.02	0.02	0.61	0.59	0.42	0.54
High pressure air (estimated)	0.05	0.04	0.07	0.07	1.39	1.86	1.67	1.82
Totals	0.35	0.38	0.41	0.385	9.67	10.82	10.18	10.43

COST OF EXCAVATION OF LAND TUNNELS, IN DOLLARS PER CUBIC YARD

	Manhattan.	Weehawken.	Total yardage and average cost.
Cubic yards excavated	42289	8311	51600
Labor:			
Surface transport	$0.49	$0.87	$0.55
Drilling and blasting	2.37	1.55	2.24
Mucking	2.49	2.08	2.42
Timbering	0.87	0.18	0.76
Total labor	$6.22	$4.68	$5.97
Material:			
Drilling	$0.15	$0.15	$0.15
Blasting	0.21	0.21	0.21
Timber	0.39	0.20	0.36
Total material	$0.75	$0.56	$0.72
Plant running	$0.76	$0.65	$0.74
Surface labor, repairs and maintenance	0.15	0.08	0.14
Field office administration	1.05	1.18	1.07
Total field charges	$8.96	$7.15	$8.64
Chief office administration	0.34	0.38	0.34
Plant depreciation	0.66	1.01	0.72
Street and building repairs	0.27	.....	0.23
Total average cost per cubic yard	$10.23	$8.54	$9.93

In working in the shield chambers in a full face of rock as much as possible of the rock excavation was done before the shields were installed in order to avoid handling the rock through the narrow shield doors. The typical working gang in the shields, of which there were two gangs per shield per 24 hours working in two 10-hour shifts, was as follows:

GENERAL

½ tunnel supt.	at	$200.00	per month
1 assistant tunnel supt.	"	5.00	per day
1 general foreman	"	5.00	"
½ electrician	"	3.50	"
½ electrician's helper	"	3.00	"
½ pipe fitter	"	3.00	"
½ pipe fitter's helper	"	2.75	"

DRILLING

1 foreman	at	$5.00	per day
3 drillers	"	4.00	"
3 drillers' helpers	"	3.00	"
1 nipper	"	2.50	"
½ water boy	"	2.50	"
½ powder boy	"	2.75	"

MUCKING

1 foreman	at	$3.50	per day
8 muckers	"	2.75	"

The duties of these gangs were as follows: The tunnel superintendent looked after both shifts of one shield; the assistant or walking boss had charge of all work in the tunnel in one shift; the general foreman had charge of the labor at the face; the electrician looked after repairs, extensions of the cables and lamp renewals; the pipe fitters worked in both tunnels, repairing the leaks in pipes between the power house and working faces, extending the pipe lines and attending to shield repairs; in the latter work the erector runner helped. The drillers stuck to their own jobs, which were not subject to interruption as long as the bottom headings lasted. One water boy and one powder boy served two tunnels. The muckers helped the iron men put up the rings of the casing, as well as looking after their own work in cleaning out the face. The rate of progress obtained was 4.2 feet per day per shield where most of the excavation had been done beforehand; and 2.1 feet per day per shield where no previous work had been done.

When the rock, gravel and hard-pan gave place to a full face of silt, the timber was removed, all the shield doors were opened, and the shield was shoved forward into the ground without any excavation being done by hand ahead of the diaphragms. As the shield advanced the silt was simply forced through the open doors into the tunnel. After the work had progressed in this way for some time, taking in about 90 per cent of the full volume of the tunnel excavation per foot of advance, the air pressure was raised from 20 to 22 pounds. As a result the silt in the face got harder and flowed less readily through the shield doors; and the amount taken in fell to about 65 per cent of the full volume. As this mode of operation caused a disturbance of the surface the air pressure was lowered to 16 pounds, when the muck became softer and the full volume of excavation was taken in. The pressure was later raised to 20 pounds.

The forcing of the shield through the silt resulted in raising the bed of the river in an amount depending on the quantity of material brought into the shield. If the whole volume of excavation was being brought in, the surface of the river bed was not affected. When about 50 per cent of the whole volume was being taken in the river bed raised about 3 feet; and when the shield was being driven blind the bed raised about 7 feet. The opening of doors in the shield was regulated to take in the minimum quantity of muck and cause no surface disturbance. In the north Manhattan tunnel all the doors were usually open; in the south tunnel five or six of the nine doors were generally open.

[1] From the paper by B. H. M. Hewett and W. L. Brown, before the American Society of Civil Engineers, June, 1910.

As soon as the south shield had passed the river bulkhead at Weehawken the silt was found to be much softer than behind the wall. It was like a fluid in many of its properties and this fluidity could be varied by changing the air pressure in the shield chamber. When the air pressure was equal to the weight of the overlying water and silt, the silt stiffened to about the consistency of a very soft clay. When the pressure was reduced to 12 or 15 pounds it became sufficiently fluid to flow through a 1½-inch grout hole at a rate running up as high as 50 gallons per minute. This was a condition which had been looked forward to by the contractor and it was anticipated that the shield doors could be closed and the shield driven across the river without taking in a shovelful of muck. This had been done in driving the Hudson and Manhattan Railroad Company's tunnels between Hoboken and New York City, but when the doors were all closed and the shield shoved forward the tunnel immediately began to rise in spite of the heaviest downward lead which the clearance at the back of the shield would permit.

The pressure caused by the shield displacing the ground as it advanced caused the iron tunnel lining to rise about 2 inches and it became distorted, the horizontal diameter decreasing and the vertical diameter increasing by as much as 1¼ inches. The shield was stopped and the hood removed as it was thought that the latter was producing these effects. Driving was then resumed, but the same troubles continued and it was not found possible to keep to grade.

By opening the doors and taking in a portion of the material these difficulties were overcome. It was found that the level of the shield could be regulated by varying the proportion of silt admitted through the doors. This quantity ranged from none at all to the full volume displaced and averaged about 33 per cent. The muck flowed into the tunnel in a thick stream, and by regulating the advance of the shield the flow was proportioned to the time which was required to load it into cars. In driving through silt the typical gang per shift of eight hours per shield was as follows:

General

$\frac{1}{3}$ tunnel supt. at $300 per month.....	$4.00	per day
Asst. supt..........................	6.00	"
General foreman....................	5.00	"
Foreman...........................	4.00	"
$\frac{1}{2}$ electrician and helper, $3.50 and 3.00	3.25	"
2 pipe fitters, $3.50..................	7.00	"
2 pipe fitters' helpers, $3.25..........	6.50	"
Cost per 8-hour shift................	35.75	

Mucking

Foreman...........................	$4.00	per day
6 muckers, $3.00....................	18.00	"
Cost per 8-hour shift................	$22.00	

Erecting Iron and Driving Shield

Foreman...........................	$4.00	per day
Erector runner.....................	3.50	"
4 iron workers, $3.00................	12.00	"
3 laborers, $3.00....................	9.00	"
Cost per 8-hour shift................	$28.50	

The total cost of labor per 8-hour shift was $85.75. Three shifts of 8 hours each were worked under an average air pressure of 25 pounds. The rate of progress in the silt under the river was 2½ feet (the width of a ring) in every 3 hours and 21 minutes or about one foot in 1 hour and 20 minutes. This was exclusive of the time during which work was suspended. The average daily advance, including all delays, was 10.8 feet per day.

The junction of the shields under the river was made as follows: When the two shields of one tunnel, which had been driven from opposite sides of the river, approached within 10 feet of each other the shields were stopped and a 10-inch pipe was driven between them in order to make a final check on lines and levels. The first traffic established was the passage of a box of cigars through this pipe.

One shield was then started up with all doors closed while the doors on the stationary shield ahead were opened so that the muck driven forward by the moving shield was taken in through the doors of the stationary shield. This was continued until the cutting edges met. All doors in both shields were then opened and the shields mucked out. The cutting edges were removed and the shields advanced till their outer skins met. The interior framing and everything except the outer skin of the shields was removed. The iron lining was then built up inside of the skins, concreted and grouted outside.

The single erector attached to the center of the shield was capable of erecting the iron lining as fast as it could be brought into the tunnel. The individual segments varied in weight from 2060 to 2580 pounds. The average time spent in erecting and bolting up for the whole length of the tube tunnels was 2 hours and 15 minutes per ring. Each ring was 2 feet 6 inches in width by 23 feet outside diameter.

After the metal lining had been built completely across the river in both tunnels the work of making it water-tight was taken up. This consisted in forming a rust joint between the plates with a mixture of sal-ammoniac and iron borings, and in taking out each bolt and placing around the shank under the washer at each end a grummet made of yarn soaked in red lead. Before caulking the joints were cleaned. The usual mixture for the joints was 2 pounds of sal-ammoniac, 1 pound of sulphur and 250 pounds of iron filings or borings. Air hammers were used with advantage in caulking this mixture into the joints.

In putting in the concrete lining in the under-river tunnels the mixture (proportions 1 to 2½ to 5) was turned over for about 1½ minutes or 20 revolutions in No. 6 Ransome mixers. A 4-bag batch consisted of one 380-lb. barrel of cement, 8.75 cubic feet of sand and 17.5 cubic feet of stone. The average quantity of water used per batch was 25 U.S. gallons. Run-of-crusher trap rock with the largest stones of a size which would pass a 2½-inch screen was generally used. The average resulting volume from each batch was 0.808 cubic yard. The force employed in mixing concrete per 10-hour shift was as follows:

Manhattan side:

Foreman	$3.00	per shift
4 men on sand and stone cars at $1.75	7.00	"
4 men handling cement at 1.75	7.00	"
2 men dumping mixers at 1.75	3.50	"
Labor per shift	$20.00	

Weehawken side:

Foreman	$3.00	per shift
2 men hauling cement at $1.75	3.50	"
2 men dumping mixers at 1.75	3.50	"
Cost of labor per 10-hour shift	$10.00	

The average quantity of concrete mixed per 10-hour shift was about 117 batches or 90 cubic yards. The maximum output of one of the mixers was 168 batches or 129 cubic yards in a 10-hour shift. The average force per shift for transportation in two tunnels while building two arches, two inverts and two duct benches consisted of two foremen, twenty-eight laborers, two switchmen and four hoisting engineers. The labor cost of this gang was $71 per shift.

The average time required to lay a 30-foot length of invert was 7 hours, but two spade men remained for an hour extra, smoothing off. The typical working force used in placing concrete in the inverts was as follows:

Foreman	$3.25	per shift
2 spaders, $2.00	4.00	"
9 laborers, $1.75	15.75	"
Total cost per shift	$23.00	

The following force, with the wages listed, was used in cutting the forms for the concrete laying:

Foreman	$4.50	per shift
5 carpenters, $3.25	16.25	"
6 carpenter's helpers, $2.25	13.50	"
Total cost per shift	$34.25	

The average time required to erect a form was 2 hours, one carpenter and one helper remaining until the concrete was finished. With the same force as used in laying the concrete in inverts the concrete duct bench was laid at a rate of 35 feet in 6 hours. An average gang for a 20-foot length of arch was one foreman, two spaders and ten laborers, at a total labor cost of $21 per shift.

Two 20-foot lengths of arch were grouted at one time, an average of three-quarters of a barrel of cement and three-quarters of a barrel of sand being used per lineal foot of tunnel. The average amount put in by one machine per shift was 15 barrels and the average length grouted was 20 feet. The typical working force on this work was as follows:

Foreman	$3.75	per shift
Laborer running grout machine	2.00	"
2 laborers handling cement and sand	1.75	"
1 laborer tending valves and pipes	1.75	"
Total labor per shift	$9.25	

After the grouting was finished the arches were rubbed down with wire brushes to remove the discoloration and the rough places at the junction of adjoining lengths were bush hammered.

The leakage after the concrete lining was in was found to be from 0.05 to 0.06 gallon per lineal foot of tunnel per 24 hours, which compares favorably with the records of other lined tunnels.

The air pressure carried during the progress of the subriver work varied from 17 to 27 pounds per square inch. Behind the river line it averaged 17 pounds and was generally kept about equal to the water head at the crown of the tunnel. Under the river the pressure averaged 26 pounds per square inch. In silt the pressure was much lower than the hydrostatic head at the crown, but if it became necessary to excavate ahead of the shields the air pressure required was about equal to the weight of the overlying material, water and silt. The silt, which weighed from 97 to 106 pounds per cubic foot, with an average of 100 pounds, acted like a fluid. The compressor plant was found to be ample for all requirements, except when passing the gravel section at Weehawken.

The quantity of free air per man per hour was in general between 1500 and 5000 cubic feet. When there was an excessive escape through open gravel the supply for a time reached 10,000 cubic feet per hour per man. For more than half of the time working in silt the supply was between 3000 and 4000 cubic feet. But when it seemed evident that any quantity beyond 2000 cubic feet had no beneficial effect on the health of the workers no attempt was made to deliver more. On two distinct occasions for two consecutive weeks it ran as low as 1000 cubic feet per man per hour without any increase in the number of cases of bends.

The amount of CO_2 in the air was also measured daily, as the specifications covering the work called for not more than one part of CO_2 per 1000 parts of air. The average ranged between 0.8 and 1.5 parts per 1000. In exceptional cases it fell as low as 0.3 and rose as high as 4.0. The temperature of the air in the tunnels usually ranged from 55 to 60 degrees Fahrenheit, which was the temperature of the surrounding silt, but when grouting was being extensively done in long sections of the tunnel in rock, the temperature varied from 85 to 110 degrees Fahrenheit.

NOTE.—From paper by B. H. M. Hewett and W.L. Brown before the American Society of Civil Engineers, April, 1910.

Various types of screw piles were sunk and tests made not only of the dead load carrying capacity, but also as to their behavior under the addition of impact. It was found that screw piles could be sunk to hard ground and would carry the required load. A screw pile having a shaft 30 inches in diameter and a blade 5 feet in diameter was loaded to 600,000 pounds, with the result that for a month (the duration of this loaded test) there was no subsidence.

After the iron tunnel lining had been constructed across the river, tests were made of two types of support. One was a screw pile 29½ inches in diameter with a blade 4 feet 8 inches in diameter; and the other was a wrought iron pipe 16 inches in diameter. Tests were made not only for their carrying capacity, but also for their value as anchorages. It was found that the screw pile was more satisfactory in every way. It could be put down much more rapidly, was more easily maintained in a vertical position, and as a support for the track could carry satisfactorily any load which could be placed upon it. The 16-inch pipe did not prove efficient either as a carrier or as an anchorage.

After the shields had met and the iron lining had been joined, various experiments and tests were made in the tunnel. Screw piles and the pipes previously referred to were inserted through the bore segments in the bottom of the tunnel. Thorough tests were made with these, levels were observed in the tunnels during construction and placing of the concrete lining, an examination was conducted of the tunnels of the Hudson and Manhattan Railroad Company under traffic, and the result was the decision not to install the screw piles. The tubes, however, were reinforced longitudinally by twisted steel rods in the invert and roof, and by transverse rods where there was a superincumbent load on the tunnels on the New York side. Where they emerge from the rock and pass into soft rock the metal shell is of cast steel instead of cast iron.

There was considerable subsidence in the tunnels during construction and lining amounting to an average of 0.34 feet between the bulkhead lines. This settlement has been constantly decreasing since construction and appears to have been due almost entirely to the disturbances of the surrounding materials while the work was being carried on. The silt weighs about

100 pounds per cubic foot and contains about 38 per cent water, this being the average of a number of samples taken from the shield door which varied in weight from 93 to 109 pounds per cubic foot. It was found that whenever this material was disturbed outside the tunnels a displacement of the tubes followed. The tubes as noted have been lined with concrete reinforced with steel rods; and prior to the placing of the concrete the joints were caulked, the bolts grummeted and the tunnels rendered practically water-tight. The present quantity of water which must be disposed of does not exceed 300 gallons per twenty-four hours in each tunnel 6100 feet long.

The quantities of some of the main items in the North River tunnels are as follows:

Excavation, in cubic yards	238,995
Cast metal used in tunnels, tons	64,265
Steel bolts used, tons	3,606
Cement used (concrete and grout) barrels	145,500
Concrete, cubic yards	75, 400
Dynamite for blasting, pounds	100,400
Brickwork, cubic yards	4,980
Structural steel (including Pier 72), pounds	3,141,000

CHAPTER XII

EXCAVATION FOR THE TERMINAL STATION OF THE PENNSYLVANIA RAILROAD

THE site of the Pennsylvania Terminal Station in New York City is between Tenth and Seventh Avenues and Thirty-first and Thirty-third Streets; it includes an area of about twenty-eight acres.

The principal contract was with the New York Contracting and Trucking Company, which was later assigned by that company to the New York Contracting Company, Pennsylvania Terminal, for the performance of the following divisions of work.

Excavation for, and construction of, the retaining walls in Seventh Avenue and Thirty-first Street, Ninth Avenue and Thirty-third Street; excavation over the entire area enclosed by the retaining wall; the building of sewers and the laying of water and gas mains; the building of trestles to support street traffic; and the construction of the two twin tunnels under Ninth Avenue.

These contracts demanded that the material excavated be delivered on board scows to be furnished by the railroad company, alongside the pier at the foot of West Thirty-second Street, North River. These scows were supplied, and the material was disposed of from the pier, by Henry Steers, Incorporated, under a contract which called for the transportation and placing of all material so delivered in the Pennsylvania Railroad Company's freight terminal at Greenville, N. J.

The disposal of the excavated material was one of the principal features of the work, and the above contract covered the disposition of material from those portions of the terminal site east of Seventh Avenue and west of Ninth Avenue, from all substructural work and from other construction.

The central power plant for conducting this section of the work consisted of the following items:

Four Ingersoll-Rand straight line air compressors.

One Ingersoll-Rand duplex Corliss steam driven compressor, cross-compound, with a capacity of 5600 cubic feet per minute compressed to 80 pounds at 70 r.p.m.

Three Ingersoll-Rand duplex electric-driven air compressors, driven by 525 h.p., 6600 volt General Electric motors, with a

Ingersoll-Rand Rock Drills in P. R. R. Terminal Excavation.

capacity of 3000 cubic feet per minute, compressed to 80 pounds at 125 r.p.m.

Two 10- by 6- by 10-inch Worthington steam pumps.

One 7½ h.p. General Electric motor, driving the coal conveyor.

One 8- by 10-inch Buffalo Forge Co's engine driving the forced draft fan.

Three 500 h.p. Stirling water tube boilers.

In the repair shop attached to this work, were two large Ajax drill sharpeners which took care of the steels from the rock drills in the excavation.

In the pit excavation equipment the following items were included:

Three 70-ton Bucyrus steam shovels.

Two 30-ton steam shovels (Marion and Ohio).

Eighty Ingersoll-Rand rock drills.

Two Ingersoll-Rand quarry bars.

Twenty-one 10- by 16-inch, 36-inch gage Porter locomotives.

Three 9- by 16-inch, 36-inch gage Davenport locomotives.

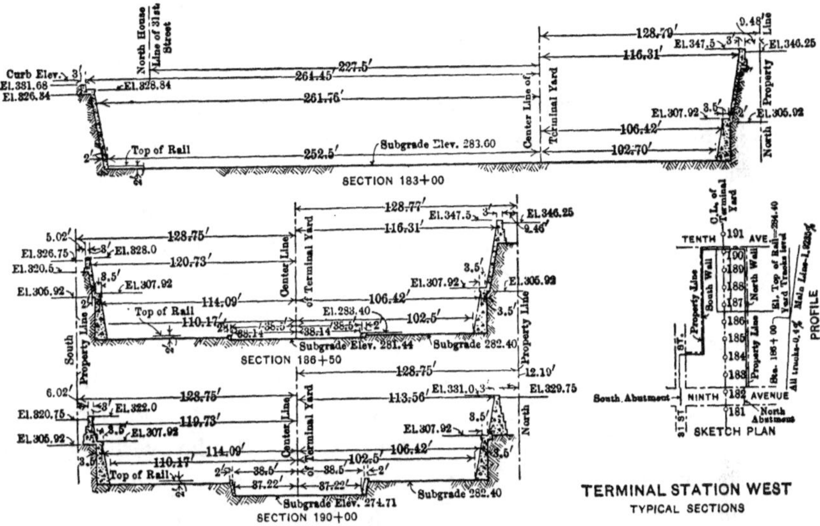

Cross-Sections of P. R. R. Terminal Excavation.

One hundred and forty four-yard Western dump cars.

One hundred and sixty-five flat cars with four-yard iron skips.

The machine equipment at the dock included six stiff-leg derricks with 35-foot masts and 40-foot booms operated by 60 h.p. three-drum Lambert hoisting engines with Northern motors, and eight Dodge electric telphers with General Electric motors.

Ground was broken under the principal contract July 9, 1904. Two methods were used in making the excavation for the retaining walls and in building these walls; construction in the trench, and construction on the bench. In general, the trench method was used wherever the rock on which the wall was to be built was twelve feet or more below the surface of the street or where the buildings adjoining the wall were not founded on rock.

In the trench method the base of the wall was staked out on the ground surface and as much width was added as was needed for sheeting and working space. All of this was then excavated to a depth of 5 feet before timbering was begun. A cable-way was erected and the spoil placed in buckets and dumped into wagons. Some very difficult material was encountered in the deeper excavations; beds of quicksand were passed through varying from 1 to 18 feet in thickness.

After encountering a fine sand in one trench no headway was made until a tight wooden cylinder was sunk through the sand by excavating the material inside of it and heavily weighting the shell with pig iron. When this cylinder had reached the gravel which lay below the sand, it was used as a sump, and the water level kept below the excavation, which permitted good progress. Sand continued to flow under the sheeting to such an extent that the front walls of four adjoining buildings were badly cracked and had to be rebuilt.

The bench method of excavation for the retaining wall was simple, and was used only when the rock lay near the surface and when the adjoining buildings had a rock foundation. As the overlying material was dry and firm, little or no shoring was required.

The concrete retaining walls were usually built in sections 50 feet long. The trenches were not allowed to be opened for the full depth. Concreting was started as soon after the necessary length of rock had been uncovered as the forms and preliminary work for a section could be prepared. Generally each section was a monolith. The concrete was mixed by power in the proportions of 1 part of cement, 3 parts of sand, and 5 parts of stone. Facing mortar 2 inches thick was deposited at the same time as the concreting, being separated from the latter by a steel diaphragm until both were in place. The diaphragm was then removed and the two spaded together. The layers of concrete never exceeded 8 inches in thickness.

After a section of the concrete wall had firmly set, both back and front forms were removed and the thrust from the

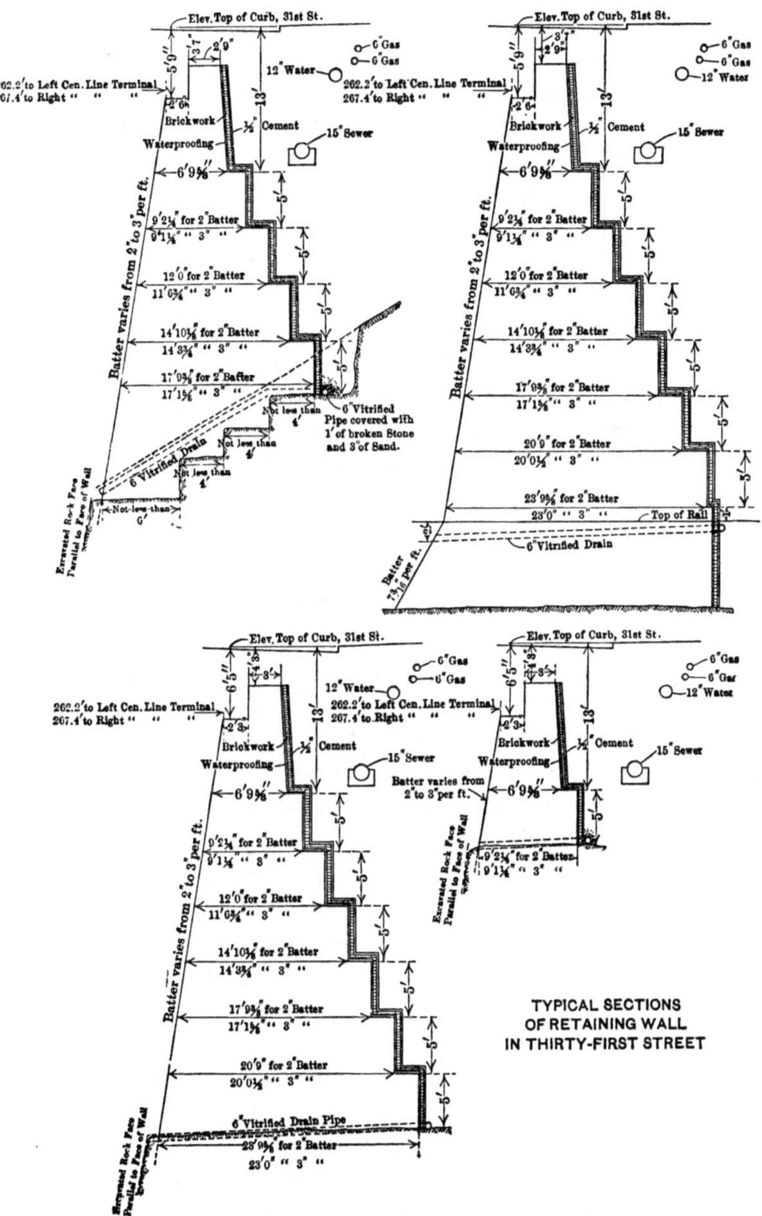

Retaining Walls for P. R. R. Terminal Excavation.

sides of the trench transferred directly to the finished wall. The face of the wall was rubbed with a cement brick to remove the marks of the planks, and washed with a thin cement grout.

Waterproofing and brick armor were then continued up the back of the wall, the waterproofing consisting of three layers of "Hydrex" felt and four layers of coal-tar pitch. The pitch contained not less than 25 per cent of carbon, softened at 60 degrees Fahrenheit and melted at between 96 and 106 degrees Fahrenheit.

In designing the concrete wall the following were assumed:

Weight of concrete, 140 pounds per cubic foot.

Weight of material from the ground surface to the depth of 12 feet, 100 pounds per cubic foot; and the angle of repose 30 degrees.

The weight of buildings back of the wall was neglected, as it was assumed to be about equal to that of the cellars filled with material weighing 100 pounds per cubic foot.

Reaction from superstructure, live and dead load, 20,000 pounds per lineal foot of wall.

Weight of materials below the 12-foot depth line, 124 pounds per cubic foot.

The resultant of both horizontal and vertical forces should, at all points, fall within the middle third of the wall; in other words, there should be no tension in the concrete.

While the pit excavation was started by hand, three 70-ton steam shovels were put to work as soon as they could be delivered. The excavated material was loaded by the shovels into 2-yard end-dump wagons and conveyed to the dumping board at Thirty-fifth Street.

The average number of teams employed was 140, 10 per cent of which were snatch teams to pull the wagons out of the pit, and to assist them up the runway at the dumping board. The teams averaged only seven trips per day of ten hours. The number of teams was not sufficient to keep the three shovels busy when in good digging; but the dumping board was taxed to the limit of its capacity.

As the shovels had three-and-one-half-yard buckets, one bucketful meant a wagon full and running over. The output from August to November inclusive averaged 40,000 cubic yards per month. One shift only was worked per day. The quantity was not large for such shovels to dig, but it was a large quantity to truck through the streets and required the passage, at a given point, of one team every 18 seconds.

At the beginning of the team transportation period, on May 22, 1905, two shifts of ten hours each were inaugurated, and the earth was handled at the rate of 85,000 to 90,000 cubic yards per month. But by the end of August, when a little more than 60 per cent of the total earth had been disposed of, the rock began to interfere with the progress. The strike of the rock was almost directly north and south, and its surface formed broken ridges in that direction with deep valleys between. The dip was almost vertical near Ninth Avenue and about 70 degrees toward the west near Seventh Avenue. This made it necessary to turn the shovels parallel to the ridges in order to strip the rock for drilling. As the ridges were very much broken the shovels continued to bump into them on all occassions, making it necessary to move back and start other cuts, or stand and wait for the rock to be drilled and blasted.

A small Vulcan steam shovel with a three-quarter-yard dipper was brought on the work to do the stripping. It was moved so readily from place to place that another shovel of smaller type was put in use and thereafter the stripping was done largely by these two small shovels and by hand. The large shovels were used almost exclusively in handling rock.

The drilling necessary to remove the rock was very large in total amount and also in amount per yard excavated. In order not to damage the retaining walls and the rock underlying them, holes spaced at five-inch centers were drilled 1 foot away from the face of the holes and on the same batter. These breaking holes alone amounted to a total of 210,000 lineal feet or 1 foot of hole for each 3½ cubic yard of rock excavated. The regulations of the Bureau of Combustibles which prohibit springing of holes compelled the placing of drilled holes very close together, making a total of about 420,000 lineal feet which, added to the other 210,000 lineal feet, brings the aggregate to 630,000 feet. If to this is added the block holes (for some of the rock broke large) it will show at least 1 foot of hole drilled for each cubic yard of rock excavated.

The excavated material was hauled from the shovels to the pier in 10-car trains. The cars were of three classes, namely, 4-yard dump cars, flat cars and flat cars carrying 4-yard skips. So far as practicable, earth and rocks of one cubic yard or less were loaded in the dump cars; larger rocks on the flat cars; and medium sized rocks in the skips. The dump cars were run at once to the hoppers, dumped and returned to the pit; the flat cars and skips were run under the derricks and telphers and the large rocks unloaded, after which they were run to the hoppers and emptied.

The total quantity of excavated material handled on this pier from May 22, 1905 to December 31, 1908 amounted to 673,800 cubic yards of earth and 1,488,000 cubic yards of rock, place measurement. This is equal to 3,208,400, cubic yards, scow measurement. In addition to this, 175,000 cubic yards of crushed stone and sand, and 6000 car loads of miscellaneous building materials were transferred from scows and lighters to smaller cars for delivery to the Terminal work.

All the earth and 570,000 cubic yards of rock, place measurement, were handled from the chutes. The remainder of the rock, amounting to 918,000 cubic yards, and all the incoming material were handled by the derricks and telphers. In materials-handling capacity one telpher was about equivalent to one derrick. A train, therefore, could be emptied or a boat loaded under the bank of eight telphers in one-quarter of the time required by the derricks, of which two only could work on one boat. The telphers were of great advantage where track room and scow berths were limited.

The material from various contracts of the Pennsylvania Railroad extension, which was transported and disposed of by Henry Steers, Incorporated, amounted to 4,457,800 cubic yards. Of this, 3,454,800 cubic yards were placed in the freight terminal yard at Greenville, N. J.; 711,900 cubic yards in the Meadows division; and 291,000 cubic yards at other points. Handling this material required the loading of from ten to twenty scows per day. The average for more than two years was fourteen per day. As the average time spent in one round trip was three and one-third days, a fleet of more than fifty scows was required to keep all points supplied. All loaded scows were towed from the docks to stake boats about one mile

Drilling for P. R. R. Terminal Excavation.

off shore at Greenville. From there they were taken to the different unloading points by smaller tugs which also returned the empty scows to the stake.

The unloading plants were similar at the different points, although that at Greenville was much larger than the others. It included five land dredges and eight traveling derricks of two types, one floating and the other mounted on wheels and traveling on a track of 16-ft gage. The derricks, which were of the "A" frame type and capable of handling 20 tons, were used for the larger rocks which were deposited by the derricks either in the channels along which they worked or in the fill along shore, without the use of cars. The land dredges had 60-foot booms, carrying two-and-one-half-yard Hayward buckets operated by a 14- by 18-inch double-drum dredging engine. They loaded into 9-yard, standard gage, side dump cars, built by the contractor; and unloaded the scows to within one foot of the deck. The material remaining was loaded by hand into skips which were dumped into the cars by small derricks, one of which was located at the rear of each dredge. The cars were hauled to the dump by 25-ton standard gage locomotives.

The cost of repairs to the scows, due to loading, transportation and unloading at all points, was about three and one-half cents per cubic yard. In addition it cost four-tenths of a cent per cubic yard for scows overturned or sunk in service, making three and nine-tenths cents in all.

The two double-track tunnels under Ninth Avenue, which were constructed to obtain 100 feet of additional tail room on each of the four tracks, required an excavation 75 feet wide. The rock was of fair quality, but not firm enough to support so great a span in a single tunnel. To obviate the necessity of timbering, the center wall was built before excavating for the full width. The dip of the rock at this point is almost 90 degrees. To prevent blowing away the entire face in excavating for the tunnel, the pit excavation was not carried west to the final face below the springing line, but a 10-foot bench was left at that elevation.

A top heading 9 by 9 feet in section was started above the bench, and when 10 feet had been penetrated it was widened to 20 feet. A cross-heading was driven in each direction at the west end of the first heading. The bench was then shut down and the first 10 feet of longitudinal heading was widened sufficiently to receive the center wall.

When the middle wall had been concreted all voids between the top and the rock were grouted through pipes left for the purpose. The wall was then protected by curtains of heavy round timber securely wired together and the remainder of the excavation was made by widening the cross-headings toward the face. The muck was carried out by cableways, one on each side of the completed wall. Each cableway was supported by a tower outside the tunnel and by a large hook-bolt grouted into the rock at the inner end of the tunnel. Forms were built for each tunnel complete, and the concrete was delivered by a

Looking east at Seventh Avenue. Approach to new Pennsylvania Terminal, with Cameron Pump removing 400 gallons drainage water per minute from the diggings to the sewer 65 feet above.

belt conveyor, running over the top of the lagging and moved out as the tunnel was keyed.*

The rock formation consisted of quartz, feldspar and mica, with some hornblende, serpentine, pyrites and tourmaline. The formation varied from mica schist to granite and may be generally classed as gneiss. The total rock excavation with an

* From a paper by George C. Clark, M.A.S.C.E., on The New York Tunnel Extension of the Pennsylvania Railroad and The Site of the Terminal Station, in the Proceedings of the A.S.C. E., March, 1910.

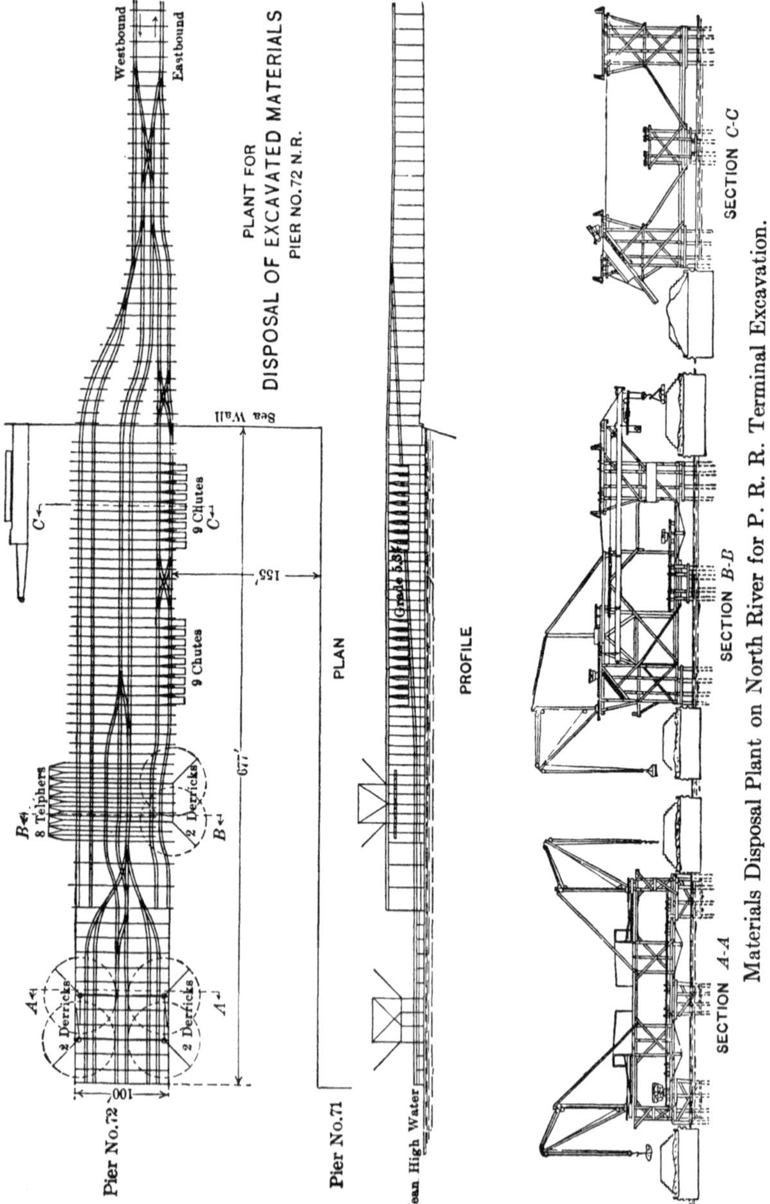

Materials Disposal Plant on North River for P. R. R. Terminal Excavation.

average depth of 50 feet was about 450,000 cubic yards in open cut. The general method of drilling for the different classes of work was as follows:

In breaking down, the holes were started about 8 feet apart, on a slight batter, so that at the bottom they would be less than 8 feet apart. They were drilled 10 feet deep, and it was necessary to load heavily to lift the cut. When a side cut of about 20 feet had been made, the side holes were drilled 20 feet deep and the holes loaded and tamped for the full 20-foot cut. The terms of the specifications required the contractor to finish the sides of the excavation by broaching holes.

For the steam shovel excavation, on portions of the work spring holes were used. These holes were 20 feet deep. Two or three sticks of dynamite were exploded at the bottom of the holes, and no tamping was used. This process was repeated with increasingly heavy charges until a cavity was formed of a size which would hold from 100 to 200 pounds of dynamite. Face and breast holes were drilled, and by this means cuts 20 feet by 15 feet thick were broken up.

The average performance from more than 25,000 drill shifts showed 33 lineal feet of hole per 8-hour shift. The average cubic yards per drill shift was 13.9. The average drilling per cubic yard was 2.4 feet. The dynamite used was 60 per cent, and the average excavation per pound of dynamite was 2.2 cubic yards. The average performance of derricks, with gangs of twelve men and one foreman, was 50 cubic yards per 8-hour shift. The cost of field engineering and office was 2.8 per cent of the cost of work executed, of which 2.7 per cent was for salaries.

The quantities of some of the main items in the excavation of the Terminal Station are as follows:

Excavation, in cubic yards	517,000
Cement used (concrete and grout), barrels	33,000
Concrete, cubic yards	18,500
Dynamite for blasting, pounds	206,000
Structural Steel (including Pier 72), pounds	1,475,000

* From a paper by B. F. Cresson, Jr., before the A.S.C.E., April 6, 1910.

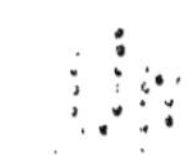

CHAPTER XIII

CROSS-TOWN TUNNELS OF THE PENNSYLVANIA RAILROAD

ON May 29, 1905, a contract was entered into with the United Engineering and Contracting Company for the construction of the tunnels for the Pennsylvania Railroad extending eastward from the easterly extension of the Terminal Station in New York City to the permanent shafts just east of First Avenue, where they connected with the East River tunnels.

These cross-town tunnels are located under Thirty-second and Thirty-third streets, from the Terminal Station to Second Avenue. Curving thence to the left, they pass under private property and under First Avenue to the shafts.

The method of handling the work adopted by the contractor was in general as follows: Excavation was carried on by modifications of the top-heading and bench method, the bench being carried as close to the face as possible in order to allow the muck from the heading to be thrown by the blast over the bench into the full tunnel section. The spoil was loaded into 3-yard buckets of a special design by means of Marion steam shovels operated by compressed air; and these buckets were hauled to the shafts by General Electric electric locomotives.

Electrically operated telphers suspended from a timber trestle hoisted the buckets and, traveling on a mono-rail track, deposited them on wagons for transportation to the dock. At the dock the buckets were lifted by electrically operated stiff-leg derricks and the contents deposited on scows for final disposal. The spoil was thus transported from the heading to the scow without breaking the bulk. When the concreting was in progress the spoil buckets were returned to the shafts loaded with stone and sand.

The power house at the corner of Thirty-first Street and Fourth Avenue supplied compressed air for operating the drills, shovels, pumps and hoists in the tunnel driven from the river shafts. It included three Laidlaw-Dunn-Gordon compressors. The largest was a 2-stage, cross-compound, direct-connected, electric unit, 32 and 20 by 30 inches, driven at 100 r.p.m. by a 480 h.p., 230-volt, direct current Fort Wayne constant speed motor. This unit was rated at 2870 cubic feet of free air per minute at a pressure of 100 pounds. It was governed by throttling the suction, the governor being controlled by the pressure in the air receiver and the motor running continuously at regular speed. The two other compressors were of smaller type; one 22½ and 14 by 18 inches, rated at 1250 cubic feet of free air per minute at 100 pounds pressure; the other 16 and 10 by 18 inches, rated at 630 cubic feet per minute. They were driven at 150 r.p.m. by 105 h.p., 220-volt, direct current General Electric motors, having a speed of 655 r.p.m. The larger of these two compressors was driven by two of the motors belted in tandem, and the smaller was belt-connected to a third motor. All of these compressors were water-jacketed and fitted with intercoolers, the water supply for cooling purposes being furnished by a water cooling tower.

The Dodge telphers used for hoisting muck from the tunnels and for lowering supplies, were hung from single rails on a timber trestle about 40 feet high spanning and connecting the two shafts. They were operated by a 75-h.p. General Electric motor for hoisting, and a 15-h.p. Northern motor for propelling. Their rated lifting capacity was 10,000 pounds, at a speed of 200 feet per minute.

During excavation the headings were supplied with forced ventilation from 12- and 14-inch Root spiral riveted asphalted pressure pipes. Canvas extensions were used beyond the ends of the pipes and air was supplied by a blower driven by a 15-h.p. motor.

The air compressing plant for the intermediate shaft was located at the rear of the Thirty-third Street shaft and supplied air for driving the tunnels east and west from the shafts, both under Thirty-second and Thirty-third Streets. Two Laidlaw-Dunn-Gordon compressors, similar to the larger machine in the First Avenue plant, were here installed, with a similar water cooling tower. The equipment also included American blowers with General Electric motors for forced ventilation.

For the receipt and disposal of materials at the Thirty-fifth Street pier, there was an equipment of four stiff-leg derricks operated by Lidgerwood and Lambert electric hoists. Two were used in lifting the muck buckets from the wagons and dumping them on the scows for final removal. The other two were fitted with clam-shell buckets for unloading sand and broken stone from the barges and for depositing the materials in large hoppers from which they were drawn into wagons for transportation to the various concrete plants.

In the tunnels the loading was done with air operated steam shovels. Four of these, Marion Model 20, were used at various points of the work. The material was carried from the shafts in buckets of special design. The buckets were carried in the tunnel on flat cars and through the streets on wagons, both cars and wagons being provided with cradles shaped to receive them. The tunnel cars were hauled by standard 10-ton General Electric electric mine locomotives, the current for which was taken at 220 volts from a pair of trolley wires suspended from the roof of the tunnel. Two eight-and-one-half-ton Davenport steam locomotives were also used toward the end of the work. The steam shovels were supplemented by two 15-ton Browning locomotive cranes which handled the spoil in places where the timbering interfered with the operation of the shovels. All tracks were of 3-foot gage and laid with 40-pound rail.

Practically all of the heavy drilling was done with Ingersoll-Rand "E-52" rock drills, the trimming being done with "Little Jap" and "Baby" drills. A large number of pumps were used at various points of the work, practically all of them being of Cameron make. The grout machines were of the vertical cylinder, air stirring type.

The sinking of the intermediate shafts was the first work undertaken. The shaft at Thirty-third Street had a cross-section of 34½ feet by 21 feet, and was 83 feet deep. The rock surface averaged 5 feet below the ground surface. Sinking was started on July 10, 1905, and was completed on October 3d of the same year, the rock throughout being hard and dry. The average daily rate of sinking was 0.73 feet and an average of 17.1 cubic yards was excavated per day with two shifts of eight hours each. The first shift was started at 6 A.M., and the second at 2:30 P.M., ending at 11 P.M. These hours were adopted to avoid undue disturbances during the night.

Before blasting the first lift of rock, channel cuts 5 or 6 feet deep were made along the sides of the shaft in order to avoid damage to the walls of the neighboring buildings. Timbering was required for a depth of only 10 feet below the surface of the ground. A drift 30 feet long, 17 feet wide and 27 feet high connected the south end of the shaft with the tunnels. This drift was excavated in three stages, a top heading and a bench in two lifts. While blasting the cut in the top heading, concussion was sufficient to break glass in the neighboring buildings. The use of a "Radialaxe" machine for making a cut to blast on open ends reduced this concussion.

The construction of the Thirty-second Street shaft was similar to that at Thirty-third Street, this shaft being 31½ by 20½ feet in section, with a depth of 71 feet. The depth of earth excavation averaged 19½ feet. Sinking was started May 15, 1905, and completed on the 26th of the following October. The daily average rate was 0.3 feet in earth and 0.52 feet in rock. The drift from shaft to tunnel was excavated in much the same manner as the one at Thirty-third Street.

For an average distance of 350 feet from the First Avenue shafts there were four single-track tunnels. The rock was sound and dry. A top heading of the full size of the tunnel and about 8 feet high was first driven, drilling being done by four drills mounted on two columns and the holes blasted in the ordinary way. The bench was 13 feet high. Drills on tripods were used on the bench, but owing to the lack of headroom, steels long enough to reach the bottom of the bench could not be used. Drills on tripods were placed as low possible and lift holes were drilled 15 degrees from the horizontal at the bottom of the bench. Headings were driven 10 to 20 feet in advance of the bench. In these single tunnels the muck was loaded by hand.

From the end of the single-track tunnel westward to Fifth Avenue on Thirty-third Street and to Madison Avenue on Thirty-second Street (with some exceptions) each pair of tunnels was excavated for the entire width at one operation. Three distinct methods were extensively used. The double heading, the center heading and the full-sized heading method. These differed only in the manner of blasting and drilling. The bench was usually within 10 or 15 feet of the face and was drilled and fired in the same way as in the single tunnels.

In the double heading method the top headings for each tunnel were driven separately, leaving a short rock core wall between them. These headings were drilled from columns in the same manner as in the single tunnels. The temporary dividing rock wall between the headings was drilled by a tripod drill on the bench of one of the headings, and was fired with the bench.

In the center heading method only one heading was driven, rectangular in shape and about 8 feet high by 14 feet wide. It was on the center line between the tunnels. In general, the face was from 6 to 12 feet (the length of one or two rounds) in advance of the face at the top. The center heading was drilled by four drills mounted on two columns. By turning these drills to the side they were used for holes at right angles to the line of the tunnel; and by means of these latter holes the remainder of the face of the heading was blasted. By turning the drills downward the bench holes under the center heading were also drilled.

Where the full heading method was employed ten drills were mounted on five columns across the face. Holes were drilled to form a cut near the center line between the tunnels. The remainder of the holes were located so that they would

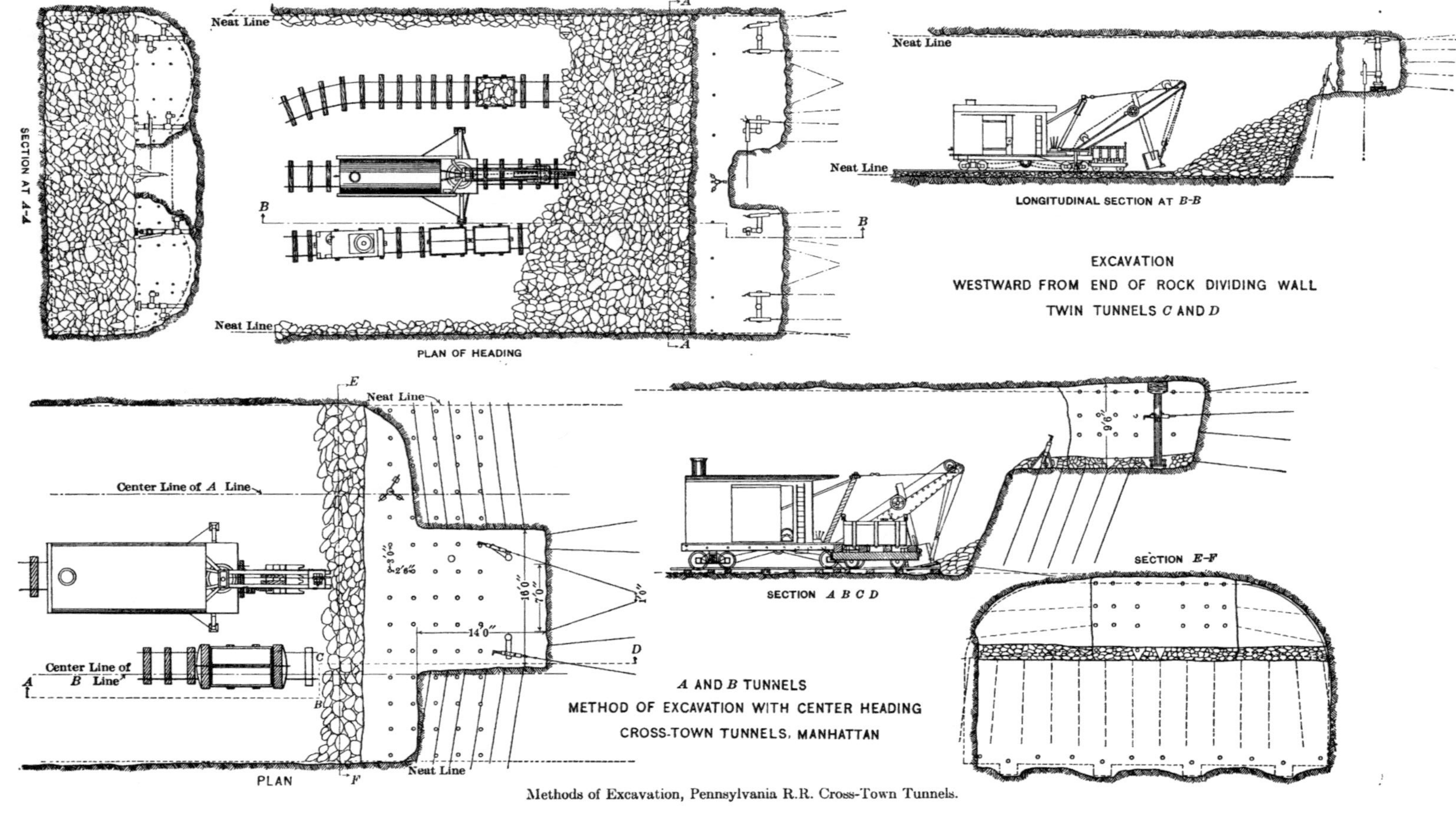

Methods of Excavation, Pennsylvania R.R. Cross-Town Tunnels.

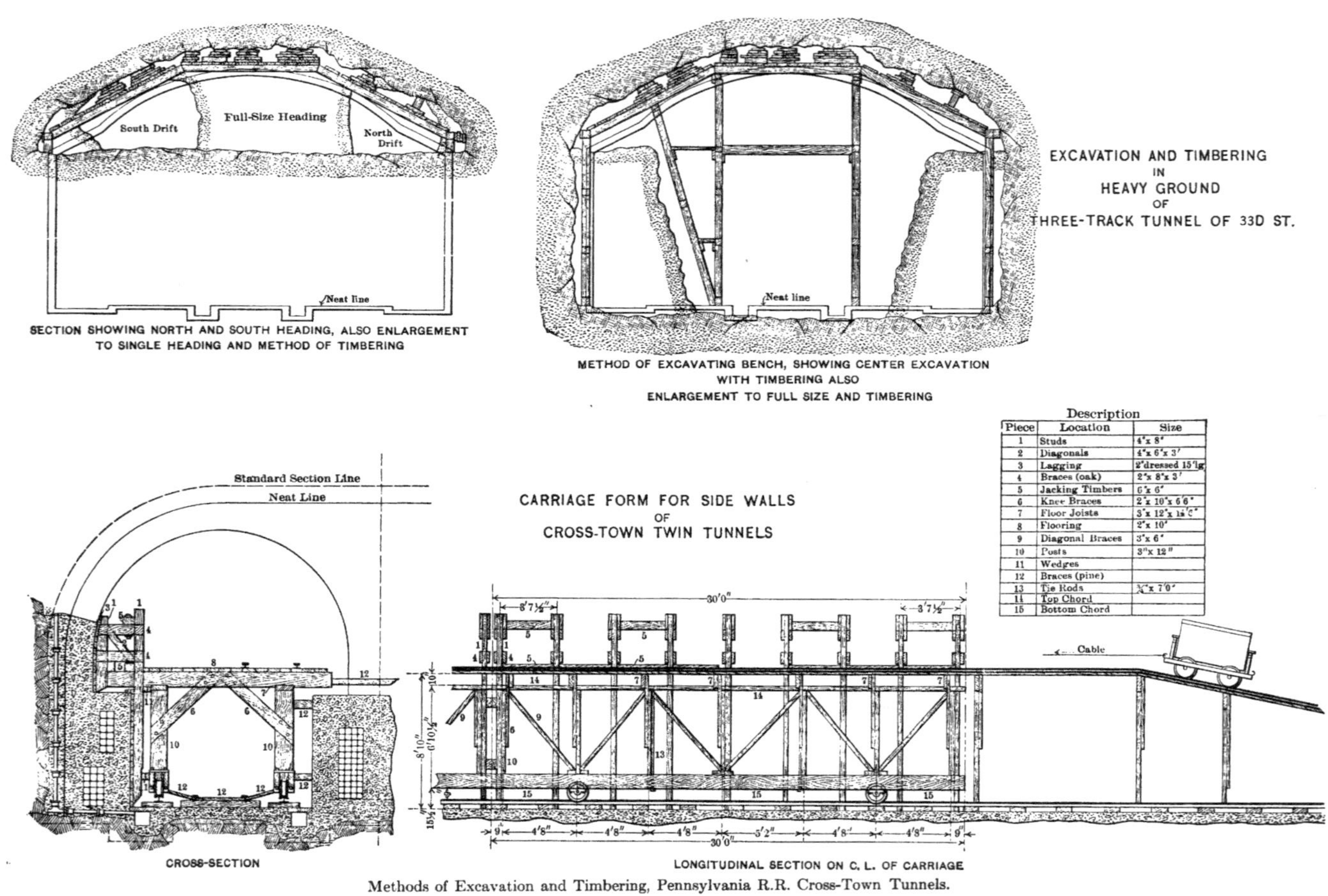

Description

Piece	Location	Size
1	Studs	4"x 8"
2	Diagonals	4"x 6"x 3'
3	Lagging	2"dressed 15'lg
4	Braces (oak)	2"x 8"x 3'
5	Jacking Timbers	6"x 6"
6	Knee Braces	2"x 10"x 6'6"
7	Floor Joists	3"x 12"x 15'0"
8	Flooring	2"x 10"
9	Diagonal Braces	3"x 6"
10	Posts	3"x 12"
11	Wedges	
12	Braces (pine)	
13	Tie Rods	¾"x 7'0"
14	Top Chord	
15	Bottom Chord	

Methods of Excavation and Timbering, Pennsylvania R.R. Cross-Town Tunnels.

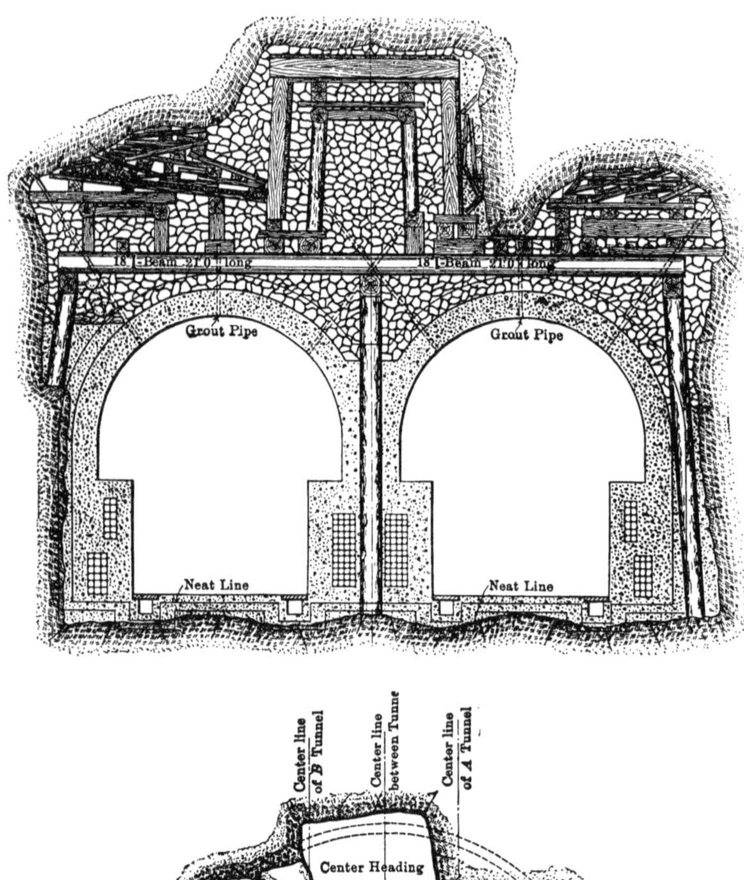

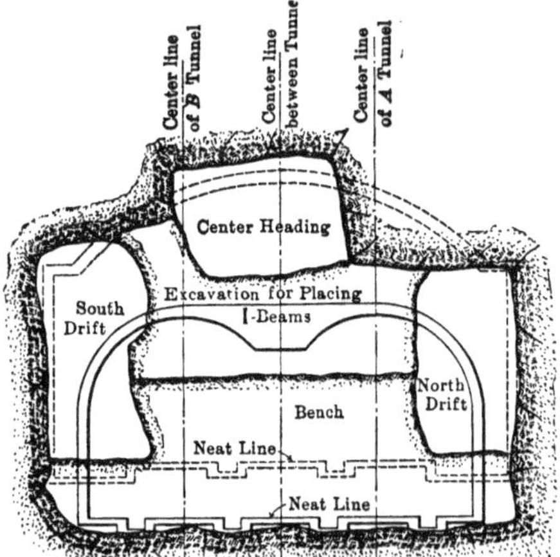

Construction of twin tunnels through excavation started for three-track tunnel in Thirty-third Street near Fifth Avenue.

draw into the center of the cut. The bench was frequently drilled from the same set-up of columns by turning the drills downward. In sound rock this method proved to be the most rapid of the three.

Practically all trimming was left until immediately before the concreting was begun. It was then taken up as a separate operation, but proved to be costly and tedious, and a hindrance to the placing of the lining. The rock encountered was Hudson schist, varying widely in character.

The material excavated from the tunnels was dumped on barges at the Thirty-fifth Street pier. These barges were towed to points near the Bayonne Peninsula where the spoil was used principally in the construction of the Greenville freight terminal. A portion was also used in building the extension across the Hackensack meadows to the Bergen Hill tunnel. The average rate of advance in the full-sized tunnels was from 3.8 to 4.7. feet per day, in the full-sized twin tunnels, from 1.4 to 5.8. feet per day, and in exploration drifts from 4.6 to 6.5 feet per day.

From a paper by James H. Brace and Francis Mason, in the Proceedings of the A.S.C.E. for October, 1909.

CHAPTER XIV

THE EAST RIVER TUNNELS OF THE PENNSYLVANIA RAILROAD

FROM the inception of the Pennsylvania Railroad project it was recognized that the most difficult and expensive section of the work would be the tunnels under the East River from Manhattan Island to Long Island. The borings along the line of the tunnel in the river bed had shown a great variety of materials to be passed through, comprising quicksand, coarse sand, gravel, boulders and bed rock, as well as some clayey materials. The rock was usually covered by a few feet of sand, gravel and boulders intermixed; but in places where the rock surface was at some distance below the tunnel grade, the material to be met was quicksand. The nearest parallel in work previously done was found in some of the tunnels under the Thames River, England, and particularly in the Blackwell tunnel, where open gravel was passed through.

The contract covering this section of the work was entered into with S. Pearson & Son on July 7, 1904. This contract covered the permanent shafts in New York City and in Long Island City, the tunnels between these shafts, and their extension eastward in Long Island City to East Avenue, involving about 23,600 feet of single-track tunnel. The contract had many novel features and seemed to be peculiarly suitable, considering the unknown risks involved and the unusual magnitude of the work.

A fixed amount was named as the contractor's profit. If the actual cost of the work when completed, including the sum named as contractor's profit, should be less than a certain estimated sum named in the contract, the contractor should have one-half of the saving. If on the other hand the actual cost of the completed work, including the fixed sum for contractor's profit, should exceed the estimated cost named in the contract, the contractor should pay one-half the excess and the railroad company the other half. The contractor's liability, however, was limited to the amount named for a profit plus $1,000,000. In other words, his maximum money loss would be $1,000,000.*

The plant assembled by S. Pearson & Son for handling this section is believed to be the most extensive ever placed on a single piece of contract work. The minimum plant to be provided by the contractors for the undertaking was specified by the railroad company in part as follows: The tunnels were to be driven eastward from shafts in Manhattan Island and westward from the temporary shaft to be built near East Avenue in Long Island City, making a total of eight headings, in all of which work was to be prosecuted simultaneously with the utmost practicable diligence. The contractor was to provide on each side of the river an adequate plant which was to include boilers, air compressors, hydraulic machinery, dynamos and all other necessary equipment, with a reasonable duplication to meet unusual and unexpected emergencies.

The air compressors were to be of sufficient capacity to deliver regularly into each heading at least 300,000 cubic feet of free air per hour at a pressure of 50 pounds per square inch above the normal air pressure; and for a larger amount if found necessary during the progress of the work. The air for the compressors was to be drawn from the exterior of the power house and the intake was to be so located as to give pure air. This air was to be cooled and freed as completely as possible from oil and other impurities before delivering into the heading.

In order to provide a reasonable margin for repairs and contingencies, a spare compressor and boiler plant was to be provided on each side of the East River, and to be kept in good condition, ready for immediate use. The capacity of these spare plants was to be 25 per cent of that required in the preceding paragraph for regular operation.

*From paper by Alfred Noble, Past President Am. Soc. C.E. in the Proceedings of the A.S. of C.E. for September, 1909.

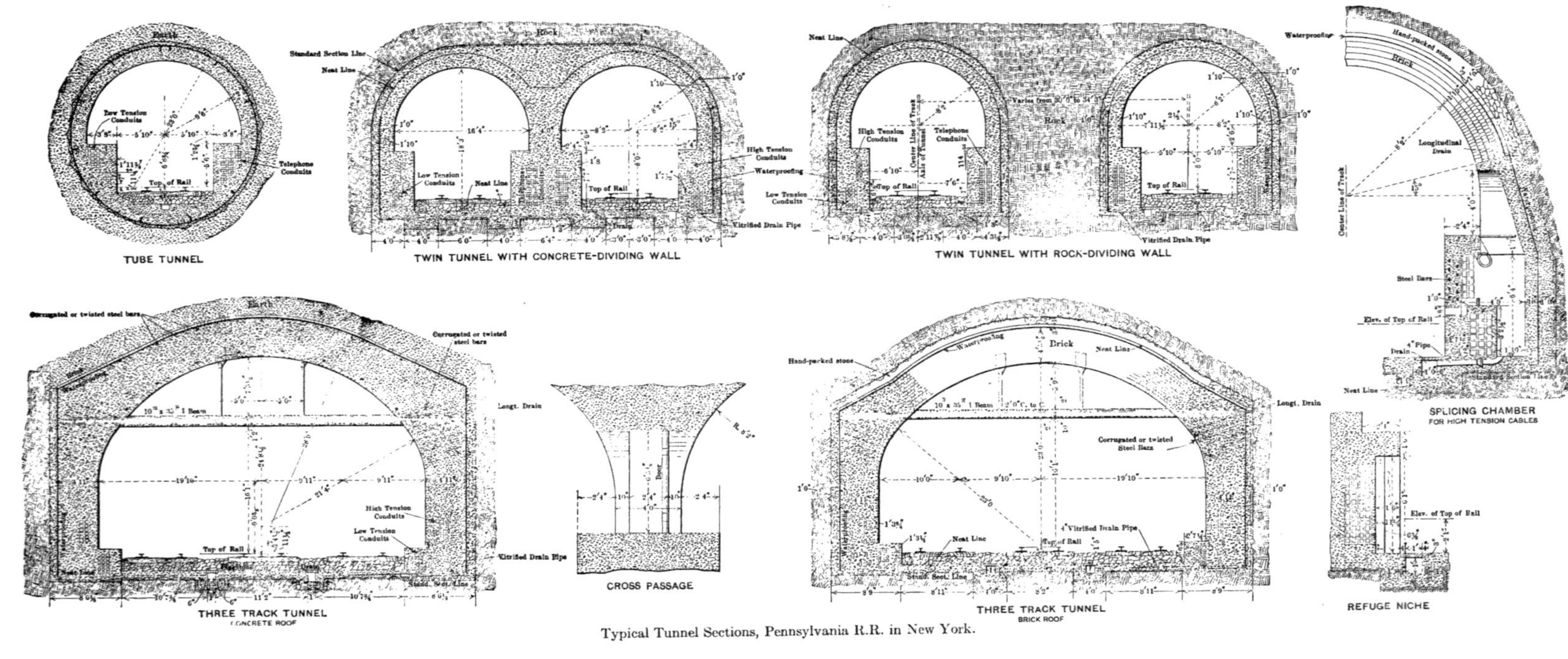

Typical Tunnel Sections, Pennsylvania R.R. in New York.

Effective means were to be used to secure proper ventilation. The amount of carbonic acid at any working face or in any chamber must never exceed one part in one thousand parts of air. Suitable devices were to be used to deaden as much as practicable the noise of the air introduced and exhausted. When blasting was to be resorted to, special means were to be provided for the rapid removal of the fumes produced.

Bulkheads were to be built in each tunnel at intervals of not more than 1000 feet; and it was specified that there should at no time be an interval of more than 1000 feet between a shield and the nearest bulkhead. These bulkheads were to be of concrete or brick set in Portland cement mortar, or of other construction to be approved by the company's engineer. Each was to be provided with two air locks near the bottom, at least 6 feet in diameter and 20 feet in length, for the passage of men and materials; one near the roof as an emergency lock for the passage of men only; and a pipe 12 inches in diameter and 30 feet long with a gate valve at each end, for passing pipes and rails. The emergency lock was to be of dimensions sufficiently ample to contain the entire force employed at any one time in the heading.

Stairways and galleries were always to be maintained to give sufficient access to the locks. All parts of the bulkheads and air locks were specified to be of sufficient strength to sustain safely a pressure of 55 pounds per square inch. The pipes necessary for air supply, ventilation, hydraulic and electric transmission, and other purposes were to be built into the bulkhead and provided with suitable connections. All of these pipes were to be standard lap welded. When a shield had been driven 500 feet or more from the shaft it was specified that at least two bulkheads should always be in use if compressed air was being used.

A safety screen extending from the roof downward into the tunnel, of a design to be approved by the company's engineer, was to be maintained within 100 feet of each working face. Others were to be built at intermediate points between the working face and the nearest bulkhead, if necessary, to maintain a chamber filled with compressed air along the tunnel roof which would give access to the emergency lock. The galleries were to extend from the safety screen nearest the working force to the first bulkhead.

The shields were to be of ample strength and of the best materials; were to be provided with hydraulic rams of sufficient power to move them along the alignment laid down on the plans and profiles; and they were to have adequate arrangements for the rapid execution of the work and for the safety of the men employed.

These outline specifications were of help to the contractors in making their bids and deciding what plant should be installed. The plant put in by S. Pearson & Son fulfilled these requirements, but it was found that the porous materials overlying the tunnels increased the demand for air beyond that specified, and it became necessary to increase the plant.

In the effort to select the best air compressors for continuous day-and-night service under the peculiarly difficult conditions of this work, the contractor made a careful investigation of plants erected by various manufacturers wherever available. Indicator cards of the steam and air cylinders were taken by the contractor's engineers where the plants were within reasonable distance; and where the plants were located too far away, indicator cards were submitted for inspection.

After an exhaustive study of all the machines proposed and of their relative merits, it was decided to adopt the type of Ingersoll-Rand air compressor fitted with the latter company's air-thrown inlet and discharge valves, on account of the larger valve areas, the free openings for inlet and discharge, and the reduced clearance spaces. This compressor was chosen in preference to other types with poppet discharge valves, as a high piston speed was necessary on account of the limited area at the disposal of the contractor for the installation of his plant. The choice of this type was amply justified as, during the four years' operation of the plant, it was never necessary to replace any of the forged steel, oil treated valves.

There were four cross-compound steam duplex air low pres-

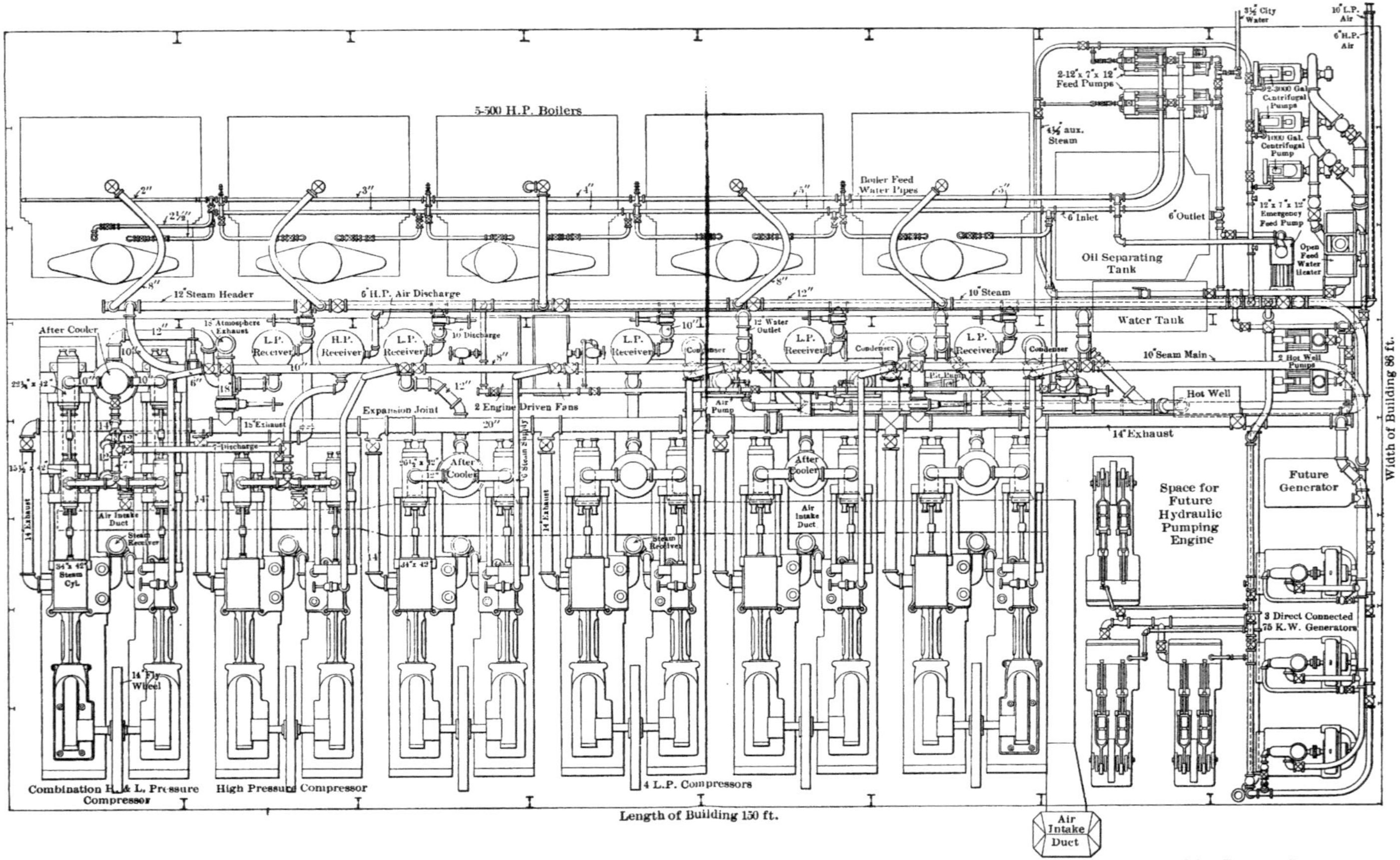

5-500 H.P. Boilers
2-12" x 7" x 12" Feed Pumps
4½" aux. Steam
Boiler Feed Water Pipes
6" Inlet
6" Outlet
Oil Separating Tank
Open Feed Water Heater
12" x 7" x 12" Emergency Feed Pump
3½" City Water
10" L.P. Air
6" H.P. Air
12" Steam Header
6" H.P. Air Discharge
10" Steam
Water Tank
10" Steam Main
2 Hot Well Pumps
Hot Well
14" Exhaust
After Cooler
L.P. Receiver
H.P. Receiver
Condenser
Air Pump
Expansion Joint
2 Engine Driven Fans
Air Intake Duct
Steam Receiver
14' Fly Wheel
Space for Future Hydraulic Pumping Engine
Future Generator
3 Direct Connected 75 K.W. Generators
Combination H. & L. Pressure Compressor
High Pressure Compressor
4 L.P. Compressors
Length of Building 150 ft.
Width of Building 86 ft.

Plan of the Manhattan Air Compressor Plant for Pennsylvania R.R. East River Tunnels. This was the Largest, Most Complete Air Power Plant ever used for Contract Work.

sure units, with steam cylinders 16 and 34 inches in diameter, air cylinders 26¼ inches in diameter, and a stroke of 42 inches. They compressed to 50 pounds pressure, with an aggregate free air capacity of 14,744 cubic feet per minute. A fifth machine was of the same type, same stroke and with steam cylinders of the same size, as the four previous units; but it had 15½-inch duplex air cylinders designed to compress to 140 pounds. The in take of this latter compressor could be at atmosphere, or

Interior of Manhattan Air Compressor Plant, P. R. R. East River Tunnels.

at the discharge pressure of the four low pressure units, the latter increasing its delivery at high pressure about four times. The piston displacement of this machine was 1310 cubic feet per minute at normal speed.

The steam ends of these air compressors were of cross-compound Corliss type with trip release gear controlled by the governor on each cylinder. The steam cylinders and intermediate receiver were steam jacketed and a steam separator was mounted on the throttle valve. Steam was admitted at a boiler pressure of 150 pounds (Stirling boilers) and the exhaust carried to Wheeler condensers at about a 26-inch vacuum. A test made to determine the steam consumption gave 14.2 pounds of steam per i.h.p. hour when compressing up to 30 pounds per square inch. An efficiency test of the low pressure compressor units on the Manhattan side showed a mechanical efficiency of over 90 per cent and a volumetric efficiency of about 96 per cent.

In order to cover the demand of the specifications for a spare plant of 25 per cent capacity, a combination machine was designed which could be used either as a high pressure machine for rock drills or as a low pressure machine for supplying tunnel air. It had the same steam end as the low pressure units, but was fitted with two low pressure cylinders of 22¼-inch diameter and two high pressure cylinders of 15½-inch diameter. Running as a low pressure machine with all four air cylinders operating, it had a capacity of 5,000 cubic feet of free air per minute. If it was desired to run it as a high pressure machine, the two low pressure cylinders could be disconnected, when the capacity was 1568 cubic feet of free air to 90 pounds pressure with atmospheric intake, and 6900 cubic feet of free air to 140 pounds pressure with an intake of 50 pounds from the low pressure units. Each air compressor was fitted with a vertical low pressure aftercooler, 57 inches in diameter and 14½ feet long, having 920 square feet of cooling surface. These aftercoolers were fitted with tinned navy-mixture brass tubes and Tobin bronze tube plates. The air from each compressor was discharged into individual low pressure air receivers, 4½ feet in diameter and 12 feet high.

In addition to the steam driven low pressure machines it became necessary on the Long Island City side to purchase two low pressure Laidlaw-Dunn-Gordon electrically driven compressors. Each of these had two air cylinders, 30 inches in diameter by 42-inch stroke, with rotative inlet valves. They were designed for a speed of 75 r.p.m. with a rope driven fly-wheel 20 feet in diameter weighing 20 tons and carrying fourteen 2-inch ropes. Horizontal aftercoolers of 1000 square

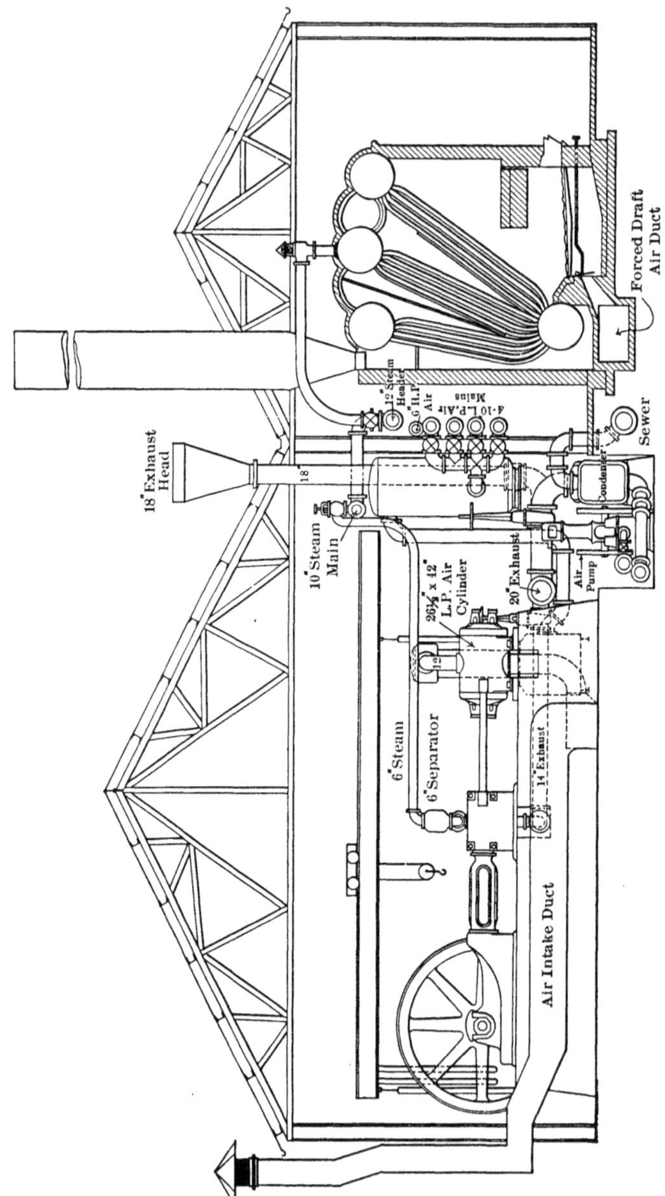

Section of Manhattan Air Compressor Plant, P. R. R. East River Tunnels.

feet of cooling surface each were attached, and the air was discharged into receivers 4½ by 12 feet. These units were driven by Westinghouse 600 h.p., 440 volt, three-phase, 25-cycle motors running at 300 r.p.m. with a rope sheave 5 feet 2 inches in diameter. The motors took their current from three transformers of 375 kw. each, oil insulated and water cooled, receiving current at 11,000 volts and transforming it down to 440 volts.

The great disadvantage of these electrically driven air compressors was that there was no way to regulate the volume of air discharged, as the speed of the motor could not be changed. The usual method of operating them was to open out on two or more tunnels requiring more than their combined capacity, and to adjust the volume of air by means of one of the steam driven units.

As stand-by high pressure machines for the Manhattan side when the combination machines were on low pressure duty, two Ingersoll-Rand duplex, simple steam, 2-stage air compressors were installed with steam cylinders 16 inches in diameter and air cylinders 25¼ and 16¼ inches in diameter. The stroke of these units was 16 inches and each had a capacity of 1205 cubic feet of free air per minute.

On the Long Island City side where little rock was encountered an Ingersoll-Rand "Imperial" compressor was installed as a stand-by while the combination machine was used on low pressure duty. This was a duplex, simple steam, 2-stage air compressor, with 16-inch steam cylinders, 15- and 25-inch air cylinders and 20-inch stroke. Its capacity was 1070 cubic feet of free air per minute at 100 pounds pressure.

For starting up the headings at the East Avenue side at Long Island City, two Ingersoll-Rand straight line compressors were used, with steam cylinder 18 inches in diameter, air cylinder 18¼ inches and a 24-inch stroke. At 90 r.p.m. each had a capacity of 656 cubic feet of free air per minute compressed to 90 pounds.

As there were ultimately two electrically driven air compressors on the Long Island side, and six low pressure units and one combination unit on each side of the river; and as these machines were guaranteed to run at 125 r.p.m. continuously for twenty-four hours, the maximum free air capacity of all the compressors, including the high pressure units, amounted to 102,922 cubic feet per minute.

Steam at 150 pounds pressure was generated in twelve Stirling water tube boilers (six on each side of the river), each having a capacity of 500 h.p. with 10 square feet of heating surface per h.p. and 0.25 square foot of grate surface per h.p. The grates were 8 feet deep, and were of the McClave shaking type. Each boiler occupied a space 19 feet 9½ inches by 18 feet 3 inches, and was about 21 feet high. Each had an independent steel stack 54 inches in diameter and 100 feet above grate level. The boilers were guaranteed to evaporate 8.7 pounds of water per pound of dry coal having a heat value of not less than 12,000 B.t.u. and not more than 15 per cent of ash, from and at 212 degrees Fahrenheit with a pressure in the ash pit of not less than 2 inches and a draft at the damper box of 0.75 inch. This result was to be obtained with either No. 2 or 1 buckwheat anthracite; and in testing it was found that the boilers exceeded this efficiency.

In computing the boiler capacity necessary, it was originally estimated, before finally deciding on the whole plant, that the i.h.p. requirements on each side of the river would be as follows: Electrical plant, 580; air compressors, 3325; hydraulic plant, 202; total, 4107 i.h.p. using 68,300 pounds of steam per hour. On the basis of eight pounds of water evaporated per pound of coal, this would represent 8500 pounds of coal per hour. Assuming four pounds of coal per boiler h.p., the capacity would be 2125 plus 531 (for the 25 per cent spare plant) or 2656 boiler h.p. This was taken to represent five boilers at 500 h.p. capacity. Ultimately it became necessary to increase the compressor plant and a sixth boiler was added on each side of the river.

The boilers were arranged for forced draft. Two 6½-foot fans driven by 7-inch by 8-inch vertical engines were provided for each plant of five boilers. At East Avenue in Long

Island City there were also four 100 h.p. locomotive boilers. These supplied steam to the two straight line compressors and also were used for driving fan engines for ventilation, the shaft pumps and steam derricks.

With five boilers in operation the highest coal consumption on the Manhattan side for any one month was at the rate of 800 tons per week. This is equivalent to 17 pounds per square

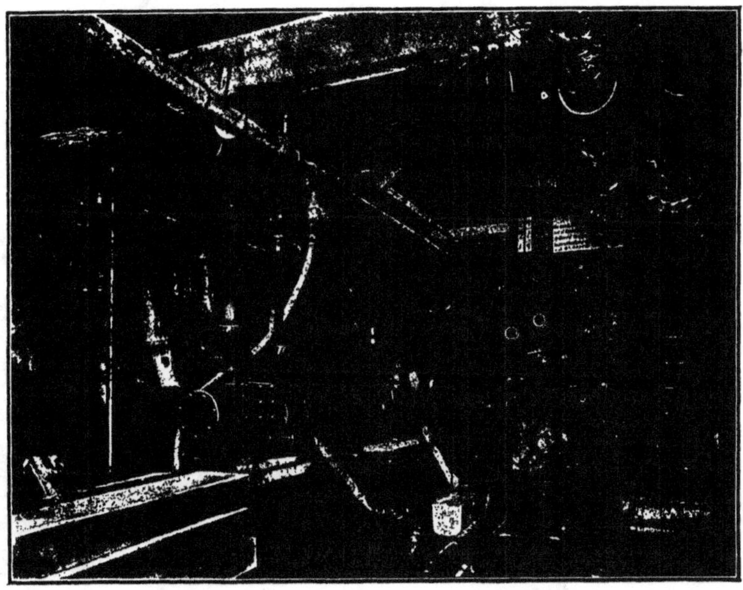

Cameron Pumping Plant in Pennsylvania and Long Island R. R. Tunnel. The pump in the rear, nearest the air lock, is equipped with motor and electrically driven, while the pump in front is operated by compressed air.

foot of grate surface per hour for five boilers. According to the records kept, the average consumption was 2.8 pounds of coal per i.h.p. per hour for all machinery.

The coal used on the Long Island City side was No. 2 buckwheat. On the Manhattan side where a greater demand was made on the plant, No. 1 buckwheat was used. The calorific value of the coal generally was from 11,500 to 12,900 B.t.u., with ash varying from 13 to 20 per cent. As a result of a combination of poor coal and inefficient firemen, the actual ash from the boiler varied from 20 to 30 per cent.*

For ordinary service work, the most suitable pump for the rough work and large volumes of water proved to be the Cameron No. 12, with 18-inch steam and 12-inch water cylinders, and 20-inch stroke. At the East Avenue site of the works, a great number of pumps were necessary in the headings and break-

Photograph taken in Pennsylvania and Long Island R. R. Tunnel. Cameron Station Pump handling the drainage water, which seeps through the rock and earth that separate the tunnel from the river bottom.

ups; and outside of the air-tight bulkheads at the lower end of this section, the No. 9 Cameron pump was generally adopted, although smaller sizes were used at various points. These pumps took up so little room that they stood at the side of the headings without interfering with the passage of cars.

* From a paper by Henry Japp, M.A.S.C.E., on the "Contractor's Plant for the East River Tunnels" in the Proceedings of the Am. Soc. C.E. for November, 1909.

Besides other qualities, the points of excellence peculiar to the Cameron design are simplicity, durability and the entire absence of outside valve gear or other moving parts. This pump has fewer working parts than any other pump; the steam mechanism consists of four stout pieces only, none of them delicate, intricate or exposed to injury. While under full pressure of steam the suction pipe may be lifted out of water and the pump allowed to run away or race as fast as steam will drive it, without danger of the piston striking the heads or any injury to the pump. Under most conditions as found on construction work, any pump is liable to have its supply of water cut off unexpectedly. With pumps of other design the sudden removal of the working load quite frequently results in the breaking of cylinder heads or other derangement that puts the machine out of service. The absence of outside gear of any kind permits the operation of this pump under adverse conditions or rough usage. Instances have occurred where this pump has started off and cleared a shaft of water when the pump itself had been buried for weeks under a mass of fallen rock and debris.

CHAPTER XV

THE EAST RIVER TUNNELS OF THE PENNSYLVANIA RAILROAD
(Continued)

THERE were two types of shields used in carrying on this section of the work: The heavy type used in the tunnels under the river, and a lighter type used in driving the land tunnels from the East Avenue shaft, Long Island City, under the Long Island Station. The type used under the river was designed by Mr. E. W. Moir, Vice President of S. Pearson & Son, and was similar to that used in the Blackwell Tunnel, England, also designed by Mr. Moir. The principal feature distinguishing these shields from those used in the land section and from others used in subaqueous work around New York was their massive construction. The cutting edges were made very heavy, yet they proved none too heavy for the work before them. The cutting edge of one of them was turned up by being pushed on an almost imperceptible incline of rock and had to be repaired under air pressure. The total weight of each of these shields, without jackets or erectors, was 185 net tons.

Eight subaqueous shields were used, 23 feet 6½ inches in outside diameter, with horizontal floors projecting 9 inches in advance of the cutting edge between the vertical diaphragms and running back to the line of the cutting edge on each side. They were divided into nine pockets by two vertical diaphragms and two horizontal floors. The latter were made up of two plates ⅝ of an inch thick, and were non-continuous for a width of 6 feet 10 inches, butting against the vertical diaphragms which were continuous for a width of 6 feet 10 inches.

The outer shield was made up of three skin plates of ¾-inch

steel, the outer and middle plates being 17 feet 6 inches long. The inner plate was 17 feet 3 inches long.

The skin plates were divided up around the circumference in such a way that the shields could be built for transportation in eight sections, including the hydraulic jack boxes. The middle and inner skin plates lapped the outer plates by 12 inches and 24 inches respectively.

In addition to the two vertical diaphragms there were two transverse bulkheads, 2 feet 6 inches apart, completely closing the shields except for openings made for doors and muck chutes. For each floor there was a pair of doors, one in each transverse bulkhead; and nine muck chutes pierced both bulkheads, with hinged doors on either end. A safety screen about 4 feet wide and 7 feet deep shrouded and surrounded the doors opening from the upper chamber. A drop safety curtain, 1 foot 6 inches deep and $\frac{3}{8}$ of an inch thick, was fixed along the roof of each chamber. The cutting edge was of cast steel, divided into segments machined on the radial joints and bolted together with turned and fitted bolts.

The benefit of having the two transverse bulkheads was to give the shield an added stiffness which it required. The smallness of the doors and the muck chutes through these bulkheads handicapped for a while the mucking-out operations, especially in rock. After it was found that there was no likelihood of this feature being required, the transverse bulkhead in all three bottom pockets was cut out and the middle bottom pocket utilized for running the tunnel cars through the shield into the heading beyond on the tunnel track.

To facilitate the passage of drill columns and timber to the upper pockets, part of the center pocket transverse bulkhead was also cut away. The 18-inch curtain suspended from the under side of each floor 18 inches in front of the bulkhead provided an air space for the men into which they could duck their heads if the shield was flooded. As the conditions obtaining under the East River had never been explored by a previous tunnel at the time this shield was started, many and varied contingencies were provided for in the accessories of the shield

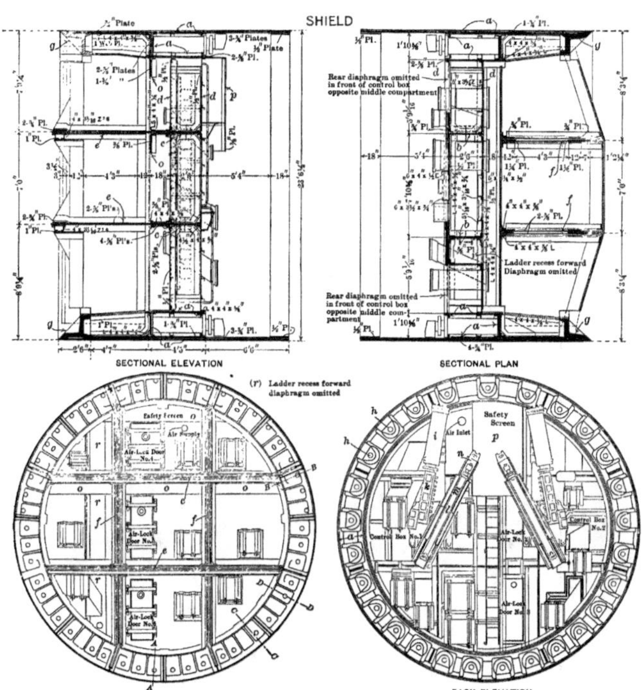

East River Tunnel Shield, Pennsylvania R.R.

which would not be necessary in future work under this river. The most satisfactory arrangement, in any type or mixture of types of materials found under the river was the bare shield, with the fixed hood projecting 3 feet in advance of the cutting edge for about two-fifths of the circumference, and no extension floors except those formed by sliding timber extensions which could readily be replaced without damage.

After extensive tests on various makes of drills the Ingersoll-Rand " E-52 " 3¼-inch rock drill was adopted for this work. It was found to use less air than any other make and to stand up to the work equally well, if not better. These machines had exceptionally hard service on account of the seamy nature of the rock. They were generally mounted on standard drill columns set up in the pockets of the shields, except where advance headings were being driven.

In addition to these standard rock drills a number of Ingersoll-Rand hand hammer or plug drills were used for trimming and breaking up lumps of rock.

In the tunnels working under compressed air, no pumps were necessary in the air chamber, as the air pressure blew the water out from the pipes to the sump. It was possible under special circumstances, by allowing air to leak into the pipe from the chamber, for the water to be delivered right up into the river without the use of pumps. But generally it was found more reliable to blow the water from the tunnel to the shafts and to pump it from there.

At the foot of each shaft, as a stand-by in the event of flooding, one special 6-inch vertical pump was installed capable of delivering 60,000 gallons per hour. Two Ajax drill sharpeners were used, one on the Manhattan side and the other at Long Island City.*

There were two permanent shafts on each side of the East River and four single-track cast-iron tube tunnels, each about 6000 feet long and consisting of about 3900 feet between shafts under the river and about 2000 feet in Long Island City, mostly

* From "Contractor's Plant for the East River Tunnels," by Henry Japp, M.A.S.C.E., in the Proceedings of the Am. Soc. C.E., November, 1909.

under the station and passenger yards of the Long Island Railroad. An average of 1760 feet of tunnel was driven from Manhattan, and 2142 feet from Long Island westward. Ground was broken on May 17, 1904. Five years later to a day, the work was finished and received final inspection for acceptance by the railroad company.

The work was carried on from three sites, as follows: From permanent shafts located near the river in Manhattan, four shields were driven eastward to about the middle of the river; from two similar shafts at the river front in Long Island City, four shields were driven westward to meet those from Manhattan; from a temporary shaft near East Avenue, Long Island City, the land section of about 2000 feet was driven westward to the river shafts.

In the description which follows the cost of work will be given under two terms. "Unit labor" will be the cost of labor directly chargeable to the operation considered. "Top charges" will include the cost of the plant and its operation, the cost of the contractor's staff and roving labor, such as electricians, pipe men, yard men and all miscellaneous labor. But it does not include materials entering into the permanent work, or contractor's profit.

Working east from the Manhattan shaft the formations were in succession as follows: 123 feet of all rock section; 87 feet of all earth and rock; 723 feet of all earth section; 515 feet of all earth and rock; 291 feet of all rock section; and 56 feet of part rock and part earth.

The rock was Hudson schist and Fordham gneiss. The latter was slightly the harder and both were badly seamed and fissured. When the rock surface was encountered it was covered with a deposit of boulders, gravel and sand varying in thickness from 4 to 10 feet. The rock near the surface on the Manhattan side was broken up and full of disintegrated seams; and it was irregular in stratification, dipping toward the west at about 60 degrees. The rock surface was very irregular and was covered with boulders and detached masses of rock bedded in coarse sand and gravel. From the latter material air escaped

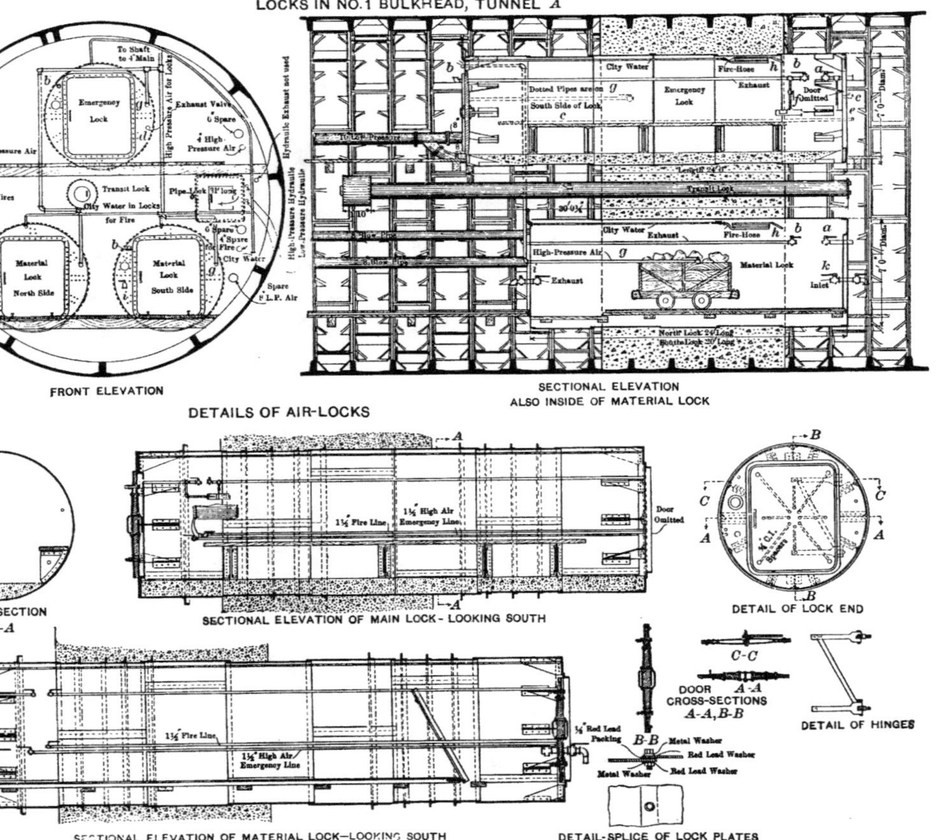

Bulkhead Construction, Pennsylvania R.R. East River Tunnels.

freely. When the shields had entirely cleared the rock the material in the face had changed to a fine sand, stratified every few inches by very thin layers of chocolate-colored clayey material. This is elsewhere referred to as quicksand. As the shield advanced eastward, the number and thickness of the layers of clay increased until the clay formed at least 20 per cent of the entire mass, and many of these layers were 2 inches in thickness. About 440 feet beyond the Manhattan ledge, the material at the bottom changed suddenly to about 98 per cent clay. The sand layers were not more than $\frac{1}{16}$ of an inch thick, averaging 2 inches apart.

The surface of the sand and gravel was irregular but rising gradually. After rock was encountered the formations of rock and clay were roughly parallel to the rock surface; as the surface of the rock rose they disappeared in order and were again encountered when the shields broke out of rock on the east side of Blackwell's Island reef. East of the reef a large quantity of coarse open sand was present in the gravel formation before the clay appeared below the top of the cutting edge. Wherever the clay extended above the top of the shield it reduced the escape of air very materially.

While sinking the lower portions of the shafts the tunnels were excavated eastward in the solid rock for a distance of about 60 feet, where the rock at the top was found to be somewhat disintegrated. This was as far as was considered prudent to go with the full-sized section without air pressure. At about the same time top headings were excavated westward from the shafts for a distance of 100 feet, and these headings enlarged to full size for a distance of about 50 feet.

The shields were erected in the shafts, and were shoved forward to the face of the excavation. Concrete bulkheads with the necessary air-locks were then built across the tunnels behind the shields. The shields were shoved eastward for about 60 feet and the permanent tunnel lining erected as the shield advanced. Before leaving the rock, air pressure was necessary in the tunnels and this necessitated the building of bulkheads with air-locks inside the cast iron linings just east of the portals. Before erecting the bulkheads it was necessary to close the annular space between the iron tunnel lining and the rock.

The space at the portal was filled with the concrete wall. After about twenty permanent rings had been erected in each tunnel, two rings were pulled apart at the tail of the shield and a second masonry wall or dam was built. The space between the two dams was then filled with grout. To avoid the possibility of pushing the iron backward, after the air pressure was put on, rings formed of segmental plates $\frac{5}{8}$ of an inch thick and $13\frac{7}{8}$ inches wide were inserted in 18 of the circumferential joints in each tunnel between the rings as they were erected. When these rings were in position they projected about 15 inches beyond the alignment and when the tunnel was grouted they were bedded in the cement. The bulkheads were completed, and the tunnels put under air pressure. In the deepest part of the river near the pier head line on the Manhattan side, there was only 8 feet of natural cover over the tops of the tunnels; and this was a fine sand which was certain to allow air to escape freely. A blanket of clay, averaging 10 or 12 feet in thickness was dumped over the line of work. It was found to be of material advantage, but its depth was insufficient to entirely stop the loss of air.

The shields in each pair of tunnels were advanced through the solid rock section about abreast with each other, until the test holes from the faces indicated soft ground within a few feet. As the distance between the sides of the tunnels was only 14 feet, the two center tunnels were given a lead of 100 feet from this point as a precaution against a blow extending from one tunnel to another.

When the shields in two of the tunnels in soft ground from Manhattan reached the bulkhead line, work was partly suspended and shutters put in place in the top and center compartments of the face of the shield. These shutters were moved in and out by screws on the ends of the shutters. Similar shutters had been used with marked success in loose open material in the Blackwell Tunnel. In operating, the shutters were forced by

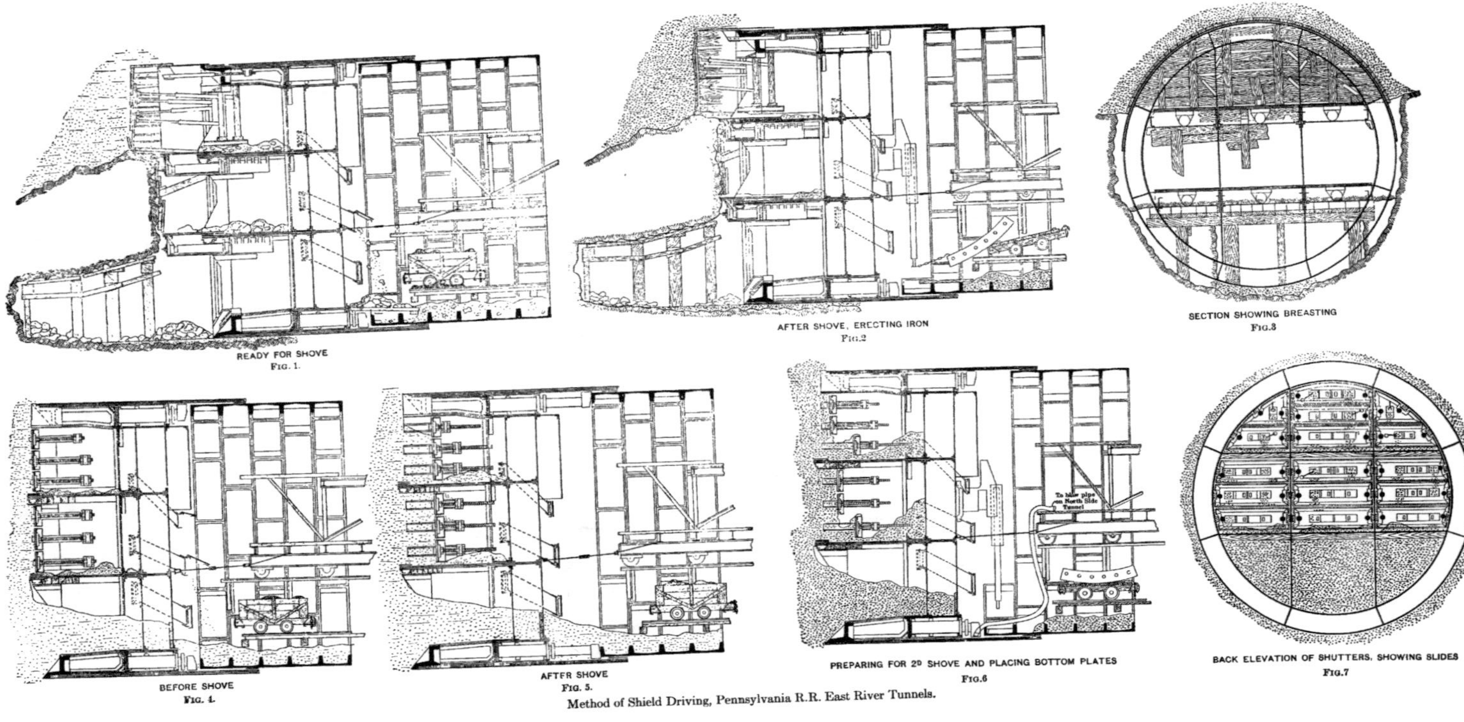

READY FOR SHOVE
FIG. 1.

AFTER SHOVE, ERECTING IRON
FIG. 2

SECTION SHOWING BREASTING
FIG. 3

BEFORE SHOVE
FIG. 4.

AFTFR SHOVE
FIG. 5.

PREPARING FOR 2D SHOVE AND PLACING BOTTOM PLATES
FIG. 6

BACK ELEVATION OF SHUTTERS, SHOWING SLIDES
FIG. 7

Method of Shield Driving, Pennsylvania R.R. East River Tunnels.

the screws against the face and material removed through the doors during the process. As pressure was applied to the shield jacks the shutters were allowed to slide back into the shield chambers, the screws being slacked back. In preparing for a new shove the slides in the shutters were opened and the material in front raked into the shield.

No shutters were placed in the bottom compartments and as the air pressure was not generally high enough to keep the

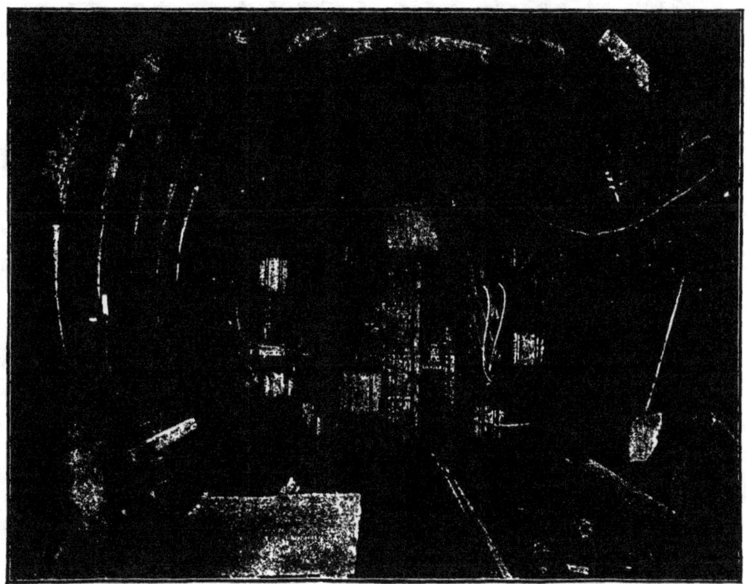

Rear of Shield showing Complete Fittings.

face dry at the bottom, these lower compartments were pretty well filled with a soft, wet quicksand. Much of the excavation in the bottom compartment was done by a blow-pipe. During the shove the material from the bottom compartment often ran back through the open door in the transverse bulkhead.

In the Blackwell Tunnel, the material was loose enough to keep in contact with the shutters at all times. This was not the condition in the East River tunnels; the sand at the top was dry and would often stand with a vertical face for some hours.

In advancing the shutters it was difficult to bring them in close contact with the face at the end of the operation. The soft material at the bottom was constantly running into the lower compartment and undermining the stiff material at the top. Under these circumstances, the air escaped freely through the unprotected sand face. The points of the shutters were plastered with clay, but this did not keep the air from passing out through the lower compartments. This condition facilitated the for-

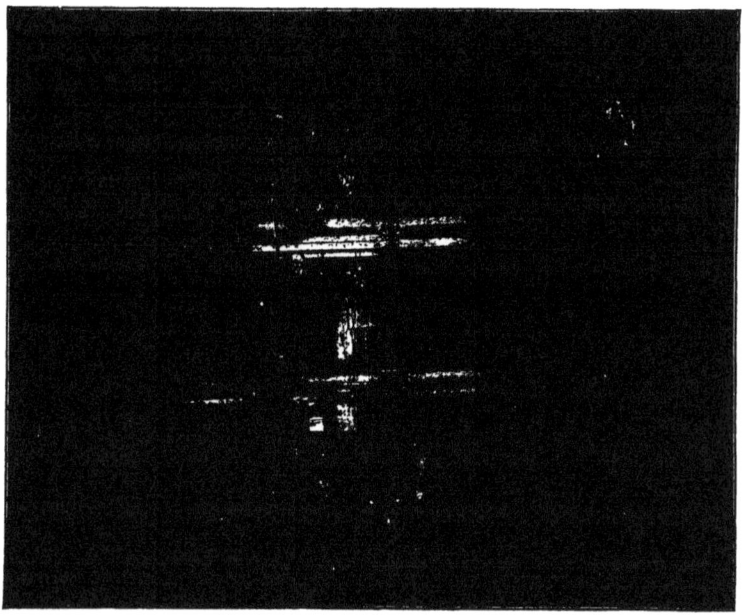

Shield Fitted with Fixed Hoods and Fixed Extensions to the Floors.

mation of blowouts which were of constant occurrence where the shutters were used in sand. In one of the tunnels, the shutters were placed in the shield but never used against the face. Excavation was carried on by poling the top and breasting the face; and this change resulted in much better progress and fewer blowouts.

Shutters were not placed on the Long Island shields. Before the shield entered soft ground a fixed hood was attached to

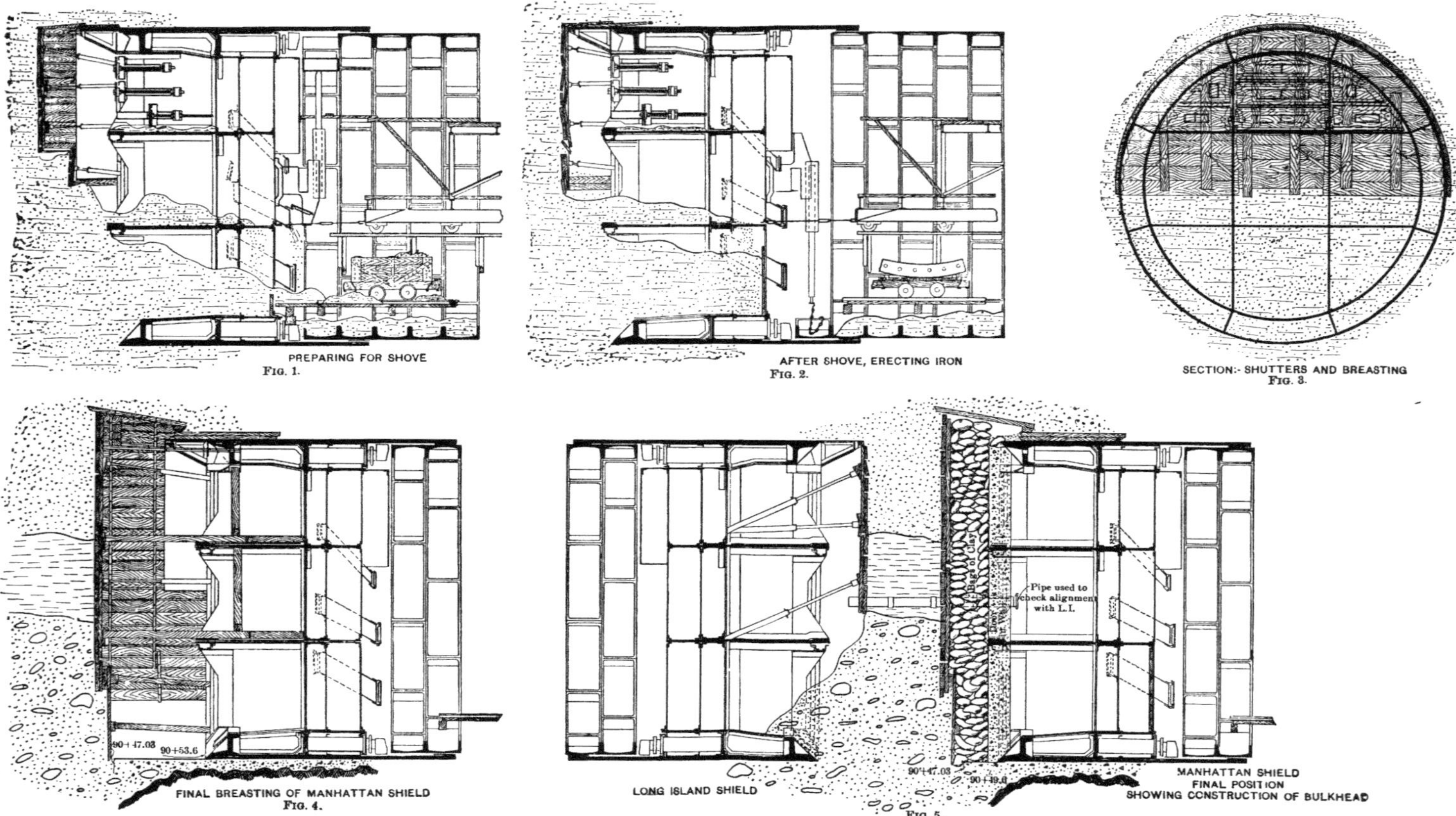

Fig. 1. Fig. 2. Fig. 3. Fig. 4. Fig. 5.

Method of Shield Driving, Pennsylvania R.R. East River Tunnels.

each. The face was mined out to the front of the hood and breasted down to a little below the floor of the top pockets of the shield. In the middle pockets the earth took a natural slope backward to the floor. In the bottom pockets it was held, at the back, by stop logs. The air pressure was always about equal to the hydrostatic head at the middle of the shield. In consequence, the face in the upper and middle pockets was dry, but in the lower pocket it was wet and flowed under the

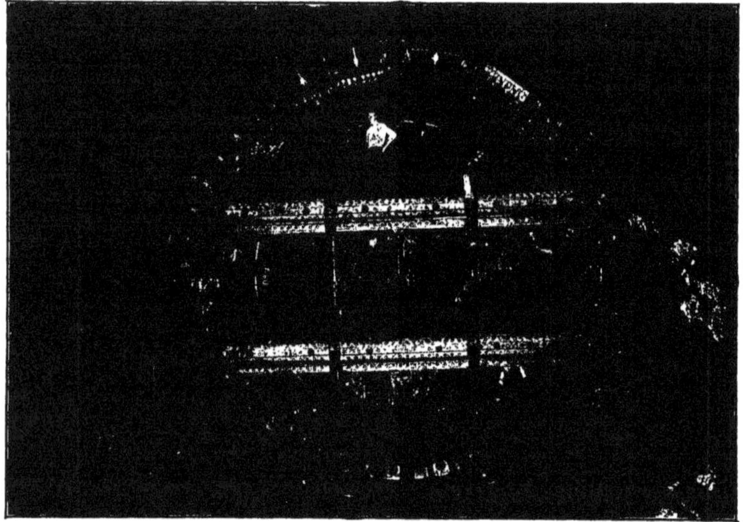

Shield Fitted with Sectional Sliding Hoods and Sliding Extensions to the Floors.

pressure of shoving the shield. By this method, 4195 lineal feet of tunnel were excavated by the four Long Island shields in 120 days between November 1, 1907 and March 7, 1908. This was an average of 8.74 feet per day per shield.

Preparatory to making the final shove with the shields, special polings were placed with unusual care. The Manhattan shields were stopped and the excavation ahead made bell shape to receive the Long Island shields. The shields being shoved into final position, the rear end of the polings rested above the hood. When this was done, bulkheads of concrete and clay bags were built to avoid blows when the shields came near each other. An 8-inch pipe was then driven forward to the bulkhead for from 30 to 100 feet, in order to check the alignment and grade between the two workings before the shields were actually shoved together. To bring the cutting edges together, it was necessary to cut away the projecting floors of the working compartments.

Operations were carried on continuously for thirteen days out of fourteen, repairs being done on alternate Sundays when the work was closed down. When it was required to have an air pressure greater than 32 pounds, four gangs were worked, each gang working two 3-hour shifts with 3-hour intermission between shifts. When the air pressure was less than 32 pounds three gangs were employed in three 8-hour shifts; ½ hour in low pressure was allowed for lunch. In soft ground during the greater portion of the work, the pressure maintained was about equal to the hydrostatic head at the axis of the tunnel. This was from 30 to 34 pounds per square inch above atmosphere. Pressures as high as 37 pounds were maintained for extended periods. In firm material 28 pounds was sufficient. While removing broken tunnel plates 42 pounds was carried for a short time; but pressures of from 37½ to 40 pounds were maintained for more than a month.

CHAPTER XVI

THE EAST RIVER TUNNELS OF THE PENNSYLVANIA RAILROAD

(*Continued.*)

THE river shafts on the Manhattan and Long Island sides were designed to serve as working shafts and permanent openings to the tunnels. As they were practically identical on both sides of the river, a description of the construction used in Long Island City will serve for both. There were two shafts on each side of the river, each shaft serving two tunnels. Each consisted of a steel caisson, 40 by 74 feet in dimensions with walls 5 feet in thickness, filled with concrete. Each shaft was divided into two compartments, 29 by 30 feet, separated by a wall 6 feet thick. Openings for the tunnels 25 feet in diameter were provided in the sides of the caisson, and these openings were closed during sinking by steel bulkheads.

The shafts were sunk as pneumatic caissons to a depth of 78 feet below mean high water mark. Most large caissons go to rock or a little below. The unusual feature of these caissons was that they were sunk 54 feet through rock. The roof of the working chamber was 7 feet above the cutting edge. Each chamber had two shafts, 3 by 5 feet in cross-section, with a diaphragm dividing it into two passages, one for men and one for the muck buckets. On top of these shafts were Moran locks. A 5-ton crane mounted on top of the caisson served both shafts and the muck cars on the ground level beside the caisson. Circular steel muck buckets 2½ feet in diameter and 3 feet high dumped the muck into the cars and returned to the bottom of the working chamber without unhooking. Work was carried on in three 8-hour shifts.

On the Long Island side earth was excavated at the rate of 67 cubic yards per caisson per day. Rock excavation amounting to about 6200 cubic yards in each caisson was done at the rate of 44.5 cubic yards per day. The average rate of sinking through earth was 0.7 foot per day; through rock, 0.48 per day in the south caisson and 0.39 in the north caisson. In sinking the caissons 100-ton hydraulic jacks and wood blocking were used. When lowering, the air pressure was reduced by about 10 pounds, which increased the net weight to more than 4,000,000 pounds. The caissons usually carried a net weight of about 870 tons. The concrete in them was generally kept about at the ground level. Water ballast 5 to 20 feet in depth was kept near the roof of the working chamber. The air pressure in the chamber was generally less than the hydrostatic head. For example, the average pressure in the caissons was 16½ pounds of air, while the average head was 62½ feet or 27 pounds per square inch. The bottom of the shaft was an inverted concrete arch 4 feet thick, waterproofed with six-ply felt and pitch.

The cost of excavation in the caisson was $15.02 per cubic yard, of which $4.48 was labor and $10.54 top charges. The cost of labor in compressed air chargeable to concreting was $3.40 per cubic yard. When the roof of each working chamber had been removed the shield was erected in a timber cradle in the bottom of the shaft, in a position to be shoved out of the opening in the side of the caisson. Temporary stays of iron lining were erected across the shaft to furnish an abutment for the jacks.

The roof of the working chamber was re-erected about 35 feet above its original position, bringing it about 8 feet above the tunnel openings. Instead of the two small shafts in use during the sinking of the caisson, a large steel T-shaped head-lock was built. This was 8 feet in diameter and contained a ladder and elevator-cage for men and for standard 1-yard tunnel cars. In the tee forming the top were two standard tunnel locks.

On the Manhattan side the south shaft was sunk in earth at the rate of about 0.5 foot per day and the north shaft at about 0.53 foot per day. Two 10-hour shifts were used. The average rate of excavation in soft material was 84 cubic yards per day;

in rock below the caisson, 125 cubic yards per day. Earth excavation cost $3.96 per cubic yard, of which $1.45 was for labor and $2.51 top charges. Rock excavation cost $8.93 per cubic yard, of which $2.83 was for labor and $6.10 for top charges.

In driving tunnels westward from the Long Island shaft, the materials were encountered in the following order: 124 feet of all rock section; 125 feet of earth and rock; 22 feet of all rock; 56 feet of earth and rock; 387 feet of all rock section; 70 feet of earth and rock; and 1333 feet of all earth section. The rock was similar to that in the Blackwell's Island reef and was covered with sand and boulders. The soft ground was of three classes. The first was of fine red sand, occurring in layers from 6 to 15 feet thick. This is the quicksand usually found in deep foundations in New York City. With surplus water this sand is a true quicksand. When the water is blown out by air pressure it is stable, stands up well and is easy to work. The second material was known as "bull's liver," consisting of thin layers of blue clay and of a very fine red sand. The clay was entirely free from sand. This was an ideal material in which to work a shield, as it stood up well, held the air about as well as clay and was much easier to work. The third material was a layer of very fine open gray sand which was encountered in the top of all the tunnels for about four hundred feet just east of Blackwell's Island reef.

The first work in air pressure was to remove the shield plug closing the opening in the side of the shaft. This being done, the shield was shoved through the opening and excavation begun. The shields were fitted with movable platforms and the hoods were not placed until the rock excavation had been completed. Shields had not been extensively used in rock up to this time and it was therefore necessary to develop methods of operation by experience. When rock was present under the shields it was required that a bed of concrete be laid in the form of a cradle, upon which the shield was moved. Three general methods were used for excavating in the all rock sections—the bottom heading method, the full face method and the center heading method.

The bottom heading method was the first one tried. A heading 8 by 12 feet wide was driven on the center line, the bottom being at the grade line of the tunnel floor. Four drills were used, mounted on a column. The face of the heading was kept from 10 to 30 feet in advance of the shield. A concrete cradle, 8 to 10 feet wide, was laid when the heading had been driven 10 feet. The excavation was enlarged to full size as the shield advanced. The drills were mounted in the forward compartments of the shields, and the sides and top of the excavation were shot downward into the heading. As the heading was completely blocked by the material blasted from the face, work had to be suspended until the face had been mucked.

The bottom heading method was as good as could be devised, with the shields equipped with two transverse bulkheads, as originally installed. All the muck had to be taken from the face by hand and passed through the chutes and doors. The closed transverse bulkheads were an obstacle to rapid progress in rock sections. These bulkheads with air locks were designed in the belief that it would be necessary to maintain the full air pressure in the working compartment only. In the case of blowouts it was thought that some form of bulkhead that could be quickly closed tight would be required to avoid flooding the tunnel. From experience gained while working in the sand from Manhattan to the Blackwell's Island reef, it was demonstrated that this design was not practicable, and that a bulkhead closed in the bottom was a hindrance. The bulkheads were cut through and altered to permit of the passage of cars through the shield.

To avoid blocking the tracks when blasting and to permit working a larger force of men at the face, the level of the heading was raised. This reduced the quantity of rock to be taken from the top and the bottom was taken out as a bench. To keep the tracks clear while blasting, a timber platform was built from the center floor of the shield. The platforms were not entirely satisfactory and later the drills in the heading were turned upward and a top bench also worked. So little excavation was left in the top that the muck was allowed to fall in the tracks, from which it was quickly cleared. This method as

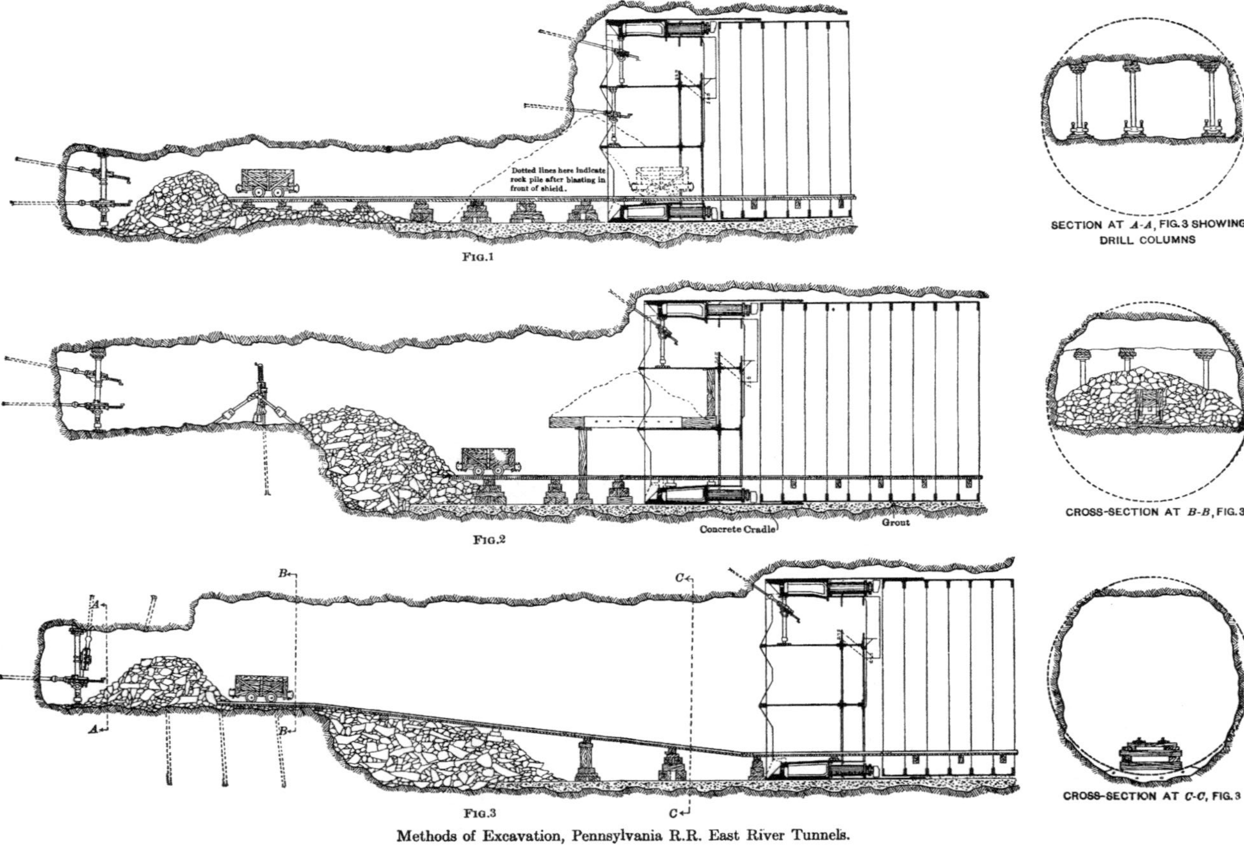

Methods of Excavation, Pennsylvania R.R. East River Tunnels.

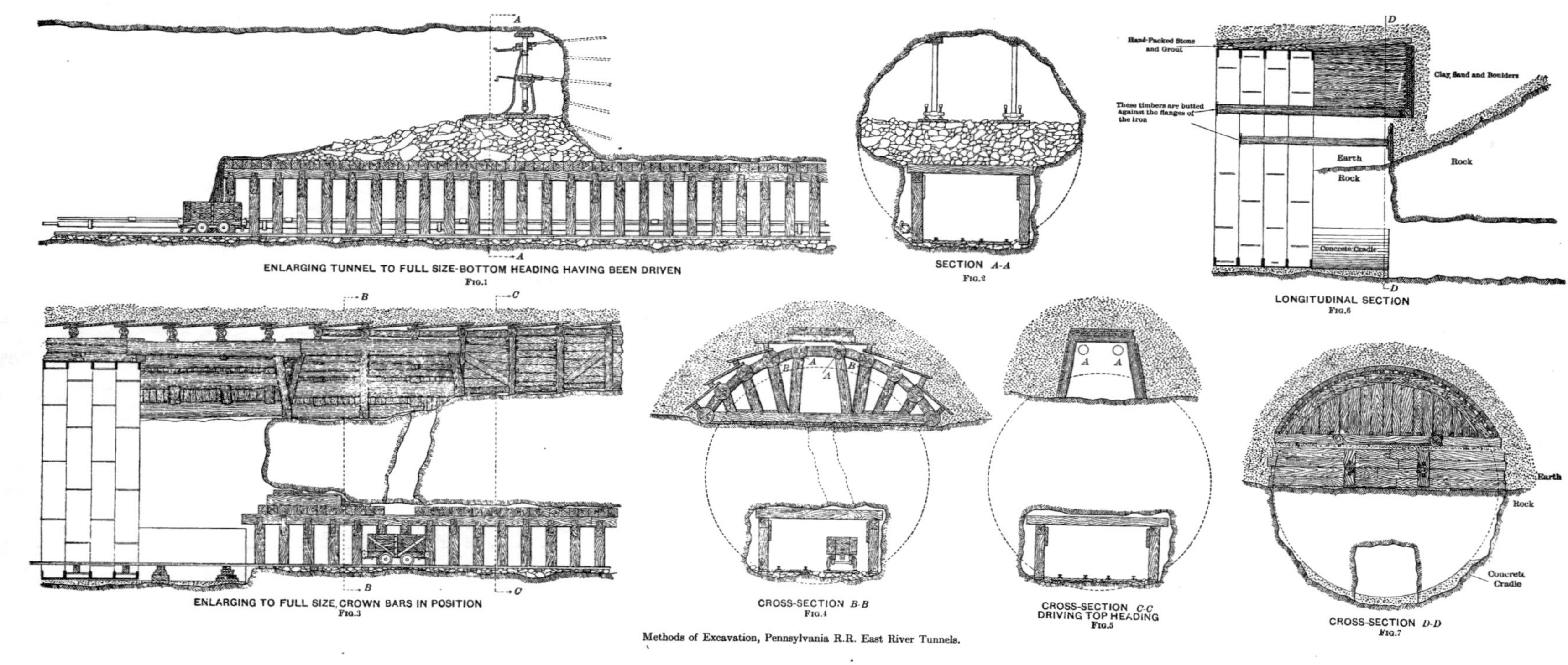

Methods of Excavation, Pennsylvania R.R. East River Tunnels.

outlined, called the center heading method, proved the most satisfactory for full rock sections.

Excavation in earth and rock was the most difficult class of work encountered, particularly when the rock was covered with boulders and coarse, sharp sand which permitted a free escape of air. Before removing the rock under soft ground it was necessary to excavate the latter in advance of the shield to a point beyond where the rock was to be disturbed, and to support the top, sides and face of the opening thus made. A fixed hood attached to and in advance of the shield was designed to support the top and sides of the excavation. With this fixed hood it was necessary either to force the hood into the undisturbed material, the distance required, or to excavate an opening. To avoid this difficulty sliding hoods were tried as an experiment, made in segments, which were forced forward by screw rods one at a time into the material as far as possible. Enough material was then removed from beneath and in front of the segment to free it when it was forced farther forward. These operations were repeated until the section had been extended far enough for a shove. When the shield was advanced the nuts on the screw rods were loosened and the hood telescoped on the shield. Owing to the transverse strains on the hood section, caused by the unequal relative movements of the top and bottom of the shield in shoving forward, this plan proved impracticable.

Fixed hoods were substituted for the sliding type and poling boards used to support the roof and sides, with breast boards for the face. In placing the poling and breasting, all voids behind them were filled with marsh hay or bags of sawdust or clay. To prevent loss of air in open material the joints between the boards were plastered with clay especially prepared in a pug mill for this purpose.

When the rock face became sufficiently high and sound, a bottom heading was driven some 20 or 30 feet in advance of the shield, and the cradle placed. The remainder of the rock face was removed by firing top and side rounds into the bottom heading after the soft ground had been excavated. To avoid a run of material great care was taken in firing not to disturb the timbering on the rock under the breast boards. In the early part of the work when a bottom heading was impracticable, the soft ground was first excavated as described above, and the rock was drilled by machines mounted on tripods and fired as a bench. By this plan no drilling could be done until the soft ground was removed. This was called the rock bench method. Later the rock cut method was devised. Drills were set up on columns in the bottom compartments of the shields and the face drilled while work was in progress in the soft ground above. This drilling was done either for horizontal or vertical cut, and side and top rounds. The drill runners were protected while at work by timber platforms built out from the floors of the compartments above. This plan, while not as economical of explosive, saved the delay due to drilling the bench.

In driving the tunnels which connected the river shafts in Long Island City with East Avenue, a temporary shaft was sunk at East Avenue. This was rectangular in shape, built of rough 6 by 12 sheet piling, 127 by 34 feet. It was braced across by heavy timber and was driven about 28 feet to rock as the excavation progressed. Below this the shaft was sunk in rock about 27 feet without timbering. When the shaft was down, bottom headings were started westward in the tunnels. When these had been driven about half way to the river shafts, soft ground was encountered; and as the latter carried considerable water it was decided to use compressed air. Bulkheads were built in the headings and with an air pressure of about 15 pounds the heading was driven through the soft ground and into rock by ordinary mining methods. The use of compressed air was then discontinued.

West of this soft ground the top heading followed by a bench was driven until soft ground was again encountered. One of the four tunnels, being higher, was more in soft ground. At first it was the intention to delay this excavation until it had been well drained by the bottom headings of the tunnels on either side; later it was decided to use a shield without compressed air. This shield had been used in excavating the stations of the Great Northern and City tunnel in London.

It was rebuilt, its diameter being changed from 24 feet 8½ inches to 23 feet 5¼ inches. But it proved too weak and after it had been flattened about 4 inches and jacked up three times, the scheme was abandoned, the shield removed and the work continued by the methods employed in the other tunnels. The description of operations in one tunnel, therefore, will serve for all.

From the bottom headings break-ups were started at several places in each tunnel where there was ample cover of rock. Where the roof was in soft ground top headings were driven from the point of break-up and timbered. As soon as the full-sized excavation was completed, the iron lining was built, usually in short lengths. At a point under the Long Island Railroad station the tunnels were in soft ground and to avoid disturbance of the surface a shield and compressed air were used. The shield was used to drive three of the tunnels, but during the driving it was found that the ground passed through was better than had been anticipated. There was considerable clay in the sand and after the water had been blown out by compressed air it was found to be very stable. The fourth tunnel was timbered and driven under air pressure without a shield.

When the tunnel was all in good rock two distinct methods were used. The first was the bottom heading and break-up, and the second the top heading and bench method. The bottom heading, 13 feet by 9 feet high, having first been driven, a break-up was started by blasting down the rock to form a chamber of the full height of the tunnel. A timber platform was then erected in the bottom heading and extended through the break-up chamber. The plan was then to drill the entire face above the top heading and blast it down upon the timber staging. In this way the passage in the bottom heading was not interfered with. The spoil was loaded into cars in the bottom heading through holes in the staging. This method had the advantage that the bottom heading could be pushed through rapidly, and from it the tunnel could be attacked at a number of points at one time. It was found to be more expensive than the top heading and bench method; and as soon as the depression of the rock was passed, a top heading about 7 feet high and roughly the segment of a 23-foot circle, was driven to the next soft ground in each of the tunnels. The remainder of the section was taken out in two benches; the first, about 4 feet high, was kept about 15 feet ahead of the lower bench, which was about 11 feet high.

For a length of about 2500 feet of tunnel the roof was in soft ground and it was excavated in normal air pressure by the usual methods of mining and timbering. In the greater part of this, rock surface was well above the middle of the tunnel. Starting from the break-up in the all-rock section, when soft ground was approached the top heading was driven from the rock into and through the earth. This was done by the usual post, cap and poling board method, giving a heading about 7 feet high by 6 feet wide. The ground was a running sand with little or no clay and with considerable water in places. All the headings required side polings. The roof poling boards were about 2½ or 3 feet above the outside limit of the tunnel lining.

The next step was placing two crown bars, usually about 20 feet long, under the caps. Posts were then placed under the bars, and poling boards at right angles to the axis of the tunnel were driven out over the bars. As these polings were being driven the side polings of the original headings were removed, and the earth mined out to the end of these new transverse polings. Breast boards were set on end under the ends of the transverse polings when they had been driven out to their limit. Side bars were then placed as far out as possible and supported on raking posts. These posts were carried down to rock, if it were near, otherwise a sill was placed beneath them.

A new set of transverse polings was driven over these side bars and the process was repeated until the sides had been carried down to rock, or to the elevation of the sills supporting the posts, which were usually about 4 feet above the axis of the tunnel. The plan then was to excavate the remainder of the section and build the iron lining in short lengths, gradually

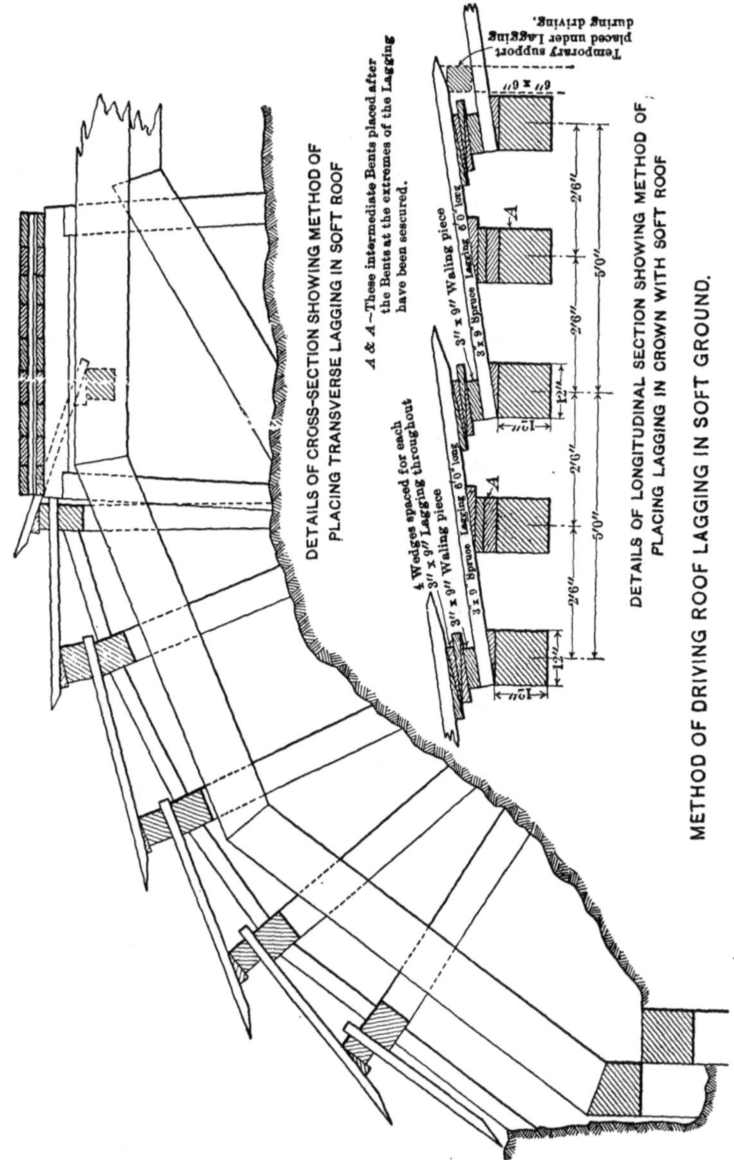

METHOD OF DRIVING ROOF LAGGING IN SOFT GROUND.

transferring the weight of the roof bars to the iron lining as the posts were taken out. Such workings were in progress at as many as eight places in one tunnel at one time.

The plan adopted in one tunnel for driving in compressed air without a shield through soft ground, while not as rapid, proved to be as cheap as the work done by the shields. The operation of this scheme was as follows: Having the iron built up to the face of the full-sized excavation, a hole or top heading about 3 feet wide and 4 or 5 feet high was excavated about 10 feet in advance. This was done in a few hours without timbering of any kind. As soon as this heading was ten feet out, 6 by-12-inch polings were put up in the roof with the rear ends resting on the iron lining and the front ends on the vertical breast boards. The heading was then widened out rapidly and the lagging was placed down to about 45 degrees from the crown. The forward ends of the lagging were then supported by a timber rib and sill. Protected by this roof, the full section was excavated and three rings of iron lining were built and grouted; and then the whole process was repeated.

CHAPTER XVII

THE EAST RIVER TUNNELS OF THE PENNSYLVANIA RAILROAD
(*Continued.*)

As already stated, the specifications of the railroad company required an air compressor plant capable of supplying not less than 300,000 cubic feet of free air per hour at 50 pounds pressure above normal atmosphere to each heading, and a reserve plant of 25 per cent of this capacity. The air compressor plants on each side of the river, installed by the Ingersoll-Rand Company of New York, met these requirements, having a rated capacity of 25,000 cubic feet of free air per minute or an average of 5260 cubic feet per minute per heading.

In tunnels B, C and D the shields broke through rock surface in November and December, 1905. The air consumption in the four tunnels exceeded 15,000 cubic feet, and in tunnel D alone on several occasions it exceeded 7000 cubic feet per minute for twenty-four hours. Blows had been frequent and it was evident that a greater volume of air would be required than was anticipated in order to drive the four tunnels simultaneously in the open material east of the Manhattan rock. Work was accordingly suspended on two of the tunnels while the rated capacity of the compressing plant was being increased from 25,000 to 35,000 cubic feet of free air per minute.

During one period of the work one, and sometimes two, tunnels were shut down. The consumption of air in the tunnels from Manhattan averaged more than 20,000 cubic feet per minute for periods of from 30 to 60 days. It was often more than 25,000 cubic feet per minute for twenty-four hours, with a maximum of nearly 29,000 cubic feet. On several occasions the quantity supplied to a single tunnel averaged more than 15,000 cubic feet throughout a 24-hour period. The greatest average for twenty-four hours was in excess of 19,000 cubic feet per minute; but conditions were so favorable in the other headings at this time that work could be carried on continuously in all of them.

The need of driving all headings simultaneously from the Long Island side was so evident that it was decided to increase the rated capacity of the Long Island City plant to 45,400 cubic feet of free air per minute, which was 10,400 cubic feet in excess of the augmented Manhattan plant.

The earth encountered on emerging from the rock when driving westward from Long Island was far more compact and less permeable to air than on the Manhattan side. But for a distance of from 400 to 600 feet immediately east of the reef a clean, open sand was met, and while the shields were passing through this the quantity of air supplied to the four headings was seldom less than 20,000 cubic feet per minute; it was usually more than 25,000 cubic feet, with a recorded maximum of 33,400 cubic feet. This was a greater volume than was ever used on the Manhattan side and it was more uniformly distributed among the several headings. In no case, however, did the air consumption per heading equal the maximum observed on the Manhattan side, the largest on the Long Island side being 12,700 cubic feet per minute for twenty-four hours. It is to be remembered that at one time only two tunnels were in progress in the bad material, working eastward from Manhattan.

It would seem that a reasonable compliance with the actual needs on the Manhattan side would have been an air compressing plant of a rated capacity of 45,400 cubic feet per minute, and on the Long Island side one of a capacity of 35,000 cubic feet per minute.

The total quantity of free air compressed for the supply of the working chambers of the tunnels and the Long Island caissons was 34,109,000,000 cubic feet. In addition 10,615,000,000 cubic feet were compressed to between 80 and 125 pounds for power purposes, of which at least 80 per cent was exhausted in the compressed air working chambers. The total supply of free air to each heading while under pressure, therefore, averaged about 3550 cubic feet per minute.

Investigation of the number of blowouts showing large

losses of pressure and with the relatively large reservoir capacity provided by the long stretch of tunnels, a maximum loss of 220,000 cubic feet of free air was known to occur in ten minutes. Of this quantity, however, probably 30 or 40 per cent escaped in the first forty-five seconds, while the remainder was a more or less steady loss up to the time when the supply could be increased sufficiently to maintain the lower pressure. Very few blows showed losses approaching this in quantity, and in this particular case the inherent inaccuracies of the observations make the figures only a rough approximation.

A clay blanket covering the open materials penetrated by the tunnels was essential throughout the work. The material used in this blanket amounted to 283,412 cubic yards, of which 117,846 cubic yards were removed from over the completed tunnels and re-deposited in advance of the shields. A total of 88,059 cubic yards of clay was dumped over blowouts. The total cost of placing and removing the clay blanket was $304,056.

The standard cast-iron tunnel lining was of the usual tube type 23 feet in outside diameter. The rings were 30 inches wide and were composed of eleven segments and a key. The webs of the segments were 1½ inches thick in the central portions and increased to 2⅜ inches at the flanges which were 11 inches deep and machined on all contact faces. Bolt holes were cored in the flanges. The segments weighed about 2020 pounds each and the key 520 pounds. The weight of the iron per foot of tunnel was 9102 pounds.

The tube of iron rings was adapted to be built in the tail of the shield. Where no shield was used, after the excavation was completed and all loose rock removed, timbers were fixed across the tunnels from which semicircular ribs were hung, below which lagging was placed. The space between this and the rough rock surface was filled with concrete forming a cradle in which the iron tube could be erected. At the same time it occupied a space that would have had to be filled with grout at a greater cost had the shield been used. These concrete cradles averaged 1.05 cubic yards per foot of tunnel and cost,

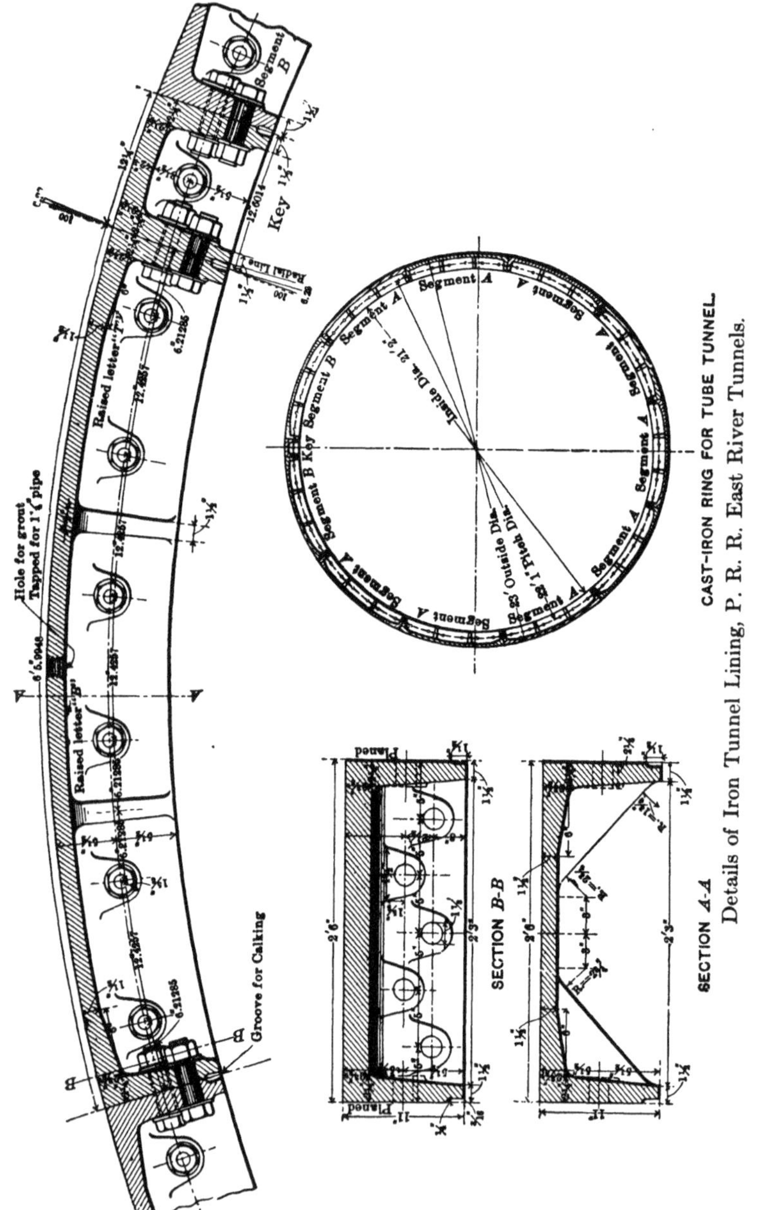

CAST-IRON RING FOR TUBE TUNNEL.

Details of Iron Tunnel Lining, P. R. R. East River Tunnels.

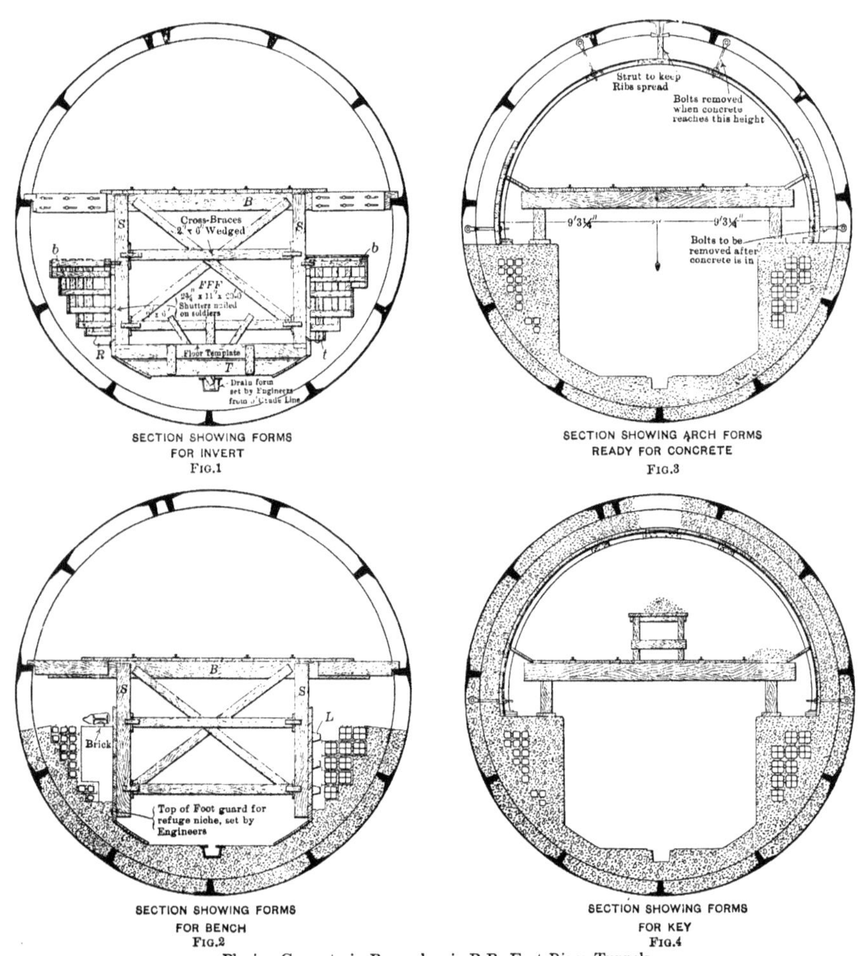

SECTION SHOWING FORMS FOR INVERT
FIG.1

SECTION SHOWING ARCH FORMS READY FOR CONCRETE
FIG.3

SECTION SHOWING FORMS FOR BENCH
FIG.2

SECTION SHOWING FORMS FOR KEY
FIG.4

Placing Concrete in Pennsylvania R.R. East River Tunnels.

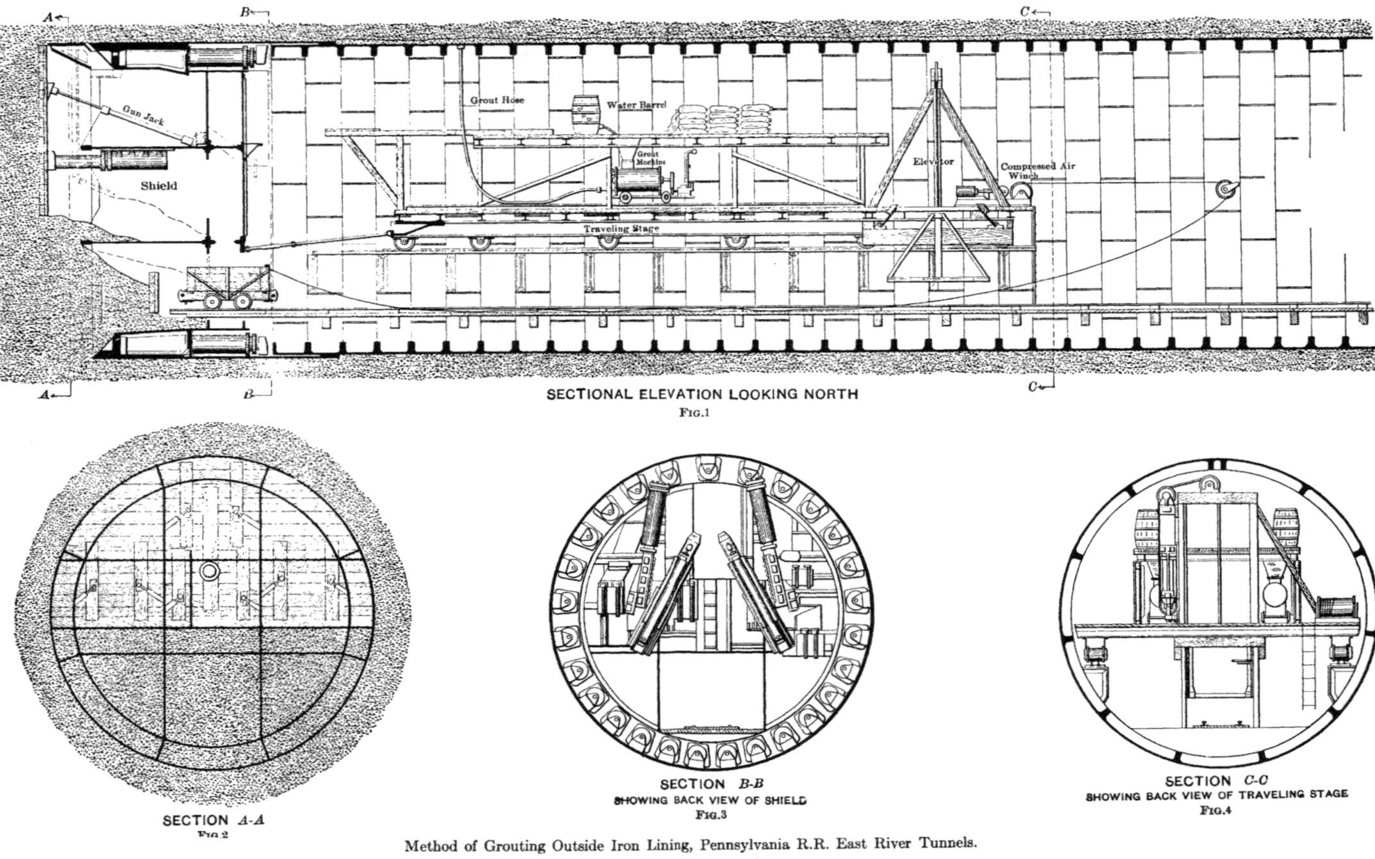

Method of Grouting Outside Iron Lining, Pennsylvania R.R. East River Tunnels.

exclusive of material, $6.70 per cubic yard, of which $2.25 was for labor and $4.45 top charges.

As soon as each ring was erected, the space between it and the roof of the excavation was filled with hand-packed stone. The interstices between the hand-packed stones were then filled with 1-to-1 grout of cement and sand injected through the iron lining. The hand-packed stone averaged 1½ cubic yards per foot of tunnel and cost $2.42 per cubic yard, of which $.98 was for labor and $1.44 for top charges.

It was planned to erect the iron lining with erectors of the same type as those used in the iron shields, but mounted on a traveling stage. There were two erectors, but as the tunnel was being worked at so many points this number was inadequate to meet the requirements. As a result about 58 per cent of the lining was done by hand. A portable hand winch was used for handling and placing the segments. The cost of erecting by hand was no greater than by the erectors. This was due to the greater power and plant charges against the erectors and to the fact that they were not in constant use.

The total amount of grout used on the work was, in set volume, equivalent to 249,647 barrels of 1-to-1 Portland cement grout, of which 233,647 barrels were injected through the iron lining. The average was 19.93 barrels per lineal foot of tunnel. The cost of the grout injected outside of the iron tunnel was $.93 per barrel for labor and $2.77 for top charges. East of the Long Island shaft the corresponding costs were $.68 and $1.63, the difference being partly due to the large percentage of work done in normal air.

Joints were at first caulked with a mixture of iron filings and sal ammoniac in the proportions by weight of 400 to 1, caulked by hand. Later, lead wire caulked cold by pneumatic hammers was substituted. The average cost of labor was $.12 per lineal foot and top charges $.218. All concrete was placed under normal air. The cost of labor chargeable to concrete was $1.80 per cubic yard and top charges were $3.92 exclusive of the cost of materials.

From Proceedings of the American Society of C. E., October, 1909.

CHAPTER XVIII

THE BELMONT TUNNELS

THE various tunnel and subway undertakings which are to vastly increase the transit facilities of Greater New York, are quite different from each other in the conditions and means of construction, and each has imposed special engineering problems to be solved. Not the least interesting was the work on the Belmont tunnels under the East River which are now completed, but at the time of writing are not yet in actual operation.

The Belmont system includes a tunnel and subway over three miles in length, extending from Park Avenue and Forty-second Street, Manhattan Island, to Jackson Avenue and Fourth Street, Long Island City. It will afford easy and quick transit between the Borough of Queens and Manhattan and will probably connect with some of the transit systems in New York City near the Grand Central Station. The first shift was started in July, 1905 and work was rushed continuously and with great vigor night and day until completion. The system consists of two single-track parallel tunnels. Part of the tubes are horseshoe shaped, while under the river they are of circular section and built of sectional cast iron rings. The contractors were the Degnon Engineering and Construction Company. The builders had an advantage as to time of construction, in that the tunnels could be driven from four headings instead of two, or, as in the case of the Cortlandt Street tunnel, from a single heading.

For driving the subaqueous tunnel from its western end and for the construction of the subway westward from Forty-second Street there were two separate compressed air installations, resulting from certain business arrangements. The plant of the O'Rourke Engineering Company which was sold to the Degnon Company included the following equipment: One Ingersoll-Rand cross-compound Corliss steam, 2-stage air compressor with steam cylinders, 24 and 40 inches in diameter, air cylinders 39 and 24 inches, stroke 48 inches and a free air capacity of 4147 cubic feet per minute; one Ingersoll-Rand cross-compound Corliss steam, 2-stage air compressor with steam

Long Island City Air Compressor Plant, Belmont Tunnels.

cylinders 22 and 40 inches, air cylinders 38 and 24 inches, stroke 42 inches and a free air apacity of 3937 cubic feet per minute.

The Degnon Contracting Company's plant at the same point included three Ingersoll-Rand cross-compound steam, duplex air compressors with steam cylinders 15 and 28 inches, air cylinders 20¼ inches, stroke 16 inches, a free air capacity of 6540 cubic feet per minute and a maximum air pressure of 50 pounds. There was also one Ingersoll-Rand cross-compound steam, 2-stage air compressor with a steam end identical with the above machine, but with compounded air cylinders $25\frac{1}{4}$ and $16\frac{1}{4}$ inches in diameter, a free air capacity of 1704 cubic feet per minute and air pressure 100 pounds.

The most interesting in some respects of all the New York tunnel plants was that installed by the Degnon Contracting Company upon Man-O'-War's Reef in the middle of the East River, opposite Forty-second Street. The existence of this reef made possible the sinking of two shafts, giving four additional working faces for the two sub-river tunnels. The first thing to be done was to get floor space, as the original area was entirely insufficient. At first a single Ingersoll-Rand straight line compressor with a portable boiler was installed and the sinking of the two shafts was begun. The material from these shafts was used for filling upon and around the reef until a sufficient area was secured for the installation of the complete plant, but with not a square foot of space to spare. The compressor room extended to the water's edge on two sides with but a small space on the New York side; while to the north enough land was made to provide for the moving of muck cars to scows on either side.

The power plant equipment used here included one Ingersoll-Rand straight line, steam driven compressor with 24-inch steam cylinder, $26\frac{1}{4}$-inch air cylinder, 30-inch stroke and a free air capacity of 1843 cubic feet per minute. In addition to this steam driven unit there were four electrically driven, belted, duplex compressors built by the Ingersoll-Rand Company. Three of these had duplex air cylinders $20\frac{1}{4}$ inches in diameter by 16-inch stroke with an aggregate free air capacity of 6540 cubic feet per minute. The fourth machine was a 2-stage compressor with air cylinders $25\frac{1}{4}$ and $16\frac{1}{4}$ inches in diameter, 16-inch stroke and a free air capacity of 1704 cubic feet per minute. This latter machine delivered air at 100 pounds pressure while the three other power driven units carried 50 pounds air pressure. These motor driven units were to run at constant speed, the air delivery being regulated by choking controllers on the intake. One straight line steam driven compressor was included in this plant, but is not shown in the illustration. The current for the electric motors was taken from a cable connecting with the Manhattan lines of the Interborough Company. The elevators in the two shafts were also driven by electric power from the same source. Locomotive boilers supplied steam for the two straight line machines, the feed water being piped from Manhattan.

While this plant, on account of its location and of its forbidding accompanying conditions, might have been regarded as more or less an emergency plant, it must not be thought

Man-O'-War's Reef Air Compressor Plant, Belmont Tunnels.

to have been a wasteful one. The electrically driven machines, taking their current from a service in which the highest possible economies are attained, and having motors especially adapted to their work, delivered their air at a lower cost than the straight line steam driven machines, notwithstanding the fact that the latter represented practice still widely prevalent.

In the Long Island City plant there were in service two Ingersoll-Rand cross-compound steam, 2-stage air compressors with steam cylinders 15 and 28 inches in diameter, air cylinders $25\frac{1}{4}$ and $16\frac{1}{4}$ inches, 16-inch stroke and a free air capacity of 3408 cubic feet per minute at 100 pounds pressure. There were also two Ingersoll-Rand straight line, steam driven compressors, 24 and $26\frac{1}{4}$ by 30 inches in dimensions, with a free air capacity of 3686 cubic feet per minute; and one Ingersoll-Rand machine of the same type, 24 and $24\frac{1}{4}$ by 30 inches, free air capacity 1570 cubic feet per minute. These last three units were low pressure compressors and were supplied with steam by Heine boilers.

While the pneumatic pressure maintained in the tunnels until completion was always equal to, or somewhat in excess of, the hydrostatic pressure due to the submergence, there was a constant accumulation of water in the workings. While the air pressure would be in excess of the water pressure at the top of the shield, it might still be insufficient at the bottom; and here the water entered. This was collected in temporary sumps in the air-locks from which it was forced out by air pressure through pipes to various pumping stations situated along the line of construction. There was also a constant seeping of water through the joints where the caulking had not been completed. The sumps were situated where the grade was the lowest and at these points the pumps were located, lifting the water to the surface or directly into the river; or, in the land sections, into sewers connecting with the river.

In several places the segments or wall plates were removed and the material forming the 8-foot partition between the two tubes was cut away to provide sump chambers and to allow room for the pumps.

Where the pumps were situated alongside the tunnel walls and in the workings, no extra room was required for their installation, as these pumps were all of the Cameron type, with their well-known and characteristic lack of protuberant parts.

The Cameron pumps were particularly well adapted for use in tunnels or other restricted quarters, or in situations exposed to flooding, or falling rock or debris from blasting or excavation.

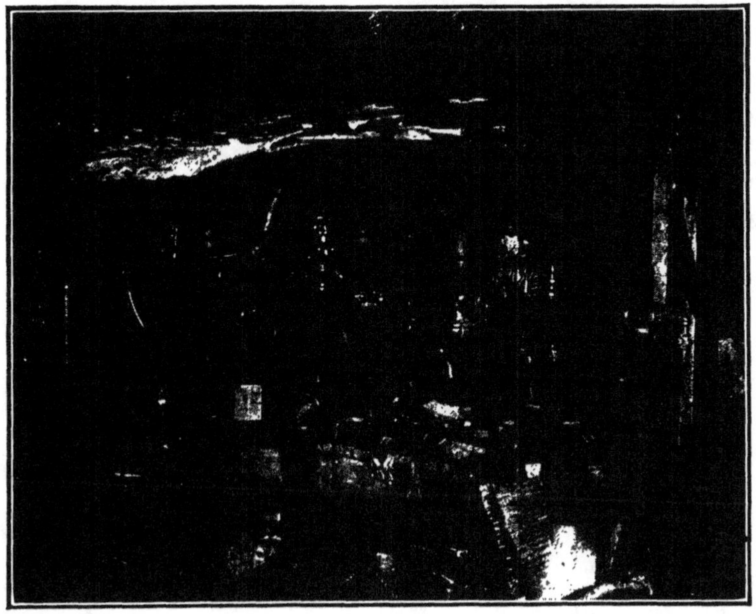

Battery of Cameron Pumps installed in "Belmont" Tunnel, under East River, under Man-O'-War's Reef.

They had no outside valve gear or moving parts to be deranged or broken by passing cars or falling material. They were reliable under all conditions, and in cases of sudden flooding would work as well when submerged to any depth as under normal conditions. In case of accident or emergency they could be run up to double their normal capacity.

A simple device was attached to the pumps to keep the exhaust compressed air from freezing and choking the passages. A small pipe was connected from the water discharge pipe to the exhaust openings of the air operated cylinder, and through it a $\frac{3}{8}$-inch nozzle discharged constantly when the pumps were running. This not only prevented freezing, but also had the effect of a muffler on the exhaust. These pumps were driven by compressed air, as were also the drills and the hoisting and other machinery employed.—Frank Richards, in *Compressed Air Magazine.*

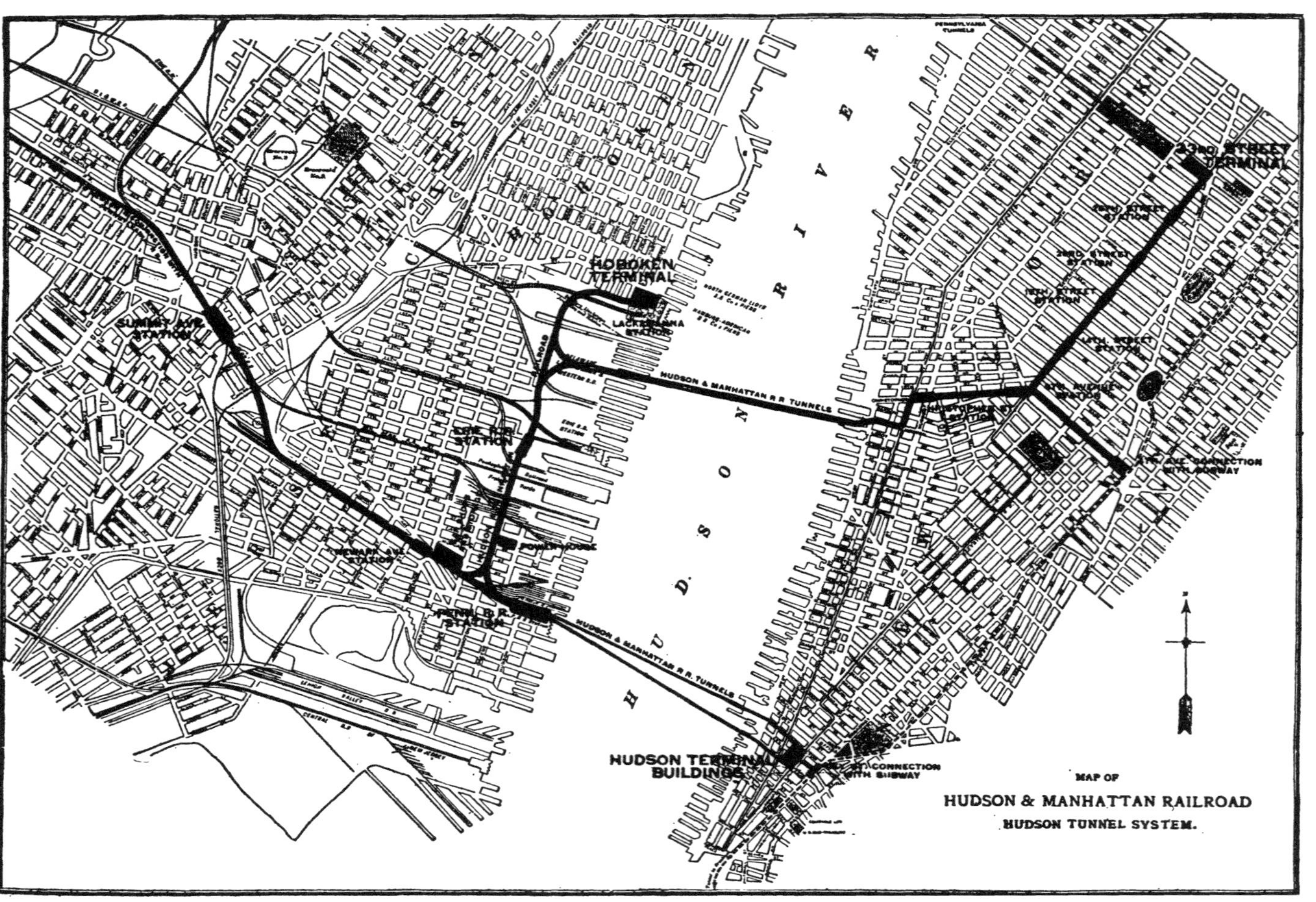
MAP OF
HUDSON & MANHATTAN RAILROAD
HUDSON TUNNEL SYSTEM.
23RD STREET TERMINAL
HOBOKEN TERMINAL
LACKAWANNA STATION
SUMMIT AVE. STATION
ERIE R.R. STATION
NEWARK AVE. STATION
PENN. R.R. STATION
POWER HOUSE
CHRISTOPHER ST. STATION
HUDSON TERMINAL BUILDINGS
CONNECTION WITH SUBWAY
HUDSON & MANHATTAN R R TUNNELS
HUDSON & MANHATTAN R R TUNNELS
H U D S O N
R I V E R

CHAPTER XIX

THE HUDSON-MANHATTAN TUNNELS

As stated in an early chapter of this book, De Witt C. Haskins began the construction of a brick walled tunnel under the Hudson River a third of a century ago. One great accident entailing serious loss of life led to legal and financial difficulties which paralyzed the undertaking. In 1902 the New York and New Jersey Railroad Company resumed serious work on the tunnel. In the following year this company was merged with the Hudson-Manhattan Railroad Company; and later the Hudson Companies were formed to conduct the construction and real estate operations involved. It was estimated that the entire project when completed would cost $70,000,000.

The accompanying map of this system makes clear its route and shows its ramifications and connections. The system as a whole may be considered as made up of four sections. The twin tubes from Hoboken, N. J. near the D. L. & W. terminal, under the river to Sixth Avenue, New York City, enter Manhattan two blocks below Christopher Street and pass up through Sixth Avenue to Thirty-third Street near the Pennsylvania Railroad terminal. The south twin tunnels, which may be called the second section, were driven entirely from the Jersey side of the river, passing from the terminal of the Pennsylvania Railroad in Jersey City, under the river and entering Manhattan Island at Cortlandt Street.

At Jersey City a large terminal station was hewn out of the solid rock, 85 feet below the present station of the Pennsylvania Railroad. The tunnel station here is 150 feet long with approaches 1000 feet in length, and is equipped with large passenger elevators to the surface. The Manhattan terminal is surmounted by the Hudson Terminal buildings, two of the largest office buildings in New York City.

The third section is a land tunnel parallel with the Hudson River, connecting the Hoboken terminal with that in Jersey City and commanding the passenger stations to four trunk railroad lines which were formerly entirely dependent on ferry service for New York connection. The fourth section is a land tunnel running from the Jersey City terminal under the Pennsylvania Railroad Station toward Newark. This passes under the most crowded portion of Jersey City, coming to the surface at the outskirts; and the tunnel trains from this point will use the Pennsylvania Railroad tracks to the transfer station at Harrison and thence to Newark, N.J. It will be noted that more than one-half of this entire system is land tunnel or, in Sixth Avenue, typical subway involving generally no unusual difficulties. The river work, however, presented unusually difficult engineering problems. The employment of compressed air as a plenum and for operating the drills, shields and other mechanism used in construction was the essential condition which made it possible to bring these tunnels to successful completion.

Messrs. Charles M. Jacobs and J. Vipond Davies were placed in charge of the engineering when the project was taken up anew by the Hudson Companies. The north tunnel had then been driven 3800 feet from the Jersey side. The shield previously used in this work was retained in service, but with necessary changes to adapt its use to a spur of rock then being approached which would require to be drilled and blasted in advance of the shield. A heavy hood or apron extending 6 feet on the upper half was added to the shield to afford protection to the laborers while working in the rock. At this point work was carried on under an air pressure of 33 pounds, there being 14 feet of silt and 65 feet of water above the shield. At places where blows occurred the river bed was covered with a clay blanket before operations could be continued.

In beginning the south tunnels, changes were made in the design of the tunnel and in the mode of procedure. The size was reduced to a diameter of 15 feet 3 inches in the clear. Cast plates bolted together insured a true circular section and the shield could be manipulated to follow the alignment. A hydraulic erector was carried by the shield for placing the lining plates or sections in position for bolting.

The forward movement of the shield was controlled by hydraulic jacks exerting an aggregate thrust of 2500 tons. It was found that the shield could be thrust forward, displacing the silt without excavating in front of the shield. Because of this quality in the silt the cost of construction became less than ever before attained in this class of work. Five feet of advance was considered good progress per twenty-four hours where the material was required to be removed from in front of the shield before shoving. On the other hand, 72 feet of progress was made in twenty-four hours in the Cortlandt Street tunnels where the material was displaced by the shield.

In an address by Mr. Jacobs, Chief Engineer, before the Yale Club of New York, the following description of some of the contingencies of subaqueous tunneling was given.

"At the beginning of the work on the south tube of the uptown tunnel, the shield from the Hoboken side was being advanced through the silt with the shield doors closed so as to save the cost of excavation. While the headings were still under the Lackawanna coal dock, the night superintendent, thinking that the shield was moving very slowly, determined (contrary to orders) to open one of the center doors so as to let the mud come in and so let the shield go ahead faster.

"The silt shot in under such pressure that it buried some of the workmen before they could escape; the rest of the shift got away through the upper emergency lock which was then 115 feet away from the shield face. The heading was lost, and the tunnel between the shield and the lock was filled solid with mud. The coal dock was crowded with shipping and, furthermore, the Lackawanna at that time was not particularly favorable to the tunnel enterprise, so that it would have been almost impossible to get permission to dredge out the bed of the river in front of the shield so that a diver could go down and timber up the exterior opening of the doorway. The problem was solved as follows:

" Two heavy mainsails were procured and a double canvas cover about 60 by 40 feet made of them. Around the edges were secured small weights of pig iron. The canvas was spread on a flat barge and lines carried to fixed points to hold the mainsail in position. The barge was withdrawn and the mainsail allowed to drop to the bed of the river, 30 feet of it covering the shield and the remaining 30 feet extending out beyond the face toward the middle of the river. One of the pipe valves in the lock was then opened and the mud, under the direct pressure of the river, shot into the tunnel westward of the lock for 40 feet. It came in a solid stream for eight days and nights. Finally it let up for a few minutes, began again and then stopped.

" A cavity had been formed in the bed of the river outside the cutting edge of the shield into which the canvas dropped and was eventually drawn into the opening of the doorway through which the mud was pouring. A small cavity was excavated in the mud-filled tube ahead of the lock and, the air pressure being put on, it immediately relieved much of the strain on the temporary canvas cover. Miners were then able to get into the tunnel and dig out the mud. In about nine days the heading was recovered and the door on the inside closed.

" The north tube is an extension of an old tunnel abandoned some years ago. Within 100 feet from the point where the shield stopped in the previous attempt was a reef of rock, standing from 1 to 16 feet above the intended grade of the tunnel.

" Before the shield arrived at this point, it was necessary to build a temporary workshop in the river ahead of the shield, so as to build on the front of it a steel apron under which the men could work in drilling the rock and blasting it out of the path of the shield. Above the rock was soft silt and, above that, from 60 to 65 feet of water. It was expected that in blasting the rock with so slight a cover, and with such a heavy water pressure, the heading would probably be blown out.

" Clay loaded on barges was, therefore, always held in readiness to be dumped into any such blowout. After a few weeks the expected blowout occurred and the 900 feet of tunnel from lock to heading was flooded. The men at work escaped. The clay scows were immediately brought over the blowout and dumped, thus blocking the hole. The water was pumped out into the western workings, and within eleven hours men were able to reach the headings on a small raft. No damages were found and work was soon again under way. In all, only twenty-one hours of time were lost. There were two more blowouts while the tunnel was being built across the 700 feet of reef, and in each case they were similarly dealt with.

" Finally, however, there was a problem which could not be dealt with by dropping these clay blankets. At the extreme eastern end of the reef the rock rose about 16 feet above the bottom of the cutting edge of the shield. The tunnel at this point is so near the bottom of the river that the clay was almost fluid and continually slipped into the pockets of the shield, so that the men could not get out underneath the apron to drill the rock. Scow after scow was dumped but the clay would not hold.

" Finally, blow-pipe flames, fed from two tanks of kerosene, were directed against the exposed clay until it was indurated, so as to hold its position while the men drilled the rock. The blow-pipe process took eight hours, during which time streams of water were continually played on the shield structure to prevent it being damaged by the high temperature. This is probably the first time that man has made brick in the bottom of a river."

CHAPTER XX

THE HUDSON-MANHATTAN TUNNELS (*Continued.*)

WHEREVER work was executed by open-cut methods the structure was waterproofed with fabric and pitch applied in the usual manner, making a complete envelope around it. As the greatest part of this work, however, was executed by tunnel methods this manner of waterproofing was not feasible, except in small portions of the work. The method adopted, therefore, was invariably to grout with Portland cement in the rear of the plate lining or concrete lining, and in the majority of cases this application answered the purpose of making the tunnels perfectly watertight. Owing to the imperviousness of neat cement this was the only water proofing adopted on the coffer-dam walls of the Church Street terminal and approaches.

In the iron-lined sections of tunnel all joints of the plate segments were first grummetted on the bolts with flax and red lead under the bolt washers, and caulking spaces between the joints of the plate lining were first caulked with a thread of lead wire, followed up and supported with rust joint cement. Throughout the concrete work, waterproofing was done by plastering the internal and exposed surface with one of the usual types of waterproofing compounds mixed with neat Portland cement and applied with a trowel, this method answering admirably in a majority of cases. At the same time, in persistent leaks, it was found necessary to cut right back into the concrete and expose the voids and then reconstruct such portion of concrete with a rich mixture of cement. As a general rule, for waterproofing of concrete work a rich mixture of cement in the concrete with thorough and efficient ramming answered the purpose and constituted the only waterproofing used.

Generally speaking, the standard track throughout all the lines of the company consists of white oak ties,laid in broken trap rock ballast on a flat surface of concrete forming the invert. This concrete invert fills the flanges between the plates in the tube tunnels and a drain is formed with a reinforced concrete slab over the same along the center line of the tunnel, which provides efficient drainage of the tunnel.

Interior of Hudson-Manhattan Tunnel.

The rails are 85-pound A.S.C.E. section with continuous rail joints, and all rails are attached to the ties with screw spikes of special design for this company's work. Goldie tie plates are used throughout, the plates being put on the ties under hydraulic pressure before the ties are sent into the tunnels, the plates being put into exact template spacing. Holes in the ties for the screw spikes were bored with a pneumatic auger before the ties were taken into the tunnels, and the screw spikes put in place and driven with a pneumatic screw driver which proved very rapid in operation and of great efficiency. This tool was designed by officers of the company for the particular use to which it was put.

All the rail used in the downtown tunnels has been 0.90 per cent. carbon manufactured by the open hearth process by the Bethlehem Steel Company; and on heavy curves either chrome nickel or manganese steel rail was used, according to the radius of curvature.

The contact (third) rail is of special type, designed by L. B. Stillwell, the company's consulting electrical engineer. This rail is carried on heavy porcelain insulators and secured by pressed steel brackets to long ties spaced about 10 feet apart. The contact rail is protected by an overhanging board of Australian jarrah wood.

At heavy curves and in the downtown terminal, as well as at special points where reinforcing was executed, the track was laid in solid concrete.

Guard rails are installed on all curves of less than 750 feet radius, these rails being 100-pound section A.S.C.E. and $\frac{9}{16}$ inches higher than the running rail. All frogs and switches are of manganese steel.

In Jersey City and Hoboken where the various tunnels of the several routes make connections between Jersey City, Hoboken and uptown New York, the elimination of grade crossings was essential to the design of the work, and to meet these conditions the tunnels were superimposed. This operation necessitated the construction of junctions in the tunnels, all of which, unfortunately, came at locations where the construction would be in loose sand or other soft foundation in which grave difficulties would have been involved in making the enlargements entirely by underground methods.

The enlargement at the junction of Sixth Avenue and Ninth Street was carried out entirely by underground methods on account of the conditions of traffic on the streets above, which would have made open-cut methods very difficult and have caused grave inconvenience to the public. This junction was

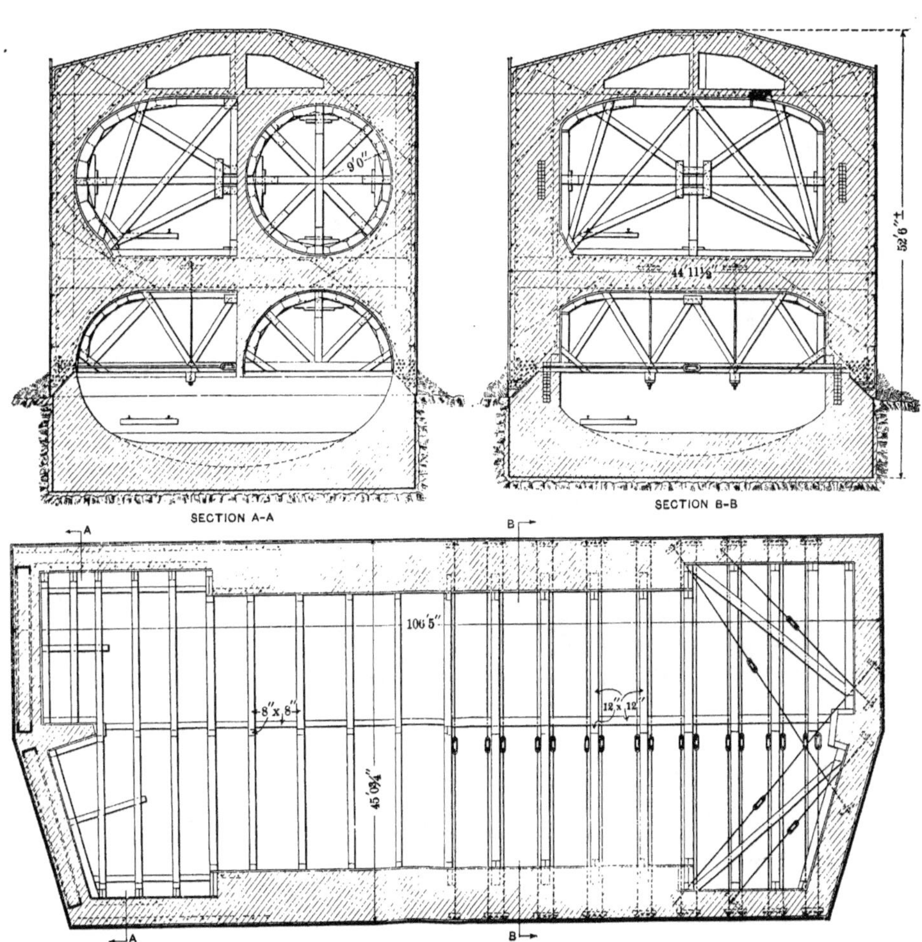

Construction of Tunnel Cross-Over, Hudson-Manhattan Tunnels.

constructed in sand formation overlying the rock, and as the location was in part on the site of a former creek there was a good deal of quicksand present to be taken care of. The entire work therefore, had to be executed under air pressure. At this point the shields in the two diverging lines were carried through continuously, forming the external lines of the enlargement; and these tubes so constructed were used to brace from, in constructing the enlargement.

Sections of lining plates were take out from the sides of these tubes and tunneling carried on between the tubes for the insertion of the heavy timbering put in place to carry the roof, maintaining the breast throughout and carrying the work on in section lengths. In this way excavation was carried on and the arch forming the permanent lining put in place in short lengths but of the full structure width, having in part a clear span of 60 feet. This work was executed with only a very slight settlement of the surface of the ground. At the same time columns of the elevated railway structure overhead were supported by long girders wedged to brackets riveted to the columns and constantly watched to take up any settlement which might occur. This method of underground enlargement (see page 156) was necessarily very expensive, and to execute similar work in the three different sites on the Jersey side, each of which was of greater dimensions than the enlargement at Sixth Avenue and Ninth Street, made a careful detail study of the possibilities desirable.

In Jersey City, fortunately, the three junction enlargements involved came below properties occupied by the Delaware, Lackawanna & Western Railroad and the Erie Railroad for yard purposes; and by arrangement with these companies the surface of the ground was occupied for the purpose of carrying on the work. In all these cases the foundations could be carried to rock.

These enlargements were made by caissons sunk from the surface. It was proposed to use concrete lined steel caissons but owing to the high cost and the time required for delivery of the steel, a reinforced concrete design was adopted which permitted the immediate commencement of work and at a much lower cost for the caisson. Three caissons fitted with locks and other necessary equipment were built on the ground and sunk from the surface, as in bridge pier practice. Where the tunnel tubes were to enter the caissons, concrete dummy drum heads were built, which were removed when the proper elevation was

Arrangement of Branch Tunnels and Cross-over on New Jersey Side, Hudson-Manhattan Tunnels.

reached; and shields were erected for the commencement of the tunnels from the caissons. In other cases shields drawn from other points were aligned to connect at the drum heads where the points were sealed with the tunnel lining before removing the drum heads.

The sizes of caisson Nos. 1 and 2 were 23 feet 5¼ inches to 45 feet 8 inches in width by 101 feet 2 inches in length by 51 feet in height. Caisson No. 3 was 106 feet long, 45 feet wide and 43 feet 11½ inches high. This caisson was arranged with eight tunnels, as follows: At the north end, two superimposed to and from Hoboken, and two superimposed to and from New York, and on the south end two superimposed tunnels to and from New Jersey and two superimposed tunnels to be used in the future when connection is made with the Erie tracks. The caisson was sunk 85 feet below tide level. Its total weight was about 10,000 tons.*

Perhaps the greatest feat in construction was the building of the tunnels at the intersection of Christopher Street, Ninth Street and Sixth Avenue, Manhattan. From this point two tunnels run east under Ninth Street and two north under Sixth Avenue. Here there was the elevated railway overhead, the Metropolitan Street Railway lines on the street surface, and buildings on each side of the street. This made the problem similar to the intersections in Hoboken, except that in this case the sinking of caissons was out of the question.

To accommodate two tubes coming up from the south and the four diverging to the east and north, it was necessary to build an arch of which the maximum width was 68 feet. The work was all in running sand and of necessity was done under air pressure. Two iron-lined tunnels were run through this intersection first, and the side walls then built in. Openings were then made at the tops of the tunnels and timbering or sheathing was carried up so that sufficiently heavy false work could be put in for springing the arch. After the arch was completed the two temporary tunnels were taken out. This work required the greatest ingenuity and care, for at least eight weeks. Any accident to the timbering, any loss of the necessary air pressure or any carelessness of the men, would have undoubtedly caused a cave-in; and the elevated structure and the surface lines, together with the streets and the buildings on each side, would have fallen into the excavation. Every square

*J. Vipond Davies, in *Railroad Age Gazette*.

inch of the treacherous ground had to be protected by wooden sheathing the moment it was exposed; otherwise the vibration of the passing trains above would start the sand running. This part of the work was the last of the excavation necessary for opening the railroad to traffic, and although it was early in December when the spring of this large arch was under way, it was finished so that trains could be operated on February 10, 1908.*

It is interesting to note that the original Ingersoll air compressor installed at the Hoboken end of the first tunnel in 1880 was continued in service until the completion of the tunnels. This compressor was overhauled in 1890 and is rated as an Ingersoll Class "A" with cylinders 20 inches and 20¼ inches by 30-inch stroke, free air capacity 1098 cubic feet per minute. The other compressors comprising the plants of the three power houses responsible for the tunnel work of the Hudson Companies all belong to the same family. Besides the compressor mentioned, the Hoboken plant included two Class "A" compressors, 22 and 26½ by 24-inch stroke, free air capacity 3686 cubic feet per minute; and one duplex Class "H" Ingersoll-Rand machine, 16 and 20¼ by 16-inch stroke, free air capacity 2178 cubic feet per minute.

The Morton Street plant at the Manhattan end of the same tunnels comprised one duplex Ingersoll-Rand compressor, 22 and 22¼ by 24-inch stroke, free air capacity 2640 cubic feet per minute; one Ingersoll-Rand Class "A" 22 and 22¼ by 24-inch, free air capacity 1320 cubic feet per minute; one 20 and 22¼ by 24-inch, free air capacity 1320 cubic feet per minute; and one 16 and 16¼ by 18-inch, free air capacity 698 cubic feet per minute.

At the Jersey City plant opposite Cortlandt Street the machines were three Ingersoll-Rand Class "H" cross-compound steam, 2-stage air compressors for high pressure air, and three Ingersoll-Rand Class "H" cross-compound steam, duplex single-stage air for the low pressure air. The former were 14- and 28-inch steam and 24¼ and 14¼-inch air, by 16-inch

* From paper by Charles M. Jacobs.

stroke, free air capacity 4170 cubic feet per minute; and the latter of the same steam cylinder dimensions with air cylinders 22¼ by 16-inch stroke, free air capacity 7920 cubic feet per minute.*

The Cameron sinking pump was used almost exclusively for taking care of the drainage water in the excavation of the Sixth Avenue subway. This pump is very light, compact and readily handled and was suspended on chains while in operation. For its purpose as a sinking pump it is particularly well adapted to care for water carrying a large proportion of sand or sediment, as the water flows steadily in one direction, and is not retarded in its passage through the valves, which have large openings. These qualities permit of a comparatively high speed of the moving parts, and of a consequently large quantity of water discharged.

The weight of the machine is reduced by discarding the valve chest and air chamber, as the valves are in the lower cylinder and plunger, and the upper part of the plunger performs the functions of an air chamber. The construction of the water end is very simple. All valves are readily accessible for inspection, but as the flow of water is continuously in one direction, the accumulation of sediment or sand around the valves is prevented. This prevention of the obstruction of the water valves eliminates the most common cause of the pump troubles experienced in sinking pumps.

* From *Compressed Air Magazine.*

CHAPTER XXI.

THE HUDSON TERMINAL STATION OF THE HUDSON-MANHATTAN TUNNELS

The provision for crossing the Hudson for the suburban population resident in New Jersey has heretofore been solely by ferry. This means of conveyance, requiring the transfer of passengers at each side of the river, is necessarily slow, due to the loading, starting, entering ferry slips and unloading, these delays being increased in case of fog or storm, or under winter conditions where the slips are jammed with ice. The ferries carry about 120,000,000 passengers per annum.

Excepting the New York Central & Hudson River Railroad, and the New York, New Haven and Hartford, all the main railway lines terminate on the west bank of the Hudson and are cut off from direct connection with New York

A tunnel connecting New York and the west shore was first practically considered in 1873, when the Hudson River Tunnel Company was organized, and laid plans for a line from a point at the foot of Fifteenth Street, Jersey City, under the Hudson to a point in Washington Square, New York City. This scheme was for a steam road with its terminal in Washington Square, the then resident district. The pronounced movement westward has necessitated the situation of the terminals in other sections.

The center of greatest concentration in Manhattan is south of the City Hall, and in locating lines for a tunnel road the problem presented was: First, to locate close to Broadway and, second, to obtain a location where the cost of the site would not be prohibitive. It was undesirable to cross Broadway, as the east side of that thoroughfare is of no greater value for handling passengers than the west side at an equal distance from Broadway, while the cost and difficulties of caring for the old buildings and their foundations would have enormously increased the costs and hazards of tunnel building; and, in addition, the connections with other city lines are better west of Broadway.

The scheme of operating the Jersey tunnels and the uptown lines fixed the train lengths at eight cars, each 48½ feet long, requiring a station track 388 feet long and platform lengths on a tangent of about 350 feet.

The small area of land required for the underground terminal was very costly. The average price was, $40.00 to $45.00 per square foot, and in addition there were the payments under the franchise provisions for lease and use in perpetuity of the underground space of the adjacent streets. The original idea was to construct a railroad station with a simple shed cover over the area at the street level; but owing to the unremunerative conditions of this plan, the investment being about $3,000,000, it was decided to improve the property by the erection of an office building that would yield an income.

The location adopted for the railroad was by a line from Jersey City eastward to the foot of Cortlandt Street, under Cortlandt Street to the private property at Church Street (the next street west of and parallel to Broadway); thence due north under this property and crossing under Dey Street to Fulton Street (420 feet between the north line of Cortlandt Street and south line of Fulton Street); thence turning west under Fulton Street and again crossing the Hudson River to Jersey City. The width of the station site averages 180 feet, and, including the widths of Cortlandt and Fulton streets, the length north and south is 530 feet.

The elevation of the tracks in the station was determined (subject to the limitations of the Rapid Transit Railroad Commissioners) as 11.7 feet below mean sea level, or at a depth of 36.86 feet below the street surface at Church and Dey streets; and this depth was altogether too great for the movements of passengers up and down without an intermediate landing. For railroad operation, the shorter the movement vertically or horizontally between the concourse or distributing floor and the cars, the better; and as the clearance needed for the cars was only 12 feet 6 inches above top of rail, and the floor depth required was only 24 inches, a grand concourse was laid out at an elevation of 4.33 feet above mean sea level. In this case there was an added advantage, as at this level the concourse could be constructed continuous under Dey Street and practically over the entire area of the station site. The only necessary function, therefore, of the street level in connection with the railroad station was to provide adequate access and egress for passengers, well distributed, to the concourse floor; and with that exception the entire surface area was available as part of the office building now developed.

The provision of platforms, stairways and openings had next to be considered. To do this intelligently it was necessary to work back from the ultimate carrying capacity of the tunnels. The capacity of each pair of tunnels is one trainload of 800 persons on a headway of 90 seconds, or, say 530 persons per minute; and this number either arriving or leaving at times of maximum movement in one direction, as the reverse movement is always comparatively light. Two terminal station tracks will easily take care of this service, allowing three minutes for the train to enter and stand in the station. As there are two pairs of tunnels provided for the future (one pair of which is now in operation), the station was laid out with four operating tracks, and an additional track, allowing only for unloading passengers, for car inspection and for storing disabled trains. The unloading platform widths and areas need to be sufficient to hold only such part of the trainload as would not have passed onto the stairs when the last portion of the train load has discharged; and obviously a floor area equal to the train itself is more than adequate providing there is no undue congestion on the stairs. In order to load a train promptly the loading platforms should have sufficient area for a trainload of passengers to stand without undue crowding, largely grouped along the edges at the points where the car doors come when the train stops, with sufficient space in addition to permit a free passage

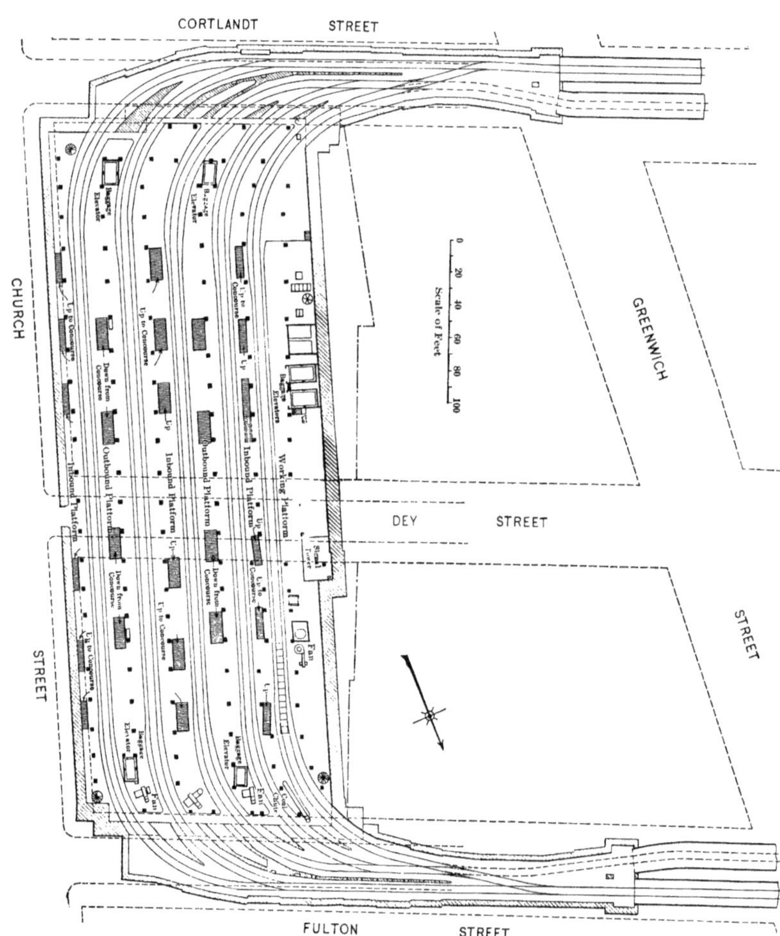

Foundation and Track Arrangement, Hudson Terminal Station.

through the crowd being maintained. The width should be greater than that of the unloading platforms and should not be less than twice the width of the trains. Alternating the platforms as before mentioned and thereby maintaining one-way movement, permits this. The platforms as finally arranged are as follows:

Along the Church Street side, an unloading platform 11½ feet wide serving one track; area 5200 square feet.

Between tracks Nos. 1 and 2, a double loading platform 22 feet wide; area 9000 square feet.

Between tracks Nos. 2 and 3, a double unloading platform 22 feet wide serving two tracks; area 9300 square feet.

Between tracks Nos. 3 and 4, a double loading platform 22 feet wide serving two tracks; area 9300 square feet.

Between tracks Nos. 4 and 5, a single unloading platform, 13 feet wide, serving No. 5 track only in emergency and being regular only for No. 4 track; area 5400 square feet.

To ascertain the necessities in respect of stairs and passages, count of actual movement of traffic at congested points in New York was made, notably at the Brooklyn Bridge. In a straight passage of ample width, the "rush hour" New York crowd moves at a rate of 300 feet per minute, walking with a step averaging 30 inches. There is only a small reduction in this speed on ramps of, say, not over 10 per cent grade. At this rate each person averages about 10 square feet of space occupied and the movement discharges about 30 persons per foot of width of passage. If the passageway becomes too congested, the space occupied per person reduces and the speed of movement also reduces, but the number discharged remains about the same, thirty per minute. Any contrary movement in a broad passage reduces the movement rather more than the relative space occupied in multiples of, say, 30 inches per person; but in narrow passages the relative reduction is much greater, notwithstanding that persons crowd into smaller space, not over 24 inches in width.

A crowd moving freely upward on stairs takes about the same number of steps per minute, say 120, but advances only about 12 inches horizontally instead of 30 inches. Upstairs movement is much more dense than downstairs, but correspondingly slower. We have counted discharge on stairs of 24 persons per foot of width per minute moving upward, but never more than 18 per foot of width moving downward. There does not appear much difference in discharging rate on stairs above 4 feet wide if the movement is all in one direction; but stairs of all widths (particularly below 8 feet wide) are seriously impeded by any contrary movement even when only four or five persons per minute are moving in the direction reverse to the heavy traffic. Generally, for stairs above 4 feet in width, all movement in one direction, actual count indicates:

Upward—Maximum, 20 persons per foot of width of stairs per minute. Average for ordinarily free-moving crowds, 15 per minute.

Downward—Maximum, 18 persons per foot of width of stairs per minute. Average for ordinarily free-moving crowds, 13 per minute.

In case of any contrary movement it is most important to force the people to a right-hand direction of movement, and speaking generally no stairs serving traffic in contrary directions for railroad service should be permitted to be installed of less than 5 feet clear width.

In unloading railroad trains in rapid transit service, it is very important to distribute passengers as quickly as possible, particularly in discharge; and, in such a problem as ours, to get them off the track platforms as rapidly as possible and with the least amount of walking along the platforms, allowing them the more easily to freely distrubute themselves on the great concourse floor. In a full train there are, say, twenty door openings in the train, all simultaneously discharging practically a single line of persons. Therefore, we located stairways on all the unloading platforms in tandem, six stairs to each, distributed as nearly uniformly along the platform lengths as possible. No. 1 platform has an aggregate of 26-foot stairs to discharge at the rate of 800 persons in a 3-minute interval, or 266 persons per minute, or say, 10 persons per foot of width of stairs. No. 3 platform has six stairs (one not fitted until needed) aggregating 48½ feet in width for discharge of 800 persons in 90 seconds, or say 9 persons per foot of width per minute.

For the loading platforms, it was important for the economical operation of the railroad to group the landings on the concourse floor, and consequently it was necessary to provide for this service only four stairs per platform in pairs. These have an aggregate width of 32½ feet, and a maximum passenger movement of 16 persons per foot of width per minute, on the assumption that the train is fully loaded at the terminal station and no consideration given to local movement at other stations.

The arrangement of stairway heads on the concourse floor tends as far as it is possible to thoroughly distribute the movement, and also to separate the incoming from the outgoing traffic. The distribution of the streams of traffic cannot be too thoroughly separated to obtain the best results. At the same time, having in mind that when the movement eastward is at its maximum and carrying 7.5 per cent of the total daily traffic between 7 A.M. and 8 A.M., the westward movement is only 1.5 per cent of the total daily traffic; and in reverse direction when between 5 P.M. and 6 P.M. the maximum westbound traffic represents 10.7 per cent of the total daily traffic, the eastbound traffic only represents 2.5 per cent of the total daily movement.

The original plan designed was to absolutely separate the movement on the street by making two main entrances on Dey Street near Church Street, each 30 feet wide, the entire entrance for all the traffic descending by arcade passages and easy stairs to the concourse; and one main exit each at Cortlandt Street and at Fulton Street, each 30 feet in width, and ascending by arcades and easy ramp sloping from 10 to 14 per cent from the concourse. As, however, the aggregate of these main entrances provided for less than 9 persons per foot of width per minute and the office buildings were greatly benefitted by making all these main approaches equally entrances and exits, the first plan was modified to that extent and the freedom of movement is much better adapted to the general approach through the streets to the station and reduces thereby the general congestion on the streets.

The first essential purpose of this railroad and station is for the operation of a purely local rapid transit passenger service, but, as before stated, the railroad was also to operate a terminal service for the various steam railroads in Jersey City and Hoboken. It was, therefore, also necessary to equip the concourse floor with ticket offices for these various trunk line railroads, enabling them to sell all classes of tickets for all points on their systems for trains departing, and to advertise schedules of trains departing, from Church Street terminal. A train leaving at an advertised time becomes the train connection for the specified steam railroad train from New Jersey. The ticket examiners at the ticket barriers on the concourse floor announce the train connection and at the leaving time of the train deliver a clearance ticket for the train to the conductor, who in turn surrenders the clearance ticket to the platform man at the respective stations on the New Jersey side, on receipt of which ticket the main line train is despatched.

The construction and design of this combined station and office building need a very brief description. The structure below the surface is the greatest example of caisson construction in existence. The soil underlying the site was quicksand down to the level of the hardpan, which was an irregular deposit overlying the bedrock (New York micaceous gneiss). All surrounding buildings were on old and inadequate foundations, and the plans for the electrical power plant to be put in below the track level required excavation to a depth of 75.8 feet below Church Street, or 50.7 feet below tide level. In addition to the building with its foundations, the approaches for the tunnels to the station at either end had also to be constructed by sinking caissons under the streets and from building line to building line without interfering with the use of the streets during construction. The main station site was first enclosed by sinking 51 rectangular caissons, joined to each other, around the external lines. All these caissons are of reinforced concrete, 8 feet thickness of wall, and all caissons were sunk through hardpan to bedrock and sealed into the rock. Rock at its deepest point is 110 feet below the surface of Church Street. Inside the area of the enclosed coffer-dam were then sunk 115 circular pits and 32 rectangular pits, in caissons down to hardpan, these pits corresponding to each column location; and in these pits were constructed the grillages and foundations for columns. Up to this point excavation had only been carried down to about the concourse floor level where water stood in the ground. The steel columns for the triple tier from foundation to street floor level were then erected in these pits; the lower length of column weighing as much as 26 tons each and carrying loading up to 1725 tons per column. The columns being erected, the steel of the concourse floor was then erected and the floor filled with solid Portland cement concrete from wall to wall. Excavation was then carried down to the train deck. From that floor the main girders on rectangular system between columns were 48 inches deep, flanges 16 inches wide. The floor had to carry the train loading as well as to be the main strut to carry the external pressures on the external walls. It was, therefore, determined to construct this of excessive mass and strength by putting in a solid slab, 36 inches thick, of reinforced Portland cement concrete, burying columns and girders in one continuous mass. The enormous external pressure may be appreciated from the fact that during excavation from the concourse to the train floor and while waiting for steel girders to be delivered, the entire wall along Church Street bowed in 10 inches without crack or apparent injury.

After the track floor construction was complete, excavation was carried down to the bottom. The bottom of the railroad's transformer sub-station No. 3 was excavated down to bedrock. The entire balance of area of basement had all quicksand removed to hardpan or rock and the area backfilled with boiler cinders and thoroughly sub-drained to the sump where automatic ejectors are installed. Since construction, it is found that the entire drainage through the walls and into the foundations is insignificant and negligible. To construct this basement it was necessary to build the coffer-dam continuous but at the same time the approaches under Cortlandt Street and Fulton Street were also being sunk in caissons connected end to end with removable steel end walls used only for sinking purposes; and these approaches involved 33 caissons having a total cubic capacity of 25,000 cubic yards. These being sunk to final grade, sealed, roofed, and in every way made secure, the trainways through the main coffer-dam walls were blasted out. This was a most difficult job, executed while the office buildings were fully occupied. The trainways represented 120 feet of regular railroad tunnel. The total quantities involved in work below the street level, as illustrating the magnitude of the undertaking, were as follows:

238,000 cubic yards excavation
80,000 cubic yards excavation in caissons
11,000 cubic yards concrete in caissons
6,267 tons structural steel

In the basement of the buildings is the following equipment:

Electric transformer sub-station transforming current generated in Jersey City power house, transmitted at 11,000 volts a.c. to current at 625 volts d.c. for railroad operation and 240 volts d.c. for the power and lighting of the buildings.

A complete school of instruction for railroad employees, fitted with a full-sized car and signal equipment.

Club, reading and dressing rooms for employees.

Suction and forced draft fans for tunnel ventilation, and also similar machinery for ventilation of the basement and the buildings.

Absorption ice-making plant (Carbondale type) for clubs, restaurants and markets.

1500 h.p. boiler plant (Babcock & Wilcox).

Isolated generating plant for supplying entire buildings.

Storage battery plant.

Hydraulic pumps for all baggage elevators.

Extensive baggage rooms and space for handling and storage of baggage or freight.

Coal bunkers, capacity 1500 tons, constructed of reinforced concrete.

In addition to the local passenger business of the Hudson-Manhattan Railroad, it is obvious from the foregoing descriptions that the railroad is also laid out to be the distributing terminal for the steam trunk lines terminating in New Jersey. This is anticipated in the fact that the company is now constructing a physical connection to the tracks of the Pennsylvania Railroad so that its electric trains can be run over the tracks of the Pennsylvania Railroad from the suburban district in New Jersey into the tunnels of the Hudson and Manhattan Railroad, either to the Church Street terminal or ultimately uptown to Forty-second Street, Grand Central Station. Further than this, a connection is anticipated from the Erie direct to the Church Street terminal.

For handling baggage there are four elevators of the Otis plunger type, the floor area of each averaging 12 by 6 feet. These elevators are equipped with rams 9½ to 12½ inches in diameter and have a lift of 23 feet; capacity of the elevators is 8000 to 13,000 pounds. One of these elevators is installed at each end of each of the loading platforms, and the main Dey Street baggage elevators serve the No. 6 platform by a door opening onto that platform direct. The means is, therefore, provided for getting baggage onto each or any one of the platforms serving the five separate tracks at either end.

The development and use for railroad purposes of the space below street level only, allowed of the full treatment above the surface of almost the entire area. This very great area permitted the design of office buildings on strictly economical lines which would be noteworthy and handsome if for no other reason than on account of their enormous mass and simplicity.

There are two of these buildings 22 stories in height above the street, the combined cubical contents of which are approximately 15,000,000 cubic feet. Both of these superstructures were so designed as to have easy access from the elevator halls to the concourse floor below.

The Sixth Avenue elevated station at Cortlandt Street

connects with the corridors on the third floor of the building on Cortlandt Street and the twin buildings are connected by a bridge on this floor crossing Dey Street.

There are 39 high-speed 1-to-1 traction elevators, 22 of which are express elevators running to the twenty-second floor, and 17 local elevators running to the eleventh floor. Three of the elevators run down to the concourse floor, but are not at present used except in cases of emergency.

The rental area of the buildings is approximately 815,000 square feet, exclusive of the valuable rental space on the entire concourse floor.

In order to construct these buildings enormous quantities of materials were required; there are approximately 17,000,000 bricks above the surface of the ground, and in the substructure and super-structure combined there are 27,000 tons of steel.

There are four entrances to the railroad station, or concourse floor. The approaches on Cortlandt and Fulton Streets are by means of ramps and the two on Dey Street by means of stairways. These approaches are very simple in design and are arranged with shop windows all around. At the ends of these approaches are four large clock panels designed by Mr. Carl Bitter. Steel and glass marquises cover the entire width of the sidewalk over all entrances. The floors of the ramps are of cement mixed with carborundum so as to avoid slipping. The stairways are of bluestone.

All renting spaces are designed on a strictly commercial basis and the entire station, including the concourse floor and the railroad platforms, are built so as to be as sanitary as possible. The floor of the concourse is of white terrazza with colored mosaic bands, and all walls and columns have a white glazed terra cotta wainscoting with sanitary base and decorative cap of the same material. The walls above the wainscoting are of hard plaster; all angles are coved or round, and the entire plaster work is painted with enamel paint.

On the concourse floor every convenience of the modern terminal station is provided for the public and every effort has been made to make it attractive. This floor is approximately 430 feet long by 185 feet wide, and of this space aisles which approximate a total of 100 feet in width are given up to the public, with ticket booths arranged at convenient points, giving an unobstructed view of the whole length of the floor. On this floor, in addition to the ticket offices of the Hudson and Manhattan Railroad Company, are the ticket offices of the Pennsylvania, Erie and Lehigh Valley Railroads. There are ample waiting rooms with first-class toilet accommodations; and baggage and parcel rooms, barber shops, bootblacks, telephone and telegraph booths, and shops at which nearly everything that the commuter requires may be purchased.

This combination of a railroad terminal and an office building above, presented problems which would not arise in the case of either proposition if handled by itself. The most serious of these is the arrangement of the columns so that as far as possible they would allow of a proper architectural treatment of the buildings and still maintain the right-of-way of the tracks in the sub-structure, This was accomplished in the main body of the plot, but at the Cortlandt and Fulton Street ends where the tracks converge to run down the streets, it was found necessary to have the building columns rest on girders, which were carried by columns extending through the track floor, which columns were located so as to leave proper clearance for the tracks. The distributing girders were placed at the concourse floor level and are made up of three single girders, each 72 inches deep, with a flange width of 10 inches; and as these girders when set up were very wide, and it being almost impossible to design proper caps for the columns which supported them, mill slabs of steel were used; these were in some cases 6 inches thick.

Another point which had to be taken care of was the multitude of pipes and wires which were necessary to connect the buildings above the track and concourse floors with the power and heating plants which were located below these floors, particularly bearing in mind that the passage through the track floor must not by any connections obstruct more than necessary the space occupied by platforms. This was accomplished by connecting up groups of pipes or wires into systems of piping which for convenience were termed sub-mains, which sub-mains were in turn connected to the mains in the basement by means of large vertical risers termed sub-main feeders. By this means the amount of room required for piping and wire shafts was reduced to a minimum; and as these are usually placed near columns, the size of the finish around columns was reduced quite materially and thereby unnecessary obtruction of the track platforms was avoided.

These sub-mains were placed near the concourse ceiling and to make proper finish for the concourse a hung ceiling was erected under same with trap doors for easy access to the control valves.

The entire lighting of the buildings and sub-structure is by means of high efficiency lamps and specially designed fixtures.

The location of these twin buildings in conjunction with the railroad station terminal has created a new center of population where previously only a small community was gathered. The present aggregation of persons transacting their daily work under these roofs is 8000 and with the complete rental of all space will amount to approximately 10,000.

The property was purchased in the early part of 1906 and some few buildings standing thereon were razed at that time. It was not, however, until May 1, 1906, that the bulk of the properties was turned over to the railroad company. The company by its own engineers carried out all work of construction of the railroad station, approaches, foundations and sub-structure below street level. The caisson and foundation work had advanced so that on May 12, 1907, the first grillage and column were set in the permanent structure, and on April 4, 1908, the company moved into its offices in the completed building. The completion of tunnel approaches, tunnels and terminal station, however, took considerably longer, the railroad going into operation July 19, 1909.

The design and construction of tunnels, station and substructure were by Jacobs & Davies, engineers of the company, while the entire design of the buildings, and treatment and decoration of the station were by Clinton & Russel, architects. George A. Fuller Company was the contractor for the buildings.

From a paper before American Institute of Architects by J. Vipond Davies and J. Hallis Wells.

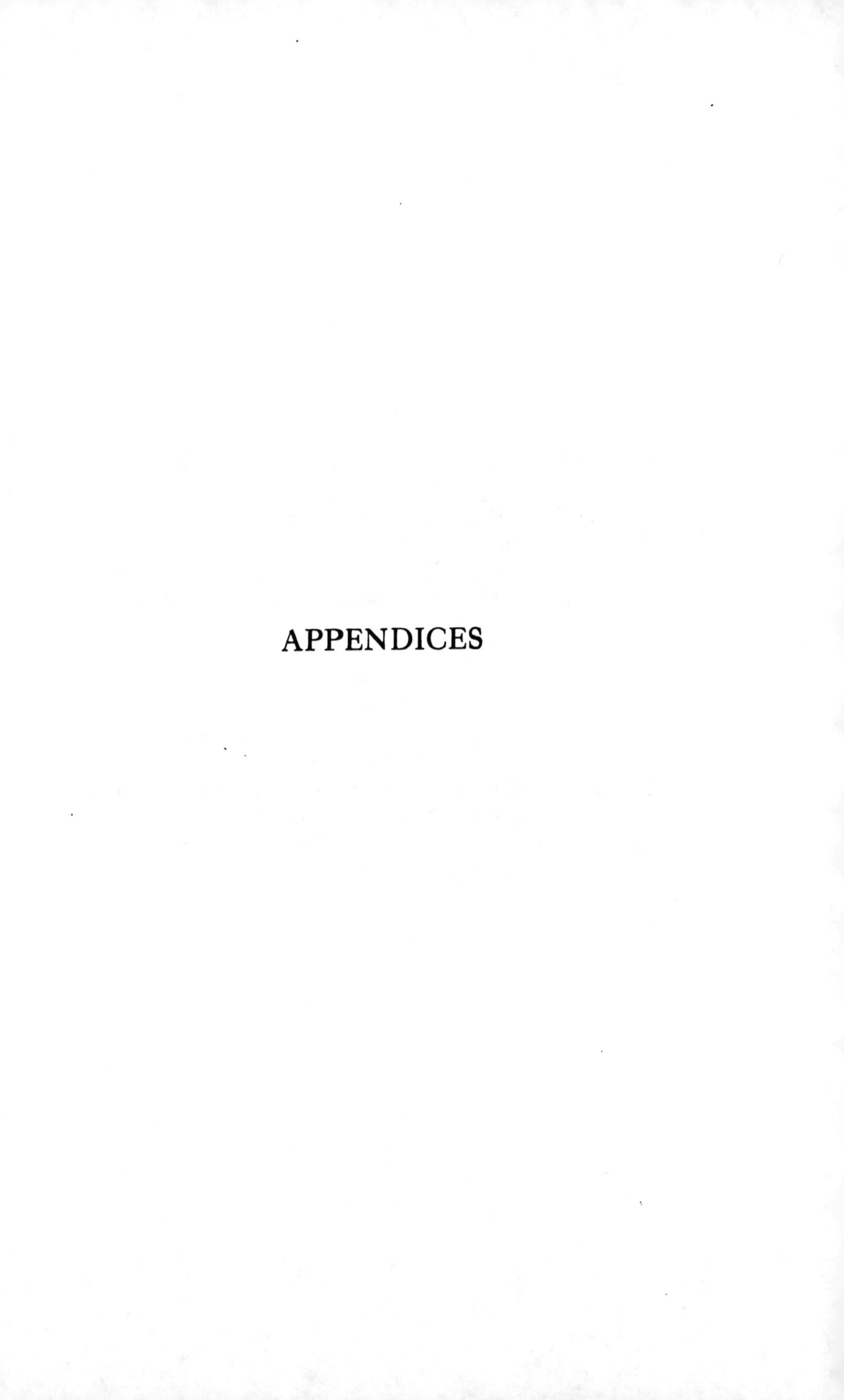

APPENDICES

APPENDICES

A. Air Compressors in the New York Tunnel Work.
B. The Compressed Air Plenum.
C. The Use of Compressed Air in Tunneling.
D. Special Types of Air Compressors.
E. Straight Line and Duplex Compound Air Compressors.
F. Compound Air Compression; Altitude Compression; Air Cylinder Lubrication.
G. Some Air Lift Data.
H. Compressed Air Locomotives.
I. Rock Drills; Hammer Drills.
J. Tunnel Carriage for Drilling; Electric-Air Drill.
K. Rock Drill Bits; Drill Sharpening.
L. Selection of Explosives; Dampness and Dynamite; Blasting Gelatine; Cost of Blasting in Open Cuts.
M. Pumps for Sinking and Tunneling; Sinking Caissons.
N. Engineering Data.

APPENDIX A

Air Compressors on New York Tunnel Work

The tunnel stage of the development of New York City may be said to have really commenced with the present century. Although the first tunnel under the North River was planned and begun a quarter of a century ago, it has but recently been completed, with also its twin tunnel for the reciprocal traffic. On account of the earlier completion of connections, other tunnels begun within the present century will be in established service before these.

The tunnels completed or approaching completion, including the two mentioned above, are as follows:

Six tunnels under the North River; the two from Morton Street, Manhattan, to Hoboken to be used for local and suburban electric train service; two near Cortlandt Street for the same system; two at about Thirty-third Street for the Pennsylvania Railroad. Eight under the East River; two from the Battery up into the heart of Brooklyn, as a continuation of the already completed subway; four to connect the Pennsylvania Railroad with the Long Island Railroad, two of these tunnels also extending across Manhattan; and the two so-called Belmont tunnels which are to connect the Forty-second Street line of the present subway with Long Island trolley lines.

This tunnel work involves not only the actual driving of the tunnels under the rivers as indicated, but greater additional lengths of subterranean tunneling for the approaches or connections. Other tunnels " too numerous to mention " in these and other directions are planned and more or less specifically provided for to supply work for at least twenty years ahead, by which time the tunnel habit will have become so established that no one now can suggest the amount of subterranean and subaqueous excavation and construction which will ultimately be required in New York and vicinity.

We have here to do with only one, although the most important, physical agency in all this tunnel work, the compressed air supply. Merely to enumerate the air compressing plants which have been installed in New York for tunnel work alone, with mention of a few of their most important details, is enough for the present paper.

It will be noted that all the air compressors herein enumerated are New York machines, machines largely developed by New York practice in the building of the Aqueduct, supplemented by mine and tunnel work throughout the world; and perfected and manufactured by the two New York companies of world-wide reputation in this line, the Ingersoll-Sergeant and the Rand, now in the natural course of business events combined in a single concern, the Ingersoll-Rand Company. The position of this company in this great metropolitan development is unique, and cannot be approached for parallel or comparison in any other line of business.

That there is plenty of tunnel work ahead for the air compressor might well be inferred from the substantial and apparently permanent character of many of the installations. Several of the plants here mentioned will undoubtedly be employed to supply the air for other tunnels besides those for which they have been originally erected. These plants accordingly have generally nothing cheap or temporary about them. They employ all the usual well-known devices of economy both in the use of steam and in the compression of the air. The boilers are all of modern design and nearly all of the water-tube type. The steam units are usually compound and condensing, and the air compression two stage with intercoolers and aftercoolers. Gravity oiling systems are installed, which constantly and perfectly lubricate every part and return the oil for repeated use. The action of the compressors is regulated automatically according to the call for the air, so that a series of machines will run constantly without handling the throttle. Recording gages are generally employed and their records are watched and filed in the offices.

While as a rule nothing has been neglected in the installation of these plants which could contribute to the reliability and economy of their operation, to the accessibility of parts and to convenience of manipulation, so that, seen within and with all the circumstances considered, many of them may be taken as models of their class, but the slightest thought has been given to the exteriors of the buildings. One plant is located in an old church, another in a dilapidated foundry, and in several cases the compressors, boilers, etc., have been completely placed in the open air and their protective sheds or buildings have been erected over them.

The perfection and endurance of the compressors may be noted as remarkable. The writer hereof more than a year ago personally visited every plant mentioned except that upon Man-O'-War's Reef, the improvised island in the East River; and while most of the compressors seen were being worked to the limits of their capacity, running at speeds which were astonishing, not one was seen out of order or undergoing repairs. The arduous work on the New York Aqueduct and in tunnels and mines everywhere has to a remarkable extent revealed and eliminated the weak spots and suggested successive improvements.

As indicating the speeds at which these compressors may be run, it may be specially noted that five duplex Corliss compressors, 42-inch stroke, in the Manhattan plant of S. Pearson & Son, Inc., were designed and guaranteed to run continuously at 100 r.p.m., or 700 feet piston speed, with a further provision that in case of emergency they would be capable of running at 125 r.p.m. for a period not exceeding twenty-four hours. This emergency has been encountered several times since the plant was installed, and in fact the machines have run as high as 135 r.p.m. or 945 feet piston speed, for long periods without apparent distress.

In the estimated free air capacities given herein for each plant the piston speed assumed for all is 500 feet per minute.

The one-quarter inch additional to the nominal diameters of the Ingersoll air cylinders is dropped out of the computations, as this normally compensates for the area of the piston inlet pipe, although in some of the compressors with mechanically operated valves this pipe is not used.

Pennsylvania Station Excavation. The work of excavating for the New York terminal of the Pennsylvania Railroad is not at all tunnel work, but it is at the point where four of the tunnels are to meet. This work was, to think of, a simple affair. It was only to dig a hole in the ground; but it was a hole measuring roughly, in the main portion of it, 1800 by 400 feet and 40 feet deep, with more than 1,500,000 cubic yards of material to be removed. A considerable portion of the top was sand and gravel, which was removed first, but most of the material is solid rock. Both steam and compressed air are employed on the work. The steam shovels, being self-contained, also some traveling derricks and of course all the locomotives, are steam operated; while rock drills, pumps, many hoists, concrete mixers, etc., are driven by compressed air; and here, as elsewhere, the compressors are driven to their full capacity.

A temporary compressor plant was first installed right upon a portion of the ground to be excavated, the exterior of the plant being shown in Fig. 1. The church and appurtenances in the background have since been pulled down and rock cutting is proceeding upon the site. There were here three Rand straight line Class " C " compressors with cylinders 24- and 26-inch diameter by 30-inch stroke, free air capacity 5529 cubic feet per minute; and one Ingersoll Class " A " piston inlet compressor 24- and 26¼- by 30-inch stroke, free air capacity 1843 cubic feet per minute. The steam cylinders had balanced valves and Meyer adjustable cut-offs and worked non-condensing. The steam pressure carried was 110 pounds and the air pressure 90 pounds, the latter not being always maintained, as the air was used as fast as it could be delivered. The rock drilling, however, was kept constantly in advance of the work of removal and many holes were always waiting to be fired when needed. The air was not cooled except by the water jacket. There were two large air receivers and a combined delivery pipe 8 inches in diameter with valves for disconnecting each compressor. The air line was carried around the excavation with distributing branches where required. There were six locomotive boilers burning small anthracite. A Cochrane feed water heater was in service and two duplex steam pumps for boiler feeding.

It was well to mention this plant first, since it was, with perhaps one exception, the least economical of any of the plants

FIG. 1.—Temporary Power House, Pennsylvania Terminal.

here enumerated. Fig. 2 shows the exterior and Fig. 3 the interior of the more permanent installation of the New York Contracting Company for this Pennsylvania terminal excavation. This is a plant of much larger capacity and does its work much cheaper. The building, as is evident, was a church, but the interior is now as unecclesiastical as could well be imagined.

There are here three 2-stage, electrically driven Rand compressors with air cylinders 30- and 19-inch diameter by 30-inch stroke; free air capacity 8983 cubic feet per minute. The induction motors are each 500 h.p. General Electric, type L.M.,

122 r.p.m., 6600 volts, 3-phase, 25-cycle. There is also one Rand Corliss, cross-compound, girder frame, 2-stage compressor with steam cylinders 22- and 40-inch and air cylinders 38- and 23-inch by 48-inch stroke; free air capacity 3937 cubic feet per minute. In addition to these are the four compressors of

Fig. 2.—Exterior of Power House, Pennsylvania Terminal Excavation

the temporary plant previously enumerated and therefore not mentioned further and not repeated in our final summary of the various plants.

Pennsylvania Railroad East River Tunnels, Manhattan Plant. The plant of the contractors, S. Pearson & Son, Inc., at Thirty-third Street and First Avenue, New York, is in marked contrast to the preceding. Fig. 4 is a snap-shot of the exterior and Fig. 5 shows the interior. The entire equipment in this case was installed under the direction of the builders of the compressors, the Ingersoll-Rand Company. There are four cross-compound Corliss compressors with steam cylinders 16- and 34- by 42-inch stroke, and duplex air cylinders 26¼-inch, for a maximum air pressure of 50 pounds; free air capacity, 14,744 cubic feet per minute. There is another cross-compound Corliss compressor

Fig. 3.—Interior of Power House for P.R.R. Terminal Excavation.

of the same stroke and with the same steam cylinder dimensions as the above, but with duplex air cylinders 15¼-inch diameter designed to compress to 140 pounds air pressure. The air for this compressor may be taken into the cylinders at the atmospheric pressure, or it may be taken in at 40 or 50 pounds pressure from the aftercooler of the low pressure service, thus increasing its delivery at the high pressure about fourfold; free air capacity, 1310 cubic feet per minute. Another compressor has a special combination feature. It is a cross-compound

Corliss compressor with the same steam cylinder dimensions as above, but with tandem air cylinders 23¼ and 15¼ inches in diameter on each side. All the air cylinders may be used to compress atmospheric air to 50 pounds pressure and deliver individually into the low pressure service; or, by disconnecting the 23¼-inch cylinders, the smaller cylinders may be used for the high pressure service, 140 pounds, precisely the same as the preceding machine. Free air capacity of this compressor is 4194 cubic feet per minute. Besides these, there are two straight line Class "A" compressors 18- and 18¼-

FIG. 4.—Manhattan Power House for P.R.R. East River Tunnels.

by 24-inch stroke used for preliminary development work and generally held in reserve; free air capacity, 1766 cubic feet per minute. This is the plant mentioned above, guaranteed to work up to a piston speed of 700 and in emergencies to 875 feet per minute, and which has been run up to 945 feet in actual work.

There are here six 500 h.p. Sterling boilers, three Wheeler condensers, with independent Edwards air pumps, three centrifugal pumps of the Buffalo Forge Company supplying water from the East River for jackets, intercoolers, aftercoolers and condensers, duplex boiler feed pumps in duplicate, a separate

Fig. 5.—Interior of Manhattan Power House for P.R.R. East River Tunnels.

system of gravity lubrication, a special loop steam system with Holly drip arrangement, and a chemical oil separator. A working steam pressure of 150 pounds is carried throughout and everything possible is run condensing except what is required for heating the feed water. The power house contains three high speed engines with direct-connected generators and three duplex high pressure hydraulic pumps automatically controlled to supply water for advancing the shields, with which we here have nothing to do. Total free air capacity of plant is 22,014 cubic feet per minute.

Fig. 6.—Long Island City Power House for P.R.R. East River Tunnels.

Pennsylvania Railroad East River Tunnels, Long Island City Plant. This plant of S. Pearson & Son, Inc., at Flushing Street and East River has the same units as the above, except that it has no Class "A" compressors, and the entire plant is quite differently arranged, the large yard space allowing great length for the power house. Fig. 6 is a snap-shot of the exterior. The vertical pipes which will be noticed, capped with strainers, are for the intake air. Instead of the Class "A" compressors an additional Corliss compressor, the same as the others for low pressure air, was installed, making the total free air capacity of the plant at 500 feet piston speed 23,934 cubic feet per minute.

Pennsylvania Railroad North River Tunnels, Manhattan Plant. The plant of the O'Rourke Engineering Construction Company at Thirty-third Street and Eleventh Avenue, New York City, the general exterior of which is shown in Fig. 7, comprises three Ingersoll-Rand Corliss compressors with steam cylinders 14- and 30- by 36-inch stroke and duplex air cylinders 23¼-inch diameter, for maximum air pressure of 50 pounds; free air capacity, 8652 cubic feet per minute. There

Fig. 7.—Manhattan Power House for P.R.R. North River Tunnels.

is also one cross-compound Corliss compressor with steam cylinders 14- and 22- by 36-inch stroke and duplex air cylinders 14¼-inch diameter to compress to 140 pounds, using either free air or air taken from the aftercoolers of the low pressure compressors. Free air capacity is 1068 cubic feet per minute.

Pennsylvania Railroad North River Tunnels, Weehawken Plant. This plant, also of the O'Rourke Engineering Construction Company, foot of Baldwin Avenue and North River, Weehawken, N. J., is an exact duplicate of the preceding. Total free air capacity is 9720 cubic feet per minute. The interior of this plant is seen in Fig. 8.

Pennsylvania Railroad Tunnel Under Bergen Hill. This plant of the John Shield's Construction Company at Hempstead, N. J., comprises one Ingersoll Class " A " compressor, 24- and 24¼- by 30-inch, free air capacity 1570 cubic feet per minute; and four Rand Class " C " 24- and 24- by 30-inch, free air capacity, 6280 cubic feet per minute.

Fig. 8.—Interior of Weehawken Power House for P.R.R. North River Tunnels.

New York and Brooklyn Subway Tunnel, Battery Park, Manhattan. The principal compressor in this plant of the New York Tunnel Company, the contractors, is an Ingersoll-Rand cross-compound Corliss, steam cylinders 24- and 44-inch diameter and 48-inch stroke, with 2-stage piston inlet air cylinders 36¼- and 22¼-inch diameter. The engine has its own air pump and condenser; free air capacity, 3534 cubic feet per minute. This compressor was originally installed at Jerome Park Reservoir, where it was in service about six years.

Besides this, there are two Ingersoll Class "A" compressors, 24- and 24¼- by 30-inch stroke, free air capacity 3140 cubic feet per minute. There are two Heine and two Hogan water tube boilers.

New York and Brooklyn Subway Tunnel, Joralemon and Forman Streets, Brooklyn. This plant, while of considerably larger total capacity than that at Battery Park, has for its largest unit the other Jerome Park Reservoir compressor, an Ingersoll cross-compound Corliss with steam cylinders 24- and 44-inch diameter by 48-inch stroke and single stage, piston inlet air cylinders 24¼-inch diameter. Free air capacity is 3140 cubic feet per minute. This compressor also has its own air pump and condenser. There are also two Ingersoll cross-compound Class "GC" compressors with steam cylinders 22- and 34-inch diameter by 24-inch stroke and single stage piston inlet air cylinders 30¼ and 28¼-inch diameter. The difference in the diameters of these cylinders is due to the exigencies of manufacture when the machines were required at very short notice. These compressors were not required to compress the air to above 25 or 30 pounds; free air capacity, 9184 cubic feet per minute.

There is one Rand Class "B-4" cross-compound compressor with single stage air cylinders, steam cylinders 20- and 32-inch diameter by 30-inch stroke and air cylinders 26-inch diameter, free air capacity, 3686 cubic feet per minute; and two Ingersoll Class "A" straight line piston inlet compressors, 24-inch steam and 24¼-inch air by 30-inch stroke, free air capacity, 3140 cubic feet per minute.

Belmont East River Tunnel Plants. As these were the subject of a previous article (see Chapter XVIII) we here merely enumerate the sizes and capacities of the compressors employed. At Forty-second Street, Manhattan, there is in one power house a Rand cross-compound Corliss 2-stage air compressor with steam cylinders 24- and 40- by 48-inch stroke and air cylinders 39- and 24-inch; free air capacity, 4147 cubic feet per minute; and an Ingersoll cross-compound Corliss 2-stage compressor with steam cylinders 22- and 40- by 42-inch stroke, and air cylinders 38- and 24-inch; free air capacity, 3937 cubic feet per minute. In the other power house there are three Ingersoll cross-compound steam, duplex air Class "H" compressors with steam cylinders 15- and 28- by 16-inch stroke and air cylinders $20\frac{1}{4}$-inch diameter, for a maximum pressure of 50 pounds; free air capacity 6540 cubic feet per minute. There is also an Ingersoll cross-compound steam, 2-stage air, Class "HC" compressor with steam cylinders and stroke as above,

Fig. 9.—Erecting Compressors in Manhattan Power House for the Belmont Tunnels.

but with air cylinders $25\frac{1}{4}$- and $16\frac{1}{4}$-inch diameter, for 100 pounds air pressure; free air capacity 1704 cubic feet per minute. Fig. 9 shows one of those compressors being set up in place before the house was built over it.

On Man-O'-War's Reef there are three duplex Class "J" Ingersoll belted compressors with air cylinders $20\frac{1}{4}$-inch diameter by 18-inch stroke, for 50 pounds pressure; aggregate free air capacity, 6540 cubic feet per minute; one electric belted 2-stage machine for 100 pounds pressure with air cylinders $25\frac{1}{4}$- and $16\frac{1}{4}$-inch diameter by 18-inch stroke; free air capacity, 1704 cubic feet per minute; and two Ingersoll Class "A" straight line compressors, 24-inch diameter steam, $26\frac{1}{4}$-inch diameter air, by 30-inch stroke; free air capacity, 3686 cubic feet per minute. See Fig. 10.

At the Long Island City plant there are two Ingersoll cross-compound steam, 2-stage air Class " H " compressors with steam cylinders 15- and 28- by 16-inch stroke, and air cylinders 25¼ and 16¼, for 100 pounds air pressure; free air capacity, 3408 cubic feet per minute. There are here also two Ingersoll Class "A" compressors 24- and 26¼- by 30-inch stroke, free air capacity, 3686 cubic feet per minute; and one Class " A " compressor 24- and 24¼- by 30-inch stroke, free air capacity, 1570 cubic feet per minute. See Fig. 11.

FIG. 10.—Power House for Belmont Tunnels on Man-o'-War's Reef.

Hudson Companies' North River Tunnels, Morton Street, Manhattan. This pair of tunnels now completed was begun, or one of them, a quarter of a century ago, the work having been stopped by serious accidents and financial difficulties. The final plant here comprised one duplex Rand compressor

22- by 24-inch stroke, free air capacity 2640 cubic feet per minute; one Ingersoll Class "A" 22- and 22¼- by 24-inch stroke, free air capacity, 1320 cubic feet; one Ingersoll 20- and 22¼- by 24-inch stroke, free air capacity, 1320 cubic feet per minute; and an Ingersoll 16- and 16¼- by 18-inch stroke, free air capacity, 698 cubic feet per minute.

Hudson Companies' North River Tunnels, Fifteenth Street, Hoboken, N. J. This plant is located immediately opposite

Fig. 11.—Interior of Long Island City Power House for Belmont Tunnels.

the preceding, working at the other ends of the same tunnels and continuing them westward into the land. There is one compressor here which was sold to the Hudson River Tunnel Company in 1880, and overhauled in 1890, which was still doing good service until the work was finished. It is now rated as an Ingersoll Class "A", 20- and 20¼- by 30-inch stroke, free air capacity 1089 cubic feet per minute. There are also two Ingersoll Class "A" compressors, 22- and 26¼- by 24-inch, free air capacity 2686 cubic feet per minute; and one Ingersoll duplex Class "H" compressor 16- and 20¼- by 16-inch stroke, free air capacity, 2178 cubic feet per minute.

Hudson Companies' North River Tunnels, Near Pennsylvania Station, Jersey City, N. J. The tunnels here being driven are to enter New York City near Cortlandt Street; there is no plant opposite, the tunnels being driven entirely from their western ends. There are here three Ingersoll Class "HC" cross-compound steam, 2-stage air compressors for high pressure air, and three Ingersoll Class "H" cross-compound steam and duplex single-stage air compressors for the low-pressure air. The former are 14- and 28-inch steam and 24¼- and 14¼-inch air by 16-inch stroke, free air capacity 4710 cubic feet per minute; and the latter are of the same steam dimensions with air cylinders 22¼- by 16-inch, free air capacity, 7920 cubic feet per minute.

Hudson Companies' No. 4 Plant, Washington Street, Jersey City, N. J. This plant has been employed upon land tunnels connecting the two preceding. It comprises two Rand Class "B" compressors, cross-compound steam cylinders 18- and 30-inch, and 2-stage air cylinders 26- and 15-inch by 30-inch stroke, free air capacity 3686 cubic feet per minute; and two Rand Class "B" compressors with steam dimensions as above and duplex air cylinders 23-inch diameter by 30-inch stroke, free air capacity 5768 cubic feet per minute.

Summary of Tunnel Plants. The total free air capacity of all the compressors here enumerated is 191,291 cubic feet per minute, which would be represented by a cube with a side of over 57 feet. The total number of compressors is eighty, most of them approaching the largest sizes built. The actual horse-power employed has not been computed on account of the differences in the air pressures, but probably is not less than 40,000. The number of steam cylinders is one hundred and twenty and the number of air cylinders, one hundred and thirty-eight. That these compressors have been kept constantly running, mostly night and day, and generally at speeds which would be considered excessive, is something for the builders, the owners and the operators to be proud of. Whatever delays have occurred, whatever accidents have happened, whatever of the unforeseen has been encountered, the air compressors have been always ready, always efficient and always to be relied upon.

FIG. 12.—One Type of Boiler Used in the New York Tunnel Plants.

It will be seen that the compressed air for this tunnel work is delivered and used at two quite different pressures, requiring two different classes of compressors and separate pipe lines for transmission. The low pressure air for the shield work is generally used at pressures of between 20 and 30 pounds and the compressors are usually guaranteed for a maximum of 50 pounds. The high pressure air for operating the drills is required to be higher than the normal for such work, as the air from them is exhausted against the air pressure in the shield. The air for this service is carried at pressures above 100 pounds up to 140 or 150 pounds, the compression being 2-stage with, of course, efficient intercooling. Many of the installations also include aftercoolers, which are found to contribute to economy of operation, giving drier air and reducing the volume during transmission without any ultimate reduction of volume when the air is used at the end of the line.

The usual conditions of steam economy are insisted upon throughout these plants. Steam is carried at pressures up to 150 pounds, the steam ends of the compressors are generally compounded, and condensing apparatus is usually installed for each entire plant whether the individual units are compounded or not. The automatic regulation of the speeds of the compressors according to the varying demands of the service has been a notable and successful feature.

Much the larger volume of the air compressed has been for the low pressure service to oppose the inrush of water, and passengers on the East River ferries have seen the water actively boiling with the escape of this air, so that most of it may in a way be said to have been lost or wasted. Under the most favorable conditions the use of air in subaqueous tunnels is a very different problem from that of the vertical caisson. In the latter the pressure adjusts itself precisely to that of the surrounding water, the air escaping under the edge when the pressure is at all in excess, and the compressor supplying a caisson has only to make up for the losses in the air lock and to renew the air sufficiently for safe respiration.

When the air pressure at the top of the tunnel is sufficient to balance the pressure of the water and hold it back, the air pressure at the bottom of the tunnel will be five or six pounds too light; and if the pressure is increased to balance the water pressure at the bottom, then it is able to blow off at the top with considerable force, and where the superincumbent material is in a soft or semi-fluid condition the air finds its way through it in all directions. The compressors in this service were constantly worked to their utmost in the struggle with the soft mud waiting to rush in, and an unstable equilibrium only could be maintained at the best.—Frank Richards, in *Compressed Air Magazine*, January, 1908.

APPENDIX B

THE COMPRESSED AIR PLENUM

The remarkable success which engineers have made in driving tunnels under rivers and other important waterways in various parts of the world, has led to a serious consideration of employing similar methods for establishing subaqueous passages beneath straits, bays and even the ocean itself. From the constructional point of view, there is not the slightest doubt of its feasibility, for what has been done so satisfactorily in many cases can be extended to a far greater degree.

At the present time financial reasons would alone seem to prevent the boring of tunnels between Europe and Africa, or Asia and North America, since the expense would be, perhaps, larger than the ultimate advantages to be secured. Furthermore, in the face of the diplomatic relations existing between world powers, such engineering feats appear to be well-nigh impossible. However, apart from this, engineers regard with confidence the proposition of sub-ocean tunneling because the achievements already attained have been due to the development of the compressed air system. At first, when this system was introduced, its possibilities were only conjectural, for its beginnings were small inasmuch as it was used for driving bores, making foundations for bridges and wharves under river beds, and in waterbearing strata generally. But it has developed steadily, until now work is carried on with safety and with certainty, as regards its final result, at depths up to nearly 120 feet below high-water level, involving an air pressure of 40 pounds per square inch above the atmosphere. In fact, in nearly every instance where water is likely to be encountered, compressed air is now adopted, for engineers prefer to use it as a safeguard against any emergency. Whether compressed air can be applied for deep-sea boring is still largely a matter of experiment. Still, the shield system has operated so accurately in all cases with such practical results, that its application to engineering problems of such magnitude as referred to above is highly probable.*

The phenomenal advances in the methods of subaqueous tunneling in the last few years are directly due to the improvements in the means of generating, and of operating with, compressed air.

The use of the plenum method for tunneling, and in sinking caissons, has become general in submarine work. The air, compressed to the required pressure, provides in itself the power to operate the drills, shovels, pumps, jacks and shields, and all other machinery employed in the tunnels, as well as providing the necessary pressure to counterbalance the weight of water and material through which the tunnel is being driven; and at the same time, air that has been used for power is producing a constant ventilation and supply of fresh air to the workmen.

Air, when compressed, is the only medium possessing the qualities which are requisite in the varied conditions and operations of subaqueous tunneling. In the East River tunnels, the average total supply of free air to each heading while under pressure was 3550 cubic feet per minute; this included the compressed air used for all purposes in the headings. In blowouts the maximum loss recorded was 220,000 cubic feet of free air in ten minutes. It is probable that 30 to 40 per cent of this loss occurred in the first forty-five seconds, the remaining loss being gradual till the supply was increased to the lowered pressure.

The silt pressure was lower than the hydrostatic head at the crown, but if it became necessary to make an excavation ahead of the shield, the air pressure required was about equal to the weight of the overlying material, namely, the water and silt. The silt weighed from 97 to 106 pounds per cubic foot, averaged 100 pounds per cubic foot, and acted like a fluid.

* From *Compressed Air Magazine*, June, 1907.

The records of the air supply proved beyond doubt that any supply per man beyond 2000 cubic feet had no beneficial effect upon health; on two occasions for two consecutive weeks it ran as low as 1000 cubic feet without increasing the number of cases of bends.

The amount of CO_2 in the air was measured daily. The average ranged between 0.8 and 1.5 parts per 1000 parts. In exceptional cases it fell as low as 0.3, and rose to 4.0. The temperature usually ranged from 55 to 60 degrees Fahrenheit, which was the temperature of the surrounding silt; when grouting extensively in the long sections in rock, it varied from 85 to 110 degrees Fahrenheit. The pressure of air varied from 17 to 37 pounds. To enable the engine room force to keep a watch on the air conditions in the tunnel, a half-inch air line connected the working chambers with recording gages in the engine room. During the greater portion of the work in soft ground, a pressure was maintained which would about balance the hydrostatic head at the axis of the tunnel. The required pressure varied from 30 to 34 pounds above that of the atmosphere. In the event of a blow, the pressure usually dropped from 2 to 8 pounds and it generally took some hours to restore the original pressure.

The rules observed for the prevention of caisson disease were, that no workman was allowed to enter the air chamber without having undergone a physical examination, sound physique being an essential requirement. The men were required not to enter the air with an empty stomach, to wear warm clothing on coming out, and to drink hot coffee. The time worked in the air chamber was limited to eight hours with half an hour for lunch, up to 32 pounds gage pressure; and two spells of three hours each with three hours' rest between, for pressures from 32 to 42 pounds; and two spells of two hours each for pressures greater than 42 pounds, with four hours' rest between.

Medical air locks were installed, well warmed dressing rooms provided for the workmen, and covered gangways for access to the shafts. Practically no cases of bends occurred until the air pressure reached 29 pounds, when, within a few days of each other, two men died.

At 30 pounds pressure, it became customary to allow one-half minute per pound of air pressure in decompression. The lengthening of the decompression period to fifteen minutes reduced the number of cases of bends, and no doubt prevented

FIG. 1.—Interior of Medical Air Lock.

many fatal ones; but they still occurred. The percentage of cases in air pressures of 31½ pounds for 8-hour shifts was no greater than the percentage in 32½ pounds for two 3-hour shifts. It was, if anything, less for the longer shift.

At atmospheric pressure, the percentage of carbon dioxide in the alveolar or expired air is 5.6 per cent and at a pressure of 2 atmospheres absolute, this is reduced to 2.8 per cent.

So the question of the percentage of carbon dioxide in the air of the working chamber is not important unless it approaches the percentage in the air cells of the lungs. To illustrate this, if the air-chamber is under an air pressure of 30 pounds, or 3 atmospheres absolute, the percentage of carbon dioxide in the air cells is 5.6 divided by 3, or 1.86 per cent; and if the percentage of carbon dioxide in the air chamber does not exceed 1 per cent, no ill effects will arise. This is ten times as much as generally specified, namely one part in 1000, and greatly reduces the amount of compressed air necessary per man per hour, which can be calculated approximately from the following formula:

$$\text{Cubic feet per man per hour} = \frac{\text{80 cubic feet}}{\text{percentage } CO_2 \text{ permitted}}.$$

Thus, if 0.04 per cent is the CO_2 in the atmosphere, and the percentage in the tunnel is allowed to go up to 0.10 per cent, the air required per man per hour equals $\frac{80}{0.06} = 1333$ cubic feet.

The death rate due to caisson disease was comparatively small, an average of 19/100 of one per cent for the whole of the compressed air work. The only recognized cure for caisson disease is recompression in a medical air lock, followed by slow decompression. This makes evident the advantage of slow decompression; and when it is at all possible, in future works, regulated decompression will in all probability be adopted.

From "Caisson Disease and Its Prevention," by Henry Japp, M. American Society C.E., Proceedings American Society C.E., December, 1909, where the subject is treated at length.

APPENDIX C

THE USE OF COMPRESSED AIR IN TUNNELING

SINCE the first recorded experiments in air compression by Hero of Alexandria, and the invention of the air pump in 1650 by Otto Von Guericke, the most decided advance in the principles of air compression are described in the application for a patent in 1829 by William Mann, as follows: "The condensing pumps used in compressing the air I make of different capacities, according to the density of the fluid to be compressed—those used to compress the higher densities being proportionally smaller than those previously used to compress it at the first or lower densities," etc. This was the precursor of the present system of stage compression.

In 1847 an English patent was granted to Van Rathen for the process of cooling the air by water in the cylinder, or by surrounding the vessel with cold water. He also describes a reservoir for storing air, a refrigerator for cooling the air after its compression, and a mode of heating the air to give it greater tension after it is compressed.

In 1853, Piatti submitted several projects to the Italian ministry relative to the construction of the Mt. Cenis tunnels, which treated especially of the employment of water power to compress air for a motor for rock drills in driving the tunnels and for running trains through the tunnel both during and after its construction. Previous to this, in 1852, Colladon of Geneva filed his petition for a patent in Italy for the use of compressed air in running machine drills in a tunnel. To Colladon is said to be due the essential features of the compressor systems of the Mt. Cenis and St. Gothard tunnels. The compressor systems of Mt. Cenis were established, and the drills put to work, during 1861. It is stated that Colladon,

Section of Ingersoll-Rand Class "AA-2" Two-stage Steam-driven Straight Line Air Compressor.

as far back as 1828, proposed to Brunnel to use compressed air to keep the water out of the first Thames tunnel.

In America, air compressors were first applied for purposes of rock drilling at the Hoosac tunnel. The first compressor used at the Hoosac tunnel consisted of four horizontal air cylinders set at right angles, run by a water turbine of 120 h.p. and driven directly from a crank on the upper end of the shaft of the turbine. Of this compressor, Mr. Thomas Doane, Chief Engineer, says in his report for 1866: "The air compressor of four horizontal cylinders, 13 by 20 inches each,

Ingersoll-Rand Class "NF-1" Single-stage Steam-driven Air Compressor.

referred to in my former report as about ready for use at the east end, has been at work night and day without cessation, except on Sundays, since March. It was intended to compress air to 60 pounds per square inch, and has run up as high as 85 pounds; but as the drilling machines require air at only 30 pounds pressure it has been run generally at that pressure. It was intended for a speed of 120 r.p.m., but as it can easily supply all our drilling machines, nine having been the highest number, at a speed of 70 revolutions, it has not usually been run faster. This compressor, making 70 revolutions, will furnish 148.01 cubic feet of air per minute, at a pressure of 42 pounds."

In selecting an air compressor, the conditions under which

it is to operate are to be carefully considered, as it is impossible to design a single compressor which will fit all conditions. The most important factors are: Pressure desired; the character of apparatus to be operated; the cost of fuel; allowable space; and quantity of air required. Generally speaking, economy has not been the most important consideration until recently.

The three classes into which reciprocating apparatus for the production of compressed air naturally fall, and considerations of convenience, first cost and economy of operation, have

Ingersoll-Rand Class "O" Duplex Double Cross-compound Duplex Air Compressor.

resulted in the development of certain distinct types of compressors, which may be classed under the general heading of self-contained steam actuated compressors, and those actuated by some external means.

Both classes may be simple, duplex or multi-compression machines. Experience, however, has sifted out the best forms, which are as follows:

(1) Straight Line; that is, steam and air cylinders in one line, mounted on a continuous girder frame. A self-contained, reliable type; a great user of steam,

but a most satisfactory type when fuel is inexpensive and where a large amount of air is not needed; usually single-stage compressors, but often built in two or three stages.

(2) Duplex; usually built with two parallel engines, connected by 90-degree cranks to a single fly-wheel shaft, with air cylinders behind each steam cylinder. Both steam and both air cylinders are of the same diameter. This type makes no great pretense at economy, but finds an extensive field in locations where fuel is not high and where simplicity and small first cost are important, and where considerable air, at low pressures only, is desired.

(3) Compound; of the same general character as the duplex except that either or both air and steam cylinders are compounded. In some cases the engine may be run condensing. This is, however, hardly necessary except for very large sizes, where it is far more desirable to use the large class of Corliss type.

(4) Corliss type; as implied in the name, this class includes compressors in which the engine portion employs the well-known Corliss valve motion. Such compressors, with few exceptions, are of the horizontal type, the air cylinder or cylinders, as the case may be, being placed tandem to the steam cylinders. They are employed where the volume of air desired and the fuel conditions demand the most economical form of engine. They are usually compounded, both for steam and air, and generally run condensing.

As air is commonly used under the same conditions and with the same machinery that uses steam, the true way of comparing the efficiency of a compressor would be to compare the volume of cold compressed air that the compressor will furnish with the volume of steam the compressor uses at the same pressure, to furnish the amount of air. On this basis, the efficiency of a straight line compressor, non-compound, would be about 60 per cent.; a duplex Corliss compressor with compound condensing steam and compound air cylinders with intercooler, about 80 or 90 per cent. in cold air, of the amount of steam used.

If the properties of cold air and steam are compared, the comparison is all in favor of air. The loss due to condensation in an exposed steam pipe line often amounts to from 15 to 30 per cent. This loss alone would make the use of air more economical.

Air pipe lines have in different places been laid for distances of fifteen miles or more, but average pipe lines in tunnels and around quarries run from 1000 to 10,000 feet.

Ingersoll-Rand Class "CH" Corliss Steam Double Cross-compound Duplex Air Compressor.

As a practical example of what would be required if 1000 cubic feet of free air compressed per minute to 80 pounds pressure were to be carried a distance of 5000 feet, a 5-inch pipe line would show a loss of pressure of about 6 pounds, and a 6-inch pipe line about 2½ pounds, all elbows in the pipe line increasing the friction. The difference in the diameter of the pipes accounts for the difference in loss of pressure.

The friction loss may be considered for ordinary purposes as being proportional to the length of pipe and to the square of the velocity of the air; where the volume passing through a pipe is doubled, the friction will be about four times as great.

Heating the air by means of a reheater increases the volume from 35 to 50 per cent; and this increase in volume costs only about one-sixth in cost of coal in reheating, as compared with the cost of coal in compressing.

When a compound condensing compressor with compound air cylinders, giving 90 per cent. in air of the volume of steam used, has the air reheated before use, it becomes evident how an

Ingersoll-Rand "Imperial X" Duplex Steam-driven Air Compressor.

efficiency 20 per cent greater than if steam were used direct may be obtained, in addition to the many advantages and conveniences in the use of air.

From "Tunneling, Explosive Compounds and Rock Drills," by Henry S. Drinker, J. J. Swann in the *Sibley Journal*, Wm. Prellwitz in *Compressed Air Information.*

APPENDIX D

SPECIAL TYPES OF AIR COMPRESSORS

Water Impulse Compressors. When water power is available at, or within several miles of, a plant where compressed air is required, the energy of the water may be employed to convert free air into compressed air at any desired pressure, and when piped to the works may be used for pumping, hoisting, drilling, and many other purposes, with considerable success and economy.

Impulse wheels range in efficiency from 85 to 90 per cent. and insure the production of compressed air energy at a cost, per unit of power, lower than by any other method.

The sizes of water wheels used depend, of course, upon the requirements of each separate case, as to the flow and head of water. Water-impulse compressors may be either of the simple straight line or duplex types. The straight line form is employed when the demand for air is light; this machine has the advantage of the straight line construction in that it takes up the stresses and strains in direct lines. The duplex machine is largely of service where the demand for air is considerable, and it has the advantage of relieving strains, by dividing the work equally between the cylinders; this machine is made with either simple or compound air cylinders, and when compounded a suitable intercooler is employed to remove the heat of compression, as the air passes from the low to the high pressure cylinders.

"Imperial XE" Air Compressor. The illustration on page 219 shows an Ingersoll-Rand "Imperial XE" direct-connected cross-compound 2-stage electrically driven air compressor, with a self-starting synchronous motor on the shaft. This is one of the most recent developments in high-duty compressor design, the direct motor drive having all the advantages, as to simplicity, compactness and high efficiency, which have long been recognized in direct-connected engine driven electric generator units.

The features of the " Imperial XE " type are: " Imperial Corliss " air inlet valves on both cylinders and " Imperial Direct Lift " air discharge valves; wholly enclosed, dust-

Ingersoll-Rand Class " PB " Direct-water-wheel-driven Duplex Air Compressor.

proof construction; flood lubrication of all principal bearings from the main crank basins, the flow of oil being proportional to the speed of the machine and all oil being returned to the system; massive construction and large bearings. The direct motor driven compressor unit of this type, and of the same company's " PE " type, return the highest economy in power driven compressors. Methods of regulation automatically proportion power to load under all variations.

The Taylor Hydraulic Air Compressor at Cobalt, Ontario. What is undoubtedly the largest single unit air compressor in the world is being constructed on the Montreal River at Ragged Chutes, about nine miles south of Cobalt, Ontario, Can. This plant operates on the now well-known Taylor system, where the air is compressed by the direct action of falling water. The following account may be accepted as

Ingersoll-Rand "Imperial XE" Duplex Direct-connected Electric-driven Air Compressor.

authoritative in every particular, having been prepared by Mr. C. H. Taylor for "Mines and Minerals," from whose pages it is here reproduced, somewhat abridged and rearranged.

The Cobalt Hydraulic Power Company, Ltd., is a commercial organization formed for the purpose of selling compressed air to the various Cobalt mines. At Ragged Chutes there is a drop in the river of 54 feet within less than a quarter of a mile. This entire head is to be utilized, furnishing 5500 h.p. and compressing 40,000 cubic feet of free air per minute to a gage pressure of 120 pounds, which is automatically reduced to, and maintained at, 100 pounds when delivered to the various mines. The air will be transmitted through nine miles of 20-inch pipe, from the end of which there are two 12-inch branch pipe lines. About seven miles from the compressor there is another 12-inch branch, so that the total length of piping, 20-, 12-, 6- and 3-inch, will be about twenty-one miles.

In order to prove that this power would be a great saving over the present cost for compressed air, about six months were spent in making exhaustive tests at a number of the larger mines, and the reports were accepted in every case by the managers. The tests showed that mines could save from one-half to one-third by buying their compressed air rather than producing it, and at the same time receive the air at a constant pressure. In addition to the advantages mentioned, it is to be understood that the air, being isothermally compressed, is, of course, as dry as possible, thus eliminating the troubles arising from freezing; further, there being no oil used in compression, the compressed air is practically odorless and ventilates the working faces, which is a distinct advantage. The various Cobalt mines will be piped independently of each other and the air will be sold by meter measurement or by the drill unit as a basis. If sold by meter, a rate of twenty-five cents per 1000 cubic feet of compressed air per minute will be charged, the air pressure being 100 pounds per square inch. The company will furnish in this case an automatic reducing valve, meter, and limit valve. When air is sold on the flat rate, the charge will be based on one drill per shift, the charge, however, decreasing with an increasing number of drills. In this case, the power company will supply the reducing and limit valves, no meter being needed.

Great care has been taken in the installation of the pipe lines, to prevent leaky joints and strains on the pipe. In the 20-inch and 12-inch diameter pipe lines, balanced expansion joints have been placed at half-mile intervals, and half-way between each two expansion joints the pipes are anchored in massive concrete piers to prevent their creeping.

After passing the gates the water flows through two 16-foot diameter intake heads, one of which is shown in Fig. 1 at *a*. In each of these heads there are sixty-six 14-inch diameter pipes *b* set in a steel disk *c*. Below the pipes, the heads gradually diminish in diameter until they become 8 feet $4\frac{3}{4}$ inches, and from this point they are 15 feet long. In this telescopic form the heads connect with the

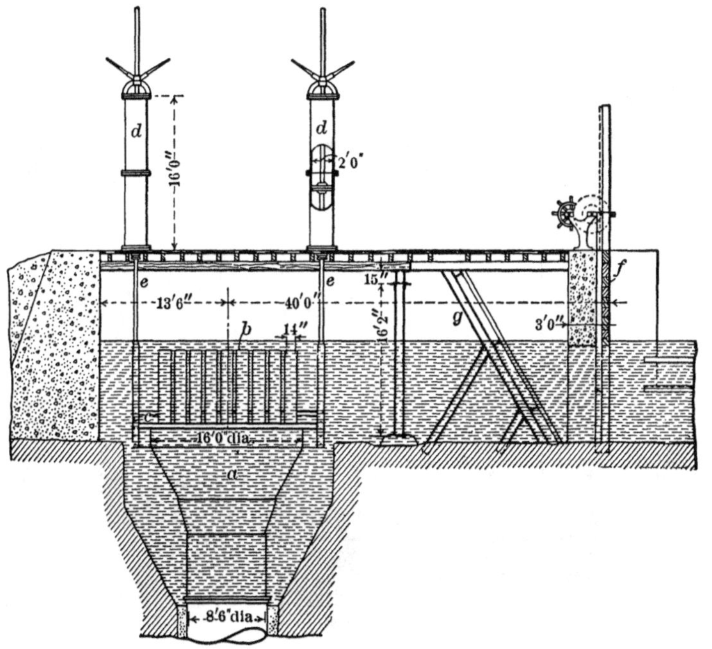

Fig. 1.

intake shafts, which are 8 feet 6 inches in diameter and 345 feet deep, with the orifice of the head at the surface of the water. This arrangement permits the heads to be raised or lowered, to conform to the level of the water in the forebay, or the heads may be raised above the level of the water by air lifts *d*, thus cutting off the supply completely. The two air-lift cylinders *d* act as governors, automatically raising and lowering the heads which are suspended from them by the hangers *e*, thereby regulating the flow of water into the intake pipes *b*, according to the demand. The head-pieces were especially designed to meet conditions due to extremely low temperatures. The gate *f* is raised by rack and pinion, and there is the usual rack *g* to prevent floating material from entering the head-pipes.

The water, with the entrained air, flows through the heads with a descending velocity of from 15 to 19 feet per second,

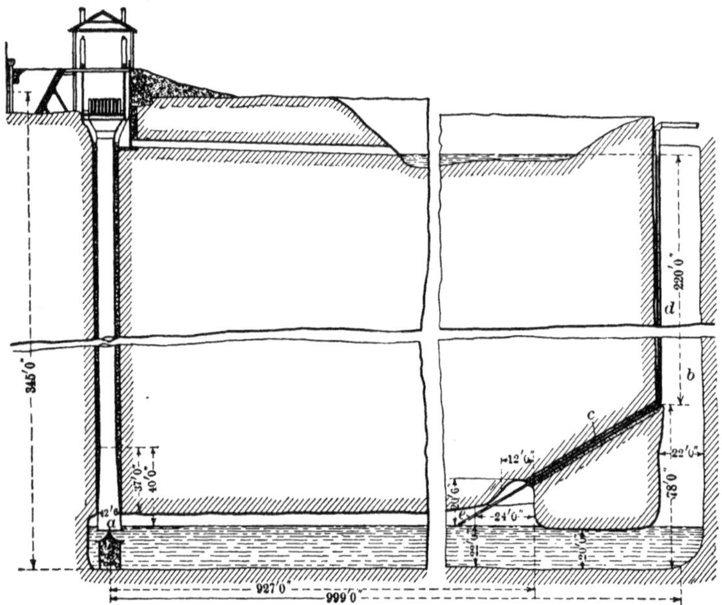

FIG. 2

gradually diminishing in the velocity of fall, owing to the compression of the volume of air; finally there is a further reduction in velocity owing to the enlarged section of the last 40 feet of fall, shown in Fig. 2. By the time the water reaches and strikes the steel-capped concrete diverting cones *a*, its velocity is so diminished by the baffle from the compressed air that there is little shock.

The cones *a* are for the purpose of spreading the flow of air and water, thereby bringing the air nearer to the top of the tunnel. The air being lighter than the water, it rises to the surface of the water under a pressure of 120 pounds per square inch. The tunnel was made 20 feet wide, 26 feet high, and 1000 feet long, the latter for the purpose of utilizing the total head of the stream, although this length was not necessary in order to give the air time to leave the water before the latter started up the outlet shaft *b*. As the velocity of the water in the tunnel is about 3 feet per second, practically all the air will leave the water in the first 300 feet. The last 75 feet of the tunnel has the height reduced to 16 feet.

The pressure given to the air is due to the height of the body of the water in the outlet shaft, which, in this case, is 298 feet deep and 22 feet in diameter. The water flows along the tunnel and up the outlet to the river, the difference in elevation between the mouth of the intake and the discharge tunnels being 47 feet. Near the outlet end of the tunnel its height is increased to 42 feet, and at this place two pipes are carried through the 30-degree riser *c* to the uptake shaft. One pipe *d*, 24 inches in diameter, carries the compressed air to the surface, where it is connected with the 20-inch main air pipe line. The other pipe *e* is 12 inches in diameter and has its end submerged at a safe distance above the roof of the outlet portion of the tunnel, to act as a blow-off in case the air in the tunnel should acquire such pressure as to force the water below the level of the tunnel outlet. If the air were allowed to escape up the outlet it would lighten the column of water in that shaft, and the air pressure would not be constant. The blow-off pipe ends at the upper level of the water in the outlet shaft, its end remaining open to the atmosphere. When the volume of air is greater than the demand, the air accumulates in the upper part of the tunnel, forcing the water down and exposing the lower end of the blow-off pipe *e* to the compressed air, thus allowing a portion of the water in this pipe to drop back, thereby decreasing the weight of the remaining water in this pipe to less than the pressure of the air. The equilibrium is now overcome and the water in the pipe is driven upward to the surface, where a most spectacular sight is witnessed, as the body of water is shot out by the air sometimes to a height of 500 feet. The blow-off continues until the pressure of the air in the tunnel is sufficiently reduced to again submerge the end of the pipe. Water now rises until an equilibrium is established between the air and the water pressure in the tunnel. The air pipe and the blow-off pipe are packed in concrete the entire length of the 30-degree riser, in order to seal them in and prevent any escape of air up the outlet shaft. Thus these arrangements permit the delivery of a large body of air at a constant pressure at all times. *Compressed Air Magazine*, June, 1910.

Lack of Oxygen in Hydraulic Air at Cobalt. When the air from the hydraulic air compressing plant at Ragged Chutes, Cobalt district, Ontario, was first turned on it was found that it was difficult to burn candles in the mines where it was used. It was claimed that this was due to the absorption of oxygen by the asphalt with which the inside of the pipes was coated, and that this effect would soon pass off. It was soon found, however, that hydraulic air contains an appreciably less percentage of oxygen than ordinary air, and analysis demonstrated that it contained only 17.7 per cent oxygen, which is 3 per cent lower than ordinary air. This is due to the oxygen going into solution in the water during compression, when a pressure of 130 to 135 pounds per square inch is maintained. The lack of oxygen does not apparently trouble the miners, but besides the difficulty experienced in keeping lights, the effect of the gases from exploded dynamite is more serious than was found to be the case with air compressed by machinery. *Engineering and Mining Journal. Compressed Air Magazine*, August, 1910.

Cost of Hydraulic Air Compression. The Taylor system of air compression, adapted to the development of waterfalls of moderate height and copious volume, has elicited much favorable comment, and where it has been installed it has been completely successful so far as the actual compressing of the air is concerned, but the cost which seems inevitable in its installation is not so familiarly known. The following account of one plant is given by Mr. Geo. C. McFarlane in *Mining and Scientific Press*.

"The most recent installation is a 5000 h.p. plant now

about completed at the Ragged Chutes of the Montreal River, nine miles south of Cobalt, Ontario. Work has been in progress on this installation for three years and for the past year a force of 200 or 300 men has been employed. The Montreal River has here, in about 1000 feet, a drop of 28 feet. The power people built a concrete jetty into the middle of the river and, to protect the opposite bank from cutting, built a concrete wall in a trench a few feet back and parallel with the bank. During the high water this summer (1909) the river current, thrown sideways by the jetty, gouged into the opposite bank as far as the concrete wall and partly undermined it, which illustrates one way of how not to attempt to raise the level of a swift river.

"Just below the jetty, at the head of the rapids, are two shafts, steel-lined, 16 feet in diameter and 360 feet deep. A 20- by 26-foot tunnel, 1000 feet long, connects these shafts with the uprise shaft at the foot of the rapids. The air is compressed to 140 pounds and is conducted to Cobalt by a 20-inch pipe. The pipe was made in 40-foot lengths, with welded flanges and sliding expansion joints set in concrete pits every half mile. Aside from the transmission pipe lines I would estimate the cost of the plant at the chutes as not far from $1,000,000. This makes the cost per horse-power for installation about $200.00 which does not compare favorably with the cost of an ordinary air plant. I know of two small plants that were installed for less than $90.00 per horse-power, including flume and pipe line, as well as wheel and compressor." *Compressed Air Magazine*, April, 1910.

APPENDIX E

STRAIGHT LINE AND DUPLEX COMPOUND AIR COMPRESSORS

THERE is nothing new about the higher expansion process, as applied to marine engines, pumping plants and general power service. But while, in the engineering world, general practice has settled down to a true appreciation of the practical value of correct steam compounding, there still is much to be said on this subject in its relation to the economical compression of air and gas.

Marine engines are almost invariably compound or triple expansion. Such engines work under high pressure, operate condensing, and run under a constant load. Compound steam cylinders are also common on pumps, even when run non-condensing, and with ordinary steam pressures. But here again is the feature of constant load. Steam engines for general power purposes are usually compounded if the units are large and condensing is practicable, but in small and medium sized units it seems generally understood that, unless pressure is high or condensation easily available, compounding is of doubtful value because of the great load variations.

In the case of the air compressor, the conditions approach those of the first two instances cited, but differ radically from the latter instance. These conditions are such as to make the compounding of steam cylinders desirable in every sense of the word, even where steam pressures are only moderate and condensation not always practicable. The discussion following will make this point more clear and may throw a new light on the subject of compressor economy to those not intimately familiar with compressor practice.

The advantages of compounding in steam engine practice everywhere are so familiar as to require not even a repetition here, but its special value in air compressing practice seems not to be fully appreciated. In view of the number of steam driven compressors in use which are neither compounded nor condensing, it seems that it is not generally understood that, while a saving of 10 to 15 per cent of the power cost is possible at the air end of the compressor by compounding, a saving of about double that percentage in fuel cost, 20 to 30 per cent, is easily possible by compounding the steam end of the same machine. If compound compression is economically practical, why neglect a saving twice as great possible by compound steam expansion?

This neglect is especially remarkable in view of the fact that the air compressor embodies load conditions which make the compounding and condensing of steam cylinders even more economically desirable than in general steam engine practice. Compound steam driven air compressors can show better results than compound stationary engines for power purposes, and for a very simple reason. To get all the economy possible from the steam, it must be admitted to the first cylinder in just such quantity that when it is finally expanded into the low pressure cylinder, its pressure there shall be such as to avoid excessive expansion and consequent heavy condensation losses. This means, of course, the admission of the same quantity of steam per stroke, for each stroke, implying a cut-off constantly fixed very close to the right point. This is entirely impossible with the stationary engine, where the constant speed under varying load must be maintained by a constantly changing cut-off, this cut-off being automatically controlled by the governor, and necessarily having a wide range to meet load conditions. There can be only one best point of cut-off, and departures from that necessarily impair the ultimate economy.

In the case of the air compressor the load is constant per stroke; for the same delivery pressure must be maintained, and the cylinders can be so proportioned and the cut-off so set as to secure and maintain the best results. The governing variations of the steam driven compressor are as to speed only, and, with air pressure constant, the changes in speed are made either by a very slight change of cut-off or with a throttling governor. In the latter case the slight "wire drawing" is about offset by the resultant superheating of the steam. As a result of these conditions the compound compressor can be made to work close to its best economy at all times.

The steam pressure used has an important bearing upon the ultimate economy. Within practical limits, the higher the pressure, the better the results. Gage pressures of 125 to 150 pounds are now quite common in new installations; but in air compressor practice, steam compounding is advantageous with steam at 80 pounds condensing, or 90 pounds non-condensing, though this may not be at all true in general power practice. When, as is often the case where compressors are used, water is costly, the smaller amount required by the compound is an argument for it; and the ultimate cost of the arrangement is also largely offset by the reduced cost of boiler installation and operation, due to the lower steam consumption.

It is unnecessary at this point to enter into a discussion of the phenomena of the application of power to resistance in compressor work. It will be enough to mention and to draw briefly the distinction between the two standard types of air compressors, designated as the straight line and duplex. In the former, steam and air cylinders, whether simple or compounded, are arranged in a straight line, and power is applied to resistance through the medium of one long piston rod. In the duplex machine there are two elements set side by side, each made up of a steam and an air cylinder, and each element in effect a straight line machine. However, the cranks of these two sections are set at an angle of 90 degrees, or one-fourth part of a circle, on the shaft. The primary object of this quartering crank arrangement is to secure a more uniform rotation effect, and to improve the regulation qualities of the machine by making it easier to run at slow speeds through the mutual assistance of the two sides. The straight line compressor may have two, three or four cylinders, but they must all be arranged in a straight line or "tandem" to one another. The duplex compressor must have four cylinders.

It is an interesting thing that when four cylinders are adopted in a duplex, to secure a more uniform rotation effect and to make it possible to keep running at the lowest speeds, the compounding of the cylinders helps to promote the original purpose of the duplex arrangement. At the steam end, because of the higher terminal pressure, the variation in working pressure is less. The result is that the effective pressure for the stroke is more uniform and continuous, and the rotation effect produced from the beginning to the end shows less difference than when the steam is used in a single cylinder. The difference of pressures in the low pressure cylinder is less for the same reason.

Aside from this reduction in range of cylinder pressures, the differences in temperatures are a powerful element in economy. These two features will be more clearly understood by a brief consideration of a specific case.

Assume that the initial steam pressure is 145 pounds gage, or 160 pounds absolute, and that a condenser gives a terminal cylinder pressure of, say, 10 pounds absolute. Ignoring for the sake of clearness the effects of clearance, condensation, etc., there are seen to be sixteen expansions of the steam. In compound steam cylinders, properly proportioned, this means four expansions in each cylinder. In the high pressure cylinder, the initial steam pressure will be 160 pounds and the terminal 40 pounds; the initial temperature will be 363 degrees and the terminal 267 degrees Fahrenheit. The difference in pressure is thus 120 pounds and in temperature 96 degrees. In the low pressure cylinder, initial and terminal pressures will be 40 and 10 pounds, respectively, corresponding to temperatures of 267 and 193 degrees Fahrenheit. The difference in pressures is here 30 pounds and in temperatures 74 degrees.

If this expansion had been applied in a single cylinder, the range of pressures would have been 150 pounds and of temperatures 170 degrees Fahrenheit. Evidently the use of compound steam cylinders in this case reduces, by approximately one-half, the cooling effect to which cylinder walls, ports, valves, etc., were subjected by the drop in temperature through expansion. The steam consumption in the former case would have been correspondingly less, and the effect of temperatures on steam economy is apparent. If a condenser had not been used, the range of pressures and temperatures would not have been so great, but, relatively, as between compound and simple cylinders, the same comparison would hold.

Looking now at the air end, the phenomena and advantages of compound air compression are so well understood as to need no extended discussion here. It will be enough to emphasize the fact that in the air cylinders inversely the same things are true of pressures and temperatures as have already been noted in connection with the steam cylinders. The result is a reduction in the differences of temperatures and pressures in the air end, all tending toward an improved operation. The cutting down and transferring of the excessive uncompensated pressures in the cylinders from the extreme ends of the stroke, and their more uniform redistribution secured by this process of double compounding, reduce the terminal and maximum stresses upon the bearings about 45 per cent., noticeably improving running conditions, making the lubrication easy and more effective, reducing wear, and giving greater durability, while still dispensing with the necessity for close attention.

Straight line compressors have been made with tandem 2-stage air compressing cylinders, and even also with tandem high and low pressure steam cylinders; but these arrangements have greatly complicated the machine, have increased its relative cost for the work it does, have made all the parts more inaccessible than before for adjustment, repair or replacement, and after all, have left the machine, in its actual running, defective in its characteristic inability to run at slow speed, and to get the expected results at any speed.

In the duplex machine, as compared to the simple straight line type, while there is a simplification by a reduction of the number of parts as regards fly-wheel, crank shaft and connecting rods, there are four cylinders in place of two. But here is where one of the most important of the advantages of the duplex machine is found. It happens that this very arrangement at once provides the possibilities for the best economy both in the development of the power from the steam and in the application of the power to the compression of the air, simply by virtue of its four cylinders. To use steam with the best economy, in this line of service, high steam pressure, compound steam cylinders, and a condenser should be used. These conditions, except the latter, may be provided for in new installations; the latter depends upon the water available. To compress the air to the usual pressures and with the least expenditure of power, compound air cylinders with an efficient intercooler between must also be provided. An economical air compressor of the present day, cannot, therefore, have less than two steam and two air cylinders; and if the duplex machine thus insists upon four cylinders, it insists only upon one of the most important conditions of practical economy in air compression. If it insists on a larger floor space, it distributes itself so well as to fully offset this factor by its better " get-at-ableness."

The duplex compressor makes possible the compounding of the cylinders either at the air or steam end, or both, without additional complication. The cylinders are there, and in the precise relative conditions most suitable for compounding. Duplex compressors may be, and are, actually made either duplex steam and duplex air, duplex steam and compound air, compound steam and compound air, or compound steam and duplex air. The third arrangement is, of course, the ideal combination for satisfactory and economical air compression, when steam and air pressures are not too low. The location of the cylinders and other parts relative to each other is precisely that most convenient for locating and connecting steam receivers, air intercoolers, aftercoolers, and other appurtenances. The attitude of the duplex machine is to invite, to make easy, and to promote the best practice in air compression. The attitude of the straight line machine, on the other hand, is just as distinctly to make difficult, and in some details, impossible, the same advanced and most approved practice.

It is really a striking array of advantageous features which can be brought out in favor of the duplex type of air compressor. The following may be recalled among them: Greater economy in steam consumption; gains by compounding both steam and air cylinders; the maintenance of a more uniform air pressure; the delivery of dry air; automatic control and efficient lubrication; reduced leakage by the partial balancing of pressures; low friction of valves and pistons; sustained adjustment and tightness of vital parts. These may easily result in a saving of 30 to 40 per cent over the simple straight line machine, and of 15 to 20 per cent over the double-compound straight line. Then the reliability and perfect accessibility of every part, and the saving in supervision and maintenance, are also to be considered in its favor. For the straight line it can be said that the first cost is perhaps less, the foundations required are less expensive, and the space occupied is small. The saving in operating the duplex machine will really cover the difference in these costs many times over and, before long, entirely pay for the machine.

Figures will actually show that the difference in the first cost of the machine and its installation is returned in a few months without any but the ordinary conditions as to fuel and labor costs.

Take an average case in which the power consumption is but 500 cubic feet of free air per minute, compressed at sea level to 90 pounds gage. In a single stage compressor this will require 94 indicated horse-power; in a 2-stage machine, 81 indicated horse-power. A straight line compressor of this size is usually operated with a simple steam cylinder; and while such machines are usually equipped with Meyer gear permitting economical cut-off, yet the practical running conditions of a straight line are such that not one out of a hundred are, in actual service, run at less than five-eighth to three-quarter cut-off. This is a fact of experience and its result is that straight line machines of this size take, in every-day service, from 40 to 50 pounds of steam per horse-power hour, and every well-informed engineer knows that they will require on an average of 45 pounds of steam or water per horse-power hour. The duplex, having no "dead center," can be run conveniently at short cut-offs; and in ordinary compressor service, small units and moderate steam pressures, duplex compound steam cylinders will require about 28 pounds of steam per horse-power hour, non-condensing.

These relative figures are as fair to one as to the other; not the best that can be done, but what can actually be expected under ordinary conditions for a term of years.

An average boiler plant will not do better than 7 pounds of water evaporated per pound of coal burned. A boiler horse-power is rated as 30 pounds of steam evaporated per hour. These are average figures, and comparisons based on them are safe and fair to all.

Results in the present case may be tabulated thus:

Simple air and simple steam: 94 indicated horse-power; multiplied by 45, equals 4230 pounds of steam per hour; divided by 30, equals 141 boiler horse-power.

Two-stage air and simple steam: 81 indicated horse-power; multiplied by 45, equals 3645 pounds of steam per hour; divided by 30, equals 122 boiler horse-power.

Duplex 2-stage air and compound steam: 81 indicated horse-power; multiplied by 28, equals 2268 pounds steam per hour; divided by 30, equals 76 boiler horse-power.

Saving by compounding air end alone (straight line or duplex): 13 indicated horse-power; 585 pounds of steam per hour, 19 boiler horse-power.

Saving by compounding steam end alone (duplex cross-compound steam simple air): 1377 pounds of steam per hour; 46 boiler horse-power.

Saving by compounding steam and air (duplex double-cross-compound only): 13 indicated horse-power; 1962 pounds of steam per hour; 65 boiler horse-power.

These figures alone are enough to prove the case, but the buyer of machinery thinks in dollars and cents rather than in horse-power. He is, to be sure, interested in knowing that the duplex compound is " more economical of power," but he knows that " it costs more " than the straight line; and even a full knowledge of the fact that the straight line " double-compound " is mechanically inferior to the duplex or " double-cross-compound " may not overcome his financial scruples.

But a complete compressor plant includes boilers and auxiliaries as well as the compressor; and boilers cost money, besides having a voracious appetite for coal. It has been demonstrated that a " double-compound " straight line is not a satisfactory machine; so further comparisons, reduced to money values, may be based on a simple steam 2-stage straight line and a " double-compound " of duplex type.

To use this straight line machine, 46 additional boiler horse-power, with larger piping, auxiliaries, etc., must be purchased. The buyer, referring to his catalogue table, will see 81 h.p. noted, but will not notice that this is indicated horse-power, and at a rating of only 30/45, or two-thirds of the boiler horse-power required. So he will probably buy a 90 h.p. boiler, force it up to 122 h.p., and then wonder why it fires so hard. This same inference made in buying a " double-compound " would have resulted in getting a good, easy-firing boiler, probably never loaded to its full capacity. The simple steam straight line, therefore, must be charged up with the cost of 46 additional boiler horse-power, with necessary auxiliaries. If their price installed is put at the moderate figure of $10.00 per horse-power, not including cost of auxiliaries and larger piping, there is a total of $460.00, which, credited to the first cost of the duplex double-compound, does not make the latter look so dear after all. In this particular size of compressor it will, probably, more than cover the difference in price of the two types. These are installation charges appearing in the items of " first cost."

Looking now at the operating charges, it will be noted that 1377 pounds less water per hour is required by the duplex compound. This is 1650 gallons per 10-hour day. In some places water charge is a serious item; at 30 cents per thousand gallons this compressor saves in water about 50 cents a day, or $150.00 per year of 300 days. When water is bad, the less there is to be handled, the less boiler repairs involved. In a larger plant, the labor of a fireman may also be saved.

The value of the water saved is important, but the amount of coal otherwise needed to evaporate this extra water is still more important. At 1 pound of coal per 7 pounds of water evaporated, this 1377 pounds would require 197 pounds of coal per hour, or 1970 pounds per day of 10 hours. With coal at $4.00 per ton, this is $3.94 per day or $1182.00 per year of 300 10-hour days. The amount saved by the use of the duplex cross-compound in fuel and water, therefore, is $1332.00 per year. In five years this amounts to $6660.00; and if the plant runs double-shift the figure is doubled. Further, as these figures are based upon only 500 cubic feet capacity, it can be estimated approximately for larger volumes. For example, 750 cubic feet equals one and one-half times, 1500 cubic feet, three times these figures, etc.

Where, now, is the economy of "the cheaper machine?" Even with coal at $2.00 per ton, or only half the figure assumed above, the saving per year in fuel and water appears at $741.00; and the duplex compound is obviously the thing, for this amount will more than overbalance the difference in cost between the two types. Even at this fuel rate its total first cost would be saved in a few years; it would pay to throw out at once a less efficient machine. When coal is at all expensive, it is evident that the buyer should go on to the most refined Corliss type of compressor, running on only about one-half the fuel required by even the good duplex double-compound used in the example—and 500 cubic feet per minute is not a large machine.

It must, however, be kept in mind that to secure these savings it is not enough that a compressor be of the "double-compound" type; but it must be a thoroughly high-class and really economical machine, well and properly designed, and well built. As there are good watches and cheap watches, so are there degrees of quality in all things. As a matter of fact, a really high-class straight line compressor has been shown by accurate tests actually to deliver its output of air at less fuel cost than duplex compounds which, on the outside, bear the appearance of economical design, and are even sold under "guarantee." Guarantees are of little protection, for once the expenses of foundations, piping, installation, etc., are incurred and the work has become dependent upon the continued use of the air, tests are not made once in a thousand times; a condition exists of which the average manufacturer is quite willing to take advantage even with impossible guarantees. If economy is really wanted, it can safely be expected and maintained only in constructions of the highest standard. —*Lucius I. Wightman, E.E.*

APPENDIX F

COMPOUND AIR COMPRESSION

It is well known that the heating of air produces an increase in its volume. This is true whatever the source of the heat. The heat produced in a cylinder by compression acts to expand the air in that cylinder, whatever may be the speed or rate of compression. In effect, this is equivalent to an increase in the volume of air being compressed and delivered. This in turn calls for an increase in the power to compress this apparently added volume of air; or, to put it differently, the heat of compression, in increasing the volume of air, makes it necessary to carry the air to a higher average or mean effective pressure in the cylinder in order to secure finally the required volume of air at the required pressure, after its temperature has fallen to that of the surrounding atmosphere. Looking at it in this way also, there is seen to be an excess of power required to meet the extra resistance mentioned.

A consideration of these facts suggests that if some means be provided for removing this heat of compression as fast as produced, there will be an important reduction in the power required to raise a given weight or volume of air to a given pressure.

When air is compressed in a cylinder without any attempt whatever to remove the heat produced, the compression is known as " adiabatic." When compression is carried on in such a way that heat is removed as fast as produced, the compression is called " isothermal." In the first case the air delivered under pressure will be at the high terminal temperature corresponding to that pressure. In the second the compressed air will have the temperature at which it entered the cylinder. The first kind of compression is the one which all pneumatic engineers seek to avoid; the second is the impossible ideal. The actual results secured in the best compressors are intermediate between these, but nearer to the adiabatic.

Other things being equal, the economy of an air compressor is proportional to the degree in which the heat of compression is removed as developed. Compressor efficiency, therefore, may be said to depend upon the effectiveness of the cooling devices adopted, provided what is gained here is not elsewhere wasted in whole or part. After long experience, bitter alike to makers and users, modern practice in compressor design recognizes only two practical methods of removing the heat of compression, viz., jacket cooling and intercooling. These will be considered in order.

Jacket cooling seeks to remove the heat of compression, as it arises, through the cylinder walls which are kept at a low temperature by cold water circulaing in a surrounding jacket. A brief consideration of the conditions will show that jacketed barrel cooling alone can be only a partial and very unsatisfactory solution of the problem.

With the piston at the beginning of its stroke, the maximum cold cylinder surface is exposed and the cylinder is filled with air at its lowest pressure and temperature. As the piston advances, pressure and temperature increase, while the exposed area of cooling surface diminishes; and when the maximum pressure and temperature are attained near the end of the stroke, there is practically none of the cylinder walls exposed except on the other, or intake, side of the piston; and if the head, too, is jacketed, it alone remains to exert any cooling influence. Furthermore, throughout the stroke only the outside layer of the air can be in contact with the cold surface and, air being a poor conductor of heat, none of the heat from the interior of the air volume is absorbed in the cooling water. Cylinder jacketing is advisable and even essential, in keeping the metal of the working parts at a low temperature, preventing the coking of lubricant upon the cylinder walls, and other evils of a hot machine. But it cannot of itself be considered as an adequate solution of the problem of cooling during compression.

However, in those constructions involving the use of a piston inlet tube and valve, not only the barrels, but the heads and inlet valves, too, are chilled; and the piston and tube themselves are kept relatively very cool. Thus the air enters through a cold passage, is in contact on all sides with cold metal throughout the stroke, and the maximum effect obtainable from jacketing alone is secured.

If, at several points in the stroke, the piston should be stopped for a moment and the air, already partially compressed and heated, be withdrawn long enough to be cooled by some external means to its initial temperature, and then returned to the cylinder to be further compressed, it is evident that a fairly uniform temperature could be maintained in the air volume throughout the range of pressures from initial to terminal. The result would in effect be nearly that of isothermal compression. Evidently mechanical considerations forbid in practice such repeated starting and stopping of the piston; but the same results may be secured by carrying on the process of compression in several cylinders, in the first of which a certain low pressure is reached and the air at this pressure discharged through a cooling device to a second cylinder; there it attains a still higher pressure and is discharged through another cooler to a third cylinder for a further compression; and so on, until the required terminal pressure is secured. Such a process developed to a practical working basis is the " compound " method of compression in multi-stage cylinders which has to-day become practically standard in air compressor work for the higher pressures.

Theoretically, there is a gain in compound compression, whatever the pressure. But with low pressures the saving is so small as to be offset by the greater expense and complication involved in several cylinders and the losses unavoidable in the operation of added parts. After extended experience, makers of air compressors have fixed upon 70 to 100 pounds gage as the maximum terminal pressure which can be best attained in simple cylinders; and for pressures from 75 pounds up, they have adopted compound compression in 2-, 3- and

4-stage machines, the number of stages increasing with the pressure. At high altitudes, however, with large volumes and expensive fuel, this dividing line may come at a lower pressure. It is elastic and depends somewhat on the conditions.

In a compound air compressor, correctly designed, the cylinder ratios are such that the final temperatures and mean effective pressures are equal in all cylinders, and all pistons are, therefore, equally loaded. The air compressed in the first cylinder to a pressure determined by the cylinder ratio is discharged through the outlet valves to an intercooler, where it is split up into thin streams passing over cold surfaces. The best practice involves a nest of tubes through which cold water circulates, and over and between which the stream of air passes, complete breaking-up and subdivision of the stream being secured by baffle-plates and the tubes themselves. In cases of very high pressure the air may pass through the tubes, for structural reasons. A properly designed intercooler having sufficient cooling area for the volume of air may reduce the temperature of the air compressed in the first cylinder to at least outgoing water temperature.

From the intercooler this air, entering the second cylinder cold, is compressed to a higher pressure and again reaches a temperature about the same as that attained in the first cylinder. In 2-stage machines this air will be discharged directly to the receiver without further cooling, unless conditions are such as to render advisable the use of an aftercooler. In 3-stage machines the second cylinder will be known as the intermediate, from which the air will pass to the second intercooler, undergo a second reduction of temperature, and enter the third cylinder for final compression to required pressure.

It is seen that multi-stage compression is in effect identical with that theoretical process suggested above, in which the compressing piston was stopped and the air cooled at intervals during the stroke. The maximum cooling effect and saving is secured by making the intercoolers of ample proportions and providing for the splitting-up of the air stream into thin sheets exposed to cooling action.

The discussion thus far has dealt with the theory of compound air compression, the conditions encountered, and the means adopted in the best practice for meeting these conditions. General statements of the gains secured by compounding have been made. It remains to discuss in detail some of the more important and specific advantages arising from stage compression.

The table appended (see page 347) gives the percentage of work lost in the heat of compression in one, two, three and four stages, at various pressures. In these figures no account is taken of jacket cooling, for the reasons already stated; nor is any allowance made for certain inevitable mechanical losses.

Taking a specific example, the saving by compounding strikingly appears. Assume that a volume of compressed air equivalent to 100 final effective horse-power is be delivered at a pressure of 100 pounds. Referring to the table, in column two the theoretical percentage of lost work in 1-stage compression is given at 36.7 per cent; but because there is bound to be some radiation of heat, this value of 36.7 per cent will not be found in practice, and 30 per cent may be assumed as a good practical value for the loss under average conditions. On this basis it is found, in the present case, that to deliver 100 available horse-power in compressed air at 100 pounds pressure by 1-stage compression, there will be required 130 indicated horse-power. Looking now at column four of the table, the percentage of loss in 2-stage compression at this pressure is found to be 16.9 per cent, which is very close to the value which will be found in practice. Applying this value, it is seen that to deliver the equivalent of 100 effective horse-power in air at 100 pounds pressure by 2-stage compression, about 117 indicated horse-power will be required. In this case, as between single and 2-stage compression, we have a direct saving of 13 indicated horse-power, or 10 per cent. Referring to column six, the percentage of loss at 100 pounds pressure in 3-stage compression appears at 1.09 per cent, showing 111 indicated horse-power required in this case. Comparing this with the power required for the same work in single-stage compression, the saving appears as 19 indicated horse-power, or 14.6 per cent. Considering the compression of the same volume to the same pressure in four stages, the percentage of loss is seen to be 7.8 per cent from column eight, implying an applied power of 108 indicated horse-power. In this case the saving, as compared to single-stage compression, is 22 horse-power, or 16.9 per cent.

From these gains something must be allowed for the friction of extra mechanical parts and of the air through additional sets of ports, valves, coolers, etc. More especially is this true when the machine belongs to that class of machine termed "compound" by courtesy, attractive in price through frugal designing, in which small coolers, insufficient valve area, the use of a hot discharge port for the air intake, small ports, etc., are all antagonistic to economy.

Reliable and repeated tests show that such machines may actually require 10 to 15 per cent more power per cubic foot of air really delivered than some well-designed, simple, single cylinder types. No more cylinders are required for the compound than for the simple machine, in duplex constructions. Yet, here, too, the economy expected is only realized from high-class designs generously proportioned, and fitted with large coolers and the other essential refinements of good practice.

When compression is carried on in a single cylinder, the difference in the pressures at the beginning and end of stroke is the total difference between initial and terminal pressures, implying a great variation in strains on the driving mechanism and the structure of the machine. The greatest strains come near the end of the stroke and are almost instantly relieved when the inlet valves open. Thus the terminal stress on a 20-inch cylinder having 314 square inches area at 100 pounds pressure will be 31,400 pounds or nearly 16 tons. At 100 revolutions this stress is repeated 200 times per minute and demands a very rugged construction. This is a condition not conducive to easy operation in any but the most massively proportioned compressors. In compound compression, on the other hand, the difference between initial and terminal pressures in each cylinder is but a fraction of the total range of pressure. The pressures, furthermore, are partially balanced in the several cylinders. The working strains on valves and other parts are consequently greatly diminished, resulting in a greatly reduced wear and liability to breakage, and securing free lubrication and a noticeable improvement in the smooth, easy operation of the machine. These are all facts which contribute to continuous and satisfactory service, with the least possible adjustment and attention.

As a matter of fact, compounding the air cylinders transfers so much of the load from the later to the earlier part of the stroke that the maximum terminal stress on bearings is reduced fully 45 per cent over those in single stage compression; in the above case, from 3140 " ton minutes " to 1727, obviously a much easier proposition, mechanically. Misled by this point, it has been common to reduce the weight and size of bearings accordingly, the mistake being evident, however, when it is remembered that the stoppage of circulating water in the cooler at once raises the load on the low pressure piston; while a broken or damaged outlet valve on the high pressure cylinder may at any moment throw the same load on all parts as with a single cylinder machine.

The more equable distribution of the load throughout the stroke in compound compression, just noted, also aids in securing a higher economy in steam consumption at the other end of the machine; for it makes possible an earlier cut-off in the steam cylinder and a consequently greater steam expansion, with its attendant saving—late cut-offs not being so necessary to prevent " centering." Multi-stage compression with effective intercoolers between stages also permits a higher piston speed, in itself a factor in steam economy by reducing the leakage and condensation in the steam end.

The air remaining in the clearance space between piston and head at the end of the stroke must be expanded on the return stroke to atmospheric pressure before free air can enter through the inlet valves. Evidently the higher the pressure in this clearance space, the greater this expanded volume and the lower the intake efficiency of the cylinder. In single stage compression clearance pressure in each cylinder is terminal pressure in that cylinder. But this terminal pressure in the intake cylinder of a compound is low, usually not over 25 pounds when the final working pressure is 100 pounds. The volumetric efficiency of compound compression cylinders is higher for this reason, the clearance in the low pressure cylinder only being in question.

Another condition conducive to high volumetric efficiency resulting from compound compression is the fact that terminal pressures, and consequently terminal temperatures, are lower than in single-stage cylinders. The cylinder walls and more particularly the heads, with the valves and ports which may be in them, are therefore kept much cooler and the entering air is not so much heated by contact with these parts. A third element entering into the question of capacity is the reduced leakage in stage compression cylinders, through valves and past piston and rods, with the incidental loss of power. It is evident that the higher the pressure the greater the liability to leakage; and the smaller range of partly balanced pressures in multi-stage cylinders reduces this loss.

One of the greatest difficulties hitherto encountered in air power transmission has been the freezing of the moisture in the air, either in the pipe line or at the exhaust ports of the air motors. One of the great advantages of the subdivision of compression into several stages lies in the opportunity it affords for cooling the compressed air at intermediate stages to a temperature at which its moisture will be precipitated. Of course, practically all of this condensation occurs in the inter- and aftercoolers; and herein appears the necessity for a design which will pass the air at low velocity with full opportunity for cooling on the water tubes. The moisture in suspension is withdrawn through the drain pipe. It is needless to say that unless some provision is made for arresting and withdrawing the condensed water from the intercooler, the value of the latter as an air drier is lost; for the moisture is carried over into the compression cylinders, producing a condition of cutting and leakage in valves and rings, and finally working out into the pipe line. Aftercoolers are in some instances as important as intercoolers in removing moisture.

If air be compressed in a single cylinder from atmospheric pressure and temperature of 60 degrees Fahrenheit to a final pressure of 100 pounds, the maximum temperature attained may be 484 degrees Fahrenheit. This temperature is manifestly destructive to common lubricants and oils of ordinary quality are burned into a solid, gritty, coke-like or gummy substance which gives the very reverse of proper lubrication, unless proper jacketing devices are employed to keep the parts cold. This deposit, moreover, collecting in ports and valves, may so obstruct and clog them as to cause leakage and throw an added load on the compressor. If, however, this same volume of air be compressed in the first cylinder to a pressure of 25 pounds, the highest temperature which can be reached is only 233 degrees, a heat which will not leave a deposit or destroy the lubricating qualities of good oils such as should be used in compressor work. This air, passing through the intercooler, will be brought back to about the original temperature of 60 degrees and compressed (in a 2-stage compressor) from 25 to 100 pounds in the second cylinder. Here the maximum temperature attained will be but little (if any) in excess of that in the first cylinder, since the heat of compression is a function of the number of compressions and is almost wholly independent of the initial pressure. In multi-stage compressors, therefore, the conditions of temperature are seen to be most conducive to thorough lubrication of pistons and valves, tending toward durability and tightness of working parts, with long life and high efficiency of the machine.

The advantages of compound air compression have gradually forced themselves upon the attention of pneumatic engineers. Not many years ago, when pressures were lower, the majority of compressors were single-stage machines. But with the growing tendency toward higher pressures, and an understanding of needed economies, compound compressors came into greater prominence; and of late much the larger percentage of installations have been machines of this style.

But it will not do to reason that a compound compressor, simply as a compound, is more economical than a high-class simple machine, for such is not the case. On the contrary, only compounds of the highest class are advantageous or deserve any consideration from an economical standpoint.

The gains depend, not simply upon stage compression and effective cooling, but also upon correct design throughout the machine and a consistent attention to every detail.

Every condition which may possibly affect the air from intake to discharge must be properly considered and provided for. Some of these defects which may offset compression economy have been noted from time to time throughout the preceding discussion. But their importance merits a repetition here; a weak structure and small bearings (based on a mistaken idea of reduced stresses) with no provision for unexpected contingencies, resulting in excessive friction losses; multiplicity of wearing parts, absorbing a large portion of the power theoretically saved; heated and restricted air passages, inefficient valves, neglect of proper jacket and head cooling; frugal and ineffective intercoolers; poor workmanship, resulting in leakage losses. Not only may these defects largely offset the saving by compression in stages, but it is a fact that compounds now on the market may require more power per cubic foot of air compressed than well-designed, high-class, simple compressors of equivalent capacity.

The term "compound" or "2-stage" as applied to air compressors should properly stand for superior economy. The buyer of a compound rightfully expects a saving by its use. But poor practice may prove the undoing of the best theory. That compressor only is a commercial and economical success which embodies a sound theory in a mechanical structure correctly designed, built by skilled and careful workmen, and so simple as to be readily understood, handled and maintained by mechanics of average intelligence.—*Lucius I. Wightman, in "Power," January, 1906.*

Altitude Compression. The height of the atmosphere surrounding the earth has been variously estimated to extend from 50 to 20,000 miles, and since air has weight it exerts upon surrounding objects a pressure of the air column above the object.

Being very elastic its weight will cause it to have a variable density throughout its height and exert varying pressures at different altitudes. At the sea level an atmospheric column balances a column of mercury 30 inches high and of equal area, which corresponds to a pressure of 14.7 pounds per square inch. The variation in pressure for different elevations has been determined by barometric observations and is given in the table following, from which it will be noted that the atmospheric pressure decreases with increasing height, and as a consequence one pound of air occupies a greater volume at an altitude than at the sea level (at the same temperature); or a cubic foot of air weighs less at a higher altitude than at a lower one.

In descending the shaft of a mine the contrary effect is noticed, but in a mine or any level below the sea increase in density is counterbalanced by increase in temperature as we approach the center of the earth. The temperature of the atmosphere also changes with increasing altitude, but is not always uniform for any two places at the same elevation.

The volumetric efficiency of an air compressor, expressed in terms of free air, is the same at all altitudes (for the displacement in a given size of cylinder is the same); but the volumetric efficiency, expressed in terms of compressed air at a given pressure, decreases as the altitude increases; for the quantity of air taken into a given cylinder per stroke being less dense at an altitude (due to lower initial or atmospheric pressure) it will be compressed into a smaller space for a given terminal pressure.

To cite an example:

300 cubic feet of air, at atmospheric pressure of 14.7 pounds, compressed to 80 pounds gage, will represent a volume of

$300 \times \frac{14.7}{94.7} = 46.5$ cubic feet.

If the atmospheric pressure was 10.10 pounds in the above

example, then the volume delivered would be $300 \times \frac{10.10}{90.10} = 33.50$ cubic feet; or the volumetric efficiency of a compressor performing the above work at an altitude of 10,000 feet would be but 72 per cent of what it would be at the sea level.

In order, therefore, that an air compressor may deliver at an altitude a volume of compressed air per stroke equal to that which it would deliver at sea level, the intake cylinder of the altitude compressor must be proportionately larger than that of the compressor at sea level.

Less power is required at an altitude than at sea level to compress the free air, taken in by a compressor of a given size, to the same terminal pressure (as shown in table following); but in order to compress a quantity of air at an altitude which is to be equivalent in effect to air at sea level, more power is required, because the reduction in power is not proportionate to the increase in volume necessary.

Example:

To compress 100 cubic feet of free air, at atmospheric pressure of 14.7 pounds, to 80 pounds gage, requires 17.75 indicated horse-power.

To compress 100 cubic feet of free air, at atmospheric pressure of 10.10 pounds, to 80 pounds gage, requires 15.25 indicated horse-power.

But the equivalent volume of 100 cubic feet of free air at an atmospheric pressure of 14.7 pounds is $\frac{100}{.72} = 139$ cubic feet at an atmospheric pressure of 10.10 pounds; and $139 \times .1525 = 21.2$ indicated horse-power; or (for the conditions assumed here) 3.45 indicated horse-power more are required at 10,000 feet altitude to produce the same effect as at sea level.

The net efficiency of a compressed air plant depends upon the type of compressor and engine or motor using the air, the working pressure and initial temperature, and whether the air is used expansively or at full stroke.

Most compressed air engines or motors (such as rock drills, pumps and hoists), working at an altitude, use the air at full stroke; in the following table the volumetric efficiencies, at different altitudes, of an air compressor supplying such engines with air at full stroke are given.

RELATIVE VOLUMETRIC EFFICIENCIES AND DIFFERENCES IN WORK DONE IN COMPRESSING AIR AT DIFFERENT ELEVATIONS COMPARED WITH CONDITIONS AT SEA LEVEL

Altitude above Sea Level in Feet.	Atmospheric Pressure.		Volume (Cubic Feet) of 1 Pound of Air (at 60° F.) under Corresponding Pressure of Atmosphere.	Percentage of Increase in Volume per Pound of Air Temperature 60° F.	Percentage of Volumetric Efficiency of an Air Compressor Delivering Air under a Pressure of 80 Pounds—referred to Sea Level Conditions (Temperature 60° F.).	Percentage of Decrease in Power in an Air Compressor of a Given Capacity, Delivering Air at 80 Pounds Pressure.	Percentage of Extra Work Required to Compress a Quantity of Air Equivalent in Effect to Air at Sea Level to 80 Pounds Pressure.
	Barometer Inches of Mercury.	Pounds per Square Inch.					
0	30.00	14.7	13.14	....	100.0	0.0	0.0
500	29.45	14.45	13.36	1.7	98.5	0.38	1.5
1000	28.90	14.12	13.66	4.0	96.5	1.38	2.5
1500	28.35	13.92	13.85	5.4	95.0	2.05	3.0
2000	27.78	13.61	14.19	8.0	93.5	2.45	4.2
3000	26.75	13.10	14.72	12.0	90.5	4.02	6.1
4000	25.75	12.61	15.31	16.5	87.5	5.27	8.5
5000	24.78	12.15	15.88	20.8	84.7	7.04	10.0
6000	23.86	11.75	16.41	24.9	82.0	8.41	11.2
7000	22.97	11.27	17.15	30.6	79.5	9.70	14.0
8000	22.10	10.85	17.78	35.4	77.0	11.05	15.5
9000	21.30	10.45	18.50	41.0	74.5	12.80	17.3
10 000	20.60	10.10	19.10	45.5	72.2	14.00	19.5

In designing an air compressor for a high altitude, the above factors have to be taken into account; in addition to these the influence of a lower back pressure in the steam cylinder will have to be considered in the proportion of cylinders. Again, a compound air compressor designed for an altitude must have a higher ratio of cylinder diameters, so as to divide the work equally.

Conditions of Air Cylinder Lubrication. The fires which sometimes occur in air compressor cylinders are due to the lubricating oil, the only combustible present. Inferior oils cause explosions by reason of the large amount of carbon and foreign substances they contain, but they are not the only oils responsible for these explosions. The conditions peculiar to a given machine may facilitate or retard combustion. For instance, in a chemical works, a copper or coal mine, foreign substances in the atmosphere may furnish something to feed the fire caused by combustion of the residual carbon. Most oxidation in all cases takes place at the junction between cylinder and discharge pipe. Continual oxidation so reduces the size of the pipe that more air is compressed in the cylinder than can pass through the pipe. Increased friction and compression cause an abnormal degree of heat in the cylinder, and trouble from fire is experienced. In all cases an oil should be used which causes the least oxidation possible, its flash-point being as high as consistent with good lubricating qualities. Ignition in the compressed air delivery pipe is not uncommon, as shown by the explosion of two air receivers during the construction of the New York aqueduct; in one case the engine-room was destroyed by the resultant fire. The explosion was caused by the use of an oil of very low flash-point. This ignition has extended in some cases to the air receiver, and in one instance the flames were carried down into the mine by the compressed air. In some cases the pressure recorded by the gage has not been so high as that equivalent to the flash-point temperature of the oil. There must, however, have been an increase in temperature, and this is due to a momentary increase caused by the constricted air passages being choked by the deposited carbon. Trouble is increased by using too much oil, either of good or bad quality. This source of trouble is rather common, for many engineers have an idea that an air cylinder requires as much oil as a steam cylinder. Consequently deposition of carbon goes on at a very rapid rate. The carbon deposit can be removed by kerosene. Care should, however, be exercised in the use of that same, for its flash-point is about 120 degrees Fahrenheit, and its careless introduction through the inlet valve has accounted for many explosions. *Engineering Times*, **London.**

APPENDIX G

SOME AIR LIFT DATA

AIR lifts are used to quite an extent in this section (Los Angeles, Cal.) for raising water and oil, in some cases operating in oil wells 2000 feet deep or more. In many cases the cost of installation is moderate, and in all cases the cost of maintenance is very low; and air lifts, with compressors of any reasonable size, can be operated more economically than ordinary deep-well pumps. There are many situations where they are really the most economical appliances that can be used.

It is necessary, however, to have a proper amount of submergence to get economical operation. The exact amount of submergence for best work varies a little with the lift and quantity of water handled. Ordinarily, for lifts of 40 feet or less I would recommend about two and one-half to one—that is, two and one-half times the amount of pipe below the surface of the water in the well when pumping the maximum quantity, to the lift above this level. With lifts of from 50 to 80 feet, two to one generally gives good results. On deeper lifts one and one-half to one is frequently used. There are situations where sufficient submergence cannot possibly be obtained, and while the pumps may be operated with considerably less submergence, it generally increases the cost of pumping somewhat.

The quantity of air required depends somewhat on the size of the installation, the proper proportioning of the pipes, flow of water in the wells, etc., and it is impossible to give the exact quantity, as it is very seldom that two wells will work exactly alike.

I give herewith a table showing the approximate quantity of air required and working pressure for all ordinary cases, but know of a number of installations that are operated successfully with from 15 to 20 per cent less air than is shown in this table, and a few installations that use more.

APPROXIMATE CUBIC FEET OF FREE AIR AND WORKING PRESSURE REQUIRED TO RAISE ONE GALLON OF WATER BY AN AIR LIFT.

	RATIO OF SUBMERGENCE TO LIFT.							
Lift in Feet.	1 to 1.		1½ to 1.		2 to 1.		2½ to 1.	
	Free Air, Cubic Feet.	Working Pressure, Pounds.	Free Air, Cubic Feet.	Working Pressure, Pounds.	Free Air, Cubic Feet.	Working Pressure, Pounds.	Free Air, Cubic Feet.	Working Pressure, Pounds.
20	0.428	9	0.31	13½	0.252	18	0.217	22½
30	0.47	13½	0.35	20	0.29	27	0.255	34
40	0.508	18	0.387	27	0.325	36	0.287	45
50	0.546	22½	0.422	34	0.36	45	0.32	56
60	0.582	27	0.457	40½	0.392	54	0.35	67½
80	0.653	36	0.522	54	0.455	72	0.41	90
100	0.72	45	0.585	67½	0.512	90	0.465	112½
120	0.785	54	0.642	81	0.567	108	0.52	135
140	0.847	63	0.697	94½	0.622	126	0.572	157½
160	0.907	72	0.755	108	0.675	144	0.624	180
180	0.965	81	0.81	121½	0.725	162	0.672	202
200	1.022	90	0.862	135	0.775	180	0.72	225

In selecting a compressor it is well to allow a surplus over the amount given in the table, as it cannot always be known before testing how much the water in the wells will fall when being pumped; and while some of the better makes of the larger sizes of compressors will give a volumetric efficiency of over 90 per cent, there are some of the smaller sizes of compressors, with poppet inlet valves, that are deficient in inlet valve area, and some of them will not deliver 60 per cent of the amount of air that is shown by piston displacement when running at full speed. This, of course, varies with the inlet valve area and speed.

The size of air pipe is not very important, providing it is large enough to carry the air without undue friction, and the working pressure given is based on there being very little friction.

The size of the pipe in which the water is lifted to the surface is, however, quite important, as there must be a fairly high velocity to work properly, and it is better to err in having the pipe a little too small than too large. The best work is generally obtained with a flow of from 12 to 18 gallons per square inch of section. Smaller pipes will not stand quite so high a velocity as larger sizes.

The arrangement of the air nozzles at the bottom is not a matter of very great importance, provided, of course, the air pipe is somewhat above the bottom of the water pipe. There are a number of different arrangements that give good results.

In some cases, where it is desired to deliver the water at some distance away from and above the well, where sufficient submergence cannot be obtained, air displacement pumps are used; that is, a cylinder or chamber is lowered into the well below the water line and provided with valves somewhat similar to pump cylinders, being alternately filled and emptied with air under pressure. What is known as the " dense air " system, by which the air is returned to the compressor under considerable pressure, increases the economy of the compressor and makes a satisfactory and very economically operated pumping plant.

Direct-acting deep-well steam pumps are generally very wasteful in the use of steam, and very seldom are any more economical to operate than a good air-lift system, properly installed. All kinds of deep-well pumps, having a long line of rods, generally are quite expensive to maintain, to say nothing of the trouble and time lost in pulling and replacing rods and buckets. They are good things to keep away from wherever it is possible, particularly where any considerable quantity of water is required from deep wells. However, when operated at very slow speeds, and large capacity is not required, their use is sometimes admissible. *Power*, New York.

Cost of Pumping with the Air Lift. This question is usually asked without giving several items which largely determine the answer. Thus, coal at $2.00 is one thing, at $4.00, another. Again, some wells are nearby, and in other plants the pipe investment is greater because of scattered wells. Speaking generally, the average cost per thousand gallons pumped depends on the size of plant and height of lift. In a 4,000,000 gallon plant, with a 50-foot lift, it is about one-third cent per 1000 gallons. In a larger plant, with a 35-foot lift, with coal at $2.00, it is about one and one-half mills. In another case, where the lift is 75 feet and the capacity one and one-third million gallons, the cost is one cent per 1000 gallons, coal costing $2.00. In a plant pumping 3,000,000 gallons 75 feet high, the cost is 4.5 cents, and where the lift is 50 feet, 3.5 cents. In Pennsylvania, a plant giving 175 gallons per minute at 75-foot lift, costs one and one-third cents per 1000 gallons. In a proposed municipal plant, 100,000,000 gallons per twenty-four hours, 50-foot lift, and with coal at $1.50 a ton, the cost figured 1 mill per 1000 gallons, including all fixed and operating expenses. In another case, involving the handling of about 15,000,000 gallons of water 30 feet high every twenty-four hours, using compound condensing compressors and with coal at $2.00 per ton, other figures being estimated on a very generous basis, the cost nets about $2.50 per 1,000,000 gallons, or about two and one-half mills per 1000 gallons. These figures cover fuel, oil, labor, sinking fund, interest and taxes.

In many cases the introduction of the air lift may be effected at little expense, often involving the purchase only of an air compressor, a receiver and a small amount of pipe; but the following is estimated on a basis which will cover the greatest amount of expense likely to be incurred, with a view of showing particularly that the interest and depreciation charges under the most extreme conditions are not likely to develop into formidable figures. The following is a list of the complete equipment for an air lift plant to raise 1,500,000 gallons per twenty hours, or 1250 gallons per minute. Total lift, 75 feet; air compressor, complete, ready for foundation and piping; air receiver; boiler, 85 h.p., with feed pumps, etc., bricked up and ready for use, including building and value of ground so occupied; tank, 19,000 gallons capacity, including suitable timber framework to bring tank 75 feet above water level; two

12-inch wells, each 135 feet deep, cased; casing, 450 feet 7⅝-inch light pipe; air pipe, 500 feet of 3-inch air pipe in wells; air pipe, 1000 feet of 4-inch air line from receiver to wells; water pipe, 1250 feet of 12, 10 and 8-inch cast-iron distributing main, leaded joints, from tank to works, laid below frost (air line laid in same trench); all other pipe and fittings; compressor, receiver and tank foundations, laid in cement; special automatic governing mechanism; total estimated cost of complete plant, ready to run, as above, $8750. This is intended to include everything which may be considered as a legitimate expense in this connection. In many cases the buildings, boilers, tanks, wells, pipe lines, ground space, and other items do not represent a present expense, being already on the ground.

We may estimate the cost of operation as follows: Engineer, double shift, at $2.25 per day, $4.50, one-fifth time chargeable to pumping plant, per day, $0.90; fireman, double shift, at $1.75 per day, $3.50, on the basis of one man required for each 250 h.p. of boiler, for 85 h.p. per day, $1.19; fuel, 85 h.p., twenty hours, say four and one-quarter tons, at $2.00 per ton, per day, $8.50; oil, waste and sundries, say, 60 cents; interest on investment of $8750 at 5 per cent, figuring eleven 25-day months, or 275 working days per year, per day, $1.91; deterioration, covering sinking fund, repairs, etc., providing for renewal of complete plant every ten years, same basis as interest but 10 per cent, per day, $3.18; insurance and taxes at 1 per cent, as above, per day, thirty-two cents; total estimated cost of pumping 1,500,000 gallons per day, 75 feet high, under the above conditions, $16.60. Cost of each 1000 gallons $16.60÷1500=$0.01107. *Engineering Record.*

APPENDIX H

COMPRESSED AIR LOCOMOTIVES

Two Compressed Air Mine Locomotives. The halftones herewith show two interesting compressed air locomotives recently built for mine service by the Baldwin Locomotive Works. Both these engines are of the four-coupled type, but they differ from each other more than the half tones suggest, both in size and in many constructive details.

The locomotive for the Lehigh Valley Coal Company is built within a width limit of 5 feet 6 inches and a height limit of 5 feet 7 inches, the length over the bumpers being 14 feet. The frames are of forged iron, and they have a slab section ahead of the leading driving pedestals. This construction provides a ready means for supporting the cylinders, which are placed between the frames and are securely bolted to them. The cylinders are set on an incline of one in ten, so that the main rods will clear the leading axle. The driving axle, of course, has two cranks inside and is a steel forging made in a single piece. There are two similar air tanks with a combined capacity of 95 cubic feet. Air is stored in these tanks at an initial prescure of 800 pounds, and a reducer keeps an auxiliary reservoir constantly charged to a working pressure of 140 pounds. Safety valves are provided for both the main and the auxiliary reservoirs at their respective pressures. The equipment includes air brakes for all the wheels, also four sand-boxes with spouts to all the wheels. The principal dimensions are as follows:

Gage, 4 feet.
Cylinder, 8 by 12 inches.
Driving-wheels, 28 inches diameter.
Wheel-base, 4 feet.

Tractive force, 3260 pounds.
Weight, 18,000 pounds.

The locomotive for the Gilson Asphaltum Company, Mack, Col., may be said to be about one-half the size or capacity

of the preceding. It is lighter and more compact. In the mine where this locomotive is used the air is charged with gilsonite or asphalt dust, rendering it dangerously explosive, so that compressed air haulage was adopted as a safety precaution independently of other considerations. The narrowness of the gage permitted only a single air storage tank which has a capacity of 39 cubic feet. The charging pressure is 800 pounds and the working pressure of the auxiliary tank 140 pounds. The frames are of plate steel, supported on coiled

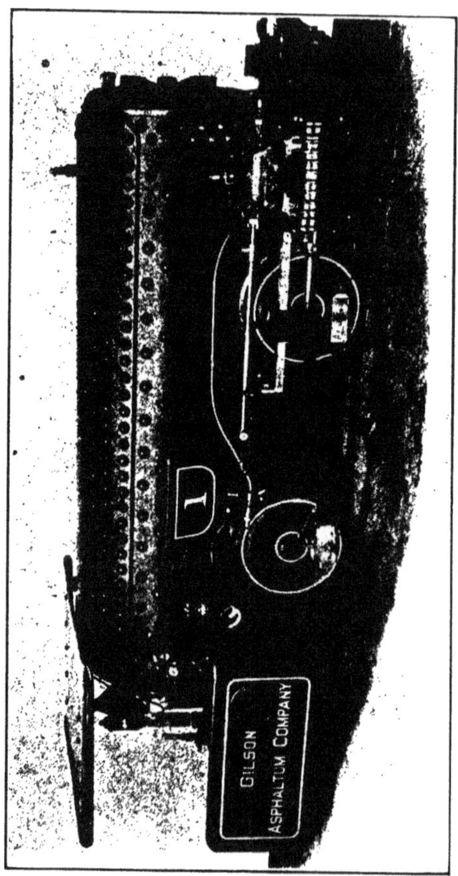

springs. The air tank rests directly on the frames, the points of support being over the springs. The cylinders are placed outside the frames in a horizontal position. The function of the heat radiating rings cast around the cylinders is in this case reversed, as the cylinders cool in working and the rings absorb heat from the atmosphere and help maintain the temperature at a workable point within.

This engine is provided with a sand-box on each side, and sand can be blown under either front or back wheels. Air-brake equipment also is provided with shoes on all the wheels. The auxiliary air tank is placed on the left side and is fitted with a safety valve, as is also the main tank. The nozzle and valve for recharging are seen on the side. The principal dimensions of this engine are as follows:

Gage, 2 feet 6 inches.
Cylinders, $5\frac{1}{2}$ by 10 inches.
Driving-wheels, 20 inches diameter.
Wheel base, 3 feet 6 inches.
Weight, 8650 pounds.
Tractive force, 1800 pounds.

From *Compressed Air Magazine.*

German Compressed Air Mine Locomotives. We illustrate on these pages a type of compressed air locomotive introduced by the Berliner Maschinenbau-Actiengesellschaft, Figs. 1 and 2 being end and side outline elevations respectively, not to the same scale, and the half tone, Fig. 3, showing a locomotive in actual service and stopped at a charging station for a fresh supply of air.

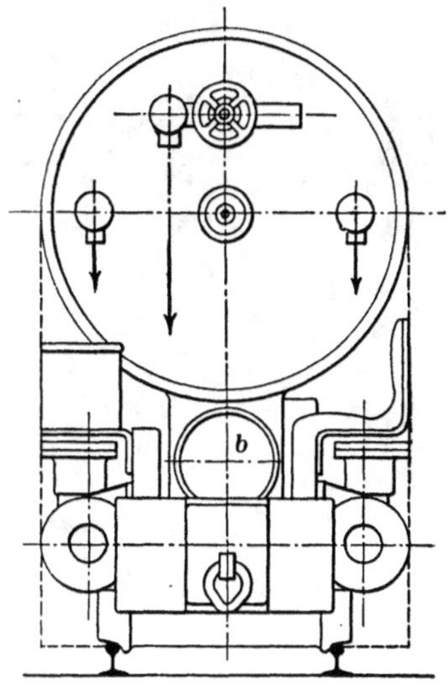

Fig. 1.

The standard pattern of the machine is of 8 to 12 nominal horse-power, but is capable of working up to 24 h.p. as a maximum, and, under ordinary conditions of gradient, will haul about forty full tubs, each with a net load of 11 cwts., at a speed of five and one-half miles per hour. It will run a distance of about

1600 to 3200 yards with a single charge of air, the pressure sinking from about 750 pounds per square inch to 150 pounds.

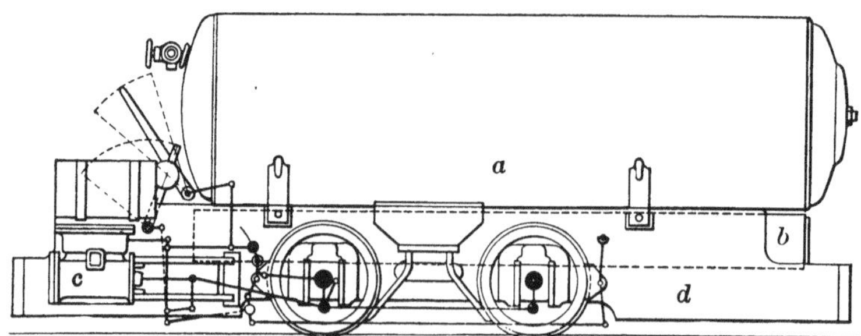

Fig. 2.

Even under the latter conditions, however, the engine can run empty for another 1500 to 2000 yards, so that the driver can

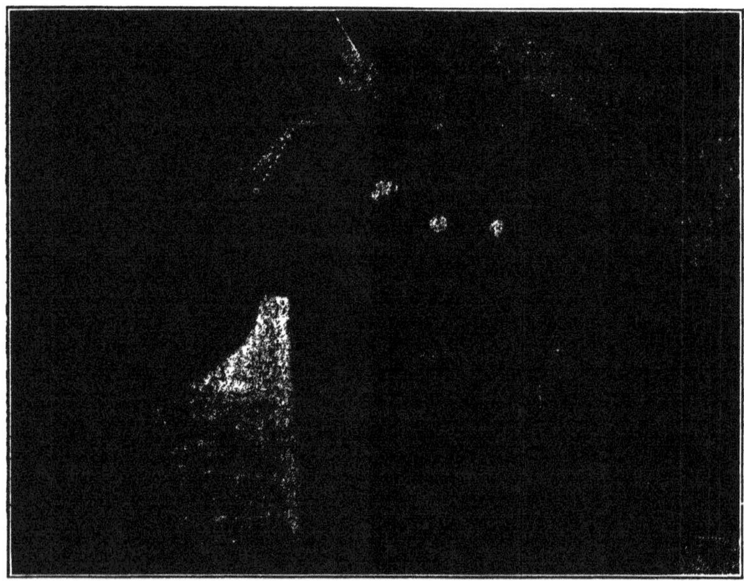

Fig. 3.

easily reach a recharging station should the locomotive be unable to haul the train at any point of its course.

The dimensions of the locomotive are as follows: Total length over buffers, 13 feet; maximum height above the rails, 5 feet; maximum width, 3 feet; wheel-base, 40 inches. With these dimensions curves of 33 feet radius can be negotiated without difficulty. The effective adhesion weight of the locomotive is about five and one-half tons, so that it is capable of exerting considerable tractive force, even on greasy rails, without slipping.

As shown in Figs. 1 and 2, the locomotive consists of the main air receiver, *a*, auxiliary receiver, *b*, the motion, *c*, and the frame, *d*, with the requisite valves and fittings, including safety valves and pressure gages for both air vessels, a reducing valve, signal bell, sanding appliances, powerful brake, lamp, etc. The driver's seat is above the driving cylinders, and all parts of the motion are easy of access. The air supply is compressed to 1125 or 1500 pounds per square inch, and stored in reservoirs. These are connected by air mains with charging reservoirs (Fig. 3), situated at a convenient place for recharging. This latter operation is effected in a very short time; in fact, it is claimed that one to one and one-half minutes will be sufficient, on account of the high pressure in the recharging cylinders. The difference between the pressure of 750 pounds in the locomotive air cylinder and 1500 pounds in the compressor equalizes the work of the latter, so that it can be kept running continuously, even when the loads to be hauled are subjected to considerable fluctuation. In the event of the compressor supplying more air than is being consumed by the locomotives, an automatic valve on the former opens and allows the compressor to run empty until the pressure in the reservoirs has fallen below the limit of 1500 pounds.

The working pressure in the engine cylinders is lowered to 150 pounds by a reducing valve of special design, the air being passed through an auxiliary air chamber. An early cut-off permits the expansive power of the air to be fully utilized.

From *Compressed Air Magazine.*

APPENDIX I

ROCK DRILLS AND MOUNTINGS

THE percussive rock drill, as distinguished from all other types, is an American invention, the first practical patents having been taken out by J. J. Couch, of Philadelphia, in 1849. Couch was assisted in building this drill by Joseph W. Fowle, later of Boston, their experiments being carried on during the year 1848. The Couch drill was a crank-and-fly-wheel machine,

Rand "Little Giant" Tappet Valve Rock Drill with Plain Slide Valve.

and its application to practical work was therefore limited to surface hole drilling.

In 1848 Couch and Fowle separated, Fowle filing a caveat in 1849. This caveat describes the type of successful power rock drill used to-day. The chief point was that Fowle first showed a drill where the cutting tool is attached directly to the piston or to the cross-head connected with the piston. This important invention was described by William Fowle, in his testimony before the Massachusetts Legislative Committee in the contest with Burleigh in 1874, as follows:

" My first idea of ever driving a rock drill by direct action came about in this way: I was sitting in my office one day, after my business had failed, and happening to take up an old steam cylinder, I unconsciously put it in my mouth and blew the rod in and out, using it to drive in some tacks with which a few circulars were fastened to the walls."

The nearest approach to rock drill inventions abroad was in the German work of Schumann in 1854. Fowle being without means, but a genius in the true sense, his inventions remained in obscurity until Charles Burleigh purchased his patents and produced the Burleigh drill, about the year 1866. This drill was used in the Hoosac Tunnel in 1867.

Following these inventions came Haupt, De Volson Wood, and Simon Ingersoll, and after these men Sergeant, Waring and

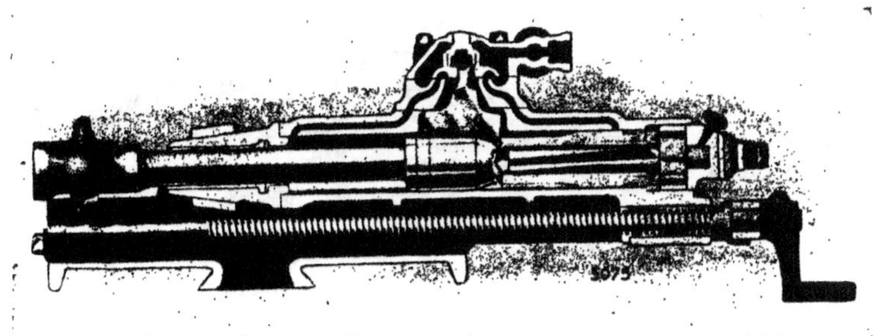

Rand "Little Giant" Tappet Valve Rock Drill with Balanced Valve.

Githens, Githens being the inventor of the Rand drill. The Ingersoll drill was invented in 1871.*

The percussive rock drill as used to-day may be divided generally into three types, distinguished by the operation of the valve.

The three types are: where the valves are operated by tappets or rockers, by steam or air, or a combination of the tappet and air-thrown system. The three types are exemplified by the Rand, the Ingersoll, and the Sergeant drills, respectively.

The valve mechanism of the Rand drill is made up of three pieces—the valve, the rocker, and the rocker pin. The rocker, turning on the rocker pin, is in contact with the piston at one

* From "The History of the Rock Drill," by W. L. Saunders.

point and projects into the valve in its upper arm, which ends in a globular form. When the piston moves, a curved surface slides under a rocker contact, pushing the rocker upward and swinging the valve in the same direction as the piston moves. On the reverse travel of the piston this series of movements is exactly reversed.

The distinguishing characteristic of this drill is the positive character of its valve movement. There is no lost motion, no incomplete travel, no fluttering of the valve, no uncertainty in the machine movement. When steam or air is admitted to the cylinder the piston must move; and when the piston moves, the valve must be thrown.

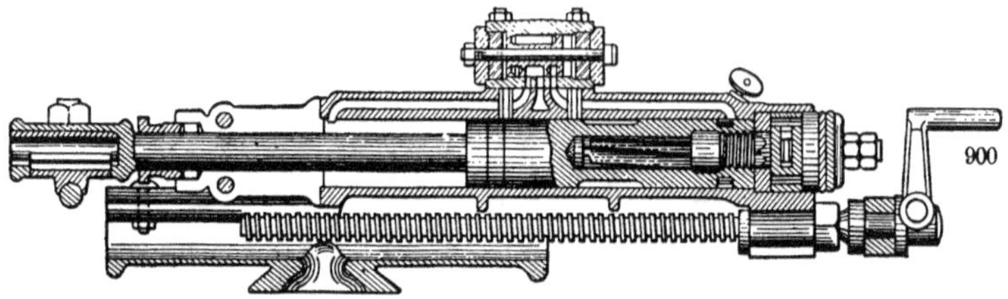

"New Ingersoll" Air-thrown Valve Rock Drill.

While the tappet movement is adapted to the use of either steam or air, it is as a steam-driven machine that the tappet drill shows its peculiar superiority. Steam pressure may not be high and the steam may be "wet." Under such conditions the "steam thrown" valve is slow in action and labors under the burden of releasing water of condensation. The tappet valve, however, is superior to these difficulties encountered with the use of steam.

The Ingersoll drill has an independent air-thrown valve, the action or which is controlled by the movement of the piston. It has the variable stroke so necessary in working in caving, seamy or broken ground; while its quick return "muds" the hole well. The blow is practically uncushioned. With compressed air or with reasonably dry steam this drill will give excellent results in any ordinary material to which percussion drills are suited.

In certain classes of work there are several positive advantages in the " tappet " principle as applied to rock drill valve movements. But the mechanical tappet, struck hundreds of blows per minute and millions of blows per month by a heavy piston moving at high velocity, demands qualities of design and material possible of attainment only to a long experience. Long practice has demonstrated that in the majority of cases the " independent" valve action gives a better machine, using less air or steam per foot of hole drilled than any other pattern. Yet the positive quality of the tappet movement holds an important place in many classes of work.

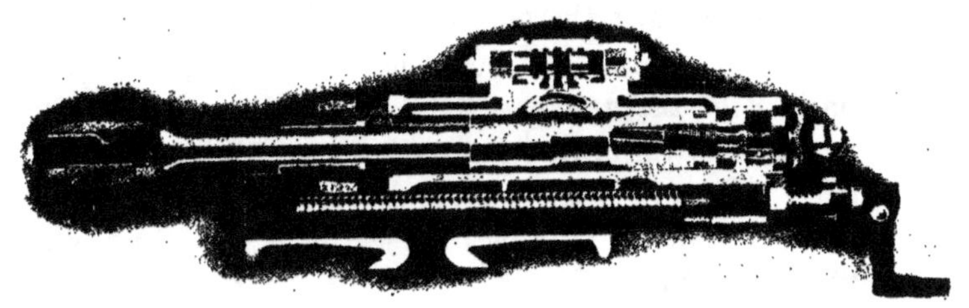

" Sergeant " Auxiliary Valve Rock Drill.

The " Sergeant " drill is a successful combination of the " independent " air-thrown valve of spool type with an improved modification of the tappet action. It retains certain advantages, while avoiding defects, of both valve movements. The valve movement is one in which the strains, shocks and jars to which the tappet or rocker is subjected are transferred from the main valve, with its vital and delicate functions, to a smaller auxiliary valve weighing only a few ounces, specially designed to withstand this service to best advantage, and cheaply replaced when worn. But the wear upon it is almost imperceptible. A valve seat between valve chest and cylinder carries an extension fitting into a recess in the latter. In this extension is milled an arc-shaped groove or slot in which the light auxiliary valve slides freely. The main valve is of the balanced air-thrown spool type, with wearing surfaces ground to a plug fit in a reamed valve chest. One end or other of the auxiliary valve projects slightly into the cylinder bore and is pushed or lifted by the piston in its travel. This movement is perfectly free and very short—only enough to uncover a small port which releases pressure from one end of the main valve; full pressure on the other end then throws this main valve, opening wide the main port and admitting full pressure to the piston for the return stroke.

The auxiliary valve is simply a trigger which releases the main valve. It is accurately machined from the best tool steel, and is hardened. Being very light, its impact cannot injure or retard the piston; nor is there any of that crowding of the piston against the opposite cylinder wall which has been such a fruitful source of trouble in ordinary tappet drills and responsible for the rapid wear of rings, pistons and cylinders in machines with ordinary unbalanced, hard-moving tappet motions. Pressure being on the back of the auxiliary valve, continued wear only improves its seating. Its action is quick, positive and perfectly free.

The main valve is accurately ground from hardened tool steel and is protected by buffers at the end of its travel; breakage is unknown. Being perfectly balanced, it moves freely with little wear, and the full port opening is secured almost instantly. The combined action of these two valves is such that admission and exhaust ports, instantly opened, retain full opening to the end of the stroke. There is therefore no cushion pressure to retard the stroke and diminish the blow; and for a given diameter of cylinder and a given weight, this is by all odds the most powerful drill made.

The " Sergeant " drill has a wide variation of stroke, secured simply by " cranking " the machine forward, without any valves or other regulating devices. The blow is absolutely dead, and no machine of equal cylinder diameter can match it in its effective penetrating quality. The ability of this drill to run on a very short stroke is of special advantage in starting a hole on an oblique surface and in avoiding a glancing blow, with consequent breakage of the starter shanks; it also admits of the hole being quickly started without "funneling" or "rifling." This feature is of vital importance under many drilling conditions—such as working through seams, in shelly or caving material where pebbles fall under the bit, in crevices or alternate layers of hard and soft rock, and in many other circumstances familiar to drill runners and likely to be encountered anywhere. The drill also "muds" or cleans the cuttings out of the hole in a most effective manner.

Another most important advantage of the variable stroke of the "Sergeant" drill, and one appealing to the practical man, is that it makes possible the use of odd steels which, by wear or breakage, have become of uneven length. Some other drills cannot use steels differing more than 2 inches from standard lengths. Steels shortened as much as 5 inches can be used with this drill. This fact allows more leeway in starting the machine after changing steels, without moving the setting, wasting time in getting an odd steel shortened, or hunting up a steel of the right length. Drills of other types are compelled to start on practically full stroke.

Another valuable feature of design in this drill is that the valve action is not dependent upon the condition of cylinder, piston or rings. It has an absolutely positive and independent valve movement. Other types of independent valve machines operate well only so long as the piston is a good plug fit in the cylinder; and, cylinder walls, piston and rings being inevitably subject to wear and consequent leakage, the valve action is soon at a serious disadvantage and requires very extensive repairs or entire rebuilding. The auxiliary valve, in striking contrast to this, will perform its functions perfectly, even with a loose piston or with the rings entirely absent from the machine. To this exclusive feature of design is largely due the sustained capacity of this drill. But it is almost unnecessary to state that a tight piston is always advisable in the interest of highest efficiency and good air or steam economy.

Remarkable records have been made in the hardest rock by drills of this type; performances just as remarkable have been noted in soft and medium rocks—facts leading to the belief that this can be justifiably called an "all-around" drill. For rapid tunnel driving and hard service anywhere it is without doubt the best machine to-day. It is a rapid and economical drill under almost any condition, except where its dead, stunning blow loses effect in "springy" or elastic material. The best results are always secured with live, active air; but dry steam brings out a good performance also. It is a simple, rugged machine, and the frequent remark about it is that "any blacksmith can keep it in good running order." All bolts and threads

Ingersoll-Rand "Universal" Tripod for Rock Drills.

are standard; there is nothing "special" about it. In long-continued service under the most severe conditions its repairs have been found to be less than upon any other model of drill; while recent improvements in details have added to its ecomony and power.

Rock Drill Mountings. The essentials of a successful tripod are: a flexibility adapting it to rough surfaces, a wide and ready adjustment, and a great strength and rigidity in service. The "Sergeant" tripod, here illustrated, meets the requirements. All adjustments are independent, and a single wrench fits all nuts. At all joints a wedge effect is secured by the use of cone-shaped clamping surfaces of large area. The legs are telescopic and the weights can be adjusted at any height.

In tunnel work, in shaft sinking, in mining, and, to a more limited extent, in quarry work, the column or bar has become an indispensable form of drill mounting. It is simply an extra heavy wrought steel tube, carrying at one end a rosette-shaped head, and at the other one or two jack screws suitably mounted. One or more column arms may be mounted and clamped on the column, carrying the drills; or, the drill may be mounted directly on the column. In either case, a safety clamp, secured on the column below the column arm or drill, prevents the latter from falling when the clamp bolts are loosened to swing around the column in changing steels. Under this general classification there are three distinct types, described as follows:

Ingersoll-Rand Double-Screw Column.

In tunnel work, with a heading or drift of 8 or 9 feet, a double-screw column is the usual mounting for drills. Each column may carry two or more machines, the number of the latter required depending upon the size of heading and the rate of advance. In tunnels 27 feet wide and 24 feet high, with 8-foot headings, it is customary to use four drills on columns in the heading and two on tripods on the bench. In tunnels 15 feet wide and 18 feet high, with 8-foot headings, three drills are ordinarily used. The double-screw column has two jack screws at the base, which give great security and rigidity. The drill on the column has a great range of adjustability; it may be shifted sideways on the arm, and the arm may be raised or lowered or swung completely about the column.

The single-screw column or shaft bar is a mounting designed for rapid and economical shaft sinking. The various lengths of bar accommodate various shaft openings. This device has but one jack screw, which is fitted with a patent lock nut, giving perfect security against working loose. For shafts less than 8 feet across, the bar should carry but one drill. For larger shafts, two drills on a bar may be used, the latter being supported by center legs. The arms permit of lengthening or shortening, can be swiveled to any position, or may be swung completely over to drill on both sides of the bar. Drills, arm and bar may be folded compactly together and removed bodily when a blast is to be fired.

Ingersoll-Rand Double-Screw Column with Arm and Saddle for Rock Drill.

The stoping bar is simply a short bar upon which the drill is mounted directly without any column arm. It has one jackscrew, secured by a lock nut, and is designed for stoping work in mines or for light drilling in a drift or heading.

Hammer or Plug Drills. The hammer drill or "buzzer" is undoubtedly playing a most important part in the economical working of modern mines. It has passed through a long and expensive development period. It is natural that in the creation of an entirely new device experience alone can work out the best features both of practical design and of practical application of the tool. Many designs have failed; and while the correct principles were being traced out, much has been learned as to the proper field of use of the hammer drill, builders and users alike learning its limitations and its possibilities.

The standard piston rock drills have no equal in the class of work for which they are properly adapted, viz., the drilling of comparatively large and deep holes at all angles. But as the diameter and depth of hole best suited to move a given amount of rock diminish, a point is reached where the economical field

"Little Giant" Drill on Single-screw Column or Shaft Bar.

of the standard drill merges into one best covered by the hammer drill. The dividing line is reached, in mining work for instance, where narrow stopes are encountered, where upraises have to be driven, as in the caving system, in underhand stoping, where a thin vein must be worked with a minimum breaking of waste rock, or wherever small, comparatively shallow holes (usually "up" holes), easy placing of the machine used and economical drilling through reduced "dead time" become determining factors. This means that as large a proportion of the time as possible shall be spent in actual drilling rather than in setting up and moving. From the line here defined the field of the hammer drill extends down to the drilling of the smallest holes for trimming, pop shots and similar work.

The diameter of the hole has everything to do with the question of economical rock drilling. With the hammer drill, as with all other classes of rock drills, the drilling speed and consequent cost of air and labor, and the strains, breakage and endurance of steel and parts are greatly affected by the diameter of the hole drilled. No attempt should be made to drill large holes with these small machines, but the smallest holes which will break the ground should be adhered to, as in hand drilling. But failure to appreciate this simple point is at the root of most of the complaints of high cost of work with any class of rock drills.

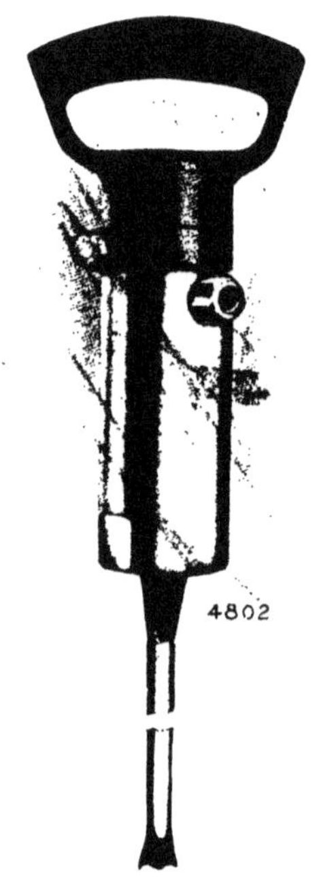

"Imperial" Hand Hammer Drill.

The term "hammer drill" is here used as distinguishing those light machines in which the steel is not attached to and reciprocated with the piston, but is struck by the hammer or piston, as in hand drilling. They are usually used without any mounting, but are handled and directed simply by the operator's hands. It is to be noted, however, that there are instances where these machines are also used with fixed mountings. This classification includes not only the ordinary hand tool—the original type of "plug drill"—but also the telescope air-feed machines for "up" holes.

The hammer drill is rapidly supplanting hand drilling in every field purely on the ground of lower cost per foot of hole drilled. This type is not for one moment to be considered as a substitute for the standard piston rock drill. Its principal application is in the class of work which the larger machine never even attempted to handle, for most of the drilling in many mines and contract jobs is still done by hand.

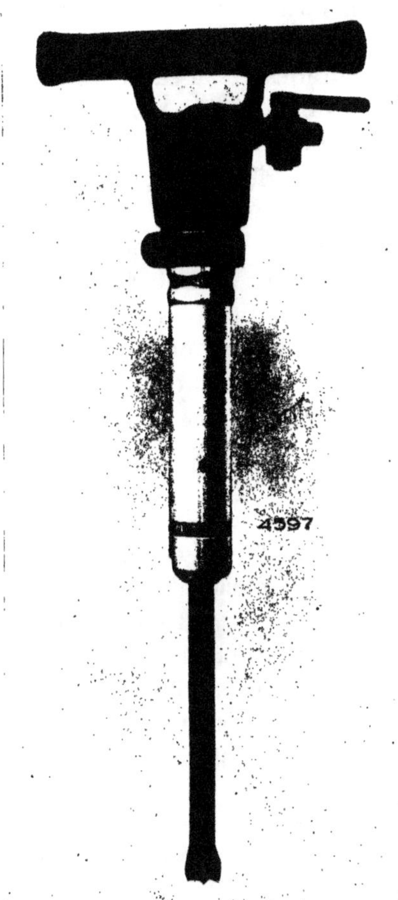

"Crown" Hand Hammer Drill.

The hammer drill is extremely simple, having only one, or at the most two, moving parts. This means a steady reliability and ease of up-keep, with low repair costs in the best types.

Requiring but a moment to change steels or start a new

hole, probably 70 to 90 per cent of the work paid for is applied in actual drilling, while with an ordinary piston drill usually not more than two thirds and often less than half the time is actual drilling time. This is a most important point in work where a large number of small, shallow and carefully placed holes are required.

The hammer drill can be used in extremely close quarters—places where no piston drill with a fixed mounting could be used, or even a hand hammer swung. Wherever a man can go he can take a hammer drill with him. It is truly a "handy" machine, easily carried anywhere under all conditions.

The air consumption of hammer drills is about one-half that of the smallest piston drill, meaning that a given compressor plant will run twice as many hammer drills, doing probably twice the work, and often more, in certain conditions; or, the initial power and plant investment for a hammer drill outfit to do a given work, as in prospecting or development, need be much less than that required for an equipment of piston drills.

No special skill is required to operate a hammer drill, and herein lies one of its greatest advantages. Only a skilled machine man can overcome a "fitchered" hole, start a difficult hole, or determine the proper feed and stroke, thus getting maximum results with the piston drill. But a half day's work will familiarize any intelligent laborer with a hammer drill. One skilled drill man can direct or "point" the holes for half a dozen or more hammer drills—a most important item where good men are hard to get.

It is a fact that one hammer drill will average an equivalent of six to fifteen hand drillers. Good labor is every year more scarce. If ten hammer drills will do the work of one hundred men, they are certainly a good investment. With a limited force provided with these drills ten times the drilling can be done and the footage correspondingly increased, thus getting cheap machine results in a short time which would otherwise take much longer.

This advantage goes still farther. Much of the economy

of blasting depends upon the holes being properly and skillfully placed to bring out the maximum quantity of rock with the minimum powder charge and with the minimum amount of

"Crown" Plug Drill with Air Jet for Blowing away Dust.

undesirable waste rock. It is certainly true that the average skill of ten selected hammer drill men will be higher than that of a gang of one hundred hand drillers. The importance of this point in its bearing on low costs and improved operating conditions will be appreciated by every contractor.

The experience of the most careful users has shown that the hammer drill brings about a most important reduction in the cost of explosives. The average powder man will load a hole to the limit, regardless of whether so much powder is needed or not. The small hole made by the hammer drill reduces the likelihood of overcharged holes or "over-shooting."

The hammer drill in the quarry is usually of the plain hand-

"Imperial" Valveless Telescope Feed Hammer Drill or Stoper.

tool type, and finds its application in drilling plug-and-feather holes, pop holes, block holes and anchor bolt holes.

In mining and tunneling practice the prevailing type is the air-feed hammer with automatic telescope feed, though the hand tool has also a limited application. Its work here is drilling in upraises, stoping, following narrow, rich veins, squaring up, cutting hitches, trimming walls, and the occasional drilling of "pop" holes and block holes.

In the coal mine the hammer drill is useful in cutting ditches, sumps, etc., levelling floors, taking off rolls or "horse backs," taking down roof, taking up floors, brushing entries, cutting through spars, drilling holes for trolley hangers or engineering points, cutting trolley cross-overs, etc.

The work of the hammer drill in contracting replaces "mud capping" and includes block holing, "pop" shooting, drilling anchor bolt holes, breaking up old concrete or masonry foundations, piers, walls, etc., dislodging the substructure of old cable or conduit railways, and removing rock in sewer, gas, water main or conduit trenches, cellars, shafts, wells, etc.

"Butterfly Valve" Telescope Feed Hammer or Stoping Drill.

A feature which cannot be too strongly insisted upon is the question of proper bits for the hammer drill. Neglect of this point alone often determines the whole difference between success and failure. The hammer drill depends upon a large number of relatively light blows. A clumsy tool or improperly dressed bit may put a hole down by main strength and brute force with a piston drill. But with a hammer drill striking up to 100,000 blows an hour, or 1,000,000 per day, a very slight difference in the quality of the steel, the exact angle of the cutting edges, the proper clearance and hardening, the number of cutting edges, whether one or eight, all are points which may make all the difference in the world. Disappointment or enthusiasm rests largely on these very points, and they should be determined exactly by intelligent experiment for every kind of rock. The conditions thus discovered should then be positively maintained.

The Ingersoll Drill and the Cameron Pump. It was in a little shop on the corner of Second Avenue and Twenty-second Street, New York, that both the Ingersoll drill and the Cameron pump originated, and the manufacture of both began under the same roof. The late Henry C. Sergeant, who is admitted to have done more in the invention and development of the rock drill than any other person, designed the first really successful Ingersoll drill, getting his fundamental ideas of the valve motion from Mr. A. S. Cameron. This was at a time when a reciprocating engine, like a pump or a rock drill, with no crank shaft to carry it over the center, was practically unknown. The first machines of this class were built on steam engine lines, the valve itself being mechanically connected with or operated by the piston. In the first Ingersoll drill, as in the first direct-acting pumps, when the piston reached the end of the stroke it reversed the valve by direct mechanical contact with knuckle joints, rods or other devices, which intervened between the piston and the valve.

Here is where great credit is due Mr. A. S. Cameron. He was seeking to perfect a pump which could be used in rough places where exposed parts were liable to wear or injury. He also wanted to design a valve which would open a large port at the end of the stroke the instant that the piston reached a certain point. This was hardly possible with a mechanically moved valve without excessive shock and wear. Cameron's invention, therefore, was to place a small tappet or knuckle in each cylinder head of the pump, which should serve as a trigger to trip and open, through contact with the piston, a small port connecting with one end or the other of the valve chamber. The valve itself was submerged in live steam pressure, equal on both ends, and hence when this tripping action took place it reduced the pressure on one end so that then the full pressure on the other end caused it to reverse. In order to do this with the minimum shock on the tappet, and also taking into consideration the importance of having a small port controlled by such action, Mr. Cameron used a plunger piston which in turn overlapped the valve itself, this plunger piston having an area on each end which might be more or less according to the resistance of the valve to the action of sliding on its seat. The valve itself was, and still is, a slide valve, which, as everybody knows, rests tightly upon its ports and does not leak through wear.

Sergeant had a problem more difficult than Cameron, because, in the first place, the piston speed of a pump is only about 100 feet per minute, while that of a rock drill is four times as great. This high speed made it difficult to use any kind of a tappet trigger, and, in order to get the quickest action of the valve, Sergeant sought to avoid the use of the slide valve and to use the plunger or valve-moving device of Cameron as the valve itself. In doing this he ran against another difficulty: the valve, in order to be tight on its seat, would press so hard that the speed of the drill became sluggish, and to remedy this he ran a bolt through the center of the valve, which relieved it of a certain portion of this pressure.

Instead of the tappet trigger, Sergeant moved his valve by causing the piston of the drill to uncover passages leading alternately to each valve end. Here we have the identical principle, so far as valve movement is concerned, which is embodied in the Cameron pump—namely, an equal pressure on both ends of the valve, and the valve moving in consequence of reduction of that pressure on one end and the other alternately, the action itself being determined by the strokes of the piston. No better evidence is needed of the success of this valve action than the fact that the Ingersoll " Eclipse " drill and the Cameron pump are at work to-day with valves of this type.

The community of interests between Cameron and Ingersoll has extended from this inception to the present day. The castings for the first air compressors of the Ingersoll make were made in the Cameron foundry on East Twenty-second Street. For many years, and until the Ingersoll works were moved to Easton, Pa., castings were made by Cameron.

Adam Scott Cameron was the youngest of four brothers, all of whom took up mechanical pursuits. While a youth serving his apprenticeship, he was a student at Cooper Institute, giving his nights and spare time to study and research. He graduated with honors, and at once applied himself to mechanical matters. He was early engaged in building the Sewall and Cameron crank-and-fly-wheel pump, which during the Civil War was in demand by the United States Navy and the merchant marine. At the close of the war the call for these pumps fell off, so that Mr. Cameron turned his attention to the design of a pump of greater adaptability and more general application. The standard Cameron pump was the result, its acorn-shaped air chamber being his trademark and continuing up to the present time. He died at an early age, but before death he stamped his ability and force of character upon the mechanical engineering of his age.

APPENDIX J

TUNNEL CARRIAGE FOR DRILLING; ELECTRIC-AIR DRILL

The illustrations herewith show two types of tunnel carriage recently brought out by the Ingersoll-Rand Company. The object of this device is to save time in setting up the drills in the heading, in removing them for blasting, and in starting

Fig. 1

drilling again after the blast, without serious interference with the mucking operations. The illustrations are almost self-explanatory.

It will be noted that there is a truck with flanged wheels running on the ordinary tunnel track for muck cars. Upon this truck and arranged to swing in a vertical plane, is a long arm of structural steel shapes with an upright screw rod at the rear which is run out to roof and floor of the tunnel, fixing the arm rigidly in position. Upon this arm is a carriage moved forward or back by a chain and crank; and this carriage supports a heavy drill bar swiveling in a horizontal plane. This bar carries the drills and has jack screws at its ends which are run out against the walls of the heading. A drop support beneath the long arm gives fruther rigidity to the mounting.

Fig. 1 shows the tunnel carriage ready to be run into the heading, with the drills swung sidewise, the drill bar turned parallel with the arm, and the whole drawn back over the truck. All supports are free. Fig. 2 shows the tunnel car-

Fig. 2

riage in position for operation, with supports set. It will be noted that there is ample room beneath the arms and in front of the truck to permit mucking to proceed while drilling is going on. Standard drills are used, held in saddles on the drill bar.

It will be readily seen that this type is susceptible of adaptation to various conditions. Fig. 3, for instance, shows a modification in which the long swinging arm is dispensed with and the vertical adjustment of the drill bar is secured by means of a large central screw. The drills can be swung on the bar to drill holes in any position—up, horizontal, down, or side holes. While the illustrations show a 4-drill bar, it is evident that a longer bar for more drills could readily be used on this carriage.

The Electric-Air Drill. By W. L. Saunders. Many members of the A.I.M.E., who participated in the visit made, during the Bethlehem meeting of February, 1906, to the shops of the Ingersoll-Rand Company, at Phillipsburg, N. J., inspected with interest the new Electric-Air drill, which the company had set up for the purpose of showing it in actual operation to

Fig. 3

American mining engineers. At the request of the Secretary of the Institute, I promised at that time to prepare a paper for our Transactions, describing the construction and advantages of the machine. But such a paper would then necessarily have contained much that was only expected or claimed by the designers and manufacturers of the drill, and not yet incontrovertibly proved by varied and long-continued practice. However moderate such statements might have been, they would have given inevitably to the paper, to some extent at least, the air of a prospectus, rather than of a technical contribution. I therefore decided, with the secretary's approval, to postpone the writing of the promised paper until it could set forth the results of adequate actual practice, as well as the latest details of construction, etc., based upon practical experience. That period has now arrived. The Electric-Air drill has been exhaustively tested in the field, under varied and arduous conditions, and upon the hardest rocks. It is now fairly in the field; its merits and performances are matters of unimpeachable record, and its place among established competitors can be definitely determined.

As a representative of the Ingersoll-Rand Company, as well as a member of the Institute, I may be permitted to add that my company, being largely interested in the manufacture of air compressors and machinery driven by compressed air, has no desire to injure its own business by claiming for this new machine that it should immediately supersede all existing applications of pneumatic transmission of power for drilling. On the other hand, if we had not satisfied ourselves that it has proved itself the best for given conditions, the company would not have risked its reputation by introducing it, and I, as a member of the Institute, would not have written this paper.

In former contributions I have discussed the use of compressed air, and opposed, to some extent, the claims of the advocates of electrical power transmission in mining. I need not now retract any opinion thus declared. Many features of electrical transmission are undoubtedly convenient and economical; but the direct application of the electric current in rock drilling has long been a baffling problem; of which, in my judgment, the machine here described has furnished the first, and thus far the only, satisfactory solution, by combining the acknowledged advantages of air-driven percussion with the acknowledged advantages of electric power transmission, while avoiding the acknowledged disadvantages of both systems.

The Electric-Air drill is correctly designated; it is not an electric drill, but an air drill, more completely an air drill than any other in existence, because it can be driven by air only, and not, like other air drills, by steam also. Yet, while it is thus distinctly air operated, the power of transmission is electric, and the sole connection of the drill with the power house is made by means of the electric wire, air compressors and pipe lines being entirely dispensed with.

The illustration gives a general idea of the apparatus. It shows a rock drill which at first glance looks quite like the familiar air or steam-driven drill, mounted in the usual way and doing the same kind of work. Very near the drill, and con-

Section of "Electric-Air" Drill and Pulsator.

nected to it by two short lengths of hose, is a small air compressor, or, more properly, a pulsator, mounted upon a little truck. This constitutes the entire apparatus of a single drill. Each drill is accompanied by its individual pulsator in the same way, and each pulsator is connected to the line of wire from the power house.

The usual drill shell is employed, and this may be mounted upon tripod, bar or column, according to the work. The drill cylinder fitted to slide in the shell is moved forward or backward by the feed screw. The cylinder is as simple as can be imagined: a straight bore with, at each end, a large opening and a boss to which to attach the hose. The piston also is plain, much shortened in the body, with a large piston rod which has a long bearing in a sleeve elongation of the cylinder.

Upon the truck is mounted an electric motor, geared to a horizontal shaft with 180-degree cranks, which drive two single-acting trunk pistons, making alternate strokes in vertical air cylinders. One of these air cylinders is connected by the hose to one end of the drill cylinder, and the other end of the cylinder is connected by the other hose to the other air cylinder. The air, therefore, in either air cylinder, in its hose and in the end of the drill cylinder to which it is connected, remains there constantly, playing back and forth through the hose according to the movements of the parts, being never discharged and only replenished from time to time to make up for leakage. The propriety of calling the apparatus a pulsator instead of a compressor is evident.

The essential details of the cycle of operation will be easily understood. We may assume, to begin with, that the entire system is filled with air at a pressure of 30 or 35 pounds. This pressure, being alike upon both sides of the drill piston, there will be no tendency for it to move in either direction. If now, the motor, instead of being at rest, is assumed to be in motion, one pulsator piston will be rising in its cylinder and the other piston will be descending in its cylinder; and, as a consqeuence, the pressure upon one side of the drill piston will be increased and the pressure upon the other side will be proportionately reduced, this difference of pressure causing the drill piston to move and make its stroke. Just before the drill piston reaches the end of its stroke, the movement of the pulsator pistons is reversed, preponderance of pressure is transferred to the other side of the piston, causing a stroke in the other direction, and so on continuously. The drill thus makes its double stroke, or at least receives its double impulse, for each revolution of the pulsator crank shaft.

This is a sketch of the general principle of operation; we may now consider some of the details. The drill cylinder, while generally similar to that of the air or steam operated drill, is in many respects quite different, and especially is it remarkable for its simplicity. The usual operating valve chest, the valve and the complicated means for operating it, the main air ports and the intricate little passages in and connected with the chest are all conspicuous by their absence, and nothing takes their place. The cylinder heads are both solid and both fastened securely in place. The split front head, the yielding fastenings for both heads, the buffers, the springs, the side rods, etc., of other drills are all banished. The cylinder is absolutely plain, with the boss at each end to which the hose is attached and the direct openings into the interior.

The piston also has been simplified. The rotation device is necessarily retained, but the enlargement at the end of the piston rod, which constituted the chuck and necessitated the split front head, is not. The piston rod throughout is much enlarged, and a simple but effective self-tightening chuck is slipped on the end of it.

The compressor or pulsator cylinders are as simple as the rest. There are no valves, either inlet or discharge, and there is no water jacketing nor the slightest need of any. The heating of the air upon the compression stroke is compensated for by the fall of temperature accompanying its re-expansion, so that the air does not get hot and does not heat any of the parts with which it comes in contact.

While this apparatus as a whole may appear complicated at first glance, it really is a great simplification, and the parts got rid of are those which have always been most troublesome and have entailed the most care and expense to maintain. The drill and the compressor or pulsator are each the simplest ever built.

There are some minor details of this apparatus with which it is not necessary to burden this paper, and which would involve tedious explanation that all would not follow. In our description of the principle of operation of the drill we assumed a mean air pressure of about 30 pounds in the apparatus, and it may be asked how this pressure is secured and maintained. When the pulsator is in operation the air pressure in the cylinders both rises above and falls considerably below the mean. If at a certain point it is below that of the atmosphere, then a little valve provided will admit more or less air, this process continuing until sufficient air is supplied. In the beginning of operations the influx of air is rapid, so that no time is lost in getting sufficient pressure to begin with. The admission and also the apportioning of the relative volumes of air to the two ends of the drill cylinder are easily adjusted by the operator.

With the Electric-Air drill there is no freezing up or choking of the exhaust; the air also does not accumulate moisture and the temperature does not fall to the freezing point. The air does become and remains a constant vehicle for the conveyance and distribution of the lubricant, and with a certain amount of oil contributed to the system at regular intervals the problem would be how to prevent its reaching every working part rather than the reverse.

The length of hose employed seems to be limited to about 8 feet for each, and these may be attached to either side of the drill, but each always to its own end of the cylinder. This length of hose gives all necessary liberty for the location of the pulsator truck near the drill. The truck is of steel, with wheels usually made for the standard 18-inch mine track, but may be made for any other gage. When in use there is no necessity for any care in leveling the truck, as the pulsator will work at any angle at which the truck can stand.

The motor may be either direct or alternating current, the latter being preferred because of the simple mechanical features. It is also smaller and lighter, a simpler and hardier machine and more nearly fool-proof. Several different speeds may be obtained with the direct and alternating current motor, full speed for steady running and considerably lower speeds for starting a hole or working through bad ground, with immediate transition from the one speed to another as required. The controller is on the top of the motor, and the operator at the drill can start, speed or stop the motor by simply pulling a cord, this being the only connection. The electrical connection ends at the motor; both the hose and the cord insulate the drill and the operator is never exposed to the current.

The Electric-Air drill strikes a blow normally so much harder than that of the air drill of the same capacity, that in many cases it is found advisable to dress the steels blunter or thicker to avoid breakage. The practical force of the drill was not first worked out in computation, but has been demonstrated in extensive practice and protracted experiment. The explanation has come later, but is clear and sufficient.

The drill piston when running at full speed, making a stroke for each rotation of the pulsator crank shaft, will not strike either head. The hole by which the air enters the cylinder from the hose is not located at the extreme end of the cylinder or close to the head, but a certain distance away from it, so that when the piston approaches the head a certain portion of air is enclosed and acts as a cushion which first checks the advance of the piston and then shoots it back. The piston thus starts upon its working stroke impelled by a certain amount of force which, we may say, has been saved over from the preceding stroke to be utilized for this. The piston after being thus started is driven forward by an air pressure which increases as it advances, the pulsator piston being in the attitude of chasing and gaining upon the drill piston for a considerable portion of the stroke, while in the case of the ordinary drill piston, driven by a constant flow of air which it runs away from, the pressure must constantly diminish as the piston speed is accelerated. In the same way by the action of the other pulsator piston the opposing pressure upon the advancing side of the drill piston is a diminishing pressure instead of the constant atmospheric resistance, and these combined cause a greater unbalanced difference of pressures upon the opposite sides of the drill, a more rapid acceleration of the piston movement, and a consequent higher velocity and force at the moment of impact of the steel upon the rock.

Perhaps the most gratifying, and also surprising, revelation of all in connection with the Electric-Air drill is the now indisputable fact that it takes only one-third to one-fourth of the power, at the power-house, to drive it and do the same work as a rock drill of equivalent capacity. This is accounted for by the fact that the same air is used over and over and that all of its elastic force is availed of in both directions, instead of exhausting the charge for each stroke at full pressure. There are also no large clearance spaces to fill anew at each stroke, as these spaces are never emptied.

A curious result of the mode of driving the piston of the

"Electric-Air" Rock Drill on Quarry Bar Mounting.

Electric-Air drill, and another valuable feature of it when in operation, is found in the trick the drill has of "yanking" itself free when the bit sticks in the hole and of going on with its work again. When the bit of the ordinary air or steam driven drill sticks in the hole, that is the end of it as far as the drill is concerned, and it is for the drill runner to free it as best he may. He runs the feed up and down, hammers the steel, and coaxes things in various ways until the drill gets steadily running again. With the Electric-Air drill when the bit sticks the motor and the pulsator pistons do not stop, but keep running the same as before. This means that if the drill piston is making, say, 400 strokes a minute it will, when it sticks, receive per minute 400 alternate thrusts and pulls with full force. Nothing could well be imagined more effective for freeing the bit, and often when it sticks, and before the runner can get ready to do anything about it, the drill is running right along again as if nothing had happened.

The coming of the Electric-Air drill suggests many possibilities, and ominously means much to the established interest. It necessarily suggests a revolution in methods and sometimes perhaps a superseding of the old plants throughout. In the working of the new drill the old central air compressor plants are absolutely worthless, but it is not easy to imagine any general abandonment of them. After all, the result may probably be that the new drill will not, to any great extent, drive out the old, but will make a new field of employment for itself, and in that way lead, as usual, to a considerable enlargement of the already extensive business which is behind it.

As has been shown, the Electric-Air drill is as far as can be from being an electric drill, but it makes the ordinary electric current nearly everywhere obtainable immediately available for driving it.

In the planning of installations which are new throughout, the Electric-Air drill is to be most seriously considered. The question of the relative final cost of operating this drill, or any other, is, after all, the decisive one, due recognition being given to the peculiarities of each, favorable or otherwise, which are not computable, but which still have their weight in determining our selections, " other things being equal."

When the Electric-Air drill is operated without its own generating plant, the current being taken from a large power company, some very low figures are already on record. At Idaho Springs, Colo., a mine shaft was put down 67 feet in 24 shifts and the total power cost was $24.00 for the entire work.

In making rock excavations for building purposes in New York City and elsewhere, steam drills, having a temporary boiler installation, are frequently used. The Electric-Air drill not only avoids the expense of the boiler equipment, but will do the work at a much lower cost, the current being supplied by one of the big electric power companies. *Proceedings of Am. Inst. of Mining Engrs.*

Two Electric-Air Drill Records, with Costs. The Brier Hill Collieries of Crawford, Tenn., have been using one of these drills, a "5-D," in their mines for about eighteen months for drilling holes in the roofs of several entries. The rock varies from slate to sandstone and conglomerate rock; and Mr. E. B. Taylor, general manager of the mines, who has kindly furnished us with the information regarding this drill, states that the drilling was done through the hardest roof he had ever encountered in thirty years' mining experience.

A "5-D" drill is equivalent to an Ingersoll-Rand 3½-inch air drill, and has a stroke of a little more than 8 inches. It will drill a 16-foot vertical hole from 1¾ to 2¾ inch in diameter. It has a 5½ h.p. motor. Such a drill is intended for the heaviest work in large tunnel headings, open cut work in quarries or railroad gradings, in shaft sinking, or in mining.

During sixteen months' work with this drill, holes were drilled in the roof of the main entry of one mine, a distance of 600 lineal feet; in driving three entries of another mine, a distance of 250 feet in a new haulway, 200 feet in the second left entry, and 275 feet in the third left entry.

These three entries were driven simultaneously, the drill being moved from one entry to another as it was needed. One hole was drilled in the roof of each of these entries each day, the average depth of a hole being 7 feet. It took the drill runner and a helper from twenty to thirty minutes to unload the drill from a car and set it up, while the hole was drilled in about twenty minutes. About a half day was consumed in drilling the three holes and making the necessary moves, more than three-quarters of the time being taken up in moving and setting up the drill.

With wages for the drill runner at $3.50 for a nine-hour day and $2.00 for the helper, this gives a labor cost of 13 cents per lineal foot of drilling. Upon one occasion the crew drilled seven holes in a nine-hour shift, aggregating 42 feet 6 inches, which substantiates the cost of 13 cents per lineal foot. Mr. Taylor states that during the 16 months this work was going on, outside of sharpening the steel bits, not one cent was spent in repairs or for maintaining the drill—a rather unusual record for any drill.

The Superior Portland Cement Company of Superior, Ohio, have three "5-C" drills at work in their limestone quarries. We are indebted to Mr. J. B. John, manager of the company, for the following account of work done by these drills.

The vein of limestone averages about 8 feet in thickness. To blast out this limestone, holes 6 feet deep and 2½ inches in diameter are drilled. Each drill puts down, on an average, 17 of these holes per day. Thus three drills do 306 lineal feet of drilling per day. There is blasted out an average of 500 tons of limestone per day, equivalent to 1.4 lineal feet of drilling per cubic yard of rock blasted, place measurement.

With wages for the drill runner at $3.50 per day, and helper at $2.00 per day, this gives a cost for labor for drilling of 5.4 cents per lineal foot, and 7.5 cents per cubic yard of rock blasted, which is a very low cost, accounted for, however, by the rapid drilling done by this machine.

Another factor that enters into the rapid work done by one of these drills is its tremendous back-pull or stroke, making the drill work itself loose in a bad hole and preventing it becoming "stuck." Even when the steel binds, there is a pull and push on the piston, at full power, for every revolution of the pulsator; and this works it loose almost instantly. Mr. John states that the wear and tear on these drills has been very light.

The method of moving the pulsator and motor in the quarry was very simple. These two are mounted on a common bed, which has two sets of wheels under it. A cheap wooden frame for a track was made in sections, for the truck to run on. Only a few of these sections were needed, and they were light, inexpensive and easily handled. Small steel rails can also be made up in sections and used in the same manner, and naturally they will give better service, as well as allow of a better joint being made between the sections. When a good hard bottom occurs in the mine or quarry, the pulsator and motor can be moved from place to place without any track, the wheels running directly on the rock. On tracks it can be carried over rough ground or muck piles with the aid of blocks and tackle.—*Engineering and Contracting.*

APPENDIX K

ROCK DRILL BITS

THE success of almost every drilling operation depends on the selection and treatment of the bits. Too much attention cannot be given this important part of the work. If the bits have been properly formed, sharpened, and tempered for the work, and if they are changed just as soon as their edges and gages are worn, the result will be found to be most economical. The power drill sharpener has removed many of the shortcomings attendant upon the hand-sharpening process, with the result that where these machines are used it is possible to accomplish from 25 to 100 per cent more drilling than under the old methods. The reasons for this are that the power sharpener turns out a much better bit. The saving in the blacksmith's wages should be a secondary consideration. The superior quality of the bits made in a machine will increase the capacity of the drilling machines sufficiently to pay handsome dividends on the cost of the power sharpener.

For the guidance of those unfamiliar with the forms of drill-bits used in the different sections, I have prepared a few drawings of those in use. Fig. 1 represents the square cross-bit adopted as the standard for American mining practice. It is made from either round, octagon, or cruciform steel. In the copper mines of Michigan it is usually made of a round steel. In the iron mines of Michigan and Minnesota and wherever this form of bit is used east of the Rocky Mountains, octagon steel is preferred; but in the Rocky Mountain and Pacific States cruciform steel is used. The reason for the adoption of this form of bit as a standard will be appreciated when the three requirements of a rock-drill bit are recalled. These are "to chisel out a hole in the rock," "to keep this hole round and free from rifles," and "to mud freely." There is really a fourth requirement, which is "to do as much drilling as possible before being re-sharpened."

The different kinds of rock to be drilled affect the wear of the bit. Very hard rock will blunt the chisel and reaming edges. The softer rocks do not blunt these edges, but wear the outer sides so that it loses its gage and size, still appearing to be quite sharp. For this reason a bit that is made with a

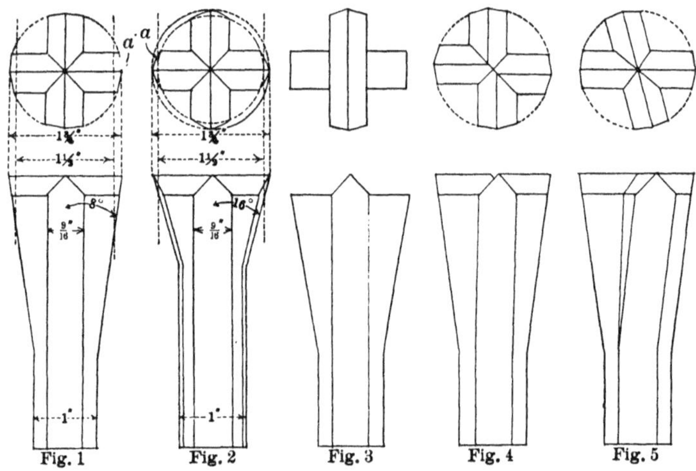

Fig. 1 Fig. 2 Fig. 3 Fig. 4 Fig. 5

square edge and a clearance angle of 8 degrees will drill about four times as long in soft rock as a bit with round edges and a clearance angle of 16 degrees, before being reduced to the size of the next bit that is to follow. Referring to Fig. 1 and Fig. 2, the latter being a round-edge bit with a clearance angle of 16 degrees, it will be seen that in Fig. 1, the corners of the bit at the base of the bevel describe a circle that is equal to the circle that the chisel edges describe. This is as it should be, as it is impossible for the chisel edge to cut out all of the rock. The reaming edge, which is that part of the bit extending from the chisel edge to the base of the bevel, marked "A" in both Fig. 1 and Fig. 2, must ream the outer edge of the hole and keep it round and free from rifles. In Fig. 2 it will be noted that the circle described by the corners of the bit at the base of the bevel is much smaller than the circle described by the chisel edges. This causes an excess of wear on the corners of the chisel edges, the bit rapidly loses its gage, as well as its efficiency, and it is almost impossible to keep the hole round. Rifles form and these cause the rotation parts of the drilling machine to break, often resulting in the loss of the hole.

The angle of the bevel of the face of the bit has to do with its life, as well as with the property of "mudding" freely. It is generally accepted that if this angle be 90 degrees it gives strength and permits the bit to "mud" or throw back the cuttings from the face of the bit when the drill is pointed downward. Bits made like Fig. 19 and Fig. 20 will not "mud" freely. Another reason why bits such as shown in Fig. 1 are preferable to those illustrated by Fig. 2, is that having a long wing they are stronger and will not break so readily as does a short bit.

The Simmons bit, used at the Champion mine at Beacon, Mich., is shown in Fig. 3. In it two of the wings are devoted entirely to reaming and keeping the hole round and free from rifles. Some tests made several years ago in jasper, the hardest rock found in the Champion mine, using a 2¾-inch Rand drill with 60-pound air pressure at the compressor, showed an average speed per minute of 0.28 inches for the ordinary cross-bit, and 0.659 inches for the Simmons bit. Both forms were hand-sharpened.

The Brunton bit, the invention of the well-known mining engineer, D. W. Brunton, is extensively used in Idaho and Montana. It is shown in Fig. 4. The object of this bit is to obtain the advantages of the X-bit without the attendant difficulties of resharpening. With this bit, as in the case of the X-bit, the piston must revolve a half turn before the cutting edges will strike in the same place a second time. It is as easily resharpened as the regular square cross-bit. The X-bit itself is shown in Fig. 5. Since the invention of power-drill sharpening machines, this bit is fast disappearing. The reason will be understood when a comparison is made with the regular square cross-bit as made with the power-sharpener, and the cross-bits as they are resharpened by hand, shown in Fig. 18, Fig. 19 and Fig. 20. The X-bit is designed to prevent rifles. This the hand-sharpened cross-bit would not do, but the machine-sharpened cross-bit effectually accomplishes. Fig. 6 shows what is commonly termed the high-center bit. This was for many years accepted as the proper form. It is still used in the mines of Cornwall and where Cornish customs prevail. Since the introduction of hammer drills this bit is again finding favor.

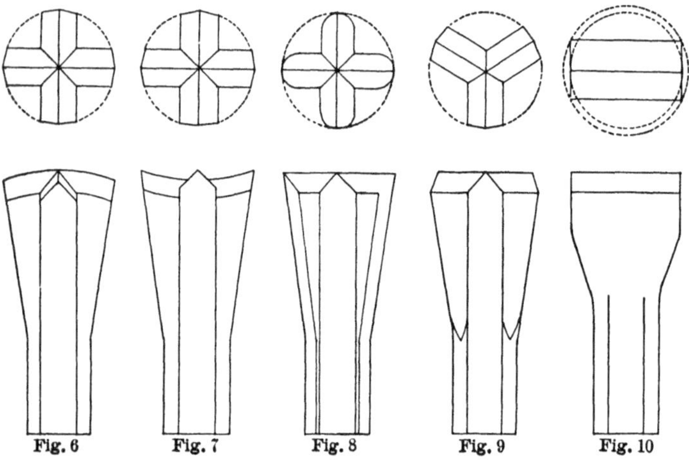
Fig. 6 Fig. 7 Fig. 8 Fig. 9 Fig. 10

It is of especial advantage in starting a hole, the high center immediately making an impression on the rock, whereas the square-faced bit requires a flat face for ready starting. For a starting bit in hammer machines it has no equal. Here, however, its advantages over the square bit end. Used as a bit to follow the starter, it is liable to follow slips and seams in the rock, causing crooked holes, which are sometimes lost before being finished. This the square bit will not do. Fig. 7 shows a bit where the corners are in advance of the center. This is a fast cutting bit. The corners break up the rock in advance of the center, and leave little for the center to do; this causes the corners to wear fast, but still not to excess when it is considered that they do most of the work. This drill will not follow slips and seams, will drill a round hole, and is easy on the drilling machine. The weak point of this form is that the leverage is so great on the corners that they are liable to break off if tempered too hard. Fig. 8 shows the round-edge bit, which is a favorite with some. In soft rock this is good, but in hard rock it permits rifles to form in the hole because there are no reaming edges.

The Y-bit shown in Fig. 9 gives the advantage of plenty of room for the cuttings to escape. It is, however, quite difficult to make and resharpen by hand. With the power-sharpener it can be made as easily as any other form. Fig. 10 shows the "bull" bit in use in the lead and zinc mines of the Joplin, Mo., district before the introduction of the power-sharpener. The extreme hardness of the limestone and flint in the sheet-ground of that district caused the ordinary cross-bit as made by hand to wear too fast. This dull bull-bit, therefore, had to be adopted. Drilling here was not a matter of cutting the rock, but of shattering it by impact. The power-sharpener has changed all this, and the American standard cross-bit as made in these machines is now used. As a result the capacity of the drills has been materially increased. In mines where hand-sharpening is still done the bull-bit is yet in use. Fig. 11 shows the Z-bit used in hand-sharpening in the southeast Missouri lead district. This bit is also used quite extensively in Germany. In both places, however, the advantage of the standard square cross-bit as made with the power-sharpener is fast causing it to be displaced. Fig. 12 shows the "six-wing rosette" bit as made in the power-sharpener in use at the Penarroya mines of Spain. It is used in hammer drills only. Of all the rosette forms of bits, this has been found to be the most satisfactory. Fig. 13 shows the square cross-bits when made up for hammer drills where a hole for the introduction of air or water to remove the cuttings apexes at a point back from the bevel of the bit in one of the recesses between the wings. Fig. 14 shows the same form where the hole ends in the center of the cross of the cutting edges. This form of bit is extensively used. Its faults are that a core is formed by this hole; this core fills the hole, and causes a stoppage of air or water. These cores have been known to become as much as 8 inches long, and are quite difficult to remove. To clear them away the core must be burned out by heating the steel the

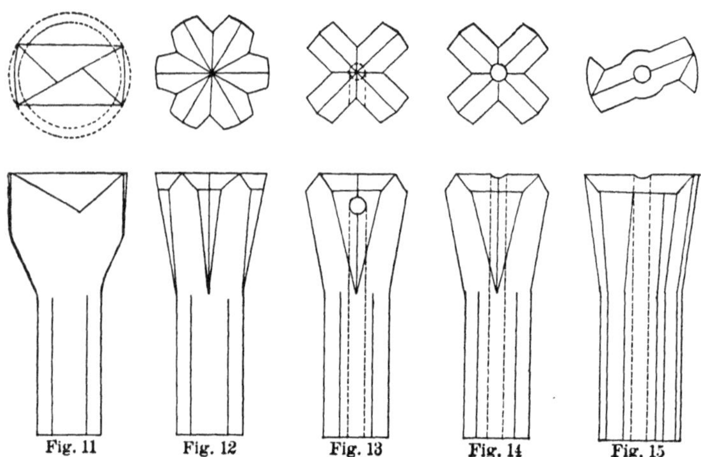

Fig. 11 Fig. 12 Fig. 13 Fig. 14 Fig. 15

full length of the core in a slow fire—a sometimes slow and tedious process. This difficulty is entirely overcome by the use of the bit shown in Fig. 13. The Z-bit, Fig. 15, is extensively used in Germany. In hammer drilling machines, the steel is formed in bars having a Z-shape. While I show this bar straight,

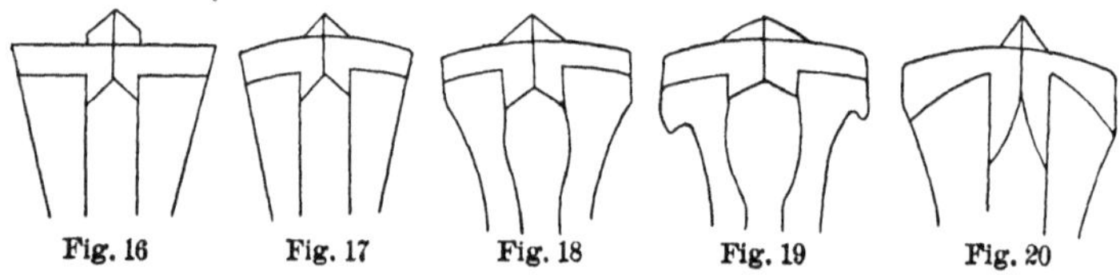

Fig. 16 Fig. 17 Fig. 18 Fig. 19 Fig. 20

it is usually twisted to form a spiral. It is an easy matter to form a Z-bit on the end of such a bar. The results obtained are excellent. Holes to a depth of 16 feet horizontal have been drilled with this form of steel. The spiral draws out the cuttings much the same as an auger. Fig. 16 to Fig. 20 are given to show the evolution of the cross-bit where hand-sharpening is employed. There are two systems of hand-sharpening. One is known as the set-hammer system. In it the steel is hammered by placing a set-hammer on the bevels and driving the steel back. The results of this method are illustrated in Fig. 16 to Fig. 19. Fig. 16 shows a bit made by cutting the bevels with a chisel, and is as it should be in form. Fig. 17 shows this bit after about the third sharpening. Fig. 18 is the same bit after about the sixth sharpening, and Fig. 19, is the same bit at about the time that the original cross that was formed on the bar of octagon steel has become exhausted. The other system of hand-sharpening is known as the fuller and dollie system. By this system the stock is first drawn sharp at the corners, as

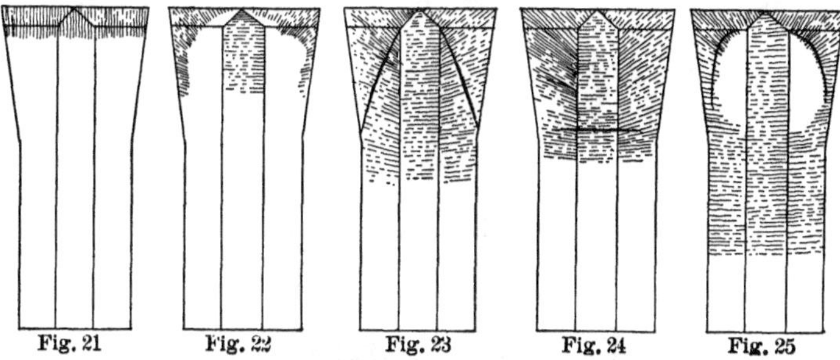
Fig. 21 Fig. 22 Fig. 23 Fig. 24 Fig. 25

shown in Fig. 20, with the fuller, after which it should be set back in the center with the dollie. Unfortunately the man swinging the sledge hammer gets tired before the bit is set back enough; the result is that the bit, partly finished, is left as shown in Fig. 20. It is because the power-sharpener has the staying power, and because it readily finishes a bit perfectly, that inferior bits like these are not to be found where machine sharpening is employed.

After a bit has been forged, it should be properly tempered, as in Fig. 21. Fig. 22 shows the result of the common method of tempering. The center of the bit is soft, while the corners are hard. When the bit is immersed in the water about an inch the large mass of metal in the center cools more slowly than the corners, since the corners have three sides exposed to the water.

Perhaps the center had not chilled at all when the bit is withdrawn for annealing, and the final result is a soft-center bit, which will flatten and retard the work of drilling. Fig. 23 and Fig 24 show the result of trying to temper the bit with the forging heat, by plunging the whole bit into the water as soon as it is sharpened. The line of tension induced by cooling is indicated. At this place the drill will break. Fig. 25 shows the checking caused by first chilling the steel back of the bit and then plunging with the forging heat.

For the purpose of tempering as shown in Fig. 21, a tank should be provided, such as is shown in section in Fig. 26. This

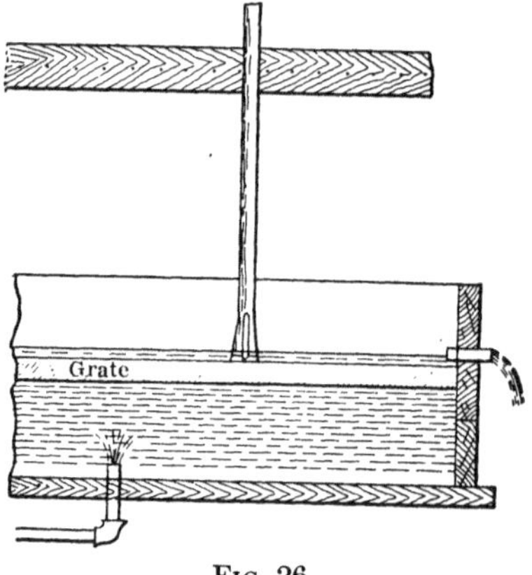

FIG. 26.

should be about 12 inches deep by 12 inches wide, and of sufficient length to accommodate whatever number of drills are to be sharpened in a day with the machine. The water inlet should be at the bottom, and the outlet should be placed about three-quarters of an inch above a grate, which itself should be about 8 inches above the bottom. This permits the bit to be immersed to a depth of about three-quarters of an inch. With a tempering tank of this construction the bit can be hardened to any desired degree. This depends on the temperature of the bit when placed on the grate. It is essential that the drill stand in a vertical position. To lean either way would cause it to harden to a greater depth on one side than on the other,

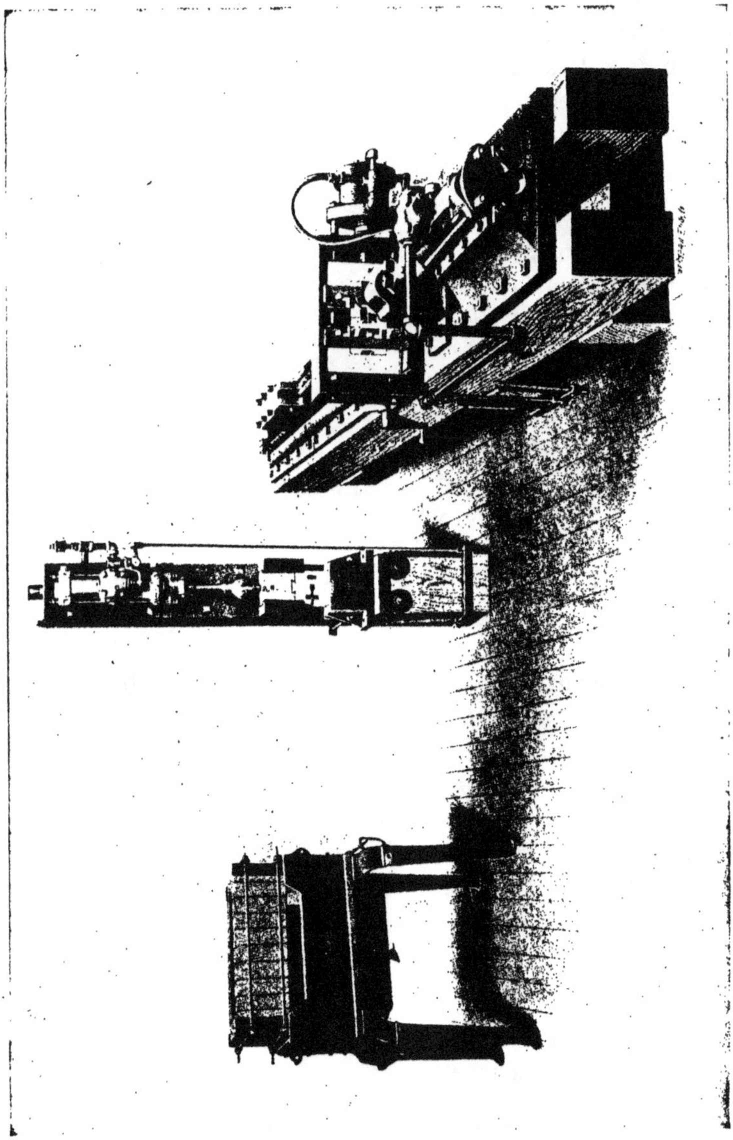

An "Ajax" Drill Sharpener and Equipment.

causing a tension that might lead to breaking of the wings. It is best to provide a rail around the tank about the distance required to hold the shortest drill, and to drive pins about 3 inches apart in this rail. By placing the drills between these pegs they can be kept in a vertical position. When using this tank a small flow sufficient to displace the water heated by the cooling of the bits should be turned on to keep the supply always cool. T. H. Proske, in *Mining and Scientific Press.*

Cost of Sharpening by Hand at the Homestake Mine, as Made up in the Office of that Company.

		Blacksmiths.		Helpers.	
Highland.....	2	$7.00	2	$6.00	
400 level.....	1	3.50	1	3.00	
600 level.....	4	14.00	4	12.00	
700 level.....	3	10.50	3	9.00	
		$35.00		$30.00	$65.00
120 drills to the man and helper.					
1,200 pounds of black coal..................					7.20
					$72.20

Cost of Sharpening with Machine, at the Homestake Mine.

		$72.00
1 machine, air to run same....................	$2.00	
2 blacksmiths, $7.00; 2 helpers, $6.00..........	13.00	
2 blacksmiths sharpening block hole steel.......	7.00	
2 extra tool packers..........................	6.00	
720 pounds coke..............................	4.75	
Fire brick to repair furnace....................	.20	
	$32.95	32.95
Saving per day..............................		$39.25

1,000 drills, 2 shifts, 10 hours each.

Machine-sharpened drills last better than those sharpened by hand and do not break as many bits, so there is a saving of steel.

"One machine is sharpening steels for one hundred drills with less waste of steel and only about one-tenth the number of broken bits to trim that there were when hand-sharpening was employed."

Rock Drill Sharpening Arrangements. Drill sharpening presents a department of mine costs to which no attention is given by stockholders, and only a moderate degree of attention by the mining companies. An important step was taken several years ago in reducing the cost in this department by the invention of the mechanical drill sharpeners, actuated by compressed air, which have now been introduced in the shops of nearly all the mining companies; but aside from this the companies themselves took no step to economize along this line except to introduce the machines and thus reduce the labor costs.

A radical departure is now being introduced, however, at a number of mines that will bring about even a greater saving than was secured when mechanical drill sharpeners were introduced. This is to alter the system of handling the drills. To show the comparison of the new system with the old, the method formerly employed will first be enumerated.

The drills are assembled underground by the drill boys, loaded on skips and hoisted to the surface. The ordinary rock skips are generally used for this purpose, and at times the long drills create a factor of danger, projecting above the skip bail and occasionally catching in the walls of the shaft.

At the surface the drills are piled out upon the floor by the drill boys, generally in disorderly heap, which at times bends the steel so that it has to be heated and straightened, thus drawing its temper. Some of the companies have special skips, with compartments in which the steel is laid in an orderly manner, and thus the danger of catching and bending is removed.

The drills are then loaded into wagons, in most cases, and hauled by teams to the drill shop, where from two to half a dozen drill sharpening machines are employed, depending on the size of the mine. Each team, driver and helper in this service costs about $5.50 per day.

After the drills are sharpened they are returned to the underground service by reversing the steps already described. This method requires that the drills be handled from six to ten times. Each drilling machine underground requires about 1500 pounds of drills every twenty-four hours, and the cost of sharpening will at times reach $7.50 per day to keep the drills of one machine sharpened.

A complete change in this system is now being devised, to be introduced later. There is being installed in each shaft house a drill sharpening shop, consisting of a fireproof room, a forge and a drill sharpening machine, with the few other necessary tools. Two drill skips will be provided at each shaft, with compartments in which the drills will be kept assorted by lengths. When a skip load of drills comes to the surface it will be detached from the hoisting cable and shunted from the tracks of the skipway into the sharpening shop, which will be inside the shaft house structure and not 20 feet from the collar of the shaft.

In the shop will be an empty drill skip; and as each drill is taken from the loaded skip and sharpened it will be placed in the empty, until the latter is full and ready to attach to the hoisting cable to be lowered into the mine, leaving the former loaded skip empty and ready for the next consignment.

There will be only one to three hours' work at each shaft, according to the volume of rock, and the sharpeners and helpers will make their rounds from shaft to shaft handling the work. No one will be employed in the service except the drill boys necessary to make the underground distribution, and the necessary sharpeners and helpers on the surface.—*Copper.*

APPENDIX L

EXPLOSIVES; DAMPNESS AND DYNAMITE; BLASTING GELATIN; COST OF BLASTING IN OPEN CUTS

Selection of Explosives for Tunnel Blasting. The selection of explosives for tunnel blasting probably requires a more careful study of conditions than for any other kind of excavating. Maximum speed in driving cannot be attained unless the explosive best adapted to the work is used. When starting a tunnel or drift, it is a good plan thoroughly to try out several explosives which are distinctly different in action before finally adopting any one of them. The results, however, from this preliminary trial will be of little or no value, unless all the explosives are used under exactly the same conditions. Care must be taken to see that no change occurs in the character of the rock, number and direction of the bore holes, strength of the detonator, kind and quantity of tamping, amount of water encountered, method of connecting up the bore holes for firing, and that the explosive is always thoroughly thawed. If a material change in any of these conditions occurs as the work progresses, further tests should be made to determine whether a quicker or slower, a stronger or weaker, explosive might not break the ground, or bottom the bore holes better, or make it possible to bring out the cut with fewer holes or deeper ones. The speed at which rock can be drilled does not indicate how it will break, and not infrequently that which can be easily drilled is very difficult to blast.

High explosives suitable for tunnel blasting should not give off objectional fumes on detonation, and accordingly gelatin dynamite, blasting gelatin or ammonia dynamite should always be selected. Gelatin dynamite is made in various grades of strength, from 25 to 80 per cent inclusive. It is comparatively slow in action, the higher grades being little, if any, quicker than the lower ones. Blasting gelatin is manufactured in only one strength, which for comparative purposes may be said to be 100 per cent. It is more powerful and quicker acting than any other blasting explosive. It should be used sparingly, therefore, until the maximum safe charge has been learned from experience. Good results will often be had in hard ground, if a few cartridges of blasting gelatin are used in the point of the bore hole, with gelatin dynamite on top. When this is done, it is best to put the detonator in one of the cartridges of blasting gelatin. Ammonia dynamite is made from 25 to 75 per cent strength. All grades are quicker than gelatin dynamites and, generally speaking, the quickness increases with the strength—that is, the stronger grades are quicker, and the lower grades of these three high explosives offer a wide range in strength and quickness to select from, and it is always possible, after a few trials, to find an explosive exactly suited to the conditions.

Railroad tunnels, mine tunnels and drifts, highway tunnels, and irrigation tunnels, are being driven daily through various kinds of "ground." Often it is a matter of first importance to finish them quickly, and consequently details in regard to methods and equipment are matter of general interest. Within the past few months, a number of speed records in tunnels of different sizes have been made, and descriptions of them have appeared in various technical magazines.

In *Engineering-Contracting* of Oct. 20, 1909, Mr. J. B. Lippincott, assistant chief engineer of the Los Angeles aqueduct, gave an interesting account of the driving of the Red Rock Tunnel of the Los Angeles aqueduct system. In August, 1909, this tunnel, which is 9 feet 10 inches by 10 feet 8½ inches in section, was advanced 1061.6 feet. Mr. Lippincott states that the explosives used were Du Pont 40 per cent ammonia dynamite and blasting powder.

In the *Engineering News* of Nov. 18, 1910, the Red Rock Tunnel is again referred to, and details are also given by Mr. C. H. Richards, division engineer, in regard to a tunnel on the

Little Lake Division of the Los Angeles aqueduct. The explosives used in this tunnel were Hercules 40 per cent and 60 per cent gelatin dynamite, the average weight of explosives per cubic yard of rock, place measurement, having been only 3.3 pounds, or about 35 pounds per lineal yard of tunnel, almost 10 by 10 feet in section.

A short time before, accounts were given in several mining magazines of a record driving speed made in the Roosevelt drainage tunnel at Cripple Creek, Colo. The explosives used in this tunnel were 40, 50 and 60 per cent Repauno gelatin dynamite and Du Pont blasting gelatin.

A very interesting description of the Rondout pressure tunnel of the Catskill Aqueduct, written by Mr. John P. Hogan, assistant engineer of the New York City Board of Water Supply, was published in the Jan. 1, 1910, number of the *Engineering Record*. Very rapid progress was made in this tunnel, and also in the Moodna pressure tunnel of the same system, described in the *Engineering Record* of June 4, 1910. The explosive which gave best results, and which was used exclusively in both of these tunnels, was 60 per cent forcite—a gelatin dynamite.

Reference to a paper by B. H. M. Hewett and W. L. Brown, on the land sections of the Pennsylvania Railroad North River tunnels, published in Vol. XXXVI of the Proceedings of the American Society of Civil Engineers, and reprinted in part in *Engineering-Contracting* of May 11, 1910, shows that 40 per cent forcite was used in blasting on the Manhattan section, and 60 per cent forcite on the Weehawken section.

The records of many other tunnels recently constructed further illustrate how many kinds and strengths of explosives are used for blasting under the different conditions encountered in one class of work.

The specific cases referred to above were all connected with large and important contracts, where equipment and methods were of the best; and several of these tunnels were driven at record speed. The fact that so many different explosives were used in the seven tunnels goes to show that care was taken to use the explosive which was best adapted to the conditions; and it is not unlikely that the speed of driving these tunnels was largely due to the attention given to the selection of the explosives.

This point is equally important when driving narrow tunnels and drifts. After a study of the rock in a cross-cut 3 feet 6 inches by 7 feet, in the Calie shaft at Cripple Creek, it was decided that best execution would be given by a 40 per cent gelatin dynamite. Repauno 40 per cent gelatin was accordingly adopted, and it was necessary to drill fourteen holes as shown in Fig. 1, from 3 feet 6 inches to 4 feet six inches deep

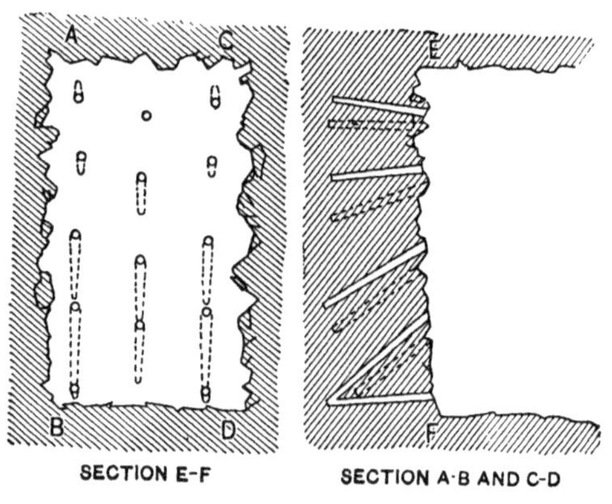

FIG. 1.

and blast them with about 35 pounds of 40 per cent gelatin dynamite, in order to advance the tunnel about 3 feet. In an attempt to increase the speed of driving, and to reduce the cost, the face was drilled with eleven holes, as shown in Fig. 2, and these holes were loaded with Du Pont blasting gelatin in the points, and Repauno 40 per cent gelatin dynamite on top. In this method of loading about 7 pounds of the blasting gelatin and 17 pounds of the gelatin dynamite were used, making a reduction of about 15 per cent in the cost of explosives, and 20 per cent in the amount of drilling, while the tunnel was still advanced fully 3 feet each shift. Here the adoption of a more suitable explosive for the work resulted in a great reduction in cost instead of increase in speed. *Engineering and Contracting*, July 27, 1910.

Dampness and Dynamite. Dynamite should never be stored in tunnels nor in any place where dampness exists. Although a tunnel may seem dry, all rock-in-place contains from 3 to 8 per cent of moisture, which is continually being brought to the wall-surface in underground workings by capillarity where it is evaporated unless, for want of ventilation, the air is saturated. Thus the rock is continually contributing moisture, which is greedily absorbed by the sodium nitrate in the dynamite, that salt being highly hygroscopic. As soon as

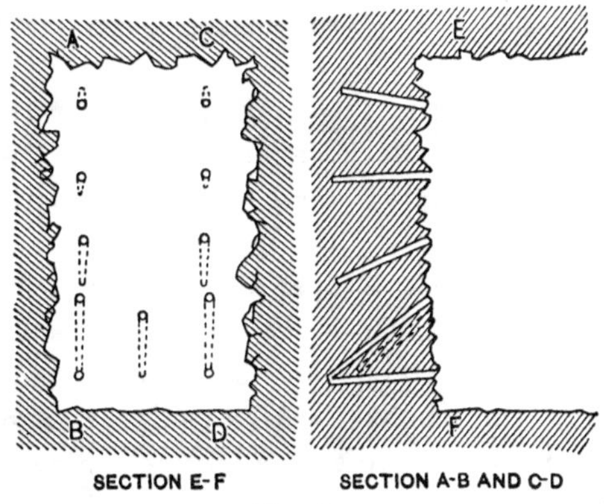

Fig. 2.

the sodium nitrate has deliquesced—that is, melted from absorption of moisture—the homogeneity of the dynamite becomes distributed, and the " dope " fails to retain the nitroglycerine, which then leaks out. The watery substance often seen on cartridge-paper, and the oily stain seen in dynamite boxes, is due to the leaking of the nitroglycerine. A cartridge in this condition is far more liable to accidental explosion than sound dynamite, and it is perilous and uneconomical in use. It will not develop the same energy as good dynamite; it is likely to burn and blow out instead of detonating properly; and it is a frequent cause of " misfires," and of the failure of a charge to explode to the bottom of a hole. *Mining and Scientific Press.*

Blasting Gelatin. Blasting gelatin consists of about 92 per cent nitroglycerine and about 8 per cent gun cotton. It is the most powerful explosive manufactured, not excepting clear nitroglycerine. Because of its high detonating power it is erroneously supposed to be more dangerous to handle than ordinary grades of dynamite; but, owing to its gelatinous composition, it is no more sensitive than 40 per cent H. G. dynamite. In appearance it is somewhat similar to gelatin dynamite, although more elastic and gelatinous. It is recommended for use when a much more powerful agent than the 60 per cent dynamite is desirable. It gave exceptionally good results in a tunnel driven through hard granite where 60 per cent gelatin dynamite failed to break out ten-foot holes satisfactorily.

The blasting gelatin in this work was used in the cut holes only, and then only made up about one-third of the charge, the remainder of the charge being of 60 per cent gelatin dynamite, which was loaded on top of the blasting gelatin.

Cost of Blasting Rock in Open Cuts. In tunnel work more explosive must be used than in open cut, yet the amount may be estimated more closely as there are records available of the quantities used. The weight of explosive used in tunneling, per cubic yard, varies from 3 to 10 pounds, according to the character of the rock, and the shape and size of the tunnel. In small mining tunnels, or adits, and in tunnels for sewers, the amount of explosive used will be much greater per cubic yard than in larger tunnels.

Some wonderful results in tunnel driving have been accomplished during the past decade by adopting definite methods of drilling, loading and firing holes.

The following data of the cost of explosive in open cuts are from Daniel J. Hauer, in *The Contractor*.

Example I. In mountainous sections of the country certain materials, such as indurated clay, cemented gravel and similar earths, frequently classed as hardpan, cannot be plowed and excavated with scrapers, owing to the steepness of the cuts and embankments. So the excavation is made with carts or small cars in a manner similar to rock work. Such was the case in this example. The material was indurated clay, with a few sandstone boulders in it. As picking was very expensive, the cut was shot with black powder, and a small amount of 40 per cent dynamite was used to spring the holes and break up some of the largest boulders. Under the specifications the material was classified as 24 per cent loose rock (there being no hardpan classification) and 76 per cent earth.

The price paid for explosives was $1.20 per keg for black powder, FF and FFF grade being used; 11¾ cents per pound for 40 per cent nitroglycerine dynamite; 42 cents per 100 feet for double tape fuse; 75 cents per hundred for caps; and from 4 to 7 cents each for electrical exploders, according to their length.

The cost per cubic yard for explosives for this piece of excavation was 2.5 cents, there being used .40 pound of black powder for each cubic yard of material excavated. The work was done in September and October, good weather prevailing.

Example II. This was a large cut in cemented gravel, with only a few sandstone boulders in it. It was almost impossible to pick the material until it was shot. Much of the gravel ran in cobble sizes. The material was harder to excavate than in Example I. About two-thirds of the cut was gravel and boulders, the rest being earth. The work was done during the months of December, January and February, when the ground was frozen.

The cut was excavated in a manner similar to the previous example, small cars being used instead of carts, and nitrogranular was used to shoot the material instead of black powder. Forty per cent strength of nitro powder was also used instead of dynamite for springing holes and breaking large boulders. The price paid for nitrogranular was nine cents per pound, and ten and one-half cents for nitro powder. The prices of other materials were the same as in the previous example.

The cost of explosive per cubic yard for this work was 1.7 cents, while .16 of a pound was used per unit. This is a low record. The costs given do not include any labor nor drilling, covering only the blasting materials.

Example III. In excavating earth with steam shovels, even where rock does not occur, it is well to do light blasting, especially when the cutting is deep. Only enough explosive should be used to shake the ground and not throw it down. Then the shovel will work faster, since the material will run to it as it digs, and time will not be lost through caving of the high banks on the shovel. This last consideration is an important one, as much time is lost by cave-ins, and in addition the shovel is frequently injured, and men are often crippled or killed.

On one job six hundredths of a pound of black powder was used per cubic yard of material. The holes were drilled to grade and sprung with light charges of dynamite, the material to be excavated being "averaged earth." The price of black powder was $1.10 per keg. The cost per cubic yard for explosives was 0.33 cents. It was found that this shooting was too light, as the material was not shaken up enough to prevent cave-ins, so on another job a new method was used. The holes, sunk with a well driller, were put from 3 to 5 feet below grade, and were not sprung. With these holes the charges were increased to two-tenths of a pound per cubic yard, making a cost of 0.9 cents per cubic yard. The material was a little harder, but cave-ins no longer occurred. However, the cost was deemed excessive, since, with the drilling and labor of loading, it amounted to about 1.5 cents per cubic yard.

Judson powder, or contractors' powder, was used in place of black powder, with the result that only six hundredths of a pound was needed, and the cost per cubic yard for explosives was 0.48 cents. Just as efficient work was done, thus proving that Judson was better adapted to this class of blasting. The Judson on this job cost seven cents per pound.

Example IV. The material in this cut was clay, shale, boulders and sandstone ledges, being classified as 35 per cent earth, 35 per cent loose rock, and 30 per cent solid rock. Black powder at $1.20 per keg was used for blasting, and 40 per cent dynamite at 11¾ cents per pound was used for springing and breaking up boulders; 0.46 pound of black powder was used for each cubic yard of material, and 0.12 pound of dynamite, making a total of 0.58 pound and a cost of 4.3 cents per cubic yard.

Example V. The material in this case was very similar to the above, there being a little less solid rock. Instead of black powder for the heavy blasting, Judson powder at 7¾ cents per pound was used. Each cubic yard took 0.26 pound of Judson, and only 0.04 pound of dynamite, a total of 0.30 pound, making a cost of 2.5 cents per cubic yard. These two examples make an interesting comparison, showing that the Judson gave more economical results, since the slight difference in the amount of solid rock would not account for the great variation in the amount of explosives used and in the cost. This statement is verified by the next record.

Example VI. Here all the material was solid sandstone ledges, there being three times as much solid rock as in Example IV. As black powder was used on this work, an easy comparison is made. In all 0.70 pound of explosives was used, 0.47 pound being black powder and 0.23 pound dynamite. The cost was five cents per cubic yard. These examples show that the black powder loosens the material, but it is necessary to use a large amount of dynamite to break up the material so that it can be moved. It must be remembered that in all of the cases given here, except the steam shovel work, the material was moved by hand, either with dump carts or small cars.

Example VII. This example and the following one are given to illustrate how expensive work can be made by the wrong method of blasting. As a rule, in excavating rock cuts, the cut is breasted, and then one or two holes are exploded, according to the material or the width of the cut. This method gives a free face for the explosives to work upon, thus obtaining from them their most effective power.

In these two examples it was decided to drill holes along the center line of cuts that were to be 20 feet wide on the bottom and to explode them all at one time. The material was a solid sandstone, occurring in ledges, being classed entirely as solid rock. In order to charge the holes sufficiently, they had to be sprung excessively, which was expensive in the use of dynamite.

Judson was used to charge the holes, sunk about 2 feet below the grade of the cut.

For this work 0.65 pound of Judson was used per cubic yard, and 0.60 pound of dynamite, making a total of 1.25 pounds, and a cost of 12.4 cents per cubic yard.

Example VIII. This too was all solid sandstone, shot in the same manner as above. A total of 1.89 pounds of explosives was used, being 0.89 pound of Judson and one pound of dynamite. The cost per cubic yard was 23 cents. In Example VII. the depth of the cut was from 16 to 20 feet, while in this case the cut was more than 30 feet in depth. In the first case the depth was not too great to have worked with one lift, but the 30 feet was too deep for one lift, especially when the cut was not worked to a breast. The result of this method of blasting was not to throw down any material, even when the large blast was made, and the entire top of the cuts had to be quarried off with dynamite, since they were ruptured so that it was not possible to use either black powder or Judson to break it up. The bottom of the cuts, where the full force of the Judson was felt, was broken up too much, as much of the rock was pulverized. If these cuts had been worked to a breast, the results would, no doubt, have been as satisfactory as those of Example V, and in the following.

Example IX. This was all sandstone, being classified as 88 per cent solid rock and 12 per cent loose rock. The work was done in the winter time, during the months of January, February, March and early April, while the work in the other two cases was done during excellent autumn weather. The rock was well breasted before being shot, and was blasted so that little dynamite was needed to break up the boulders. In nearly every case it was not permissible to waste any of the rock, else the cuts could have been blasted more heavily, and there would have been less boulder breaking.

Judson powder was used for the heavy blasting, taking 0.35 pound per cubic yard and 0.17 pound of 40 per cent dynamite, a total of 0.52 pound, making a cost of five cents per cubic yard.

Example X. A similar piece of sandstone excavation being

classed as 2 per cent earth, 15 per cent loose rock and 83 per cent solid rock was blasted with black powder, being first breasted. There was used 0.70 pound of black powder and 0.50 pound of dynamite, a total of 1.20 pounds. The cost per cubic yard was twelve cents, the work being done in the middle of winter.

Example XI. This was another case of bad judgment shown in blasting. The cut was a side hill—one of solid sandstone—with the rock at an angle of about 45 degrees. The greatest depth of cut was not over 8 or 9 feet. After shooting off the toe of the rock, holes were drilled at the upper slope and sprung. It was then found that the rock was very hard, so that the holes did not chamber readily, and when the heavy charges for springing opened up seams and cracks, the rock settled back into its old position. A considerable amount of dynamite was wasted in springing. The foreman was directed to shoot the holes with straight dynamite after springing only twice, but he continued springing, and besides loaded the holes with black powder and dynamite. The black powder cost $1.35 per keg on this job, and the dynamite twelve cents per pound. When the blast was made, the dynamite did all the work that was done, and the powder was ignited by it, burning for over five minutes after the rock was thrown down.

Two different explosives, as black powder and dynamite, should not be used in the same hole. Dynamite explodes by detonation and black powder by ignition. so the former will act a little quicker than the latter, always robbing it of its effect. This is what occurred in this case, and the black powder was a total loss. These holes should have been shot with dynamite alone.

There was used 2.05 pounds of dynamite to each cubic yard, making a cost of 27 cents per cubic yard. In addition, 2 pounds of black powder was used to each cubic yard at a cost of 10.8 cents, making a total of 4.05 pounds of explosives, and a total cost of 37.8 cents per cubic yard. To an experienced man these figures reveal incompetency.

Example XII. This was solid sandstone, but instead of

using either black powder or Judson, nitrogranular was used for the blast and nitro powder for springing the holes and breaking boulders. The granular cost 9 cents per pound and the nitro powder 10½ cents.

There was used 0.24 of a pound of nitrogranular per cubic yard and 0.17 of a pound of nitro powder, a total of 0.41 of a pound, at a cost of 3.5 cents per cubic yard. This, by comparison with the other examples given, shows a low cost.

Example XIII. This was a sandstone cliff that had to be thrown down a mountain side into a river. Nitrogranular was used, and a small amount of nitro powder to spring the holes. The blasts are successful, throwing all but a little of the material into the river, so that the labor of drilling and loading and the cost of explosives was almost the entire cost of excavation. More explosives were used in this case than in Example XII, since in that cut there was to be no waste, while in this case all the material was to be wasted.

There was used 0.31 pound of nitrogranular and 0.02 pound of nitro powder, a total of 0.33 pound, at a cost of 3.7 cents per cubic yard.

One lesson clearly indicated from these examples is that Judson powder and nitrogranular save money in blasting as compared with black powder.

In some cases money is saved in the first blast, while much dynamite is also saved in breaking up boulders and in popholing the bottom of cuts.

Another lesson is that rock cuts should always be breasted up before being shot, especially if the cuts are of considerable depth, otherwise much of the force of the explosive is lost.

APPENDIX M

PUMPS FOR SINKING AND TUNNELING; SINKING CAISSONS

THE first attempts at the construction of hydraulic machinery were made in the Greek school at Alexandria about 120 B.C., when the fountain of compression, the siphon and the forcing pump were invented by Ctesibius and Hero; and though these machines were operated by the pressure of the air, yet their inventors had no distinct notions of the preliminary branches of pneumatic science. The forcing pump was probably suggested by the Egyptian wheel or noria, which was common at that time, and which was a kind of chain pump, consisting of a number of earthen pots carried around by a wheel. In some of the machines the pots have a valve in the bottom which greatly reduces the resistance of operation; this probably was the fundamental idea which led to the invention of the forcing pump.

Till the seventeenth century, when in 1647 Pascal discovered the pressure of the atmosphere, the statement that "Nature abhors a vacuum" was accepted as good and sufficient cause for water rising into the vacuum produced by a pump. In 1601 Giovanni Batista Della Ponta describes an apparatus by which the condensation of steam in a closed vessel produces a vacuum, and may be used to suck up water from a lower level. To the Marquis of Worcester (1656) appears to be due the credit of making the first useful steam pump. It worked probably like Della Ponta's model, but with a pair of displacement chambers from which the water was displaced alternately. Thomas Savery obtained a patent in 1698 for a pumping apparatus on the same principle.

In 1690 Denis Papin suggested that the condensation of steam should be employed to make a vacuum under a piston previously raised by the expansion of steam. Papin's was the earliest cylinder-and-piston steam engine, and was afterward given practical shape in the atmospheric engine of Newcomen. About 1711 Newcomen's engine began to be introduced for pumping mines; by 1725 these engines were in common use, and held their place for about three-quarters of a century.

In 1782 Watt patented a double-action system of pumping engines. In 1781 Hornblower invented the compound engine; the compound engine was introduced widely by Woolf as a pumping engine in Cornish mines. But here it met a strong competitor in the high pressure single-cylinder engine of Trevithick, which had the advantage of greater simplicity of construction, and Woolf's engines fell into comparative disuse.

The tendency of advance up to the present time in the types of pumping engines has been towards greater compactness and simplicity in design. This in a very marked degree has been the case in the type of pump now employed for general service, and sinking pumps in construction or mining operations.

The development or evolution of the type of pump demanded by the conditions of modern tunnel construction is illustrated in the more compact and simple form of each succeeding design, from the massive atmospheric beam engines of Newcomen, the lighter beam engines with higher steam pressure of Trevithick and Watt, the rotative or fly-wheel type of pumping engine, the duplex or double-cylinder direct-acting pump of the Worthington type, the single-cylinder direct-acting pump with outside valve gear, and culminating in the compact simplicity of the Cameron pump, in which the few moving parts are within the valve chest or cylinders and not subject to injury or derangement through extraneous causes.

Before the introduction of the direct-acting pump in tunneling or mining, the installation of the pumping plant was a serious feature of the work, the machinery being heavy and not of a form that was readily movable from place to place as the driving or work advanced. The installation was kept at a fixed point, and involved the necessity of laying out and performing the driving in such a manner that sufficient grade for the proper flow of water through the drains could always be maintained through gravity to the pumps.

The maintenance of grades and drainage ditches to permit the flow of water to the pumps entailed the expenditure of much time and money. The introduction of the duplex direct-

"Cameron" Regular Pattern Piston Pump.

acting pumps and the smaller fly-wheel pumps made it possible to do away, to a great extent, with drainage ditches, as the pumps could be moved as the exigencies of the work might require or the conditions permit. But in the confined space in headings or drifts, where there is a car track or where the excavated or other material is being hauled through, it is usually necessary to cut out or widen the drift to provide space for placing and housing pumps of this type.

It is most important that all pumps having outside or exposed moving gear of any sort should be properly and securely housed as a protection against derangement of the gear by material falling from the cars, blasted stone, material from the roof or sides, grit or sand or material floating up in the case of floods. To protect the exposed moving parts of the pumps, by providing proper housing and cutting out the side of the drift if necessary to give the required width, may entail considerable outlay; but the susceptibility of the gear to derangement and the essential function of the pumps justify every means for their proper maintenance. The neglect of these precautionary measures has proven a costly experience to many engineers and contractors. The majority, if not all, of the contractors for building the cross-river tubes coming into New York, used the Cameron single-cylinder direct-acting pump for sinking and general service.

The peculiar advantages of this pump are that it has no outside gear of any sort that may be deranged and put the pump out of service; it requires no housing or protection, as its exposed parts are very much stronger and prove a better protection against injury than any housing that would be likely to be put over it. These pumps may be placed between the car track and the wall without widening of the drift or heading, or may be close to blasting operations without risk of injury. In the event of flooding or being drowned out the pump will start up no matter how deeply submerged, when the air pressure is turned on. There have been cases where this pump has been covered with broken rock and debris for weeks without interrupting its efficient operation.

Foundation Problems in New York City. C. M. Ripley. The gigantic increase in the erection of skyscrapers in the "Lower Broadway" section of New York City during the past few years has been made in the face of grave and increasing engineering difficulties. A study of the laying of the foundations for the Trust Company of America Building (see Fig. 1), in the financial section of Wall Street, will bring out forcibly: (1) what these problems are, and (2) how the talent of engineering contractors has been developed. Less than a dozen years

"Cameron" Sinking Pump.

Fig. 1.

ago the following conditions would have been considered insurmountable obstacles, making impossible the construction of a twenty-five story building on this site.

As shown in the accompanying plan (Fig. 2) this building is situated between the present United States Trust Company

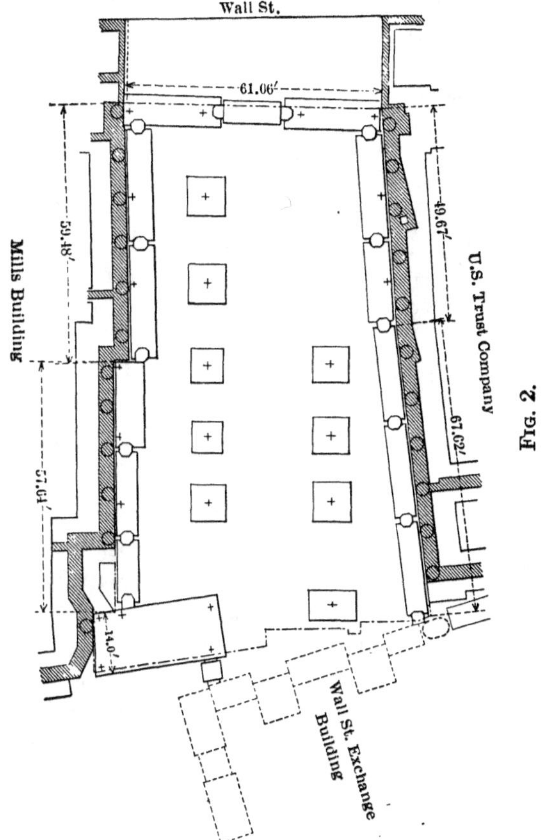

Fig. 2.

and the Mills buildings. Owing to the prevailing prices of Wall Street real estate, every inch of available space had to be utilized, with the result that the foundations of the new building practically " rub elbows " on either side with those of the old.

It is not generally understood that, as we approach the southern end of Manhattan Island, the bed-rock slopes off lower and lower below the surface, so much so that at Wall Street it is 80 feet below the curb and at the Battery between 90 and 100 feet below. It might be mentioned in this connection that the rock appears at water line at about Fourteenth Street, and continues rising as we approach upper Manhattan, so that in building projects in this latter portion of the city, it is often necessary to blast away a miniature mountain before the site is even down to street level. It is due to this characteristic of New York's geological formation that the excavation for the great Pennsylvania Railroad depot has so often been termed a veritable "quarry." In these cases the foundations are supplied by nature.

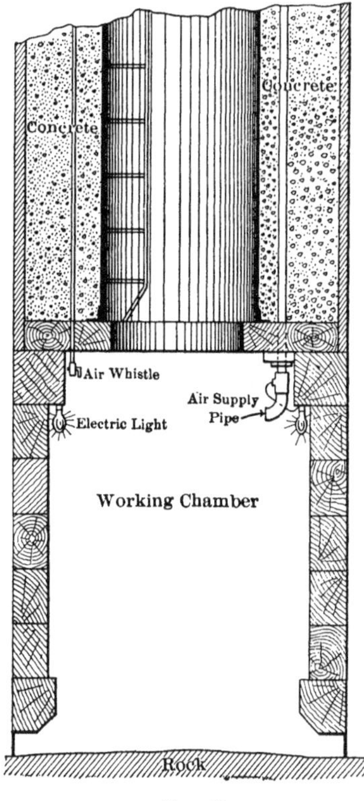

FIG. 3.

In striking contrast to such simple foundation problems, we have the case in hand. Foundations have to be laid to bed-rock, through about 80 feet of quicksand and water-bearing strata, which is already heavily loaded by adjoining ten-story buildings. In digging, water and soft mud are encountered but a few feet below the street level, and were this soft muck pumped out or removed by any of the old-time methods, more of this fluid material would enter the excavation from either side, and the adjoining structures would settle and later collapse. The Foundation Company, to whom was entrusted the responsibility both of planning and doing this work, solved these problems by employing the pneumatic caisson process, in conjunction with the Moran air lock, an invention of their vice-president, Mr. Daniel E. Moran, C.E.

The principle of the air lock was used for the underpinning of the adjoining buildings as well as for the main part of the work. Cut No. 5 shows how work was begun even while the old building was being wrecked. Niches about 5 feet above the cellar floor, and 5 feet wide, were cut in the walls of the adjoining buildings with Box electric and Ingersoll-Sergeant steam drills at intervals of about every 6 to 9 feet. These were carried downward through the old foundation, and through

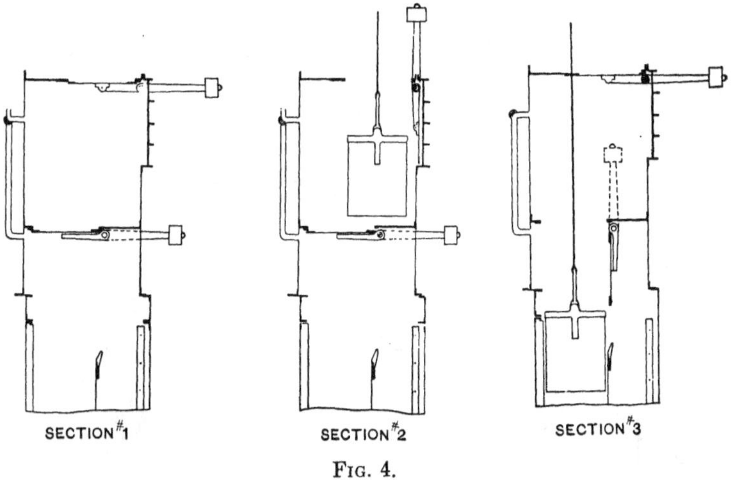

Fig. 4.

the sand under the foundation until the water line was struck. Then a 6-foot length of riveted steel pipe, 36 inches in diameter, was jacked down into the sand, thereby employing the weight of the building in constructing the new underpinning. A downward opening door was installed at the top of this length, a second length was bolted to the first, and then a second downward opening door was installed, completing the miniature air lock. As shown in Fig. 5, compressed air was supplied to the bottom chamber and the work pushed lower and lower through quicksand or hard pan, as successive lengths of pipe were bolted to the top, and material excavated. When rock was reached the entire cylinder was filled with concrete, the steel pipe remained, and when the steel beams were placed, as shown in the left side of Fig. 5, the underpinning at that point was completed. Twelve of these concrete cylinders support the wall of the Mills Building, and eleven that of the United

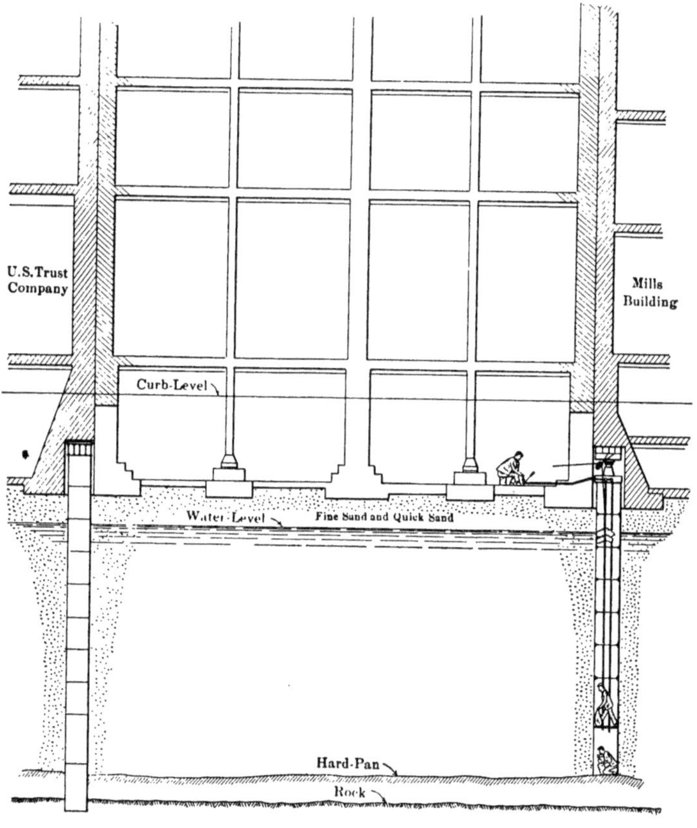

FIG. 5.

States Trust Building, as shown by the circles in the shaded portion of Fig. 2.

Twenty-seven concrete piers constitute the foundation work proper under the Trust Company of America Building. The remarkable speed with which these piers were sunk to bed-rock was made possible mainly from this one fact: The Moran air lock allows the material excavated in caisson to be hoisted to the open air in one continuous haul, being handled but once in transferring from bottom caisson up to the dumping place, generally a truck. This feat was never possible with any other equipment until Mr. Moran took the lead and perfected his device shown in Fig. 4.

The square and rectangular spaces shown in Fig. 2 give the location of the concrete piers on the site of the Trust Company of America Building. In Fig. 6 is shown the 4-boom traveler derrick, which is equipped with four double-drum Lidgerwood hoisting engines, and which effectively covered the entire area. It served to place the caissons (one of which weighed 20 tons and was 14 by 31 by 8 feet high) at their proper location. It also hoisted men and material in and out of the twenty-seven working chambers. A typical caisson or working chamber is shown in Fig. 3.

Fig. 6 shows the Moran air lock in place, near the top of the picture. The man stooping down on the ground is the gage tender, who keeps the pressure steady for the convenience of the men in the working chamber, and the man at the air lock communicates signals between the excavators and the engineers.

Having a general knowledge of the difficulties and of the apparatus to be used, and having finished the description of the underpinning, we shall take up the method employed in sinking the twenty-seven great concrete piers through this soft soil to bed-rock without weakening the adjoining foundations. See Fig. 6.

After the wooden caisson proper had been located accurately, the workmen with picks and shovels excavated inside the open topped frame, which gradually sank of its own weight. When it had sunk to water level, which was but 4 to 5 feet below the street, preparations were made to apply the compressed air as follows: The open top of the caisson was roofed over temporarily and the first 10-foot section of the steel collapsible working shaft was joined to the upper part of the caisson, as shown in Fig. 3. Section after section was added and then a

Moran air lock, as shown in Fig. 6. Then a section of temporary wooden cofferdam was built and fitted to the outside of the caisson, so as to extend its sides upward several feet. This was to act as a falsework for retaining the successive thin

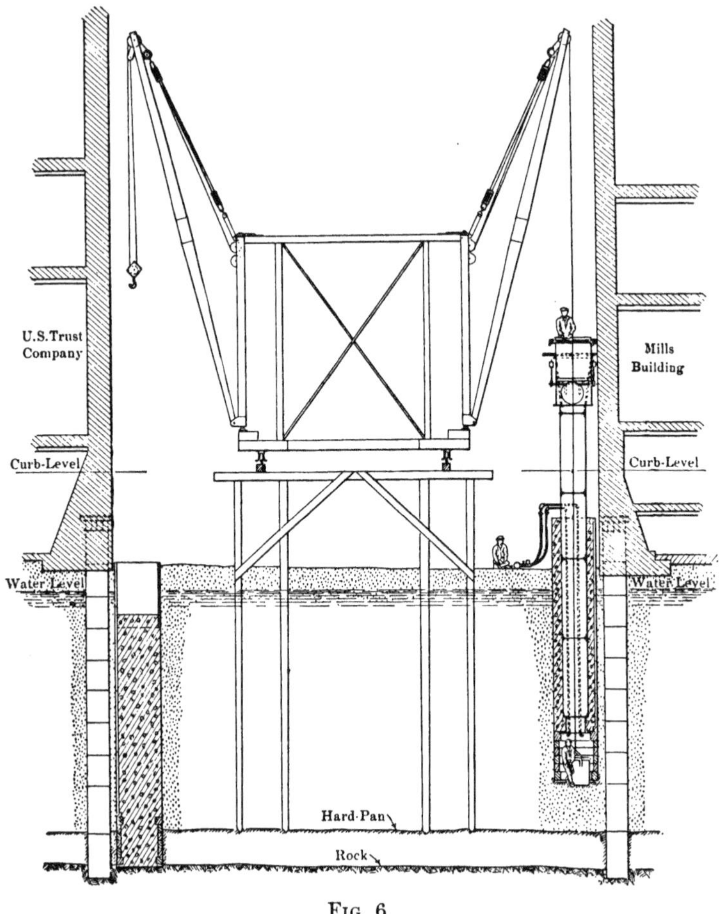

FIG. 6.

layers of concrete dumped into the annular space inside the cofferdam and on the roof of the caisson surrounding the working shaft, as will be noticed in the right hand side of section in Fig. 6. After the first 10 feet of concrete had hardened, a second cofferdam was fitted in a higher position, and the concreting continued, the first cofferdam being later removed and used as the third. One gang of men and one mixer could move from cofferdam to cofferdam, applying a 2-foot layer in each, so that by the time they returned to the first one it was hardened enough to receive its next layer without distorting the sheeting; so nearly the full height and full weight of the finished pier was used to force the caisson down to its final resting place on bed-rock, as rapidly as the excavating could be done by the men inside. Alpha Portland cement was used on this job in a 1 to 2½ to 5 mixture.

Referring again to Fig. 3, it will be noticed that the lower edges of the caisson sides are sharpened to form the "cutting edge" of the caisson, since they follow the level of the excavation and are pressed down by the great weight above. The contracting firm have prepared special 2-ton cast-iron weights, which can be piled on top of the concrete pier to further sink it, in case the "skin friction" on the sides is too great for the pier to sink of its own weight.

During this process three eight-hour shifts of the laborers were digging out material in the caisson under a pressure of from 18 to 24 pounds per square inch. This material was shoveled into buckets and hoisted up through the working shaft and the air lock out to the atmosphere, all in one continuous lift.

When bed-rock is reached, it is leveled off and, still under compressed air, the concrete is lowered into the caisson and rammed in place. The entire caisson is filled to the top, the temporary roof removed, and as the men retreat up the tube they unbolt and remove a section of the collapsible tubing and hoist it up for use in sinking another caisson. Gradually the entire space, previously used as a passage for men and material in and out of the working chamber or caisson, is filled with concrete, thus making the pier one solid monolith of concrete from bed-rock to the column base. This is shown on the left side of Fig. 6.

Referring again to plan view, Fig. 2, it is seen that these piers are sunk end to end with only a twelve-inch space between, and that the chain of piers around the entire site is made perfect by welding or bonding between the ends of each pier. This keeps the water from the surrounding soil from entering either the basement or sub-basement of the building. The method is as follows: In Fig. 7 will be seen the end faces of the two adjacent piers. The semi-octagonal groove shown in the faces was formed at the same time that the coffer-dam was put around the top of the caisson. The wooden falsework served as a "core," displacing the concrete from top to bottom of each end face of the piers. As soon as two adjacent caissons were ready to be welded or bonded the space bounded by *ABAB* was excavated. At the same time the laborers would tear off the

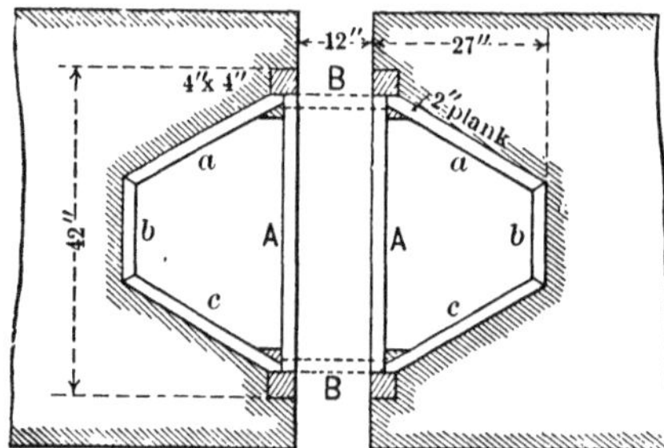

FIG. 7.

boards *AA*, saw them into the shorter lengths *BB*, and nail them in position *BB*, as shown in dotted lines. The space between the piers thus had become octagonal in shape, and was carried down the few feet to the water level. The planks *ABC* were removed. A 4-foot length of steel cylinder 30 inches in diameter was placed in the opening, and the space between it and the surrounding concrete and boards *BB* was filled in with concrete and made air tight. An air lock was bolted to the top of this cylinder and the workmen excavated the material between *A* and *B*, tearing out all the lumber as they went down, and hoisting all the material to the surface except what was needed for completing the boards *BB* down to the top of the caisson. This octagonal well was then filled to the top with concrete under pressure, and the bond was complete. When these connections between piers were completed on the north, east and west borders of the building site, it was only necessary to make the bond with the foundation piers of the Wall Street Exchange building on the south (put in by the same contractor

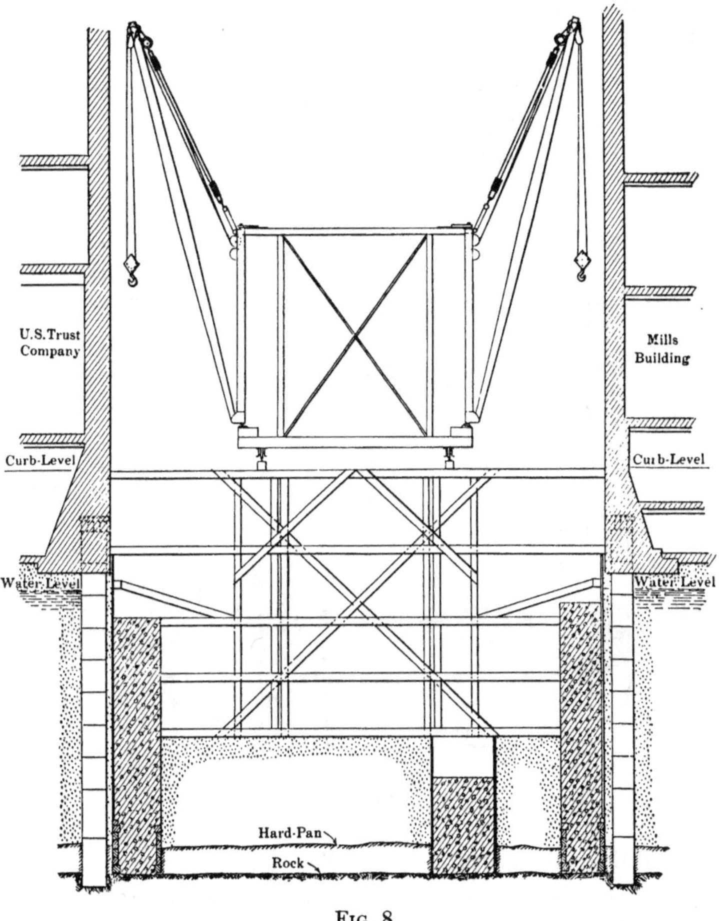

Fig. 8.

to bed-rock) in order to fully enclose the lot and prevent future flooding of the cellars, which reach to a depth of nearly 40 feet below the water level. It will be seen from Fig. 2 that this was done without expense of sinking a separate line of caissons on that side.

Another advantage in this solid wall type of bonded foundation construction is that the piers in the center of the lot can generally be sunk without the expense of the compressed air method, for there is little danger of any water seeping in from the outside, and therefore of weakening the other buildings.

At this stage of the job, the cellars can be safely dug, during which work the shoring of the neighboring building walls is done, as shown in Fig. 8. Fig. 9 illustrates the appearance

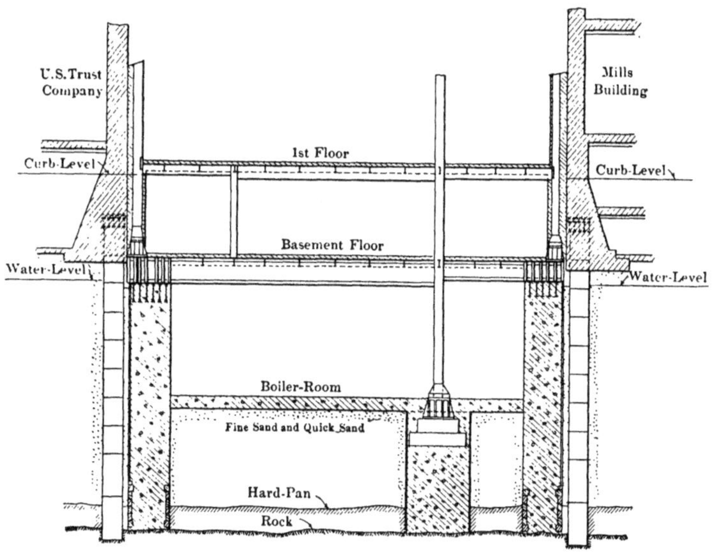

FIG. 9.

when all the substructure is completed and the cellar made ready for installing engines and boilers. The general class of work of which this job is merely one branch is civil engineering in water or water-bearing strata, including mine shafts in wet or marshy lands, bridge piers, sea walls and tunnels. *Compressed Air Magazine.*

Pneumatic Bridge Caissons in Great Britain. In a recent paper before the Institution of Engineers and Shipbuilders in

Scotland, Mr. Andrew S. Biggart described the operations in construction of a number of large bridges in Great Britain, in each of which undertakings the pneumatic caisson was a prominent feature, the work all executed by the firm of Sir William Arrol & Co. (Limited), Glasgow.

The Clyde Bridge of the Caledonian Railway Company has five deck spans from 60 to 200 feet long, carrying at one end nine tracks and at the other end thirteen tracks. Each of the river piers has five cylindrical columns seated on brick piers, with rectangular pneumatic caisson foundations. The caissons are of steel and each of them had three 3½-foot air shafts and was built on a falsework extending across the river, which also provided for the delivery and storage of materials and for the subsequent erection of the superstructure. Two wooden trestle bents were erected on the falsework on opposite sides of each caisson, and each pair supported a pair of horizontal riveted steel plate girders forming gallows frames over the caissons. Four vertical rods, one near each corner of the caisson, were connected to the caisson, and, passing between the pair of girders, engaged saddles commanded by hydraulic jacks. The caisson was lowered by the jacks to water level, concreted and again lowered and released from the suspending rods and concreted until it took bearing on the river bed. During this operation the caisson was maintained in horizontal position by guys, but rose and fell with the tide.

The bridge over the River Barrow, in the south of Ireland, has thirteen 140-foot fixed spans and one 215-foot swing span with 15 piers, each made with two 8-foot cylinders 26 feet apart on centers which had their bases extended to a diameter of from 10 to 15 feet. The lower portions of the cylinders were made with steel rings up to about the bottom of the river, and above that the cylinders were made with cast-iron rings. The cylinders were assembled on lateral extensions of a wooden falsework platform built across the river; the working chamber and the adjacent cylinder rings were lined with concrete and lowered to the river bottom by hydraulic jacks. The excavation in them was partly made by grabs, but in every case was finished under pneumatic pressure. The upper rings were added, and concreting between the air shaft and the rings was continued as the cylinders sank. Although they were carried down to an extreme depth of 120 feet below high water level, the pressure was reduced by special measures to a maximum of 45 pounds per square inch. This was mainly accomplished by the use of ejectors operated by compressed air to remove the water which came in under the cutting edge. The usual precautions were taken for the safety of the workmen by reducing the hours of work, restricting the speed of their exit, and providing warm refreshments and rest for them immediately after emerging from pressure. After the working chamber was concreted the air pressure was maintained on it for several days. The top ring of the cylinder was made of special depth to bring the upper edge to the required level. The cost of excavation at the maximum depth reached $200.00 per cubic yard.

The Suir Bridge, near the Barrow Bridge, carries the same single track railway on nine spans of about 140 feet, with cylinder piers similar to those of the Barrow Bridge, but not sunk to so great a depth. When one of the cylinders had sunk to a depth of 70 feet below the river bottom, and was subjected to a pressure of 32 pounds, one of the cast-iron rings just below the bed of the river burst, under a tensile stress of about 1000 pounds per square inch. The casting had been satisfactorily tested before acceptance, and pieces of it were tested after the accident and gave results up to the specifications without disclosing any flaw in the metal. No explanation has been offered for the break. A wooden cofferdam was built around the top of the cylinder and pumped out, and the broken ring was removed and replaced by a new one, and a concentric steel shaft 3 feet in diameter was set in it and extended down through the concrete lining to a point 5 feet below the upper end of the steel portion of the cylinder. The lower 9 feet of this shaft was then grouted to the concrete filling, the air-lock was placed on top of it, and sinking successfully completed.

The Black Friars Bridge over the Thames, in London, has five flat steel arch spans of 155 to 185 feet, which were recently enlarged by extending the width of the structure from 43 to 73 feet. This involved a corresponding extension of 30 feet at one end of all the piers, which were of masonry and were each supported on several rectangular pneumatic caissons and one triangular caisson forming a cut-water at the upstream end, where the extension was made. Pile falsework platforms were made enclosing the up-stream ends of the piers and extending 10 feet beyond it up-stream. Steel pneumatic caissons for the foundations of the pier extensions, with a semicircular cut-water on the up-stream end and a recess on the down-stream end to fit the nose of the old cut-water, were assembled and riveted on the falsework. The downstream end of the caisson did not, however, reach entirely to the main part of the old pier, but left a narrow gap there on each side of the down-stream end of the old cut-water. The caissons were assembled by steel stiff-leg derricks installed on the falsework platforms. A timber trestle was built parallel to the axis of the caisson on each side of it on the deck of the falsework platforms, and two pairs of steel-plate girders were seated on them, one at each end of the caissons, provided with vertical rods and hydraulic jacks by which the caisson was slightly lifted, while the supports under it were removed. Concrete was filled into the cutting edge and on the roof of the caisson and it was lowered to the bottom of the river, the sides being carried up by a temporary steel cofferdam continuous with them and heavily braced with interior timbers as it descended. The caissons were sunk just below the bottom of the river and the side spaces between the old and new caissons were enclosed by wooden cofferdams which were pumped out, allowing them to be excavated and concreted.

After one of the caissons had been lowered a few feet below high water, and was still suspended from the overhead girders, the hydraulic jack which supported one of its corners was prematurely exhausted, relieving the opposite diagonal jack of its load, throwing the entire 250-ton weight of the caisson on the remaining two jacks, and settling the piles under one of them a few inches. This movement caused the caisson to swing and the falsework to collapse, precipitating the caisson to the bottom of the river. The caisson was then braced by interior cross-girders and web plate brackets, and the point was lifted by hydraulic jacks operating bars suspended from two box girders braced together on the falsework platform. The caisson was then moved to proper position on sliding bearings, and was sunk in the usual manner. *Compressed Air Magazine.*

Pit Sinking through Frozen Quicksand. Mr. E. Seymour Wood recently read a paper before the North of England Institution of Mining Engineers describing a remarkable feat of shaft sinking through quicksand by the aid of the freezing process. The coal mine is located close to the east coast of the county of Durham, which lies south of Newcastle-on-the-Tyne.

The difficulties of sinking shafts in the East Durham district arise from the occurrence of magnesian limestone and underlying yellow sands, the latter being usually found as a quicksand, and both of these strata contain large quantities of water. At Dawdon, the magnesian limestone is 356 feet thick, and the yellow sand 92 feet thick. The limestone, as is usual, is full of gullets, giving off large quantities of water. Some of these gullets are connected with the sea, the water issuing from them being salt. The question was therefore considered whether to erect additional pumping plant or to carry out the sinking of the shafts through the sands in a frozen state. It was decided to adopt the freezing process. Accordingly, the shafts, each enclosed in a wooden shed, were handed over to the contractors, Messrs. Gebhardt and Koenig, Nordhausen, in April, 1903. This firm undertook the freezing of the ground through which the two shafts were to be sunk, and also the adjoining ground, to such an extent as to enable the owners of the colliery to carry out their sinking arrangements without the aid of pumps, until each shaft was sunk to a depth of 484 feet from the surface, and to establish and maintain a solid wall of ice around each shaft, so long as should be necessary for the purpose of sinking. Twenty-eight bore holes were marked off in a circle 30 feet in diameter surrounding the shafts, and were bored to a depth of 484 feet. After the whole of the freezing tubes were inserted, they were connected to the inner and outer collectors, for the circulation of brine. The length of time required to form the ice wall at the Castlereagh shaft was 185 days. The ice wall was maintained 353 days, and the total time of freezing was 538 days. The sand was struck at a depth of 371 feet and found to be frozen hard. In the shaft bottom the frozen sand was so hard that blasting had to be continued throughout the deposits. The temperature of the frozen sand at the bottom of the pit was 14°C. (+6° F.). The thawing of the frozen ground was accomplished by circulating warm brine through the freezing tubes. Once through the frozen sand the progress of the operations was very brisk. *Compressed Air Magazine.*

APPENDIX N

ENGINEERING DATA

CUBIC FEET OF FREE AIR REQUIRED TO RUN ONE DRILL OF THE SIZE AND AT THE PRESSURE STATED BELOW

Gage Pressure Pounds.	Size and Cylinder Diameter of Drill.												
	A35	A32	B	C	D	D	D	E	F	F	G	H	H9
	2″	2¼″	2½″	2¾″	3″	3⅛″	3 3/16″	3¼″	3½″	3⅝″	4¼″	5″	5½″
60	50	60	68	82	90	95	97	100	108	113	130	150	164
70	56	68	77	93	102	108	110	113	124	129	147	170	181
80	63	76	86	104	114	120	123	127	131	143	164	190	207
90	70	84	95	115	126	133	136	141	152	159	182	210	230
100	77	92	104	126	138	146	149	154	166	174	199	240	252

MULTIPLIERS TO DETERMINE CAPACITY OF COMPRESSOR REQUIRED TO OPERATE FROM ONE TO SEVENTY ROCK DRILLS AT ALTITUDES COMPARED WITH SEA LEVEL

Altitude Above Sea Level.	Number of Drills.																		
	1	2	3	4	5	6	7	8	9	10	12	15	20	25	30	40	50	60	70
Feet.	Multipliers.																		
0	1.	1.8	2.7	3.4	4.1	4.8	5.4	6.0	6.5	7.1	8.1	9.5	11.7	13.7	15.8	21.4	25.5	29.4	33.2
1000	1.03	1.85	2.78	3.5	4.22	4.94	5.56	6.18	6.69	7.3	8.34	9.78	12.05	14.1	16.3	22.0	26.26	30.3	34.2
2000	1.07	1.92	2.89	3.64	4.39	5.14	5.78	6.42	6.95	7.60	8.67	10.17	12.52	14.66	16.9	22.9	27.28	31.46	35.52
3000	1.10	1.98	2.97	3.74	4.51	5.28	5.94	6.6	7.15	7.81	8.91	10.45	12.87	15.07	17.38	23.54	28.05	32.34	36.52
4000	1.14	2.05	3.08	3.88	4.67	5.47	6.15	6.84	7.41	8.09	9.23	10.83	13.34	15.62	18.01	24.4	29.07	33.52	37.8
5000	1.17	2.10	3.16	3.98	4.8	5.62	6.32	7.02	7.61	8.31	9.48	11.12	13.69	16.03	18.49	25.04	29.84	34.4	38.84
6000	1.20	2.16	3.24	4.08	4.9	5.76	6.48	7.2	7.8	8.52	9.72	11.4	14.04	16.44	18.96	25.68	30.6	35.4	39.84
7000	1.23	2.21	3.32	4.18	5.04	5.9	6.64	7.38	7.99	8.73	9.96	11.68	14.39	16.85	19.43	26.32	31.36	36.16	40.84
8000	1.26	2.27	3.40	4.28	5.17	6.05	6.8	7.56	8.19	8.95	10.21	11.97	14.74	17.26	19.9	26.96	32.13	37.04	41.83
9000	1.29	2.32	3.48	4.39	5.29	6.19	6.96	7.74	8.38	9.16	10.45	12.26	15.09	17.67	20.38	27.6	32.9	37.92	42.83
10000	1.32	2.38	3.56	4.49	5.41	6.34	7.13	7.92	8.58	9.37	10.69	12.54	15.44	18.08	20.86	28.25	33.66	38.8	43.82
12000	1.37	2.47	3.7	4.66	5.62	6.57	7.4	8.22	8.9	9.73	11.1	13.02	16.03	18.77	21.64	29.32	34.94	40.28	45.48
15000	1.43	2.57	3.86	4.86	5.86	6.86	7.72	8.58	9.3	10.15	11.58	13.58	16.73	19.59	22.59	30.6	36.46	42.04	47.47

Example. Required the amount of free air necessary to operate thirty 5-inch drills at 9000 feet altitude, using to operate these drills air at a gage pressure of 80 pounds per square inch.

From page 340 we find when operating the drills at 80 pounds gage pressure at sea level, that one 5-inch "H" drill requires 190 cubic feet of free air per minute.

From above we also find that the factor for 30 drills at 9000 feet altitude is 20.38; multiplying 190 cubic feet by 20.38 gives 3872 cubic feet free air per minute, which is the displacement of a compressor for the above outfit under average conditions, to which must be added pipe line losses, such as friction and leakage.

LOSS OF PRESSURE IN POUNDS BY FRICTION IN TRANS

INITIAL AIR PRESSURE

Size Pipe Inches	DELIVERY IN CUBIC FEET OF												
	9.84	14.73	19.64	24.60	29.45	34.44	39.35	49.20	58.90	68.6	78.6	88.4	98.4
	EQUIVALENT DELIVERY IN CUBIC												
	50	75	100	125	150	175	200	250	300	350	400	450	500
1	18.24	.....	.....	.....	.....	.....	.....	.....	.....	.....	.....	.....	.....
1¼	5.06	11.34	20.16	.....	.....	.....	.....	.....	.....	.....	.....	.....	.....
1½	1.95	4.33	7.79	12.23	17.53	.....	.....	.....	.....	.....	.....	.....	.....
2	0.42	0.95	1.69	2.65	3.80	5.17	6.77	10.61	15.20	.....	.....	.....	.....
2½	0.13	0.29	0.52	0.81	1.16	1.58	2.09	3.24	4.65	6.31	8.28	10.47	.....
3	0.05	0.11	0.19	0.30	0.44	0.59	0.78	1.22	1.78	2.37	3.11	3.94	4.88
3½	.....	0.05	0.08	0.13	0.19	0.26	0.36	0.55	0.78	1.07	1.40	1.77	2.20
4	.....	.....	0.04	0.07	0.09	0.13	0.17	0.27	0.38	0.53	0.69	0.88	1.08
4½	.....	.....	.....	0.03	0.05	0.07	0.09	0.15	0.21	0.29	0. 9	0.48	0.60
5	.....	.....	.....	.....	0.03	0.04	0.06	0.08	0.12	0.17	0.22	0.28	0.34
6	.....	.....	.....	.....	.....	0.01	0.02	0.03	0.05	0.06	0.08	0.11	0.14
7	.....	.....	.....	.....	.....	.....	0.01	0.01	0.02	0.03	0.04	0.05	0.06
8	.....	.....	.....	.....	.....	.....	.....	.....	0.01	0.01	0.01	0.02	0.03
9	.....	.....	.....	.....	.....	.....	.....	.....	.....	.....	.....	0.01	0.01
10	.....	.....	.....	.....	.....	.....	.....	.....	.....	.....	.....	.....	.....
12	.....	.....	.....	.....	.....	.....	.....	.....	.....	.....	.....	.....	.....
14	.....	.....	.....	.....	.....	.....	.....	.....	.....	.....	.....	.....	.....
16	.....	.....	.....	.....	.....	.....	.....	.....	.....	.....	.....	.....	.....

INITIAL AIR PRESSURE

Size Pipe Inches	DELIVERY IN CUBIC FEET OF												
	7.74	11.3	15.2	19.4	23.2	27.2	31.0	38.7	46.5	54.2	62.0	69.7	77.4
	EQUIVALENT DELIVERY IN CUBIC												
	50	75	100	125	150	175	200	250	300	350	400	450	500
1	14.31	.....	.....	.....	.....	.....	.....	.....	.....	.....	.....	.....	.....
1¼	3.96	8.46	15.31	.....	.....	.....	.....	.....	.....	.....	.....	.....	.....
1½	1.53	3.26	5.92	9.64	13.79	.....	.....	.....	.....	.....	.....	.....	.....
2	0.33	0.71	1.28	2.09	2.99	4.09	5.34	8.32	12.01	.....	.....	.....	.....
2½	0.10	0.21	0.39	0.64	0.91	1.25	1.63	2.54	3.67	4.99	6.53	8.25	10.81
3	0.03	0.08	0.14	0.24	0.34	0.47	0.61	0.96	1.38	1.88	2.45	3.13	3.83
3½	0.01	0.03	0.06	0.11	0.15	0.21	0.27	0.43	0.62	0.84	1.11	1.40	1.73
4	.....	0.01	0.03	0.05	0.07	0.10	0.13	0.21	0.30	0.41	0.54	0.69	0.85
4½	.....	.....	0.02	0.03	0.04	0.06	0.07	0.12	0 17	0.23	0.30	0.38	0.47
5	.....	.....	0.01	0.01	0.02	0.03	0.04	0.07	0.09	0.13	0.17	0.22	0.27
6	.....	.....	.....	.....	.0.01	0.01	0.01	0.02	0.03	0.05	0.06	0.08	0.10
7	.....	.....	.....	.....	.....	.....	.....	0.01	0.01	0.02	0.03	0.04	0.05
8	.....	.....	.....	.....	.....	.....	.....	.....	.....	0.01	0.01	0.01	0.02
9	.....	.....	.....	.....	.....	.....	.....	.....	.....	.....	.....	.....	0.01
10	.....	.....	.....	.....	.....	.....	.....	.....	.....	.....	.....	.....	.....
12	.....	.....	.....	.....	.....	.....	.....	.....	.....	.....	.....	.....	.....
14	.....	.....	.....	.....	.....	.....	.....	.....	.....	.....	.....	.....	.....
16	.....	.....	.....	.....	.....	.....	.....	.....	.....	.....	.....	.....	.....

For longer or shorter pipes the friction loss is proportional to the length, *i. e.*,

MISSION OF AIR THROUGH PIPES 1000 FEET LONG.

60 POUNDS GAGE.

Compressed Air Per Minute.													
118.1	137.5	156.6	176.5	196.4	294.5	393.7	492	589	686	786	884	984	Size Pipe Inches
Feet of Free Air Per Minute.													
600	700	800	900	1000	1500	2000	2500	3000	3500	4000	4500	5000	
....	....	....	....	....	....	....	....	....	....	....	....	....	1
....	....	....	....	....	....	....	....	....	....	....	....	....	1¼
....	....	....	....	....	....	....	....	....	....	....	....	....	1½
....	....	....	....	....	....	....	....	....	....	....	....	....	2
....	....	....	....	....	....	....	....	....	....	....	....	....	2½
7.03	9.52	....	....	....	....	....	....	....	....	....	....	....	3
3.17	4.29	5.57	7.08	8.77	....	....	....	....	....	....	....	....	3½
1.56	2.12	2.75	3.49	4.33	9.73	....	....	....	....	....	....	....	4
0.87	1.17	1.52	1.94	2.40	5.39	9.65	....	....	....	....	....	....	4½
0.49	0.67	0.87	1.17	1.37	3.08	5.51	8.61	....	....	....	....	....	5
0.19	0.27	0.34	0.43	0.54	1.20	2.16	3.36	4.82	6.54	....	....	....	6
0.09	0.12	0.15	0.19	0.24	0.55	0.98	1.53	2.19	2.97	3.91	4.94	6.19	7
0.04	0.06	0.08	0.09	0.12	0.27	0.41	0.77	1.11	1.50	1.98	2.51	3.10	8
0.02	0.03	0.04	0.05	0.06	0.15	0.27	0.42	0.61	0.83	1.08	1.36	1.69	9
0.01	0.02	0.03	0.03	0.04	0.09	0.16	0.25	0.36	0.48	0.63	0.79	0.99	10
....	....	0.01	0.01	0.02	0.03	0.06	0.09	0.14	0.19	0.25	0.32	0.39	12
....	....	....	....	0.01	0.01	0.03	0.04	0.06	0.09	0.11	0.15	0.18	14
....	....	....	....	....	....	0.01	0.02	0.03	0.04	0.05	0.07	0.09	16

80 POUNDS GAGE.

Compressed Air Per Minute.													
92.9	108.2	124.0	139.5	152	232	310	387	465	542	620	697	774	Size Pipe Inches
Feet of Free Air Per Minute.													
600	700	800	900	1000	1500	2000	2500	3000	3500	4000	4500	5000	
....	....	....	....	....	....	....	....	....	....	....	....	....	1
....	....	....	....	....	....	....	....	....	....	....	....	....	1¼
....	....	....	....	....	....	....	....	....	....	....	....	....	1½
....	....	....	....	....	....	....	....	....	....	....	....	....	2
....	....	....	....	....	....	....	....	....	....	....	....	....	2½
5.61	7.46	9.86	....	....	....	....	....	....	....	....	....	....	3
2.46	3.37	4.42	5.61	6.64	15.41	....	....	....	....	....	....	....	3½
1.22	1.66	2.18	2.77	3.29	7.62	13.62	....	....	....	....	....	....	4
0.68	0.92	1.19	1.54	1.82	4.24	7.58	11.79	....	....	....	....	....	4½
0.39	0.53	0.69	0.88	1.04	2.43	4.32	6.88	9.72	13.25	....	....	....	5
0.15	0.20	0.27	0.34	0.40	0.95	1.69	2.64	3.79	5.27	6.78	8.54	10.55	6
0.06	0.09	0.12	0.15	0.18	0.43	0.77	1.19	1.73	2.35	3.07	3.89	4.79	7
0.03	0.04	0.06	0.08	0.09	0.22	0.39	0.60	0.87	1.19	1.55	1.97	2.46	8
0.02	0.02	0.03	0.04	0.05	0.12	0.21	0.33	0.48	0.65	0.85	1.08	1.33	9
0.01	0.01	0.02	0.02	0.03	0.06	0.12	0.19	0.28	0.37	0.49	0.66	0.77	10
....	....	0.01	0.01	0.01	0.02	0.04	0.07	0.11	0.15	0.19	0.25	0.30	12
....	....	....	....	....	0.01	0.02	0.03	0.05	0.06	0.09	0.11	0.14	14
....	....	....	....	....	....	0.01	0.01	0.02	0.03	0.04	0.05	0.07	16

for 500 feet one-half of the above; for 4000 feet four times the above, etc.

LOSS OF PRESSURE IN POUNDS BY FRICTION IN

INITIAL AIR PRESSURE

Size Pipe Inches	Delivery in Cubic Feet of												
	6.41	9.61	12.81	15.81	19.22	22.39	25.62	31.62	38.44	44.78	51.24	57.65	63.24
	Equivalent Delivery in Cubic												
	50	75	100	125	150	175	200	250	300	350	400	450	500
1	11.89	....	....	....	....	....	....	....	....	....	....	....	....
1¼	3.29	7.42	13.20	....	....	....	....	....	....	....	....	....	....
1½	1.28	2.87	5.11	7.75	11.42	....	....	....	....	....	....	....	....
2	0.27	0.62	1.15	1.68	2.48	3.36	4.43	6.72	9.95	13.41	....	....	....
2½	0.08	0.19	0.34	0.52	0.76	1.03	1.36	2.06	3.04	4.11	5.40	6.85	8.21
3	0.03	0.07	0.12	0.19	0.29	0.39	0.51	0.77	1.14	1.54	2.06	2.57	3.08
3½	0.01	0.03	0.05	0.08	0.13	0.17	0.23	0.35	0.51	0.69	0.92	1.16	1.39
4	....	0.01	0.02	0.04	0.06	0.09	0.12	0.17	0.25	0.34	0.45	0.57	0.68
4½	....	....	0.01	0.02	0.03	0 04	0.06	0.09	0.14	0.19	0.25	0.32	0.38
5	....	....	....	0.01	0.02	0.03	0.04	0.05	0.08	0.11	0.15	0.18	0.22
6	....	....	....	....	0.01	0.01	0.02	0.02	0.03	0.04	0.05	0.07	0.08
7	....	....	....	....	....	....	0.01	0.01	0.01	0.02	0.03	0.03	0.04
8	....	....	....	....	....	....	....	....	....	0.01	0.01	0.02	0.02
9	....	....	....	....	....	....	....	....	....	....	....	..01	0.01
10	....	....	....	....	....	....	....	....	....	....	....	....	....
12	....	....	....	....	....	....	....	....	....	....	....	....	....
14	....	....	....	....	....	....	....	....	....	....	....	....	....
16	....	....	....	....	....	....	....	....	....	....	....	....	....

INITIAL AIR PRESSURE

Size Pipe Inches	Delivery in Cubic Feet of												
	5.26	7.89	10.51	13.15	15.79	18.41	21.05	26.30	31.58	36.81	42.10	47.30	52.60
	Equivalent Delivery in Cubic												
	50	75	100	125	150	175	200	250	300	350	400	450	500
1	9.88	22.20	39.50	....	....	....	....	....	....	....	....	....	....
1¼	2.70	6.07	10.82	16.88	24.33	33.05	....	....	....	....	....	....	....
1½	1.05	2.37	4.22	6.58	9.47	12.90	16.84	26.30	37.90	....	....	....	....
2	0.23	0.51	0.91	1.42	2.04	2.78	3.63	5.68	8.18	11.08	14.51	18.38	22.68
2½	0.07	0.16	0.28	0.43	0.63	0.85	1.11	1.73	2.51	3.39	4.44	5.61	6.95
3	0.03	0.06	0.10	0.16	0.23	0.32	0.42	0.65	0.94	1.27	1.67	2.11	2.61
3½	0.01	0.03	0.05	0.07	0.11	0.14	0.19	0.29	0.42	0.58	0.75	0.95	1.18
4	....	0.01	0.02	0.04	0.05	0.07	0.09	0.15	0.21	0.28	0.37	0.47	0.58
4½	....	....	0.01	0.02	0.03	0.04	0.05	0.08	0.12	0.16	0.21	0.26	0.32
5	....	....	....	0.01	0.02	0.02	0.03	0.05	0.07	0.09	0.12	0.15	0.18
6	....	....	....	....	0.01	0.01	0.01	0.02	0.03	0.04	0.05	0.06	0.07
7	....	....	....	....	....	....	....	0.01	0.01	0.02	0.02	0.03	0.03
8	....	....	....	....	....	....	....	....	....	0.01	0.01	0.01	0.02
9	....	....	....	....	....	....	....	....	....	....	....	0.01	0.01
10	....	....	....	....	....	....	....	....	....	....	....	....	....
12	....	....	....	....	....	....	....	....	....	....	....	....	....
14	....	....	....	....	....	....	....	....	....	....	....	....	....
16	....	....	....	....	....	....	....	....	....	....	....	....	....

For longer or shorter pipes the friction loss is proportional to the length—*i.e.*,

TRANSMISSION OF AIR THROUGH PIPES 1000 FEET LONG

100 Pounds Gage.

Compressed Air per Minute.													Size Pipe Inches
76.88	89.56	102.5	115.3	126.5	192.2	256.2	316.2	384.4	447.8	512.4	576.5	632.4	
Feet of Free Air per Minute.													
600	700	800	900	1000	1500	2000	2500	3000	3500	4000	4500	5000	
....	....	....	....	....	....	....	....	....	....	....	....	....	1
....	....	....	....	....	....	....	....	....	....	....	....	....	1¼
....	....	....	....	....	....	....	....	....	....	....	....	....	1½
....	....	....	....	....	....	....	....	....	....	....	....	....	2
12.21	....	....	....	....	....	....	....	....	....	....	....	....	2½
4.58	6.19	8.13	10.23	12.39	....	....	....	....	....	....	....	....	3
2.14	2.79	3.67	4.64	5.60	12.81	....	....	....	....	....	....	....	3½
1.03	1.38	1.81	2.29	2.76	6.68	11.35	....	....	....	....	....	....	4
0.57	0.77	1.00	1.27	1.23	3.51	6.61	9.56	14.04	....	....	....	....	4½
0.33	0.44	0.57	0.76	0.88	2.03	3.62	5.51	8.11	10.95	14.48	....	....	5
0.12	0.17	0.22	0.28	0.34	0.78	1.41	2.14	3.16	4.26	5.59	7.04	8.51	6
0.05	0.07	0.10	0.13	0.16	0.36	0.67	0.97	1.44	1.93	2.55	3.22	3.88	7
0.03	0.04	0.05	0.06	0.08	0.18	0.33	0.49	0.76	0.98	1.30	1.84	1.98	8
0.02	0.02	0.03	0.04	0.04	0.09	0.18	0.27	0.39	0.53	0.72	0.89	1.07	9
0.01	0.01	0.02	0.02	0.03	0.05	0.10	0.16	0.23	0.31	0.41	0.52	0.63	10
....	....	0.01	0.01	0.01	0.02	0.04	0.06	0.09	0.12	0.16	0.21	0.25	12
....	....	....	....	....	0.01	0.02	0.03	0.04	0.05	0.07	0.09	0.11	14
....	....	....	....	....	....	0.01	0.01	0.02	0.03	0.04	0.05	0.06	16

125 Pounds Gage.

Compressed Air per Minute.													Size Pipe Inches
63.20	73.70	84.20	94.70	105.1	157.9	210.5	263.0	315.8	368.1	422.0	473.0	526.0	
Feet of Free Air per Minute.													
600	700	800	900	1000	1500	2000	2500	3000	3500	4000	4500	5000	
....	....	....	....	....	....	....	....	....	....	....	....	....	1
....	....	....	....	....	....	....	....	....	....	....	....	....	1¼
....	....	....	....	....	....	....	....	....	....	....	....	....	1½
....	....	....	....	....	....	....	....	....	....	....	....	....	2
10.00	13.60	17.80	....	....	....	....	....	....	....	....	....	....	2½
3.76	5.11	6.68	8.45	10.42	23.48	....	....	....	....	....	....	....	3
1.69	2.31	3.01	3.81	4.71	10.59	18.81	29.40	....	....	....	....	....	3½
0.84	1.14	1.49	1.88	2.32	5.23	9.30	14.52	20.90	28.51	....	....	....	4
0.46	0.63	0.83	1.04	1.29	2.90	5.15	8.05	11.59	15.78	20.61	26.10	32.20	4½
0.27	0.36	0.47	0.60	0.74	1.65	2.94	4.60	6.63	9.01	11. 0	14.90	18.45	5
0.10	0.14	0.18	0.23	0.29	0.64	1.15	1.80	2.59	3.53	4.61	5.83	7.20	6
0.05	0.06	0.08	0.11	0.13	0.29	0.52	0.82	1.18	1.61	2.19	2.65	3.27	7
0.02	0.03	0.04	0.05	0.07	0.15	0.26	0.41	0.60	0.81	1.06	1.34	1.65	8
0.01	0.02	0.02	0.03	0.04	0.08	0.15	0.23	0.33	0.45	0.58	0.73	0.90	9
0.01	0.01	0.01	0.02	0.02	0.05	0.08	0.13	0.19	0.26	0.34	0.43	0.53	10
....	....	0.01	0.01	0.01	0.02	0.03	0.05	0.07	0.10	0.13	0.17	0.21	12
....	....	....	....	....	0.01	0.02	0.02	0.03	0.04	0.06	0.08	0.10	14
....	....	....	....	....	....	0.01	0.01	0.02	0.02	0.03	0.04	0.05	16

for 500 feet one-half of the above; for 4000 feet four times the above, etc.

HORSE-POWER DEVELOPED IN COMPRESSING ONE CUBIC FOOT OF FREE AIR FROM ATMOSPHERIC PRESSURE (14.7 POUNDS) TO VARIOUS GAGE PRESSURES

Initial Temperature of the Air in Each Cylinder Taken as 60° F
(Jacket Cooling not Considered).

Gage Pressure.	Isothermal Compression.	Adiabatic Compression.			
		One Stage.	Two Stage.	Three Stage.	Four Stage.
10	.0332	.0358	....	....	....
20	.0551	.0623	....	....	....
30	.0713	.0842	....	....	....
40	.0842	.1026	....	....	....
50	.0950	.1187	....	....	....
60	.1042	.1331	....	....	....
70	.1122	.1465	.128	.122	.119
80	.1194	.1585	.137	.131	.127
90	.1258	.1695	.146	.139	.135
100	.1317	.1800	.154	.146	.142
125	.1443	.2036	.171	.161	.157
150	.1549	.2244	.186	.174	.169
200	.1719	.2600	.210	.196	.190
300	.1964	.3164	.247	.229	.220
400	.2141	.3613	.276	.253	.242
500	.2279	.3889	.299	.272	.260
600	.2393	.4318	.318	.288	.275
700	.2489	.4608	.335	.302	.289
800	.2573	.4873	.349	.314	.299
900	.2649	.5114	.363	.325	.310
1000	.2720	.5337	.375	.335	.318
1200	.2829	.5742	.397	.353	.333
1400	.2924	.6102	.414	.368	.347
1600	.3012	.6427	.432	.381	.359
1800	.3087	.6724	.447	.393	.369
2000	.3154	.7003	.460	.403	.379

Note. The above values are for sea-level conditions only.

GLOBE VALVES, TEES, AND ELBOWS

The reduction of pressure produced by globe valves is the same as that caused by the following additional lengths of straight pipe, as calculated by the formula:

$$\text{Additional length of pipe} = \frac{114 \times \text{diameter of pipe}}{1 + (3.6 \div \text{diameter})}$$

Diameter of pipe	1	1½	2	2½	3	3½	4	5	6	inches
Additional length	2	4	7	10	13	16	20	28	36	feet
	7	8	10	12	15	18	20	22	24	inches
	44	53	70	88	115	143	162	181	200	feet

The reduction of pressure produced by elbows and tees is equal to two-thirds of that caused by globe valves. The following are the additional lengths of straight pipe to be taken into account for elbows and tees. For globe valves multiply by $\frac{3}{2}$:

Diameter of pipe	1	1½	2	2½	3	3½	4	5	6	inches
Additional length	2	3	5	7	9	11	13	19	24	feet
	7	8	10	12	15	18	20	22	24	inches
	30	35	47	59	77	96	108	120	134	feet

These additional lengths of pipe for globe valves, elbows, and tees must be added in each case to the actual length of straight pipe. Thus a 6-inch pipe, 500 feet long, with 1 globe valve, 2 elbows and 3 tees, would be equivalent to a straight pipe $500+36+(2\times 24)+(3\times 24)=656$ feet long.

LOSS OF WORK DUE TO HEAT IN COMPRESSING AIR FROM ATMOSPHERIC PRESSURE TO VARIOUS GAGE PRESSURES BY SIMPLE AND COMPOUND COMPRESSION

AIR IN EACH CYLINDER; INITIAL TEMPERATURE 60° F.

Gage Pressure.	One Stage.		Two Stage.		Three Stage.		Four Stage.	
	Percentage of Work Lost in Terms of							
	Isothermal Compression.	Adiabatic Compression.	Isothermal Compression.	Adiabatic Compression.	Isothermal Compression.	Adiabatic Compression.	Isothermal Compression.	Adiabatic Compression.
60	29.9	23.0	13.4	11.8	8.6	7.9	4.7	4.5
70	30.6	23.4	14.1	12.4	8.7	8.0	6.1	5.7
80	32.7	24.6	14.7	12.8	9.7	8.9	6.4	6.0
90	34.7	25.8	16.1	13.8	10.5	9.5	7.3	6.8
100	36.7	26.8	16.9	14.5	10.9	9.8	7.8	7.3
125	41.1	29.2	18.5	15.6	11.6	10.4	8.8	8.1
150	44.8	30.9	20.1	16.7	12.3	10.9	9.1	8.4
200	51.2	33.9	22.2	18.1	14.0	12.3	10.5	9.5
300	61.2	37.9	25.7	20.5	16.6	14.2	12.0	10.7
400	68.7	40.7	28.9	22.4	18.2	15.4	13.1	11.5
500	70.6	41.4	31.2	23.8	19.3	16.2	14.1	12.3
600	80.4	44.5	32.8	24.7	20.4	16.9	14.9	13.0
700	85.0	46.0	34.6	25.7	21.3	17.6	16.1	13.8
800	89.5	47.2	35.7	26.3	22.0	18.1	16.2	13.9
900	93.0	48.2	37.1	27.0	22.6	18.5	16.6	14.4
1000	96.1	49.0	37.9	27.5	23.2	18.8	16.9	14.5
1200	102.8	50.7	40.3	28.8	24.8	19.9	17.7	15.0
1400	108.6	52.0	41.5	29.3	25.9	20.5	18.6	15.7
1600	113.4	53.1	43.5	30.3	26.5	20.9	19.2	16.1
1800	117.5	54.0	44.8	31.0	27.3	21.2	19.6	16.4
2000	122.0	55.0	45.8	31.4	27.5	21.5	19.9	16.5

FLOW OF AIR THROUGH AN ORIFICE,

In Cubic Feet of Free Air per Minute, Flowing from a Round Hole in Receiver into the Atmosphere

Diameter of Orifice, Inches.	Receiver Gage Pressure.								
	2 lbs.	5 lbs.	10 lbs.	15 lbs.	20 lbs.	25 lbs.	30 lbs.	35 lbs.	40 lbs.
1/64	.038	.0597	.0842	.103	.119	.133	.156	.173	.19
1/32	.153	.242	.342	.418	.485	.54	.632	.71	.77
1/16	.647	.965	1.36	1.67	1.93	2.16	2.52	2.80	3.07
1/8	2.435	3.86	5.45	6.65	7.7	8.6	10.	11.2	12.27
1/4	9.74	15.40	21.8	26.70	30.8	34.5	40.	44.7	49.09
3/8	21.95	34.60	49.	60.	69.	77.	90.	100.	110.45
1/2	39.00	61.60	87.	107.	123.	138.	161.	179.	196.35
5/8	61.00	96.50	136.	167.	193.	216.	252.	280.	306.80
3/4	87.60	133.	196.	240.	277.	310.	362.	400.	441.79
7/8	119.50	189.	267.	326.	378.	422.	493.	550.	601.32
1	156.	247.	350.	427.	494.	550.	645.	715.	785.40
1¼	242.	384.	543.	665.	770.	860.	1000.		
1½	350.	550.	780.	960.					
2	625.	985.							
	45 lbs.	50 lbs.	60 lbs.	70 lbs.	80 lbs.	90 lbs.	100 lbs.	125 lbs.	
1/64	.208	.225	.26	.295	.33	.364	.40	.486	
1/32	.843	.914	1.05	1.19	1.33	1.47	1.61	1.97	
1/16	3.36	3.64	4.2	4.76	5.32	5.87	6.45	7.85	
1/8	13.4	14.50	16.8	19.0	21.2	23.50	25.8	31.4	
1/4	53.8	58.2	67.	76.	85.	94.	103.	125.	
3/8	121.	130.	151.	171.	191.	211.	231.	282.	
1/2	215.	232.	268.	304.	340.	376.	412.	502.	
5/8	336.	364.	420.	476.	532.	587.	645.	785.	
3/4	482.	522.	604.	685.	765.	843.	925.		
7/8	658.	710.	622.	930.	1004.				
1	860.	930.							

DENSITY OF GASES AND VAPORS

Air at Same Temperature and Pressure being 1.0; also Weight of a Cubic Foot at 62° F. Under Atmospheric Pressure 29.92 Inches Mercury

	Density, Air at Same Temp. and Pres. being 1.0 (Regnault)	Specific Gravity or Density, Water at 62° being 1.0.	Weight of a Cubic Foot in Pounds.	Cubic Feet at 62° in One Pound.
Air (atmospheric)	1.00000	.001221 or 1/819	.07610	13.14
Hydrogen gas	.06926	.0000846 or 1/11820	.00527	189.70
Oxygen gas	1.10563	.001350 or 1/741	.08414	11.88
Nitrogen gas	.97137	.001185 or 1/844	.07383	13.54
Carbonic acid gas	1.52901	.001870 or 1/535	.11636	8.59
Carbonic oxide gas	.9674	.00118 or 1/847	.07364	13.60
Vapor of water	.6235	.0007613 or 1/1313	.04745	21.07
Vapor of alcohol	1.589	.00194 or 1/515	.12092	8.27
Vapor of sulphuric ether	2.586	.00316 or 1/316	.19680	5.08
Vapor of oil of turpentine	4.760	.00581 or 1/172	.36224	2.76
Vapor of mercury	6.976	.00850 or 1/118	.52987	1.88

COMPRESSED AIR TABLE FOR PUMPING PLANTS

For the convenience of engineers and others figuring on pumping plants to be operated by compressed air, a table is subjoined by which the pressure and volume of air required for any size pump can be readily ascertained. Reasonable allowances have been made for loss due to clearances in pump and friction in pipe.

Ratio of Diameters.	Perpendicular Height, in Feet, to which the Water is to be Pumped.															
	25	50	75	100	125	150	175	200	225	250	300	350	400	450	500	
1 to 1	13.75	27.5	41.25	55.0	68.25	82.5	96.25	110.0	......	......	......	......	......	......	......	Air Pressure at pump
	.21	.45	.60	.75	.89	1.04	1.20	1.34	......	......	......	......	......	......	......	Cubic feet of free air per gallon of water
1½ to 1	......	12.22	18.33	24.44	30.33	36.66	42.76	48.88	55.0	61.11	73.32	85.4	97.66	......	......	Air pressure at pump
	......	.65	.80	.95	1.09	1.24	1.39	1.53	1.68	1.83	2.12	2.41	2.70	......	......	Cubic feet of free air per gallon of water
1¾ to 1	......	......	13.75	19.8	22.8	27.5	32.1	36.66	41.25	45.83	55.0	64.16	73.33	82.5	......	Air pressure at pump
	......	......	.94	1.14	1.24	1.30	1.54	1.69	1.84	1.99	2.39	2.59	2.88	3.19	......	Cubic feet of free air per gallon of water
2 to 1	......	......	......	13.75	17.19	20.63	24.06	27.5	30.94	34.38	41.25	48.13	55.0	61.88	68.75	Air pressure at pump
	......	......	......	1.23	1.37	1.52	1.66	1.81	1.96	2.11	2.40	2.69	2.98	3.28	3.57	Cubic feet of free air per gallon of water
2¼ to 1	......	......	......	......	13.75	16.5	19.25	22.0	24.75	27.5	33.0	38.5	44.0	49.5	55.0	Air pressure at pump
	......	......	......	......	1.533	1.68	1.83	1.97	2.12	2.26	2.56	2.85	3.15	3.44	3.73	Cubic feet of free air per gallon of water
2½ to 1	......	......	......	......	......	13.2	15.4	17.6	19.8	22.0	26.4	30.8	35.2	39.6	44.0	Air pressure at pump
	......	......	......	......	......	1.79	1.98	2.06	2.104	2.34	2.62	2.88	3.18	3.36	3.23	Cubic feet of free air per gallon of water

To find the amount of air and pressure required to pump a given quantity of water a given height, find the ratio of diameters between water and air cylinders, and multiply the number of gallons of water by the figure found in the column for the required lift. The result is the number of cubic feet of free air. The pressure required on the pump will be found directly above in the same column. For example: The ratio between cylinders being 2 to 1, required to pump 100 gallons, height of lift 250 feet. We find under 250 at ratio 2 to 1, the figures 2.11; $2.11 \times 100 = 211$ cubic feet of free air. The pressure required is 34.38 pounds.

USEFUL INFORMATION—STEAM

A cubic inch of water evaporated under atmospheric pressure is approximately converted into one cubic foot of steam.

The horse-power of boilers, as per standard adopted by the A. S.M.E., is 30 pounds of water evaporated per hour at a pressure of 70 pounds per square inch and from a temperature of 100 degrees Fahrenheit.

Well designed boilers, under successful operation, will evaporate from 7 to 10 pounds of water per pound of first-class coal.

Each square foot of heating surface is considered sufficient to evaporate 2 pounds of water; therefore with an engine using 30 pounds of water per horse-power per hour, each horse-power of the engine requires 15 square feet heating surface in the boiler.

On 1 square foot of fire grate can be burned on an average from 10 to 12 pounds of hard coal, or 18 to 20 pounds of soft coal, per hour, with natural draft.

Two and one-quarter pounds of dry wood is equal to one pound of average quality soft coal.

Steam engines consume fron 12 to 50 pounds of feed water, and from 1¼ to 7 pounds of coal, per hour per indicated horse-power.

Condensing engines require from 20 to 30 times the amount of feed water for condensing purposes; approximately for most engines, 1 to 1½ gallons condensing water per minute per indicated horse-power.

Surface condensers for compound steam engines require about 2 square feet of cooling surface per horse-power; ordinary engines will require more surface according to their economy in the use of steam. It is absolutely necessary that the air pump should be set lower than the condenser for satisfactory results.

The effect of a good air pump and condenser should be to get 25 inches of vacuum and to make available about 10 pounds more mean effective pressure with the same terminal pressure, or to give the same mean effective pressure with a correspondingly less terminal pressure. Approximately, a good condenser will save one-fourth of the fuel consumed, or, in other words, increase the power of the engine one-fourth, the fuel consumption remaining the same.

USEFUL INFORMATION—WATER

One cubic inch weighs .0361 pound.

One pound equals 27.7 cubic inches.

One cubic foot equals 62.4245 pounds at 39 degrees Fahrenheit; 7.48 U. S. gallons; 6.2321 imperial gallons.

One U. S. gallon equals 8.33111 pounds; 231 cubic inches; .13368 cubic foot.

One imperial gallon equals 10 pounds at 62 degrees Fahrenheit; 277.274 cubic inches; .16046 cubic feet.

One pound pressure equals 2.31 feet in height.

One foot in height equals .433 pound pressure.

Petroleum weighs 6½ pounds per U. S. gallon, 42 gallons to the barrel.

To convert imperial gallons into U. S. gallons, multiply by the factor 1.2. To convert U. S. gallons into imperial gallons multiply by the factor .8333.

A miner's inch is a measure for flow of water, and is the quantity of water that will flow in one minute through an opening 1 inch square in a plank 2 inches thick under a head of 6½ inches to the center of the orifice. This is equivalent approximately to 1.53 cubic feet, or 11½ gallons per minute.

To find the diameter of pump plungers to pump a given quantity of water at 100 feet piston speed per minute, divide the number of gallons by 4, then extract the square root, and the result will be the diameter in inches of the plungers.

To find the number of gallons delivered per minute by a single double-acting pump at 100 feet piston speed per minute, square the diameter of the plungers, then multiply by 4.

To find the horse-power necessary to elevate water to a given height, multiply the weight of the water elevated per minute by the height in feet and divide the product by 33,000 (an allowance should be made for water friction and a further allowance for losses in the steam cylinder, say, from 20 to 30 per cent).

The mean pressure of the atmosphere is usually estimated at 14.7 pounds per square inch, so that with a perfect vacuum it will sustain a column of mercury 29.9 inches, or a column of water 33.9 feet high at sea level.

To determine the proportion between the steam and pump cylinder, multiply the given area of the pump cylinder by the resistance on the pump in pounds per square inch, and divide the product by the available pressure of steam in pounds per square inch. The product equals the area of the steam cylinder. To this must be added an extra area to overcome the friction, which is usually taken at 25 per cent.

The resistance of friction to the flow of water through pipes of uniform diameter is independent of the pressure and increases directly as the length and the square of the velocity of the flow, and inversely as the diameter of the pipe. With wooden pipes the friction is 1.75 times greater than in metallic. Doubling the diameter increases the capacity four times.

To determine the velocity in feet per minute necessary to discharge a given volume of water in a given time, multiply the number of cubic feet of water by 144 and divide the product by the area of the pipe in inches.

To determine the area of a required pipe, the volume and velocity of water being given, multiply the number of cubic feet of water by 144 and divide the product by the velocity in feet per minute. *Cameron Steam Pump Works.*

PRESSURE OF WATER

The pressure of water in pounds per square inch for every foot in height to 260 feet; and then, by intervals, to 3000 feet head. By this table, from the pounds pressure per square inch, the feet head is readily obtained, and *vice versa*.

Feet Head.	Pressure per Square Inch.	Feet Head.	Pressure per Square Inch.	Feet Head.	Pressure per Square Inch.	Feet Head.	Pressure per Square Inch.	Feet Head.	Pressure per Square Inch.	Feet Head.	Pressure per Square Inch.
1	0.43	54	23.39	107	46.34	160	69.31	213	92.20	285	123.45
2	0.86	55	23.82	108	46.78	161	69.74	214	92.69	290	125.62
3	1.30	56	24.26	109	47.21	162	70.17	215	93.13	295	127.78
4	1.73	57	24.69	110	47.64	163	70.61	216	93.56	300	129.95
5	2.16	58	25.12	111	48.08	164	71.04	217	93.99	305	132.12
6	2.59	59	25.55	112	48.51	165	71.47	218	94.43	310	134.28
7	3.03	60	25.99	113	48.94	166	71.91	219	94.86	315	136.46
8	3.46	61	26.42	114	49.38	167	72.34	220	95.30	320	138.62
9	3.89	62	26.85	115	49.81	168	72.77	221	95.73	325	140.79
10	4.33	63	27.29	116	50.24	169	73.20	222	96.16	330	142.95
11	4.76	64	27.72	117	50.68	170	73.64	223	96.60	335	145.12
12	5.20	65	28.15	118	51.11	171	74.07	224	97.03	340	147.28
13	5.63	66	28.58	119	51.54	172	74.50	225	97.46	345	149.45
14	6.06	67	29.02	120	51.98	173	74.94	226	97.90	350	151.61
15	6.49	68	29.45	121	52.41	174	75.37	227	98.33	355	153.78
16	6.93	69	29.88	122	52.84	175	75.80	228	98.76	360	155.94
17	7.36	70	30.32	123	53.28	176	76.23	229	99.20	365	158.10
18	7.79	71	30.75	124	53.71	177	76.67	230	99.63	370	160.27
19	8.22	72	31.18	125	54.15	178	77.10	231	100.00	375	162.45
20	8.66	73	31.62	126	54.58	179	77.53	232	100.49	380	164.61
21	9.09	74	32.05	127	55.01	180	77.97	233	100.93	385	166.78
22	9.53	75	32.48	128	55.44	181	78.40	234	101.36	390	168.94
23	9.96	76	32.92	129	55.88	182	78.84	235	101.70	395	171.11
24	10.39	77	33.35	130	56.31	183	79.27	236	102.23	400	173.27
25	10.82	78	33.78	131	56.74	184	79.70	237	102.66	425	184.10
26	11.26	79	34.21	132	57.18	185	80.14	238	103.09	450	195.00
27	11.69	80	34.65	133	57.61	186	80.57	239	103.53	475	205.77
28	12.12	81	35.08	134	58.04	187	81.00	240	103.96	500	216.58
29	12.55	82	35.52	135	58.48	188	81.43	241	104.39	525	227.42
30	12.99	83	35.95	136	58.91	189	81.87	242	104.83	550	238.25
31	13.42	84	36.39	137	59.34	190	82.30	243	105.26	575	249.09
32	13.86	85	36.82	138	59.77	191	82.73	244	105.69	600	259.90
33	14.29	86	37.25	139	60.21	192	83.17	245	106.13	625	270.73
34	14.72	87	37.68	140	60.64	193	83.60	246	106.56	650	281.56
35	15.16	88	38.12	141	61.07	194	84.03	247	106.99	675	292.40
36	15.59	89	38.55	142	61.51	195	84.47	248	107.43	700	303.22
37	16.02	90	38.98	143	61.94	196	84.90	249	107.86	725	314.05
38	16.45	91	39.42	144	62.37	197	85.33	250	108.29	750	324.88
39	16.89	92	39.85	145	62.81	198	85.76	251	108.73	775	335.72
40	17.32	93	40.28	146	63.24	199	86.20	252	109.16	800	346.54
41	17.75	94	40.72	147	63.67	200	86.63	253	109.59	825	357.37
42	18.19	95	41.15	148	64.10	201	87.07	254	110.03	850	368.20
43	18.62	96	41.58	149	64.54	202	87.50	255	110.46	875	379.03
44	19.05	97	42.01	150	64.97	203	87.93	256	110.89	900	389.86
45	19.49	98	42.45	151	65.40	204	88.36	257	111.32	925	400.70
46	19.92	99	42.88	152	65.84	205	88.80	258	111.76	950	411.54
47	20.35	100	43.31	153	66.27	206	89.21	259	112.19	975	422.35
48	20.79	101	43.75	154	66.70	207	89.66	260	112.62	1000	433.18
49	21.22	102	44.18	155	67.14	208	90.10	261	113.06	1500	649.70
50	21.65	103	44.61	156	67.57	209	90.53	262	113.49	2000	866.30
51	22.09	104	45.05	157	68.00	210	90.96	270	116.96	3000	1299.50
52	22.52	105	45.48	158	68.43	211	91.39	275	119.12		
53	22.95	106	45.91	159	68.87	212	91.83	280	121.29		

AREAS OF CIRCLES, ADVANCING BY EIGHTHS

AREAS

Diam.	0	⅛	¼	⅜	½	⅝	¾	⅞
0	.0	.0123	.0491	.1105	.1964	.3068	.4418	.6013
1	.7854	.9940	1.2272	1.4849	1.7671	2.0739	2.4053	2.7612
2	3.14	3.55	3.98	4.43	4.91	5.41	5.94	6.49
3	7.07	7.67	8.30	8.95	9.62	10.32	11.05	11.79
4	12.57	13.36	14.19	15.03	15.90	16.80	17.72	18.67
5	19.64	20.63	21.65	22.69	23.76	24.85	25.97	27.11
6	28.27	29.47	30.68	31.92	33.18	34.47	35.79	37.12
7	38.49	39.87	41.28	42.72	44.18	45.66	47.17	48.71
8	50.27	51.85	53.46	55.09	56.75	58.43	60.13	61.86
9	63.62	65.40	67.20	69.03	70.88	72.76	74.66	76.59
10	78.54	80.52	82.52	84.54	86.59	88.66	90.76	92.89
11	95.03	97.21	99.40	101.62	103.87	106.14	108.43	110.75
12	113.10	115.47	117.86	120.28	122.72	125.19	127.68	130.19
13	132.73	135.30	137.89	140.50	143.14	145.80	148.49	151.20
14	153.94	156.70	159.48	162.30	165.13	167.99	170.87	173.78
15	176.71	179.67	182.65	185.66	188.69	191.75	194.83	197.93
16	201.06	204.22	207.39	210.60	213.82	217.08	220.35	223.65
17	226.98	230.33	233.71	237.10	240.53	243.98	247.45	250.95
18	254.47	258.02	261.59	265.18	268.80	272.45	276.12	279.81
19	283.53	287.27	291.04	294.83	298.65	302.49	306.35	310.24
20	314.16	318.10	322.06	326.05	330.06	334.10	338.16	342.25
21	346.36	350.50	354.66	358.84	363.05	367.28	371.54	375.83
22	380.13	384.46	388.82	393.20	397.61	402.04	406.49	410.97
23	415.48	420.00	424.56	429.13	433.74	438.36	443.01	447.69
24	452.39	457.11	461.86	466.64	471.44	476.26	481.11	485.98
25	490.87	495.79	500.74	505.71	510.71	515.72	520.77	525.84
26	530.93	536.05	541.19	546.35	551.55	556.76	562.00	567.27
27	572.56	577.87	583.21	588.57	593.96	599.37	604.81	610.27
28	615.75	621.26	626.80	632.36	637.94	643.55	649.18	654.84
29	660.52	666.23	671.96	677.71	683.49	689.30	695.13	700.98
30	706.86	712.76	718.69	724.64	730.62	736.62	742.64	748.69
31	754.77	760.87	766.99	773.14	779.31	785.51	791.73	797.98
32	804.25	810.54	816.86	823.21	829.58	835.97	842.39	848.83
33	855.30	861.79	868.31	874.85	881.41	888.00	894.62	901.26
34	907.92	914.61	921.32	928.06	934.82	941.61	948.42	955.25
35	962.11	969.00	975.91	982.84	989.80	996.78	1003.8	1010.8
36	1017.9	1025.0	1032.1	1039.2	1046.3	1053.5	1060.7	1068.0
37	1075.2	1082.5	1089.8	1097.1	1104.5	1111.8	1119.2	1126.7
38	1134.1	1141.6	1149.01	1156.6	1164.2	1171.7	1179.3	1186.9
39	1194.6	1202.3	1210.0	1217.7	1225.4	1233.2	1241.0	1248.8
40	1256.6	1264.5	1272.4	1280.3	1288.2	1296.2	1304.2	1312.2
41	1320.3	1328.3	1336.4	1344.5	1352.7	1360.8	1369.0	1377.2
42	1385.4	1393.7	1402.0	1410.3	1418.6	1427.0	1435.4	1443.8
43	1452.2	1460.7	1469.1	1477.6	1486.2	1494.7	1503.3	1511.9
44	1520.5	1529.2	1537.9	1546.6	1555.3	1564.0	1572.8	1581.6
45	1590.4	1599.3	1608.2	1617.0	1626.0	1634.9	1643.9	1652.9
46	1661.9	1670.9	1680.0	1689.1	1698.2	1707.4	1716.5	1725.7
47	1734.9	1744.2	1753.5	1762.7	1772.1	1781.4	1790.8	1800.1
48	1809.6	1819.0	1828.5	1837.9	1847.5	1857.0	1866.5	1876.1
49	1885.7	1895.4	1905.0	1914.7	1924.4	1934.2	1943.9	1953.7
50	1963.5	1973.3	1983.2	1993.1	2203.0	2012.9	2022.8	2032.8

TABLE GIVING RATIOS OF AREAS

For given diameters of steam and water cylinders.

Diameter of Water Cylinders.	Diameter of Steam Cylinders.										
	3	3½	4	5	6	7	8	9	10	12	14
⅝	23.04	31.36	40.97	64.01	92.16	125.45	163.85	207.37	256.00	368.64	501.76
¾	16.00	21.77	28.45	44.45	64.00	87.12	113.78	144.00	177.77	256.00	348.44
⅞	11.75	16.00	20.90	32.66	47.02	64.01	83.60	105.80	130.61	188.09	256.00
1	9.00	12.25	16.00	25.00	36.00	49.01	64.00	81.00	100.00	144.00	196.00
1⅛	7.11	9.68	12.65	19.76	28.44	38.73	50.57	64.00	79.01	113.77	154.87
1¼	5.76	7.84	10.24	16.00	23.04	31.37	40.97	51.85	64.00	92.18	125.46
1⅜	4.76	6.48	8.46	13.23	19.04	25.92	33.85	42.84	52.89	76.16	103.66
1½	4.00	5.44	7.11	11.12	16.00	21.78	28.45	36.00	44.45	64.00	87.12
1⅝	3.41	4.64	6.06	9.47	13.63	18.56	24.24	30.68	37.87	54.53	74.22
1¾	2.94	4.00	5.23	8.17	11.75	16.00	20.90	26.45	32.66	47.03	64.00
1⅞	2.56	3.48	4.55	7.11	10.24	13.94	18.21	23.04	28.44	40.96	55.75
2	2.25	3.06	4.00	6.25	9.00	12.26	16.00	20.26	25.00	36.00	48.09
2¼	1.78	2.42	3.16	4.93	7.10	9.67	12.63	15.98	19.73	28.42	38.68
2½	1.44	1.96	2.56	4.00	5.76	7.84	10.24	12.96	16.00	23.04	31.35
2¾	1.19	1.62	2.12	3.31	4.76	6.48	8.46	10.72	13.22	19.04	25.92
3	1.00	1.36	1.78	2.78	4.00	5.43	7.11	9.00	11.11	16.00	21.77
3¼	.85	1.16	1.51	2.37	3.40	4.64	6.06	7.67	9.46	13.63	18.55
3½	.73	1.00	1.31	2.04	2.94	4.00	5.23	6.61	8.17	11.76	16.00
3¾	.64	.87	1.14	1.78	2.56	3.48	4.55	5.76	7.11	10.24	13.93
4	.56	.77	1.00	1.56	2.25	3.06	4.00	5.06	6.25	9.00	12.25
4¼	.50	.68	.89	1.38	1.99	2.71	3.54	4.49	5.53	7.97	10.85
4½	.44	.61	.79	1.23	1.78	2.42	3.16	4.00	4.94	7.11	9.68
4¾	.40	.54	.71	1.11	1.60	2.17	2.84	3.59	4.43	6.38	8.68
5	.36	.49	.64	1.00	1.44	1.96	2.56	3.24	4.00	5.76	7.84
5½	.30	.40	.53	1.00	1.19	1.62	2.12	2.68	3.30	4.76	6.48
6	.25	.34	.45	.83	1.00	1.36	1.78	2.25	2.78	4.00	5.45
6½	......	.29	.38	.69	.85	1.16	1.51	1.92	2.37	3.40	4.64
7	......	.25	.33	.59	.73	1.00	1.31	1.65	2.04	2.94	4.00
7½	......	......	.28	.51	.64	.87	1.14	1.44	1.78	2.56	3.48
8	......	......	.25	.44	.56	.77	1.00	1.27	1.56	2.25	3.06
8½	......	......	......	.39	.50	.68	.89	1.12	1.38	1.99	2.71
9	......	......	......	.35	.44	.60	.79	1.00	1.23	1.78	2.42
9½	......	......	......	.31	.40	.54	.71	.90	1.11	1.60	2.17
10	......	......	......	.28	.36	.49	.64	.81	1.00	1.44	1.96
10½	......	......	......	.25	.33	.44	.58	.73	.91	1.31	1.77
11	......	......	......	......	.30	.40	.53	.67	.83	1.19	1.62
12	......	......	......	......	.25	.34	.44	.56	.69	1.00	1.36
13	......	......	......	......	......	.29	.38	.48	.59	.85	1.16
14	......	......	......	......	......	.25	.33	.41	.51	.74	1.00
15	......	......	......	......	......	......	.28	.36	.44	.64	.87
16	......	......	......	......	......	......	.25	.32	.39	.56	.76
17	......	......	......	......	......	......	......	.28	.35	.50	.68
18	......	......	......	......	......	......	......	.25	.31	.45	.60

TABLE GIVING RATIOS OF AREAS—(*Continued*)

Diamater of Water Cylinders.	Diameter of Steam Cylinders.										
	16	18	20	22	24	26	28	30	32	34	36
5/8											
3/4	455.09										
7/8	334.37										
1	256.00	324.00	400.00								
1 1/8	202.27	256.00	316.05								
1 1/4	163.86	207.38	256.00	309.81							
1 3/8	135.39	171.47	211.69	256.00							
1 1/2	113.78	144.00	177.77	215.11	256.00						
1 5/8	96.94	122.72	151.54	183.37	218.22						
1 3/4	83.60	105.79	130.61	158.05	188.10	220.71					
1 7/8	72.82	92.16	113.78	137.67	163.85	192.29					
2	64.00	81.00	100.00	121.00	144.00	169.00	196.00	225.00	256.00		
2 1/4	50.56	64.00	79.01	95.60	113.78	131.56	154.87	177.77	202.27		
2 1/2	40.96	51.84	64.00	77.44	92.16	108.16	125.44	144.00	163.84	184.97	
2 3/4	33.85	42.84	52.89	64.00	76.17	89.39	103.66	119.01	135.41	152.86	
3	28.44	36.00	44.44	53.77	64.00	75.11	87.11	100.00	113.77	128.44	144.00
3 1/4	24.23	30.67	37.87	45.83	54.54	64.00	74.24	85.22	96.96	109.46	122.72
3 1/2	20.90	26.44	32.65	39.42	47.02	55.18	64.00	73.47	83.59	94.36	105.79
3 3/4	18.20	23.04	28.44	34.42	40.96	48.07	55.75	64.00	72.82	82.21	92.16
4	16.00	20.25	25.00	30.25	36.00	42.25	49.00	56.25	64.00	72.25	81.00
4 1/4	14.17	17.93	22.14	26.79	31.89	37.43	43.41	46.51	56.69	64.00	71.76
4 1/2	12.64	16.00	19.75	23.90	28.44	33.33	38.71	44.44	50.56	57.08	64.00
4 3/4	11.34	14.36	17.73	21.45	25.53	29.96	34.75	39.89	45.38	51.24	57.44
5	10.24	12.96	16.00	19.20	23.04	27.04	31.36	36.00	40.96	46.24	51.84
5 1/2	8.46	10.71	13.22	16.00	19.04	22.33	25.91	29.75	33.85	38.21	42.84
6	7.11	9.00	11.11	13.44	16.00	18.77	21.77	25.00	28.44	32.11	36.00
6 1/2	6.06	7.66	9.46	11.45	13.63	16.00	18.56	21.30	24.23	27.36	30.67
7	5.22	6.61	8.16	9.87	11.75	13.79	16.00	18.37	20.90	23.59	26.44
7 1/2	4.55	5.76	7.11	8.60	10.24	12.00	13.93	16.00	18.20	20.55	23.04
8	4.00	5.06	6.25	7.25	9.00	10.56	12.25	14.06	16.00	18.06	20.25
8 1/2	3.54	4.48	5.53	6.69	7.97	9.35	10.85	12.45	14.17	16.00	17.92
9	3.15	4.00	4.93	5.85	7.11	8.34	9.67	11.11	12.64	14.27	16.00
9 1/2	2.83	3.59	4.43	5.36	6.38	7.49	8.68	9.97	11.34	12.88	14.36
10	2.56	3.24	4.00	4.84	5.76	6.76	7.84	9.00	10.24	11.56	12.96
10 1/2	2.32	2.94	3.63	4.39	5.22	6.13	7.10	8.16	9.29	10.48	11.75
11	2.11	2.67	3.30	4.00	4.76	5.58	6.47	7.43	8.46	9.55	10.71
12	1.77	2.25	2.77	3.36	4.00	4.67	5.44	6.25	7.11	8.02	9.00
13	1.51	1.91	2.37	2.86	3.40	4.00	4.63	5.32	6.06	6.83	7.66
14	1.30	1.65	2.04	2.46	2.93	3.44	4.00	4.59	5.22	5.89	6.61
15	1.13	1.44	1.77	2.13	2.56	3.00	3.48	4.00	4.55	5.13	5.76
16	1.00	1.26	1.56	1.89	2.25	2.64	3.06	3.51	4.00	4.51	5.06
17	.88	1.12	1.38	1.67	1.99	2.34	2.71	3.11	3.54	4.00	4.48
18	.79	1.00	1.23	1.49	1.77	2.08	2.41	2.77	3.15	3.56	4.00

TABLE OF CAPACITY OF PUMPS

The figures at the extreme left of the table are piston or plunger diameters; the line of figures across the top are piston or plunger strokes; the figures in the body of the table are the capacity or displacement in gallons, corresponding to a single stroke. To find the capacity for one revolution, multiply the capacity for a single stroke by two.

Diam. of Cylinder Inches.	Length of Stroke in Inches.															
	2	3	4	5	6	7	12	13	16	18	20	24	25	33	36	38
1¼	.0106	.0159	.0212	.0266	.0319	.0372	.0638	.0691	.085	.0956	.1062	.1274	.1328	.1753	.1912	.2021
1⅜	.0129	.0193	.0257	.0321	.0386	.045	.0771	.0835	.1029	.1156	.1286	.1543	.1607	.2121	.2314	.2442
1½	.0153	.0229	.0306	.0382	.0459	.0535	.0918	.0994	.1224	.1377	.1530	.1836	.1912	.2524	.2754	.2907
1¾	.0208	.0312	.0416	.0521	.0625	.0729	.1249	.1353	.1666	.1874	.2082	.2499	.2603	.3436	.3748	.3956
2	.0272	.0408	.0544	.068	.0816	.0952	.1632	.1768	.2176	.2448	.2720	.3264	.340	.4489	.4897	.5169
2¼	.0344	.0516	.0688	.086	.1033	.1205	.2065	.2238	.2754	.3098	.3442	.4131	.4303	.568	.6196	.6541
2½	.0425	.0638	.0850	.1063	.1275	.1488	.255	.2763	.340	.3825	.425	.51	.5313	.7013	.765	.8075
2¾	.0514	.0771	.1029	.1286	.1543	.18	.3086	.3343	.4114	.4628	.5143	.6171	.6429	.8486	.9257	.9771
3	.0612	.0918	.1224	.1530	.1836	.2142	.3672	.3978	.4896	.5508	.612	.7344	.765	1.01	1.02	1.163
3¼	.0718	.1077	.1437	.1796	.2154	.2514	.431	.4668	.5746	.6464	.7183	.8619	.8978	1.185	1.293	1.365
3½	.0833	.1249	.1666	.2082	.2499	.2915	.4997	.5414	.6663	.7496	.833	.9995	1.041	1.374	1.499	1.583
3¾	.0957	.1435	.1913	.2392	.287	.3348	.574	.6214	.7653	.8610	.9561	1.148	1.196	1.579	1.722	1.818
4	.1088	.1632	.2176	.272	.3265	.3809	.653	.7074	.8706	.9795	1.088	1.306	1.36	1.796	1.959	2.068
4¼	.1229	.1843	.2457	.3071	.3684	.4300	.7371	.7986	.9828	1.106	1.229	1.474	1.536	2.027	2.211	2.333
4½	.1377	.2065	.2753	.3443	.413	.4818	.826	.8948	1.101	1.239	1.377	1.652	1.721	2.271	2.478	2.616
4¾	.1534	.2301	.3068	.3835	.4603	.537	.9205	.9972	1.227	1.378	1.534	1.841	1.918	2.531	2.762	2.915
5	.17	.2550	.34	.4250	.51	.5950	1.02	1.105	1.36	1.53	1.7	2.04	2.125	2.805	3.060	3.23
5¼	.1874	.2812	.3749	.4686	.5623	.6561	1.125	1.218	1.5	1.687	1.874	2.249	2.343	3.093	3.374	3.561
5½	.2057	.3086	.4114	.5143	.6171	.72	1.234	1.337	1.646	1.851	2.057	2.468	2.571	3.394	3.703	3.908
5¾	.2248	.3373	.4497	.5621	.6745	.787	1.349	1.461	1.799	2.023	2.248	2.698	2.811	3.71	4.047	4.272
6	.2448	.3672	.4896	.612	.7343	.8567	1.469	1.59	1.958	2.203	2.448	2.938	3.06	4.038	4.406	4.65
6¼	.2656	.3984	.5312	.6641	.7969	.9297	1.594	1.727	2.125	2.39	2.656	3.188	3.32	4.383	4.781	5.047
6½	.2872	.4309	.5745	.7182	.8618	1.005	1.724	1.867	2.298	2.585	2.873	3.447	3.591	4.74	5.171	5.458
6¾	.3099	.4648	.6197	.7747	.9296	1.085	1.859	2.014	2.479	2.788	3.099	3.718	3.873	5.113	5.578	5.887
7	.3332	.4999	.6665	.8331	.9997	1.166	1.999	2.166	2.666	2.999	3.332	3.999	4.165	5.499	5.998	6.332
7¾	.4084	.6126	.8168	1.021	1.225	1.429	2.45	2.654	3.267	3.675	4.084	4.9	5.105	6.739	7.351	7.759
8	.4352	.6529	.8704	1.089	1.306	1.523	2.611	2.829	3.482	3.917	4.352	5.223	5.44	7.181	7.834	8.269
9	.5508	.8263	1.102	1.377	1.652	1.928	3.305	3.580	4.406	4.957	5.508	6.610	6.885	9.089	9.915	10.46
10	.68	1.02	1.36	1.7	2.04	2.38	4.08	4.42	5.44	6.12	6.8	8.16	8.5	11.22	12.24	12.92
10½	.7497	1.125	1.499	1.874	2.249	2.624	4.498	4.873	5.998	6.747	7.497	8.996	9.37	12.37	13.49	14.24
11	.8228	1.234	1.646	2.057	2.468	2.88	4.957	5.348	6.582	7.405	8.228	9.873	10.28	13.58	14.81	15.63
12	.9792	1.469	1.958	2.488	2.938	3.427	5.875	6.365	7.834	8.813	9.792	11.75	12.24	16.16	17.63	18.6
13	1.149	1.723	2.297	2.872	3.445	4.022	6.894	7.467	9.192	10.34	11.49	13.78	14.36	18.96	20.69	21.83
14	1.332	1.998	2.665	3.331	3.977	4.664	7.994	8.661	10.66	11.99	13.32	15.98	16.66	21.99	23.99	25.32
15	1.53	2.295	3.06	3.825	4.59	5.354	9.18	9.943	12.23	13.77	15.29	18.36	19.12	25.24	27.54	29.07
16	1.74	2.61	3.48	4.35	5.22	6.09	10.44	11.31	13.92	15.66	17.40	20.88	21.76	28.72	31.33	33.07
18	2.203	3.305	4.406	5.508	6.61	7.711	13.22	14.32	17.62	19.82	22.03	26.44	27.54	36.35	39.66	41.86
20	2.720	4.08	5.440	6.8	8.16	9.52	16.32	17.68	21.76	24.48	27.2	32.64	34.00	44.88	48.96	51.68
22	3.291	4.936	6.582	8.228	9.874	11.52	19.75	21.39	26.33	29.62	32.91	39.49	41.14	54.3	59.24	62.53
24	39.16	5.875	7.833	9.792	11.75	13.71	23.5	25.46	31.33	35.25	39.16	47.0	48.96	64.63	70.50	74.42

CONTENTS OF CYLINDERS IN CUBIC FEET AND IN U. S. GALLONS FOR ONE FOOT OF LENGTH

231 Cubic Inches Equal one Gallon, and 7.4805 Gallons Equal one Cubic Foot

For the contents of a greater diameter than any in the table, take the quantity opposite *one-half* said diameter and multiply it by 4.

Diameter in Inches.	Diameter in Decimals of a Foot.	For 1 Foot in Length.		Diameter in Inches.	Diameter in Decimals of a Foot.	For 1 Foot in Length.		Diameter in Inches.	Diameter in Decimals of a Foot.	For 1 Foot in Length.	
		Cubic Ft. Also Area in Sq. Ft.	Gallons of 231 Cubic Inches.			Cubic Ft. Also Area in Sq. Ft.	Gallons of 231 Cubic Inches.			Cubic Ft. Also Area in Sq. Ft.	Gallons of 231 Cubic Inches.
1/4	.0208	.0003	.0025	3/4	.5625	.2485	1.859	19	1.583	1.969	14.73
5/16	.0260	.0005	.0040	7	.5833	.2673	1.999	1/2	1.625	2.074	15.51
3/8	.0313	.0008	.0057	1/4	.6042	.2867	2.145	20	1.667	2.182	16.32
7/16	.0365	.0010	.0078	1/2	.6250	.3068	2.295	1/2	1.708	2.292	17.15
1/2	.0417	.0014	.0102	3/4	.6458	.3276	2.450	21	1.750	2.405	17.99
9/16	.0469	.0017	.0129	8	.6667	.3491	2.611	1/2	1.792	2.521	18.86
5/8	.0521	.0021	.0159	1/4	.6875	.3712	2.777	22	1.833	2.640	19.75
11/16	.0573	.0026	.0193	1/2	.7083	.3941	2.948	1/2	1.875	2.761	20.66
3/4	.0625	.0031	.0230	3/4	.7292	.4176	3.125	23	1.917	2.885	21.58
13/16	.0677	.0036	.0269	9	.7500	.4418	3.305	1/2	1.958	3.012	22.53
7/8	.0729	.0042	.0312	1/4	.7708	.4667	3.491	24	2.000	3.142	23.50
15/16	.0781	.0048	.0359	1/2	.7917	.4922	3.682	25	2.083	3.409	25.50
1	.0833	.0055	.0408	3/4	.8125	.5185	3.879	26	2.167	3.687	27.58
1/4	.1042	.0085	.0638	10	.8333	.5454	4.080	27	2.250	3.976	29.74
1/2	.1250	.0123	.0918	1/4	.8542	.5730	4.286	28	2.333	4.276	31.99
3/4	.1458	.0167	.1249	1/2	.8750	.6013	4.498	29	2.417	4.587	34.31
2	.1667	.0218	.1632	3/4	.8958	.6303	4.715	30	2.500	4.909	36.72
1/4	.1875	.0276	.2066	11	.9167	.6600	4.937	31	2.583	5.241	39.21
1/2	.2083	.0341	.2550	1/4	.9375	.6903	5.164	32	2.667	5.585	41.78
3/4	.2292	.0412	.3085	1/2	.9583	.7213	5.396	33	2.750	5.940	44.43
3	.2500	.0491	.3672	3/4	.9792	.7530	5.633	34	2.833	6.305	47.16
1/4	.2708	.0576	.4310	12	1.000	.7854	5.875	35	2.917	6.681	49.98
1/2	.2917	.0668	.4998	1/2	1.042	.8522	6.375	36	3.000	7.069	52.88
3/4	.3125	.0767	.5738	13	1.083	.9218	6.895	37	3.083	7.467	55.86
4	.3333	.0873	.6528	1/2	1.125	.9940	7.436	38	3.167	7.876	58.92
1/4	.3542	.0985	.7369	14	1.167	1.069	7.997	39	3.250	8.296	62.06
1/2	.3750	.1104	.8263	1/2	1.208	1.147	8.578	40	3.333	8.727	65.28
3/4	.3958	.1231	.9206	15	1.250	1.227	9.180	41	3.417	9.168	68.58
5	.4167	.1364	1.020	1/2	1.292	1.310	9.801	42	3.500	9.621	71.97
1/4	.4375	.1503	1.125	16	1.333	1.396	10.44	43	3.583	10.085	75.44
1/2	.4583	.1650	1.234	1/2	1.375	1.485	11.11	44	3.667	10.559	78.99
3/4	.4792	.1803	1.349	17	1.417	1.576	11.79	45	3.750	11.045	82.62
6	.5000	.1963	1.469	1/2	1.458	1.670	12.49	46	3.833	11.541	86.33
1/4	.5208	.2131	1.594	18	1.500	1.767	13.22	47	3.917	12.048	90.13
1/2	.5417	.2304	1.724	1/2	1.542	1.867	13.96	48	4.000	12.566	94.00

HEIGHT IN FEET TO WHICH PUMPS WILL ELEVATE WATER

Steam pressure, 50 pounds per square inch at the pump. No allowance made for friction in pipes, etc.

Diameter of Steam Cylinders	Diameter of Water Cylinders.																
	2 inch	2½ inch	3 inch	3½ inch	4 inch	5 inch	6 inch	7 inch	8 inch	9 inch	10 inch	10½ inch	12 inch	14 inch	16 inch	18 inch	20 inch
3½	230	147	102	75	58	37											
4	300	192	134	134	75	48	34										
5	469	300	209	153	117	75	52	38									
6	675	432	300	221	169	108	75	55	42	33							
7	920	588	408	300	230	147	102	75	57	45	37						
8	......	768	533	344	300	192	141	98	75	59	48	44					
9	......	972	675	496	380	243	169	124	95	75	61	55	42				
10	......	......	833	612	469	300	208	153	117	94	75	68	50	38			
12	......	......	......	881	675	432	300	220	169	133	108	97	75	55	42		
14	......	......	......	......	920	588	408	300	228	182	147	133	102	75	57	45	
16	......	......	......	......	......	768	564	392	300	236	192	174	141	98	75	59	48
18	......	......	......	......	......	972	650	490	379	300	243	220	162	122	95	75	61
20	......	......	......	......	......	......	833	600	469	370	300	272	208	150	117	92	75
22	......	......	......	......	......	......	1008	741	567	448	364	329	252	185	142	112	91
24	......	......	......	......	......	......	......	882	675	533	432	392	300	220	169	133	108
26	......	......	......	......	......	......	......	1034	788	626	508	460	356	258	197	156	127
28	......	......	......	......	......	......	......	......	919	726	588	533	407	300	230	181	147
30	......	......	......	......	......	......	......	......	1054	834	676	612	468	345	263	208	169
32	......	......	......	......	......	......	......	......	......	948	798	697	533	391	300	237	192
34	......	......	......	......	......	......	......	......	......	1070	868	786	603	442	339	268	217
36	......	......	......	......	......	......	......	......	......	......	972	881	675	495	380	300	243

The maximum limit of piston speed depends upon the head pumped against.

WROUGHT IRON PIPE FOR STEAM, GAS, OR WATER

Table of Standard Dimensions

Nominal Inside Diameter.	Actual Inside Diameter. Inches.	Actual Outside Diameter. Inches.	Internal Circumference. Inches.	External Circumference. Inches.	Length of Pipe per Square Foot of Inside Surface. Feet.	Length of Pipe per Square Foot of Outside Surface. Feet.	Internal Area. Inches.	External Area. Inches.	Length of Pipe Containing 1 Cubic Foot. Feet.	Nominal Weight per Foot. Pounds.	Number of Threads per Inch. of Screw.	Contents in Gallons. per Foot.
1/8	.270	.405	.848	1.272	14.15	9.44	.0572	.129	2500.0	0.243	27	.0006
1/4	.364	.54	1.144	1.696	10.50	7.075	.1041	.229	1385.0	.422	18	.0026
3/8	.494	.675	1.552	2.121	7.67	5.657	.1916	.358	751.5	.561	18	.0057
1/2	.623	.84	1.957	2.652	6.13	4.502	.3048	.554	472.4	.845	14	.0102
3/4	.824	1.05	2.589	3.299	4.635	3.637	.5333	.866	270.0	1.126	14	.0230
1	1.048	1.315	3.292	4.134	3.679	2.903	.8627	1.357	166.9	1.67	11½	.0408
1¼	1.380	1.66	4.335	5.215	2.768	2.301	1.496	2.164	96.25	2.258	11½	.0638
1½	1.611	1.9	5.061	5.969	2.371	2.01	2.038	2.835	70.65	2.694	11½	.0918
2	2.067	2.375	6.494	7.461	1.848	1.611	3.355	4.430	42.36	3.667	11½	.1632
2½	2.468	2.875	7.754	9.032	1.547	1.328	4.783	6.491	30.11	5.773	8	.2550
3	3.067	3.5	9.636	10.996	1.245	1.091	7.388	9.621	19.49	7.547	8	.3673
3½	3.518	4.0	11.146	12.566	1.077	.955	9.887	12.566	14.56	9.055	8	.4998
4	4.026	4.5	12.648	14.137	.949	.849	12.730	15.904	11.31	10.728	8	.6528
4½	4.508	5.0	14.153	15.708	.848	.765	15.939	19.635	9.03	12.34	8	.8263
5	5.045	5.563	15.849	17.475	.757	.629	19.990	24.299	7.20	14.564	8	1.020
6	6.065	6.625	19.054	20.813	.63	.577	28.889	34.471	4.98	18.767	8	1.469
7	7.023	7.625	22.063	23.954	.544	.505	38.737	45.663	3.72	23.41	8	1.999
8	7.982	8.625	25.076	27.096	.478	.444	50.039	58.426	2.88	28.348	8	2.611
9	9.001	9.688	28.277	30.433	.425	.394	63.633	73.715	2.26	34.077	8	3.300
10	10.019	10.75	31.475	33.772	.381	.355	78.838	90.762	1.80	40.641	8	4.081
11	11.0	11.75	34.55	36.91	.34	.32	95.03	108.43	1.50	45.0	8	4.93
12	12.0	12.75	37.70	40.05	.32	.30	113.0	127.67	1.27	48.98	8	5.87

FRICTION LOSS IN POUNDS PRESSURE PER SQUARE INCH

For each 100 feet of length in different size clean iron pipes discharging given quantities of water per minute.

Gallons Dis-charged per Minute.	½ inch.	¾ inch.	1 inch.	1¼ inch.	1½ inch.	2 inch.	2½ inch.	3 inch.	3½ inch.	4 inch.	5 inch.	6 inch.	Gallons Dis-charged per Minute.
	Friction Loss in Pounds.	Friction Loss in Pounds.	Friction Loss in Pounds.	Friction Loss in Pounds.	Friction Loss in Pounds.	Friction Loss in Pounds.	Friction Loss in Pounds.	Friction Loss in Pounds.	Friction Loss in Pounds.	Friction Loss in Pounds.	Friction Loss in Pounds.	Friction Loss in Pounds.	
5	24.6	3.3	.84	.31	.12	......	......	......	......	......	......	......	5
10	96.0	13.0	3.16	1.05	.47	.12	......	......	......	......	......	......	10
15	......	28.7	6.98	2.38	.97	......	......	......	......	......	......	......	15
20	......	50.4	12.3	4.07	1.66	.42	......	......	......	......	......	......	20
25	......	78.0	19.0	6.40	2.62	......	.21	.10	......	......	......	......	25
30	......	......	27.5	9.15	3.75	.91	......	......	......	......	......	......	30
35	......	......	37.0	12.04	5.05	......	......	......	......	......	......	......	35
40	......	......	48.0	16.1	6.52	1.60	......	......	......	......	......	......	40
45	......	......	......	20.2	8.15	......	......	......	......	......	......	......	45
50	......	......	......	24.9	10.0	2.44	.81	.35	.16	.09	.03	......	50
75	......	......	......	56.1	22.4	5.32	1.80	.74	.34	......	......	......	75
100	......	......	......	......	39.0	9.46	3.20	1.31	.60	.33	.12	.05	100
125	......	......	......	......	......	14.9	4.89	1.99	.90	......	......	......	125
150	......	......	......	......	......	21.2	7.0	2.85	1.32	.69	.25	.10	150
175	......	......	......	......	......	28.1	9.46	3.85	1.78	......	......	......	175
200	......	......	......	......	......	37.5	12.48	5.02	2.32	1.22	.42	.17	200
250	......	......	......	......	......	......	19.66	7.76	3.55	1.89	.65	.46	250
300	......	......	......	......	......	......	28.06	11.2	5.23	2.66	.93	.37	300
350	......	......	......	......	......	......	......	15.2	7.0	3.65	1.28	.50	350
400	......	......	......	......	......	......	......	19.5	9.0	4.73	1.68	.65	400
450	......	......	......	......	......	......	......	25.0	11.60	6.01	2.10	.81	450
500	......	......	......	......	......	......	......	30.8	14.26	7.43	2.70	.96	500

FRICTION LOSS IN POUNDS PRESSURE PER SQUARE INCH

For each 100 feet of length in different size clean iron pipes discharging given quantities of water per minute.

Gallons Discharged per Minute.	5 inch.	6 inch.	8 inch.	10 inch.	12 inch.	14 inch.	16 inch.	18 inch.	20 inch.	24 inch.	30 inch.	Gallons Discharged per Minute.
	Friction Loss in Pounds.	Friction Loss in Pounds.	Friction Loss in Pounds.	Friction Loss in Pounds.	Friction Loss in Pounds.	Friction Loss in Pounds.	Friction Loss in Pounds.	Friction Loss in Pounds.	Friction Loss in Pounds.	Friction Loss in Pounds.	Friction Loss in Pounds.	
250	.65	.26	.07	.03	.01							250
500	2.70	.96	.25	.09	.04	.017	.009	.005				500
750	5.40	2.21	.53	.18	.08							750
1000	9.60	3.88	.94	.32	.13	.062	.036	.020	.012	.005	.002	1000
1250			1.46	.49	.20							1250
1500			2.09	.70	.29	.135	.071	.040				1500
1750				.95	.38							1750
2000				1.23	.49	.234	.123	.071	.042	.020	.006	2000
2250					.63							2250
2500					.77	.362	.188	.107				2500
3000					1.11	.515	.267	.150	.091	.047	.012	3000
3500						.697	.365	.204				3500
4000						.910	.472	.263	.158	.067	.022	4000
4500							.593	.333				4500
5000							.730	.408	.244	.102	.035	5000
6000								.585	.348	.146	.048	6000
7000									.472	.196	.065	7000
8000									.612	.255	.083	8000
9000										.323	.105	9000
10000										.396	.131	10000

POUNDS PRESSURE LOST BY FRICTION

In each 100 feet of 2½-inch fire hose, for given discharges of water per minute.

Diameter of Nozzle, Inches.	Pressure at Hose Nozzle.									
	Head in pounds per sq in.	20	30	40	50	60	70	80	90	100
	Head in feet	46.2	69.3	92.4	115.5	138.6	161.7	184.8	207.9	231.0
1	Gallons discharged	110	134	155	173	189	205	219	232	245
	Rubber hose, pounds	4.35	6.40	8.40	10.20	12.80	14.80	17.0	19.20	20.50
	Leather hose, pounds	6.33	8.53	10.83	13.10	15.34	17.79	20.11	22.40	24.83
1⅛	Gallons discharged	139	170	196	219	240	259	277	294	310
	Rubber hose, pounds	6.79	10.16	13.60	17.05	20.59	24.0	27.0	30.0	33.0
	Leather hose, pounds	9.05	12.71	16.38	20.11	23.88	27.61	31.41	35.24	39.07
1¼	Gallons discharged	171	210	242	271	297	320	342	363	383
	Rubber hose, pounds	10.28	15.64	20.85	25.46	29.50	39.0	43.81	49.42	55.0
	Leather hose, pounds	12.84	19.0	24.07	30.11	35.94	41.57	47.36	53.25	59.20
1⅜	Gallons discharged	207	253	293	327	358	387	413	439	462
	Rubber hose, pounds	15.0	22.96	29.40	40.50	48.20	55.70	64.70	72.0	79.26
	Leather hose, pounds	18.81	26.39	35.01	43.38	52.0	60.40	68.59	76.73	84.87

HORIZONTAL AND VERTICAL DISTANCES REACHED BY JETS

Diameter of Nozzle, Inches.	Pressure at Nozzle.									
	Head in pounds per sq. in.	20	30	40	50	60	70	80	90	100
	Head in feet	46.2	69.3	92.4	115.5	138.6	161.7	184.8	207.9	231.0
1	Gallons discharged	110	134	155	173	189	205	219	232	245
	Horiz. distance of jet	70	90	109	126	142	156	168	178	186
	Vertical distance of jet	43	62	79	94	108	121	131	140	148
1⅛	Gallons discharged	131	170	196	219	240	259	277	294	310
	Horiz. distance of jet	71	93	113	132	148	163	175	186	193
	Vertical distance of jet	43	63	81	97	112	125	137	148	157
1¼	Gallons discharged	171	210	242	271	297	320	342	363	383
	Horiz. distance of jet	73	96	118	138	156	172	186	198	207
	Vertical distance of jet	43	63	82	99	115	129	142	154	164
1⅜	Gallons discharged	207	253	293	327	358	387	413	439	462
	Horiz. distance of jet	75	100	124	146	166	184	200	213	224
	Vertical distance of jet	44	65	85	102	118	133	146	158	169

FRENCH OR METRIC MEASURES

The metric unit of length is the meter = 39.37 inches.

The metric unit of weight is the gram = 15.432 grains.

The following prefixes are used for sub-divisions and multiples: Milli = $\frac{1}{1000}$, Centi = $\frac{1}{100}$, Deci = $\frac{1}{10}$, Deca = 10, Hecto = 100, Kilo = 1000, Myria = 10,000.

FRENCH AND BRITISH (AND AMERICAN) EQUIVALENT MEASURES

MEASURES OF LENGTH

French.		British and U. S.
1 meter	=	39.37 inches, or 3.28083 feet, 1.09361 yards.
.3048 meter	=	1 foot.
1 centimeter	=	.3937 inch.
2.54 centimeters	=	1 inch.
1 millimeter	=	.03937 inch, or $\frac{1}{25}$ inch nearly.
25.4 millimeters	=	1 inch.
1 kilometer	=	1093.61 yards, or .62137 mile.

MEASURES OF CAPACITY

1 liter (= 1 cubic decimeter)	=	61.023 cubic inches. .03531 cubic foot. .2642 gallon (American). 2.202 pounds of water at 62° F.
28.317 liters	=	1 cubic foot.
4.543 liters	=	1 gallon (British).
3.785 liters	=	1 gallon (American).

MEASURES OF WEIGHT

French.		British and U. S.
1 gram	=	15.432 grains.
.0648 gram	=	1 grain.
28.35 gram	=	1 ounce avoirdupois.
1 kilogram	=	2.2046 pounds.
.4536 kilogram	=	1 pound.
1 tonne or metric ton 1000 kilograms	=	.9842 ton of 2240 pounds. 19.68 cwts. 2204.6 pounds.
1.016 metric tons 1016 kilograms	=	1 ton of 2240 pounds.

COAL CONSUMPTION

The average coal consumption may be taken as follows, an evaporation of 8 pounds of water to 1 pound of coal being assumed:

For non-condensing engines	3 to $5\frac{1}{2}$	per I.H.P.	per Hour.
For condensing engines	2 to 4	"	"
For compound non-condensing engines	2.5 to 3	"	"
For compound condensing engines	1.6 to 2.75	"	"
For triple condensing engines	1.25 to 1.75	"	"
For quadruple condensing engines	1 to 1.5	"	"

HEAT OF COMBUSTION OF FUELS

	Air Required per Pound of Fuel in Cubic Feet at 62° F.	Total Heat of Combustion of 1 Pound of Fuel in B.T.U.
Coal	140	14.700
Coke	142	13.548
Lignite	116	13.108
Asphalt	156	17.040
Wood, dry	80	10.974
Wood, 20 per cent moisture	60	7.951
Wood charcoal, dry	125	13.006
Peat, dry	99	12.279
Peat, 30 per cent moisture	69	8.260
Straw	56	8.144
Petroleum	188	20.411
Petroleum oils	235	27.531
Coal gas, per cubic foot at 62° F.		.630

In practice it is found that from 18 to 24 pounds of air is required for the combustion of each pound of coal, according to whether forced or natural draft is used.

FEED-WATER CONSUMPTION

Average weight of feed-water used per I.H.P. per hour, in pounds.

Type of Engine.		Boiler Pressure.	Water Consumption.
Slide valve, throttling	N.C.	80	35 to 45
Automatic expansion gear	N.C.	80	30 to 35
Automatic expansion gear	N.C.	100	26 to 30
Compound automatic expansion gear	N.C.	100	24 to 28
Compound automatic expansion gear	C.	100	18 to 24
Compound automatic expansion gear	N.C.	125	21 to 25
Compound automatic expansion gear	C.	125	16 to 20
Simple Corliss	N.C.	80	25 to 30
Simple Corliss	C.	80	22 to 25
Compound Corliss	C.	100	16 to 20
Compound Corliss	C.	125	15 to 19
Triple expansion	C.	125	14 to 16
Triple expansion	C.	150	13 to 15
Compound superheated steam	C.	180	10 to 12

C., condensing; N.C., non-condensing.

INDEX

PAGES

www.ingramcontent.com/pod-product-compliance
Lightning Source LLC
LaVergne TN
LVHW020558110826
845149LV00002B/296

* 9 7 8 1 4 1 8 1 8 8 3 8 2 *